The Definitive Guide to Complying with the HIPAA/HITECH Privacy and Security Rules

The Definitive Guide to Complying with the HIPAA/HITECH Privacy and Security Rules

John J. Trinckes, Jr.

CRC Press
Taylor & Francis Group
Boca Raton   London   New York

CRC Press is an imprint of the
Taylor & Francis Group, an **informa** business
AN AUERBACH BOOK

CRC Press
Taylor & Francis Group
6000 Broken Sound Parkway NW, Suite 300
Boca Raton, FL 33487-2742

© 2013 by Taylor & Francis Group, LLC
CRC Press is an imprint of Taylor & Francis Group, an Informa business

No claim to original U.S. Government works

Printed in the United States of America on acid-free paper
Version Date: 20121008

International Standard Book Number: 978-1-4665-0767-8 (Hardback)

Visit the Taylor & Francis Web site at
http://www.taylorandfrancis.com

and the CRC Press Web site at
http://www.crcpress.com

The time is running short for those diehards that continue to believe that this "privacy and security" obsession is something that will pass. It won't. We live in an entirely different world now and privacy and security best practices are simply a cost of doing business. Something that both regulators and patients have come to expect.

Carlos Leyva, *Esquire* **(Leyva 2012)**

I will respect the privacy of my patients, for their problems are not disclosed to me that the world may know.

Hippocratic Oath (Modern Version), by Dr. Louis Lasagna

There are only two types of companies: Those that have been hacked, and those that will be.

FBI Director Robert Mueller (*Fox News* **2012)**

Results require action, not excuses!

Amy Cotta (Cotta 2011)

Contents

Foreword

The Health Insurance Portability and Accountability Act (HIPAA) was signed into law by President Clinton in 1996, and the son of HIPAA, the Health Information Technology for Economic and Clinical Health (HITECH) Act was signed into law in 2009 by President Obama as part of the American Recovery and Reinvestment Act.

One of the most often heard complaints about HIPAA is that it is far too broad, without adequate details and directives, which in turn leads to way too much interpretation in relation to HIPAA compliance.

That grievance seems to bear fruit in the fact that in 2011 half of the most significant data breaches involved stolen patient health data, according to a report by the consumer advocacy group Privacy Rights Clearinghouse.

In *The Definitive Guide to Complying with the HIPAA/HITECH Privacy and Security Rules,* Jay Trinckes is providing a tremendous service to any HIPAA-covered entity in particularizing the gory technical details around HIPAA and HITECH that the U.S. Department of Health and Human Services never got around to documenting.

Why are medical systems such a target? For the attacker, a large metropolitan hospital billing system contains hundreds of thousands of credit card records in its database. It will have detailed medical information about politicians, entertainers, public officials, and more. It will have a storage area network (SAN) with perhaps a few terabytes of free space in which to store files, illegal content, and more.

Given that medical systems are such an enticing target, it is incumbent on the chief information officers and chief information security officers of those systems to ensure that they are adequately secured— and this book is a good place for them to start.

Ben Rothke, CISSP, CISM

Preface

The Department of Health and Human Services (HHS) has published four major rules implementing a number of provisions and regulations set out by the Health Insurance Portability and Accountability Act of 1996 (HIPAA) and amended by the Health Information Technology for Economic and Clinical Health (HITECH) Act of 1999 as part of the American Recovery and Reinvestment Act (ARRA). These rules are the Privacy Rule; the Electronic Transactions and Code Sets Rule; the National Identifier requirements for employers, providers, and health plans; and the Security Rule. It also includes more regulatory control over enforcement actions and stiffer penalties for noncompliance. There are many healthcare providers, healthcare clearinghouses, and health plans that are required to implement and comply with these rules, especially the Security Rule. Failure to implement or comply with these rules can leave the covered entity or others that need to comply open to large monetary fines, civil lawsuits, and other penalties.

With the rise of security breaches and other high-profile incidents regarding successful hacking events, it is very apparent that information has become a valuable commodity. The United States has transformed from a nation built on manufacturing and industry into an information/knowledge powerhouse. With the advancement in technology comes the opportunity for criminals to find another source of income by exploiting vulnerabilities within this technology. Retail, financial, and governmental entities have been the target and have fallen victim to these types of crimes; however, these industries are not the only industries susceptible. Technology has made companies more efficient and even now healthcare providers are required to submit Medicaid and Medicare reimbursement requests electronically. These capabilities have brought with them additional regulations for the healthcare industry. These regulations have brought to the forefront the importance of securing electronic protected health information (EPHI).

Just as a credit report is used to determine the credit worthiness for an individual, so will patient information eventually be used or already may be used to determine the health status of individuals. There has been a boom in the market of selling patient information to health and life insurance companies. These insurance

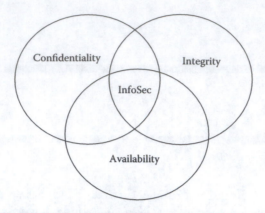

Figure 0.1 The information security triad.

companies will rate individuals on their "health score" to determine their eligibility for a specific healthcare product or service.

Wherever there is money or financial gain to be made, there will be individuals who will attempt to get into the market. This can be done legally or illegally. Since the name of the game is information, the information becomes very valuable. This raises one major question: How well do you, as a healthcare provider, protect your clients' medical records and patient information?

The Security Standards in HIPAA were developed to implement appropriate security safeguards for the protection of certain EPHI that may be at risk, while permitting authorized individuals to access and use this information under allowable uses.

Assessing these standards takes into consideration three fundamental security parameters: confidentiality, integrity, and availability (Figure 0.1).

This book was designed to assist the healthcare provider, or covered entity, in reviewing the accessibility of EPHI to verify that it is not altered or destroyed in an unauthorized manner and that it is available as needed by authorized individuals for authorized use. This book covers the following implementation standards and provides recommendations on how to comply with these standards, if required, to strengthen the security posture of the organization:

- Administrative safeguards
- Physical safeguards
- Technical safeguards
- Organizational requirements
- Policies/procedures and documentation requirements

Following the recommendations in this book will provide a covered entity the assurance that it is complying with the implementation standards of the Privacy and Security Rule of HIPAA/HITECH, along with providing recommendations based on other related regulations and industry best practices. This book can also help those entities that may not be covered but want to assure their customers that they are doing their due diligence to protect their personal and private information. Due to the fact that the HIPAA/HITECH rules apply to all covered entities and will most likely apply to business associates and subcontractors of business associates, it may not be long until these rules become the de facto standards for all companies to follow.

One of the most valuable parts of this book is the sample documents that are required and directions in using these policies/procedures to establish proof of compliance. This book will not take the place of a qualified individual conducting HIPAA assessments on the covered entity; however, the entity will be better prepared when the assessment is conducted or if an HHS auditor arrives at the door. The entity will also be well informed about taking the proper steps to protect its client's information and strengthen its security posture. This can provide a strategic advantage to the organization, not only demonstrating to clients that it cares about their health and well-being but also cares about their privacy.

Acknowledgments

I would like to thank a number of individuals who assisted me in writing this book. First, I would like to thank my wife, Wendy. Without your support and encouragement, this book would have never been written. I will love you always and forever. Second, I thank my children, Traci and Brandon, for their understanding in allowing me to have the time needed to write.

I also thank my publisher, Richard O'Hanley, and all the members of CRC Press for their hard work. Your dedication to this project is unbeatable. I think we had some good success on our first book together and believe we have hit another home run with this one.

Finally, I thank all of my contributing authors and reviewers for their expertise and contributions.

About the Author

John (Jay) Trinckes, Jr., CISSP, CISM, CRISC, CEH, NSA-IAM/IEM, MCSE-NT, A+, is the chief information security officer (CISO) for Path Forward IT, a managed service provider of IT and security services for the healthcare industry. Jay has previously worked as a senior information security consultant and authored *The Executive MBA in Information Security*, published by CRC Press, 2009. Trinckes has developed enterprise-level information security management programs for multiple clients along with conducting countless successful internal/external vulnerability/penetration assessments and other specific technical compliance audits. Trinckes has been instrumental in developing policies/procedures, audit plans, compliance assessments, business impact analyses, and business continuity and disaster recovery plans for several clients. He also conducts security awareness training and other presentations related to information security.

Trinckes is a Certified Information Systems Security Professional (CISSP), Certified Information Security Manager (CISM), Certified in Risk and Information Systems Control (CRISC), and a Certified Ethical Hacker (C-EH). He holds certifications in the National Security Agency (NSA) INFOSEC Assessment Methodology (IAM) and INFOSEC Evaluation Methodology (IEM), along with Microsoft Certified Systems Engineer (MCSE-NT) and Comptia A+ Certifications. Trinckes provides a unique perspective on compliance as a result of his previous work experience as an information security risk analyst, IT manager, system administrator, and law enforcement officer.

Trinckes graduated with a bachelor's degree in business administration/management information systems from the Union Institute and University with a 4.0 GPA and is currently working on multiple network- and security-related certifications. Trinckes is a member of numerous highly recognized security industry associations such as the FBI's InfraGard®, Information Systems Audit and Controls Association (ISACA®), and the International Information Systems Security Certification Consortium (ISC²).

When Trinckes is not consulting or writing books, he likes to spend his spare time cooking, working out with his wife, and playing video games with his kids. Trinckes can be reached for assistance or comments related to this book at hitechpo@windstream.net.

Contributors

Michael Stankiewicz, CISSP, CRISC, MBCI, is the vice president of security services for CastleGarde, Inc. He manages a team of six engineers to ensure CastleGarde's 150-plus credit union clients are properly serviced. CastleGarde conducts internal and external vulnerability/penetration assessments, general IT controls assessments, online banking assessments, and specific technical compliance audits. In addition, Stankiewicz writes, updates, and performs independent analyses of business continuity plans and business continuity plan testing. He also conducts security awareness training and other presentations related to information security. Stankiewicz is a Certified Information Systems Security Professional (CISSP), Certified in Risk and Information Systems Control (CRISC), and a member of the Business Continuity Institute (MBCI). Prior to his time at CastleGarde, Stankiewicz's notable work experience included time spent as the IT and forensic audit manager for the largest casino in the United States, vice president of information technology at a financial institution, security operations center engineer, and system administrator. He graduated with a bachelor's degree in business administration from the University of Phoenix in Arizona. His personal interests include spending time with his wife and child, and extended family and friends, and participating in sports, including the historical re-enactment of baseball from the 1860s (http://vbba.org/), and home improvements. Stankiewicz can be contacted by e-mailing mike_stankiewicz@hotmail.com.

Chris Hadnagy (also known as loganWHD) is a professional social engineer who spends his time helping companies be secure and educated. He is a student of Paul Ekman's training classes on micro expressions and has spent time learning and educating others on the values of nonverbal communication. He is also the lead developer of social-engineer.org as well as the author of the best-selling book *Social Engineering: The Art of Human Hacking*. He has launched a line of professional social engineering training and pen testing services at social-engineer.com. His goal is to help companies remain secure by educating them on the methods the "bad guys" use. Analyzing, studying, dissecting, then performing the very same attacks used by malicious hackers in some of the most recent attacks (i.e., Sony,

HB Gary, Lockheed Martin), Hadnagy is able to help companies stay informed and more secure. He runs one of the Web's most successful security podcasts, *The Social-Engineer.org Podcast*, which spends time each month analyzing someone who has to use influence and persuasion in his or her daily life. By dissecting what he or she does, viewers can learn how to enhance their abilities. That same analysis runs over to the equally popular SEORG Newsletter. After two years, both of these have become a staple in most serious security practices and are used by Fortune 500 companies around the world to educate their staff. Hadnagy can be found online at www.social-engineer.com and on Twitter as @humanhacker.

Ben Rothke, CISSP, CISM (Twitter @benrothke), is an information security manager for a major hospitality firm and the author of *Computer Security: 20 Things Every Employee Should Know* (McGraw-Hill Professional Education, 2004).

Reviewer

Elizabeth Lamkin, MHA, is CEO of PACE Healthcare Consulting, LLC (www.pacehcc.com) in Hilton Head, South Carolina. After 20 years as a highly innovative hospital CEO, she now brings effective solutions to all types of hospitals and healthcare providers. Lamkin specializes in system development, quality, HIPAA, and billing compliance. Throughout her career, she has been repeatedly recognized for quality job performance as well as patient, staff, and physician satisfaction. She has extensive experience in both startups and turnarounds.

She is a nationally known speaker and author on billing compliance including CMS Recovery Auditors.

Lamkin brings enterprise-wide solutions that begin with establishing clear directives for the governing board and creating strategic plans. Her techniques are based on performance improvement within a team of stakeholders, resulting in practical and sustainable solutions. These result-oriented techniques are relevant and transferable to any hospital or provider because each solution is based on the provider's current systems and culture.

Lamkin received her bachelor of arts in interdisciplinary studies (BAIS), cum laude, from the University of South Carolina and a master's in healthcare administration (MHA), also from University of South Carolina. She was named outstanding MHA student and won the Suzie James Yates scholarship.

Author's Note

It has been my goal throughout this book to be as accurate in my writing as possible. I have attempted to explain the requirements of the HIPAA/HITECH regulations as clearly as possible and capture the intent of the requirements. In my research, I went to the official source of each regulation and if I thought the requirement was self-explanatory I cited it accordingly. In addition, if I believed any summation or paraphrasing of the requirement distorted the meaning, I cited the specific regulation in its entirety. It was not my intent to copy all of the regulations into this book since I trust that readers can look this information up for themselves; however, I would be remiss if I did not assist the reader by providing the detailed requirements as they are mandated in the regulations. To this end, it was my purpose to guide the reader through the intricacies of the HIPAA/HITECH regulations and to pave the way for an easier path to compliance. I hope that you will find that I have accomplished this goal.

Legal Disclaimer

The material in this book is for informational purposes only and not for the purpose of providing legal advice. Readers should contact their own attorney to obtain advice with respect to any particular issue or problem related to the material discussed in this book. The opinions expressed by this author may not reflect the opinions of the publisher of this book or any other individual attorney. Sample policies or procedures included in this book are for guidance purposes only and should be reviewed by legal staff to verify compliance with local, state, or federal laws and regulations.

Chapter 1

HIPAA/HITECH Overview

Objectives

The objectives of this chapter are as follows:

- Understand terminology used in the HIPAA/HITECH Privacy and Security Rule regulations and implementation standards such as: disclosure, electronic form, electronic protected health information, direct identifiers, group health plan, healthcare, individual, use, and organized healthcare arrangements.
- Understand the term *required by law* and how it is implied in the context of HIPAA.
- Determine what qualifies an organization as a covered entity.
- Determine what qualifies an organization as a business associate and the elements required in a business associate contract.
- Understand permitted and authorized use and disclosure of protected health information along with minimum necessary standard applicability under the HIPAA Privacy Rule.
- Determine what notices are required and understand the individual rights of patients related to their health information.
- Determine the administrative requirements of a covered entity.
- Understand the options available to a covered entity related to HIPAA Privacy compliance.
- Understand enforcement actions and penalties that a covered entity could face as a result of noncompliance with the HIPAA Privacy Rule.
- Understand covered electronic transactions and the Code Set Rule.
- Understand the requirements for the National Provider Identification program.
- Understand what is required under the HIPAA Security Rule.

- Determine what types of safeguards (i.e., administrative, physical, and technical) the covered entity has to implement to become compliant with the HIPAA Security Rule.
- Understand what is meant by "Meaningful Use."
- Understand what is required by the Breach Notification Rule.
- Understand enforcement actions and penalties that a covered entity could face as a result of noncompliance with the HIPAA Security Rule.
- Understand the Anti-Kickback Statute as it pertains to federal healthcare programs, the penalties for violation, and the "safe harbor" exemptions that apply.
- Understand the Patient Safety Rule and how it pertains to the protection of patient safety work product.
- Understand some requirements of the Federal Rules of Civil Procedures.

Background

Like many other industries, the healthcare industry has faced its share of challenges. From regulations to fraud, from data breaches to substantial inflation in costs, the healthcare industry is not immune to these different factors. At one time, every state in the union established different rules and regulations regarding the healthcare providers in their state. Since insurance companies and healthcare providers were isolated regionally, regulations were not uniform, and oftentimes state laws contradicted federal regulations.

With the increased use of technology, it became apparent to the United States Congress that there could be potential fraud or compromise of sensitive information leading the way to the establishment of security and privacy standards. In 1996, Congress enacted the Health Insurance Portability and Accountability Act (HIPAA) in response to these concerns. The Department of Health and Human Services (HHS) was assigned the responsibility and oversight for the implementation and enforcement of these regulations.

In the years that followed, the Privacy Rule, the Electronic Transactions and Code Sets Rule, the National Identifier Requirements, and the Security Rule were published and finalized as a result of the Administrative Simplification provisions of HIPAA. Figure 1.1 shows the components that make up HIPAA.

In 1999, as part of the American Recovery and Reinvestment Act (ARRA), the Health Information Technology for Economic and Clinical Health (HITECH) Act revised HIPAA and amended the enforcement regulations as related to civil monetary penalties. This new rule making gave HHS more control over enforcement and compliance of the HIPAA regulations, with stiffer penalties. It also paved the way for the attorney generals of each state to take enforcement actions for violations of these regulations.

Monetary penalties are not the only ways in which Congress forces mandatory compliance with the HIPAA/HITECH regulations. The Centers for Medicare

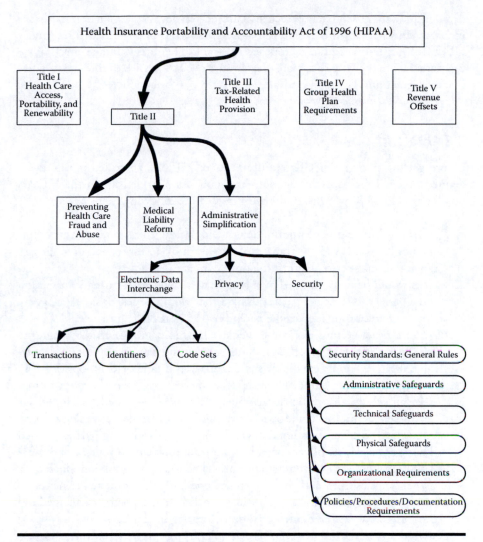

Figure 1.1   Components of the HIPAA Act.

& Medicaid Services (CMS) has developed an Electronic Health Records (EHR) Incentive Program. This incentive program provides a monetary incentive to comply with the HIPAA/HITECH regulations and will also create payment adjustments in Medicare reimbursements for eligible entities that do not successfully demonstrate meaningful use by the year 2015.

To demonstrate the seriousness by which HHS wanted covered entities to comply with these regulations, a multimillion-dollar contract was awarded to KPMG, LLP, to conduct audits on 150 covered entities by the end of 2012. In addition to fulfilling the enforcement requirements of HHS, these audits will also provide a detailed analysis into the state of security currently in development in the healthcare industry. These audits also extend to business associates of covered entities (under HITECH Act 13411) and new proposed rule-making efforts will take effect. Since the statistics are showing that more breaches are occurring with business associates, stricter regulations will apply and more oversight will be conducted.

1.1 Definitions

Before getting into the specific requirements of HIPAA, some terms should be defined that will be used throughout this book. As provided for in the HIPAA regulations (45 CFR § 160.103), the meanings of the following terms are:

Disclosure—The release of information outside of the entity holding that information. It also covers the transfer of, provision of, access to, and divulging in any other manner of that information. For example, a disclosure of information would be demonstrated by a healthcare provider providing information on a patient to the patient's health plan that would be responsible for paying for the services provided to the patient by the healthcare provider.

Electronic form—Using electronic media, electronic storage media including memory devices in computers (hard drives) and any removable/transportable digital memory medium, such as magnetic tape or disk, optical disk, or digital memory card; or transmission media used to exchange information already in electronic storage media. Transmission media includes, for example, the Internet (wide open), extranet (using Internet technology to link a business with information accessible only to collaborating parties), leased lines, dial-up lines, private networks, and the physical movement of removable/transportable electronic storage media. Certain transmissions, including paper (via facsimile) and voice (via telephone) are not considered to be transmissions via electronic media, because the information being exchanged did not originally exist in electronic form before the transmission.

Electronic protected health information (*EPHI*) or *protected health information* (*PHI*)—Individually identifiable health information transmitted by electronic media, maintained in electronic media, or transmitted or maintained in any other form or medium, whether electronic, paper, or oral. *Health information* is broadly defined as any information, in any form or medium, that relates to the past, present, or future physical or mental health, condition, provision of healthcare, or future payment for the provision of healthcare of or to an individual. Individually identifiable health information includes many common identifiers such as name, address, and Social Security number. *Protected health information* excludes individually identifiable health information in: education records covered by the Family Educational Rights and Privacy Act, as amended, 20 U.S.C. 1232g; records described at 20 U.S.C. 1232g(a)(4)(B)(iv): "records on a student who is eighteen years of age or older, or is attending an institution of postsecondary education, which are made or maintained by a physician, psychiatrist, psychologist, or other recognized professional or paraprofessional acting in his professional or paraprofessional capacity, or assisting in that capacity, and which are made, maintained, or used only in connection with the provision of treatment to the student, and are not available to anyone other than persons providing such treatment, except that such records can be personally reviewed by a physician or other appropriate professional of the student's choice"; and employment records held by a covered entity in its role as employer.

Direct identifiers of the individual or of relatives, employers, or household members of the individual are defined under 45 CFR § 164.514(e)(2) and include the following 18 items:

1. Names
2. All geographic subdivisions smaller than a state, including street address, city, county, precinct, zip code, and their equivalent geo-codes, except for the initial three digits of a zip code if, according to the current publicly available data from the Bureau of the Census:
    a. The geographic unit formed by combining all zip codes with the same three initial digits contains more than 20,000 people
    b. The initial three digits of a zip code for all such geographic units containing 20,000 or fewer people are changed to "000"
3. All elements of dates (except year) for dates directly related to an individual, including birth date, admission date, discharge date, date of death; and all ages over 89 and all elements of dates (including year) indicative of such age, except that such ages and elements may be aggregated into a single category of age 90 or older
4. Telephone numbers
5. Fax numbers
6. Electronic mail addresses
7. Social Security numbers
8. Medical record numbers
9. Health plan beneficiary numbers
10. Account numbers
11. Certificate/license numbers
12. Vehicle identifiers and serial numbers, including license plate numbers
13. Device identifiers and serial numbers
14. Web Universal Resource Locators (URLs)
15. Internet Protocol (IP) address numbers
16. Biometric identifiers, including finger and voice prints
17. Full-face photographic images and any comparable images
18. Any other unique identifying number, characteristic, or code

Group health plan—An employee welfare benefit plan that includes insured and self-insured plans with 50 or more participants that is not administered by the employer for the purpose of providing medical care to include items and services paid for as medical care. An *employee welfare plan*, as defined in section 3(1) of the Employee Retirement Income and Security Act of 1974 (ERISA), 29 U.S.C. 1002(1)), "is any plan fund or program established by an employer, union, or both that provides a wide variety of benefits including medical, sickness, accident, unemployment, vacation, disability, day care, scholarships, training programs and prepaid legal services." *Medical care* is defined under 42 U.S.C. 3000gg-91(a)(2) as the "amounts paid for the diagnosis, cure, mitigation, treatment or prevention of disease, or amounts paid for the purpose of affecting any structure or function of the body," and includes transportation primarily for and essential to this medical care and for insurance covering this medical care. A *participant* is defined as any employee (or former employee) of an employer or a member (or former member of an employee organization) that is eligible to receive benefits under an employer benefit plan. It also covers someone who may become eligible or whose beneficiaries may be eligible to receive benefits.

Healthcare—"Care, services, or supplies related to the health of an individual. It includes, but is not limited to, the following:

(1) Preventive, diagnostic, rehabilitative, maintenance, or palliative care, and counseling, service, assessment, or procedure with respect to the physical or mental condition, or functional status, of an individual or that affects the structure or function of the body; and

(2) Sale or dispensing of a drug, device, equipment, or other item in accordance with a prescription."

Individual—"The person who is the subject of protected health information."

Use—"With respect to individually identifiable health information, the sharing, employment, application, utilization, examination, or analysis of such information within an entity that maintains such information."

Organized healthcare arrangement—"(1) A clinically integrated care setting in which individuals typically receive healthcare from more than one healthcare provider;

(2) An organized system of healthcare in which more than one covered entity participates and in which the participating covered entities:

  (i) Hold themselves out to the public as participating in a joint arrangement; and

  (ii) Participate in joint activities that include at least one of the following:

    (A) Utilization review, in which healthcare decisions by participating covered entities are reviewed by other participating covered entities or by a third party on their behalf;

    (B) Quality assessment and improvement activities, in which treatment provided by participating covered entities is assessed by other participating covered entities or by a third party on their behalf; or

(C) Payment activities, if the financial risk for delivering healthcare is shared, in part or in whole, by participating covered entities through the joint arrangement and if protected health information created or received by a covered entity is reviewed by other participating covered entities or by a third party on their behalf for the purpose of administering the sharing of financial risk.

(3) A group health plan and a health insurance issuer or HMO with respect to such group health plan, but only with respect to protected health information created or received by such health insurance issuer or HMO that relates to individuals who are or who have been participants or beneficiaries in such group health plan;

(4) A group health plan and one or more other group health plans each of which are maintained by the same plan sponsor; or

(5) The group health plans described in paragraph (4) of this definition and health insurance issuers or HMOs with respect to such group health plans, but only with respect to protected health information created or received by such health insurance issuers or HMOs that relates to individuals who are or have been participants or beneficiaries in any of such group health plans."

As a note of reference, it is important to understand the definitions of these terms and how they apply to HIPAA regulations. As may be found throughout this book, some situations may arise that will require certain actions to be taken in accordance with the regulations. It may be the case, however, based on these definitions that the actions do not apply. For example, there are certain breach notification rules that apply to certain protected health information being disclosed in an unauthorized fashion. If the information disclosed did not fall under the definition of protected health information, then the breach notification requirements will not apply. Such determination is essential and could prevent the covered entity, or other organization that must comply with the HIPAA regulations, from taking undue actions.

1.2 Required by Law

The HIPAA/HITECH standards, in most cases, are required by law. In 45 CFR § 164.103, *required by law* is defined as "a mandate contained in law that compels an entity to make a use or disclosure of protected health information and that is enforceable in a court of law." It includes any court orders, warrants, subpoenas, or summons issued by a court, grand jury, government (or tribal) inspector general, or an authorized administrative body that requires the production of information. It could also include a civil or authorized investigative demand. As a condition to participate in Medicare or to receive payment under a government program providing public benefits, a covered entity has to comply with the HIPAA/HITECH regulations.

1.3 Covered Entities Defined

Since this book will discuss what these HIPAA/HITECH regulations are, it is best to determine to what types of organizations do these laws apply? An organization (or an individual) that meets one or more of the definitions to follow is considered a covered entity and must comply with the HIPAA/HITECH requirements:

- A *health plan* (or a group health plan as discussed earlier). Some examples of covered health plans are health insurance companies, HMOs, company health plans, and government programs that pay for healthcare (i.e., Medicare, Medicaid, and the military and veterans healthcare programs).
- A *healthcare clearinghouse* as defined in 45 CFR § 160.103 is a "public or private entity … that performs either of the following functions:
  (1) Processes or facilitates the processing of health information … in a nonstandard format or containing nonstandard data content into standard data elements or a standard transaction.
  (2) Receives a standard transaction … and processes or facilitates the processing of health information [in the standard transaction] into nonstandard format or nonstandard data content for the receiving entity."
- A *covered healthcare provider*—A *healthcare provider* that transmits any information in an *electronic form* in connection with a *covered transaction*. Some examples of a covered healthcare provider are doctors, clinics, psychologists, dentists, chiropractors, nursing homes, and pharmacies. There are three elements that need to be fulfilled to be defined as a covered healthcare provider and required to comply with HIPAA/HITECH regulations. The three elements are italicized above. First, to be a covered healthcare provider, the organization or individual has to provide healthcare as defined earlier: "care, services, or supplies related to the health of an individual." Second, information must be transmitted in an electronic form or using electronic media, electronic storage media including memory devices in computers (hard drives) and any removable/transportable digital memory medium, such as magnetic tape or disk, optical disk, or digital memory card; or transmission media used to exchange information already in electronic storage media. Finally, the electronic exchange of information has to be related to a covered transaction. Covered transactions are defined in Section 1.4.

As of July 2010, Table 1.1 demonstrates the number of organizations, by the North American Industry Classification System (NAICS) Code, that are defined as covered entities.

Table 1.1 Covered Entities

NAICS	Description	Totals
622	Hospitals	4,060
623	Nursing facilities	34,400
6211-6213	Medical offices	419,286
6214	Outpatient centers	13,962
6215	Medical diagnostics and imaging services	7,879
6216	Home health services	15,329
6219	Other ambulatory care services	5,879
N/A	Durable medical equipment suppliers	107,567
4611	Pharmacies	88,396
524114	Health insurance carriers	1,045
524292	Third-party administrators (working on behalf of covered health plans)	3,522
TOTALS		701,325

1.4 Covered Transactions Defined

As seen with certain organizations that are required to comply with the HIPAA/ HITECH regulations, there are also certain transactions that fall under the umbrella of HIPAA/HITECH compliance. The following explains the type of transactions considered covered transactions:

■ *Healthcare claims* or equivalent *encounter information transactions* as defined in 45 CFR § 162.1101 are either "a request to obtain payment, and necessary accompanying information, from a healthcare provider to a health plan, for healthcare," or "if there is no direct claim, because the reimbursement contract is based on a mechanism other than charges or reimbursement rates for specific services, the transaction is the transmission of encounter information for the purpose of reporting healthcare."
■ The *eligibility for a health plan transaction* as defined in 45 CFR § 162.1201 is either "an inquiry from a healthcare provider to a health plan or from one health plan to another health plan, to obtain any of the following information about a benefit plan for an enrollee: eligibility to receive healthcare under the health plan; coverage of healthcare under the health plan; or benefits associated with the benefit plan," or "a response from a health plan to a healthcare provider's (or another health plan's) inquiry" for the information already described.

- The *referral certification* and *authorization transaction* as defined in 45 CFR § 162.1301 is "a request for the review of healthcare to obtain an authorization for the healthcare, a request to obtain authorization for referring an individual to another healthcare provider, or a response to a request" for such information.
- A *healthcare claim status transaction* as defined in 45 CFR § 162.1401 is "an inquiry to determine the status of a healthcare claim or a response about the status of a healthcare claim."
- The *enrollment* or *disenrollment in a health plan transaction* as defined in 45 CFR §162.1501 is "the transmission of subscriber enrollment information to a health plan to establish or terminate insurance coverage."
- The *healthcare payment* and *remittance advice transaction*, as paraphrased from 45 CFR § 162.1601, is the transmission of payment, information about the transfer of funds, or payment processing information from a health plan to a healthcare provider's financial institution, or the transmission of the explanation of benefits or remittance of advice from a health plan to a healthcare provider.
- The *health plan premium payment transaction* as defined in 45 CFR § 162.1701 "is the transmission of payment, information about the transfer of funds, detailed remittance information about individuals for whom premiums are being paid, or payment processing information to transmit healthcare premium payments (to include, payroll deductions, other group premium payments, or associated group premium payment information) from the entity that is arranging for the provision of healthcare or is providing healthcare covered payments for an individual to a health plan."
- The *coordination of benefits transaction* as defined in 45 CFR § 162.1801 "is the transmission from any entity to a health plan for the purpose of determining the relative payment responsibilities of the health plan of claims or payment information for healthcare."

1.5 Are You a Covered Entity?

In this section, a step-by-step process will be described to determine if an organization is considered or defined as a covered entity under the HIPAA/HITECH regulations. Throughout this process, an organization will answer some questions about its status based on the previous definitions. Included in this section are some flow charts to make this process easier to follow and to assist the organization in determining their status as a covered entity. With this in mind, here is the process to determine an organization's covered entity status. Note: Throughout this section, the term *organization* will be used. An organization can also be a single individual that provides certain healthcare related services.

1.5.1 Covered Healthcare Provider

Does the organization furnish, receive payments for, or bill for healthcare as a normal course of business? If the answer is no, then the organization is not a covered healthcare provider. This, however, does not necessarily mean that the organization is not required to comply with the HIPAA/HITECH regulations. Continue on.

If the answer is yes, then does the organization transmit any covered transactions (as discussed earlier) electronically? If the answer is no, then the organization is not a covered healthcare provider. If the answer is yes, then the organization is considered a covered healthcare provider and is required to comply with the HIPAA/HITECH Security Standards. See Figure 1.2.

One important note of reference is that healthcare providers that may not submit HIPAA transactions in standard form will become covered entities under the HIPAA Security Rule when another entity, such as a billing service or hospital, transmits this standard electronic transaction on their behalf. The regulations imply that providers cannot circumvent the requirements by assigning these responsibilities to their business associates. The business associates are considered to be acting on behalf of the provider in providing these services and as such must also comply with the HIPAA Security Rule as discussed in Section 1.6. Business associates must also comply with the HIPAA Privacy Rules as part of the Privacy Rules provisions incorporated into the business associate contract governed under HITECH Act 1304.

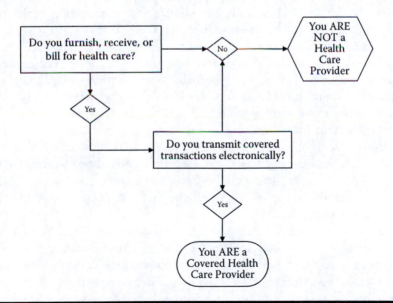

Figure 1.2   Covered healthcare provider.

Although there may be other entities that use or disclose individually identifiable health information, the Department of Health and Human Services only has jurisdiction over health plans, healthcare clearinghouses, and healthcare providers that electronically transmit health information as it relates to standard financial or administrative transactions (i.e., covered transactions). The function of the entity under the regulations dictates the qualifications as a covered entity. For instance, a social service worker that provides healthcare or transmits information in a standard HIPAA transaction would be considered a covered entity. On the other hand, if a social service worker does not provide any healthcare as defined or transmit any standard transactions, they would not be considered a covered entity. Again, it does not matter what title the individual may have, it is the activity or function that qualifies.

For additional clarifications, normally employers and marketing firms are not covered entities. In cases where employers are plan sponsors under a group health plan, the employer would be considered a covered entity under the HIPAA Privacy and Security Rule as it relates to a group health plan sponsor.

Although life and casualty insurers may use and disclose individually identifiable health information, they are not considered health plans for the purpose of the HIPAA Privacy and Security Rule. They are not considered covered entities (Department of Health and Human Services n.d.)

Related to manufacturer suppliers of healthcare devices, if the supplier is a Medicare supplier, it would be considered a covered entity if it conducts standard transactions defined under the HIPAA regulations. To clarify, the manufacturer supplier is considered a healthcare provider since it is providing healthcare as defined in the HIPAA rules. The manufacturer is only a covered entity if it is conducting standard transactions. If the manufacturer is supplying only generic (not customizable) products, then it is not providing healthcare and not a covered entity. In cases where a manufacturer is considered a covered entity, it may be considered an indirect treatment provider and not subject to all the requirements.

Likewise, for pharmaceutical manufacturers, the same rules would apply. Unless the pharmaceutical manufacturer is providing support to doctors or patients and meets the definition of providing healthcare and conducting standard transactions related to these services (which would make them a covered entity), then the pharmaceutical manufacturer would not be considered a covered entity. For instance, if the pharmaceutical company is only offering free samples, then it would not be considered a covered entity.

In cases where doctors, nurses, or other healthcare providers work for a hospital or other larger organization and do not conduct standard transactions on their own, but the larger organization submits these transactions on the provider's behalf, they are considered workforce members of the larger organization (i.e., covered entity). These workforce members are not considered covered entities themselves. There is not a blanket rule that describes all arrangements between all entities. The HIPAA Rules will apply depending on the purposes for sharing protected health information, ownership or control of the participants, and other similar matters. Just because a physician has staff privileges of a covered hospital (or entity) does not mean that the physician becomes a part of the covered entity by having these privileges.

In cases where a bank (or financial institution as defined by Congress in 12 USC § 3401, the Right to Financial Privacy Act) processes consumer side transactions for payment of healthcare services such as debit, credit, or other card payments, check processing, electronic fund transfers, or other activity that facilitates the transfer of funds, it will not be considered a covered entity or acting on behalf of a covered entity for such transactions. Now, if the bank operates an accounts payable system (or other back-office function) that is not described in section USC 1179, the bank would be considered a business associate under the rules and subject to meeting the requirements of a business associate contract.

1.5.2 Healthcare Clearinghouse

Does the organization process or facilitate the process of changing the content of health information from a nonstandard format into a standard format, or vice versa? If the answer is no, then the organization is not a healthcare clearinghouse.

If the answer is yes, does the organization perform this function for another entity? If the answer is no, then the organization is not a healthcare clearinghouse. If the answer is yes to this question, then the organization is considered a healthcare clearinghouse as defined by 45 CFR § 160.103 and is required to comply with the HIPAA/HITECH Security Standards. See Figure 1.3.

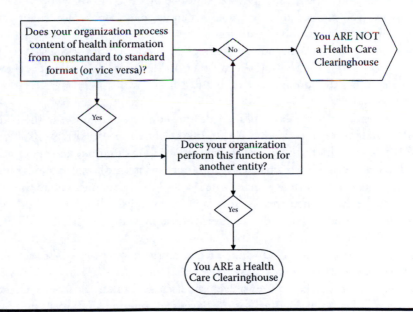

Figure 1.3   Healthcare clearinghouse.

1.5.3 Health Plan

Does the organization provide or pay for the cost of medical care as part of an individual health plan, a group health plan, or a combination thereof? If the answer is no, then the plan is not a covered health plan.

If the answer is yes, is the plan a group health plan (as discussed earlier and defined by 45 CFR § 160.103)? If the plan is a group health plan, does it have fewer than 50 participants and is it self-administered? If both of these conditions are met, then the plan is not considered a covered health plan. If, on the other hand, the plan has more than 50 participants or it is self-administered, then the plan is considered a covered health plan and is required to comply with the HIPAA/HITECH Security Standards.

If the plan is not a group health plan, is the plan a health insurance insurer? As defined in 45 CFR § 160.103, a *health insurance insurer* "is an insurance company, insurance service, or insurance organization (including an HMO) that is licensed to engage in the business of insurance in a state and is subject to state law that regulates insurance." If the answer to this question is yes, then the plan is considered a health plan and is required to comply with the HIPAA/HITECH Security Standards.

If the plan is not a health insurance insurer, is the plan an issuer of a Medicare supplemental policy? "An *issuer of a Medicare supplemental policy* is: a private entity that offers a health insurance policy or other health benefit plan, to individuals who are entitled to have payments made under Medicare, which provides reimbursement for expenses incurred for services and items for which payment may be made under Medicare, but which are not reimbursable by reason of the applicability of deductibles, coinsurance amounts, or other limitations imposed pursuant to or other limitations imposed by Medicare. A Medicare supplemental policy does not include policies or plans excluded under section 1882(g)(1) of the Social Security Act. See 42 U.S.C. 1395ss (g)(1)." An issuer of Medicare supplemental policy is considered a health plan and is required to comply with the HIPAA/HITECH Security Standards.

If the plan is not an issuer of a Medicare supplemental policy, is the plan a health maintenance organization (HMO)? As defined in 45 CFR §160.103, an *HMO* "is a federally qualified health maintenance organization, an organization recognized as a health maintenance organization under state law, or a similar organization regulated for solvency under state law in the same manner and to the same extent as a health maintenance organization as previously described." An HMO is considered a health plan and is required to comply with the HIPAA/HITECH Security Standards.

If the plan is not an HMO, is the plan a multiemployer welfare benefit plan? A *multiemployer welfare benefit plan* is defined under 45 CFR § 160.03 as "an employee welfare benefit plan [as previously discussed] or any other arrangement that is established or maintained for the purpose of offering and providing health benefits to the employees of two or more employers." A multiemployer welfare benefit plan is considered a health plan and is required to comply with the HIPAA/ HITECH Security Standards.

If the plan is not a multiemployer welfare benefit plan, is the plan an issuer of long-term care policies? If the plan provides only nursing home fixed-indemnity policies then the plan is not a health plan. If, on the other hand, the plan provides more than just nursing home fixed-indemnity policies, it is considered a health plan and is required to comply with the HIPAA/HITECH Security Standards.

If the plan is not an issuer of long-term care policies, does the plan provide only excepted benefits? As defined under 42 U.S.C. 300gg-91(c)(1), *excepted benefits* are "coverage for accident, or disability income insurance, or any combination thereof; coverage issued as a supplement to liability insurance; liability insurance, including general liability insurance and automotive liability insurance; workers' compensation or similar insurance; automobile medical payment insurance; credit only insurance; coverage for on-site medical clinics; other similar insurance coverage, specified in regulations, under which benefits for medical care are secondary or incidental to other insurance benefits." If the plan provides only excepted benefits, then the plan is not a health plan. Otherwise, the plan is considered a health plan and is required to comply with the HIPAA/HITECH Security Standards. See Figure 1.4.

1.5.4 Government Health Plans

The following government-funded health plans are all considered a covered health plan required to comply with the HIPAA/HITECH Security Standards:

- The Medicare program under Title XVIII of the Social Security Act (Parts A, B, and C) (42U.S.C. 1395, et seq.)
- The Medicaid program under Title XIX of the Social Security Act (42 U.S.C. 1396, et seq.)
- The healthcare program for active military personnel (10 U.S.C. 1074, et seq.)
- The veterans' healthcare program (38 U.S.C. Ch.17)
- The Civilian Health and Medical Program of the Uniformed Services (CHAMPUS) (10 U.S.C. 1061, et seq.)
- The Indian Health Service program under the Indian Healthcare Improvement Act (25 U.S.C. 1601)
- The Federal Employees Health Benefit Program (5 U.S.C. Ch. 89)
- Approved state child health programs under Title XXI of the Social Security Act (42 U.S.C. 1397, et seq.) (SCHIP)

If the program is not one of these listed, is the program an individual or group plan that pays the cost or provides medical care as previously defined? If not, then the plan is not considered a health plan. Otherwise, is the program a high risk pool? A *high risk pool* is a mechanism established under state law to provide health

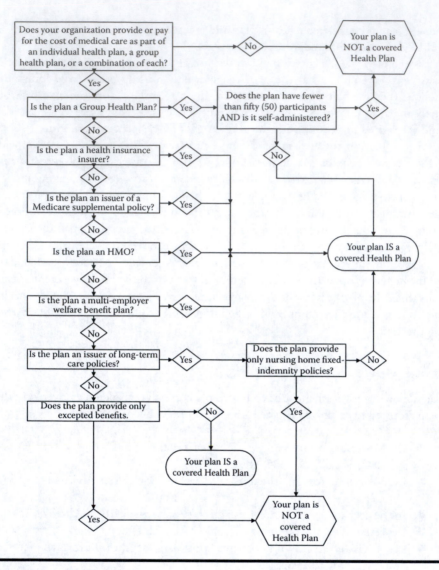

Figure 1.4 Health plans.

insurance coverage or comparable coverage to eligible individuals. If the program is a high risk pool, then it is considered a covered health plan required to comply with the HIPAA/HITECH Security Standards.

If the program is not a high risk pool, then is the plan an HMO as defined earlier? If the program is an HMO, it is considered a covered health plan required to comply with the HIPAA/HITECH Security Standards. If the plan is not an HMO, is the principal activity of the program providing healthcare directly? If it is providing healthcare directly then the plan is not considered a health plan.

If the program does not provide healthcare directly, is the principal activity of the program the making of grants to fund the direct provision of healthcare such as providing grants to fund a health clinic? If this is the case, the plan is not a health plan. If the principal purpose of the program is to provide something other than providing or paying the cost of healthcare such as operating a prison system or running a scholarship or fellowship program, then the plan is also not a health plan. If the program provides only excepted benefits, then the plan is not a health plan. If any one of these conditions is not met, then the plan would be considered a health plan with the requirement to comply with the HIPAA/HITECH Security Standards. See Figure 1.5.

1.6 Business Associates

At times, covered entities require certain functions, activities, and services be performed from other companies that are not a member of a covered entity's workforce and that may involve the use or disclosure of individually identifiable health information. Some of these functions, activities, and services may include, but are not limited to, claims processing, data analysis, utilization review, billing legal services, accounting/financial services, consulting, administrative services, accreditation, or other types of services. Companies that provide these types of functions, activities, and services to covered entities are known as business associates as defined in 45 CFR § 160.103. In addition, a covered entity may provide these types of services and be a business associate to other covered entities. If services of a company do not involve the use or disclosure of protected health information or if access to such information is incidental, then the organization or person providing these services are not considered a business associate. Some examples of a business associate that would have access to protected health information may include consultants, certified public accountants (CPAs), lawyers, medical transcriptionists, benefit administrators, and claim processors. As of July 2010, there were an estimated 1.5 million organizations that were considered business associates of covered entities. As a point of reference, the new Omnibus Rule, which will be described later, will require these business associates to be HIPAA/HITECH compliant along with any subcontractors or other associates of these business associates that may have access to electronic protected health information, and they will also need to comply with the HIPAA/HITECH regulations.

1.6.1 Business Associate Contracts

For a covered entity to utilize another company for business-associate-type services, the covered entity must have a contract or other agreement in place with the business associate. This is to ensure the safeguarding of the covered entities' individually identifiable health information. The covered entity must obtain satisfactory

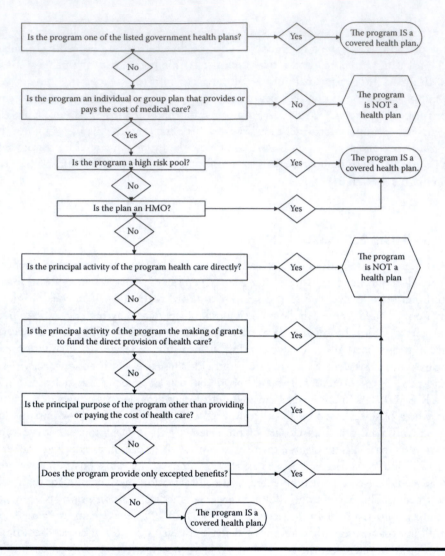

Figure 1.5   Government health plans.

assurance that the business associates will use the protected health information only for its intended use, will safeguard the information from inappropriate use, and will assist the covered entity in complying with the HIPAA/HITECH Privacy and Security Rule. A written contract complies with the satisfactory assurance requirements of the HIPAA/HITECH Privacy Rule; however, it may lack the necessary assurance for the new Omnibus Rule related to due diligence under the HIPAA/HITECH Security Rule.

Per 45 CFR § 164.504(e), the business associate contract must contain, at a minimum, the following elements:

- "Describe the permitted and required uses of protected health information by the business associate;
- Provide that the business [associate] will not use or further disclose the protected health information other than as permitted or required by the contract or as required by law; and
- Require the business associate to use appropriate safeguards to prevent a use or disclosure of the protected health information other than as provided for by the contract."

In addition, "where a covered entity knows of a material breach or violation by the business associate of the contract or agreement, the covered entity is required to take reasonable steps to cure the breach or end the violation, and if such steps are unsuccessful to terminate the contract or arrangement. If termination of the contract or agreement is not feasible, a covered entity is required to report the problem to the Department of Health and Human Services (HHS) Office for Civil Rights (OCR)."

1.7 Privacy Rule Overview

The HIPAA/HITECH Privacy Rule requires a covered entity to implement appropriate and reasonable administrative, physical, and technical safeguards for the protection of protected health information. The major purpose of the Privacy Rule is defining or limiting the use or disclosure of an individual's protected health information by a covered entity. A covered entity must disclose protected health information in only two situations: first, to individuals or authorized personal representatives when they specifically request access to or an accounting of disclosure of their protected health information; or second, to the Department of Health and Human Services when it is undertaking a compliance investigation, review, or other enforcement action.

1.7.1 Permitted Use and Disclosures Overview

There are, of course, some purposes or situations where a covered entity is permitted to use and disclose protected health information without specific authorization from an individual. Details on these permitted uses and disclosures will be discussed later, but for now, here is a list of these permitted or authorized use and disclosure situations:

- To the individual
- Treatment, payment, healthcare operations
- Uses and disclosures with opportunity to agree or object
- Incidental use and disclosure
- Public interest and benefit activities
- Limited data set

1.7.2 Authorized Uses and Disclosures Overview

Use and disclosure of protected health information is authorized for treatment, payment, or healthcare operations. For example, a doctor would be authorized to look into a patient's medical record to diagnose and provide treatment to the patient. In addition, a healthcare claims billing clerk could contact an individual's health plan and utilize the individual's information to obtain payment for provided healthcare services. These are just a couple of examples that demonstrate authorized uses and disclosure of protected health information. A covered entity must obtain an individual's written authorization for any other purposes. This written authorization must be in plain language and contain specific terms that an individual can understand. After an individual signs a written authorization, the covered entity is authorized to use or disclose the individual's information as provided for in the written authorization. There are a couple of special considerations for psychotherapy notes and marketing activities that will be discussed in detail later.

1.7.3 Minimum Necessary Overview

A covered entity must make a reasonable effort to allow only the minimum necessary use and disclosure of protected health information. There are several circumstances in which the minimum necessary requirement does not apply; however, in most instances, the covered entity must develop and implement policies and procedures to comply with the minimum necessary requirement regarding the access, use, disclosure, and requests for disclosure of protected health information. In the simplest of terms, minimum necessary means that the covered entity's workforce members will only be provided the least amount of an individual's information that is necessary for them to perform their jobs. For instance, if a receptionist at a doctor's office only needs to know the name of patients that are going to be seen on specific days at certain times, then the receptionist should not have access to the patient's full medical records. The receptionist should only have access to the patient's name and maybe their phone number so a reminder call could be made to confirm an appointment. In some cases, the receptionist may also know the reason for the visit, but this is probably the extent of the information required for him or her to perform his or her job duties. This example demonstrates the "need to know" rule of thumb that should be utilized for using or disclosing protected health information. This rule is consistent with the minimum necessary principle.

1.7.4 Notice and Other Individual Rights Overview

A covered entity must provide a notice of privacy practices to individuals as provided for in 45 CFR § 164.520. This notice must contain certain elements related to the use and disclosure of protected health information and the rights the individual has to such information. The individual has the right to receive the notification at any time upon request and the covered entity should make every reasonable attempt to acknowledge such receipt of notification. In most situations, the individual has the right to access, amend, and restrict the use or disclosure of their protected health information. An individual also has the right to receive an accounting of disclosure, with certain limitations, and to request to receive confidential communications in an alternative method.

1.7.5 Administrative Requirements Overview

The HIPAA/HITECH Privacy Rule maintains some flexibility in regard to how a covered entity will pursue compliance with these rules. There are some general requirements pertaining to the development and implementation of privacy policies and procedures, but the Privacy Rule will not specifically define how a covered entity should comply.

In addition to privacy policies and procedures, a covered entity must designate a privacy official responsible for the development and implementation of these policies and procedures. The privacy official may have other job duties and responsibilities, but the Privacy Rule indicates that a workforce member should be formally designated and assigned certain responsibilities related to the development and implementation of privacy policies and procedures.

A covered entity is also responsible for training its workforce members and management in these policies and procedures. This may be done upon hiring a new workforce member and refresher training could be provided periodically for existing workforce members. The Privacy Rule also requires retraining for workforce members whenever there is a material change to the covered entities' policies/procedures or rules/regulations as per 45 CFR § 164.530(b).

Furthermore, a covered entity must implement data safeguards to secure protected health information and develop mitigation strategies in case a breach occurs, to minimize the harm caused by the breach. This book will go into detail about the implementation of data safeguards along with mitigation strategies. These requirements are further discussed throughout the HIPAA/HITECH Security Rule standards.

A covered entity must establish procedures for individuals to report a suspected violation of the covered entity's privacy policies and procedures. A covered entity cannot retaliate against a person making a complaint. For instance, a covered entity could not terminate treatment of a patient that makes a complaint against the covered entity for a privacy policy violation.

Finally, a covered entity must document and retain records in accordance with its privacy policy. There are some exceptions to this requirement for a fully insured group health plan that will be discussed later.

1.7.6 Organizational Options Overview

As there are many ways to comply with the HIPAA/HITECH Privacy Rule, there are also many varied types of organizations and options by which these organizations can choose to comply. Some of these organizations have special considerations and provisions defined in the Privacy Rule that cover hybrid entities, affiliated covered entities, organization healthcare arrangements, covered entities with multiple covered functions, and disclosures to plan sponsors of group health plans. All of these options will be discussed in further detail later in this book.

1.7.7 Other Provisions: Personal Representatives and Minors Overview

There are special ways in which personal representatives are handled, especially when they involve minors. In most cases, a parent is considered a personal representative of their minor children; however, there are some exceptions such as in the case where child abuse or neglect is suspected. These special handling provisions are normally established by state laws as provided for in 45 § 164.502(g).

1.7.8 State Law Overview

In most cases, the federal HIPAA/HITECH Privacy Rule regulations preempt state laws if there is a discrepancy between state and federal regulations and where the federal regulations are more stringent than state laws. Where State laws are more restrictive and provide greater protection of the protected health information or where State laws require certain reporting requirements, then compliance with both the federal and state laws must be met. In most cases, state laws are written to be more stringent than federal regulations, and, therefore, federal laws seldom preempt state laws. The need to comply with both federal and state laws increases the regulatory burden for covered entities and business associates.

As previously described, the HITECH Act enabled attorney generals of each state to bring enforcement actions for violation of the HIPAA/HITECH Privacy and Security Rules. In many states, privacy regulations are much stricter than federal requirements and even though a company may not operate directly out of a certain state, if a resident of the state had their information breached, they are entitled to notification under the individual's state laws. This could create some obstacles for companies conducting business in certain states and these businesses have to be aware of the different regulations that they must follow for each area they service.

1.7.9 Enforcement and Penalties for Noncompliance Overview

The Department of Health and Human Services is responsible for enforcing compliance with the HIPAA/HITECH Privacy Rule (and Security Rule) for covered entities and business associates. There are severe civil and criminal penalties that can be imposed and as of October 30, 2009, these penalties have increased. HHS is now pursuing stricter enforcement and regulatory actions against covered entities to force compliance, including business associates that may do business with these covered entities.

1.7.10 Compliance Dates Overview

As of the date of this book's publication, all covered entities are required to comply with the HIPAA Privacy Rule and Security Rule and modifications made by the HITECH Act. These regulations have been around for almost 7 years; however, a lot of covered entities are still not compliant. Unfortunately for these covered entities, the regulators are getting stricter and 2012 may be known as the year for HIPAA/HITECH compliance enforcement efforts.

1.8 Electronic Transactions and Code Sets Rule Overview

If a covered entity performs any covered electronic transactions, the entity must comply with the standard for that transaction. A *standard transaction* is a transaction that complies with the standard for that transaction that the HHS Secretary adopted in 45 CFR § 162.103. To specify electronic transactions, the American National Standards Institute (ANSI) chartered several organizations, including the Accredited Standards Committee (ASC) X12N Subcommittee and the National Council for Prescription Drug Programs (NCPDP). There are eight standard transactions covered under the HIPAA rules:

- Claims or equivalent encounter information
- Payment and remittance advice
- Claim status inquiry and response
- Eligibility inquiry and response
- Referral certification and authorization inquiry and response
- Enrollment and disenrollment in a health plan
- Health plan premium payments
- Coordination of benefits

Note: Claims attachments and first report of injury are pending approval.

In addition, there are six code sets or clinical codes uses in transactions to identify the type of procedures, services, and diagnoses pertaining to patient encounters. The following code sets are currently in use:

- Healthcare Common Procedural Coding System (HCPCS) and Current Procedural Terminology, 4th edition, (CPT-4), combination of both, are used for physician services/other health services
- Healthcare Common Procedural Coding System (HCPCS) is used for ambulance services, durable medical equipment, prosthetics, orthotics, and supplies used outside of a physician's office
- International Classification of Diseases, 9th edition, Clinical Modification (ICD-9-CM), Volumes 1 and 2 for diagnosis codes

■ International Classification of Diseases, 9th edition, Clinical Modification (ICD-9-CM), Volume 3 for inpatient hospital procedures
■ Current Dental Terminology (CDT), Code on Dental Procedures and Nomenclature, version 3, for dental services
■ National Drug Codes (NDC) for retail pharmacy for drugs and biologics

1.9 National Provider Identifier Requirements Overview

The National Provider Identifier (NPI) is a unique 10-digit intelligence-free number assigned to all covered healthcare providers. As part of the HIPAA Administrative Simplification Standard, all covered healthcare providers, health plans, and health-care clearinghouses must use their NPIs in any administrative or financial transactions. For any HIPAA standard transaction, the NPI must be utilized. For billing purposes, covered providers must share their NPI with other providers, health plans, or healthcare clearinghouses.

1.10 Security Rule Overview

Security is ever changing and evolving. It is a dynamic and ongoing struggle to keep information secure as new technology is introduced to the industry. This new technology is usually introduced to make things more efficient, but sometimes the technology is not properly vetted and can create security issues. There were two primary purposes for the development of the HIPAA/HITECH Security Rule. First, the Security Rule was intended to protect certain electronic healthcare information. Second, this information is supposed to be protected while allowing the proper access and use of the information. It was the goal of the Security Rule, by following these objectives, to promote the expanded use of electronic health information in the healthcare industry.

This health insurance reform or, more specifically, the Security Standards of this reform are required under three parts (specifically, parts 160, 162, and 164) of Chapter 45 of the Code of Federal Regulations (CFR). These Security Standards were published February 20, 2003. All covered entities, except small health plans, were required to be in compliance by April 21, 2005. Small health plans had until April 21, 2006.

The Security Rule is different from the Privacy Rule in that the Security Rule set the requirements for only allowing those who should have access to electronically protected health information (EPHI) to actually have access to this information. The Security Rule only applies to protected health information (EPHI), whereas the Privacy Rule applies to PHI that could be found in many different forms such as electronic, oral, or paper. The Security Rule defines administrative, physical, and technical controls to be implemented to protect the confidentiality, integrity, and availability of the EPHI. As may have already been determined, the Security Rule is a more detailed, comprehensive requirement than is found in the Privacy Rule and is essentially a subset of the Privacy Rule.

The Security Rule is divided into three different safeguard categories: administrative safeguards, physical safeguards, and technical safeguards. These safeguards were developed to protect the confidentiality, integrity, and availability of electronic protected health information. Due to the details involved in the Security Rule, this book will spend a majority of its time addressing these rules specifically. This section is dedicated to providing an overview of the Security Rule while detailed explanations will be provided later.

1.10.1 Administrative Safeguards Overview

Administrative safeguards are defined under 45 CFR § 164.304 as "administrative actions, and policies and procedures, to manage the selection, development, implementation, and maintenance of security measures to protect electronic protected health information and to manage the conduct of the covered entity's workforce in relation to the protection of that information." The administrative safeguards encompass the following:

- Security management processes—Includes risk analysis, risk management, sanction policies, and information system activity reviews
- Assigned security responsibility—Includes assigning a security official
- Workforce security—Includes authorization and/or supervision, workforce clearance procedures, and termination procedures
- Information access management—Includes isolating healthcare clearinghouse functions, access authorization, and access establishment and modification
- Security awareness and training—Includes security reminders, protection from malicious software, log-in monitoring, and password management
- Security incident procedures—Includes response and reporting
- Contingency plan—Includes data backup plan, disaster recovery plan, emergency mode operation plan, testing and revision procedures, and applications and data criticality analysis
- Evaluation—Includes periodic technical and nontechnical evaluations
- Business associate contracts and other arrangements—Includes written contract or other arrangements

1.10.2 Physical Safeguards Overview

Physical safeguards are defined under 45 CFR § 164.304 as "physical measures, policies, and procedures to protect a covered entity's electronic information systems and related buildings and equipment, from natural and environmental hazards, and unauthorized intrusion." A covered entity must identify all of the places where electronic protected health information may be located. Electronic protected health information may be stored or maintained at the covered entity's main office, at the covered entity's remote locations, or at the homes of the covered entity's workforce members. A covered entity must consider all physical access to this electronic protected health information when implementing the required standards.

The physical safeguard standard of the HIPAA/HITECH Security Rule includes:

- Facility access controls—Includes contingency operations, facility security planning, access control and validation procedures, and maintenance records
- Workstation use—Includes the functions, manner, and location of workstations with respect to their access to electronic protected health information
- Workstation security—Includes physical safeguards surrounding workstations
- Device and media controls—Includes disposal, media re-use, accountability, and data backup and storage

1.10.3 Technical Safeguards Overview

Technical safeguards are defined under 45 CFR § 164.304 as "the technology and the policy and procedures for its use that protect electronic protected health information and control access to it." Due to the fact that there are so many different types of technology and solutions available to safeguard electronic information along with new technology being developed every day, the technical safeguard standards are flexible. A covered entity must consider several factors when implementing these standards. These factors include the size, complexity, and capabilities of the covered entity along with the cost of implementing solutions. A covered entity has to establish a reasonable balance between any identified risks and known vulnerabilities to the security of their electronic protected health information.

The areas of concern addressed in the technical safeguards standards of the Security Rule are as follows:

- Access control—Includes unique user identification, emergency access procedures, automatic logoff, and encryption/decryption
- Audit controls—Includes review of information system activities
- Integrity—Includes mechanisms to authenticate electronic protected health information
- Person or entity controls—Includes authentication mechanisms used
- Transmission security—Includes integrity controls and encryption during transit

1.10.4 National Institute of Standards and Technology (NIST) Special Publications

The Information Technology Laboratory (ITL) at the National Institute of Standards and Technology (NIST) provides the nation with measurements and standards involved in the advancement and productive use of information technology. Through NIST's Special Publication 800-series reports, organizations across a varied number of industries can utilize their standards and guidelines to implement cost-effective security and privacy solutions. Throughout this book, several references will be made to these publications, including NIST SP 800-53 Revision 4—Recommended Security Controls for Federal Information Systems and Organizations, and NIST SP 800-66—An Introductory Resource Guide for Implementing the Health Insurance Portability and Accountability Act (HIPAA) Security Rule.

NIST SP 800-53—Recommended Security Controls for Federal Information Systems and Organizations, Revision 4, lists 18 different families of controls over 3 different classes in an effort to standardize the framework of an organization's information security management process. There are 36 controls identified under the families of controls that make up the NIST SP 800-53 Control Set. Table 1.2 lists these security control classes along with their families and identifiers.

NIST SP 800-66—An Introductory Resource Guide for Implementing the Health Insurance Portability and Accountability Act (HIPAA) Security Rule summarizes the HIPAA security standards and helps to improve the understanding of the security standards required under the Security Rule. Both the NIST SP 800-53 and NIST SP 800-66, along with a couple of other special publications, will be referenced when discussing how these controls are applied to the protection of electronic protected health information.

1.11 Meaningful Use Overview

To achieve health and efficiency goals, the Centers for Medicare & Medicaid Services (CMS) has implemented an Electronic Health Records (EHR) Incentive Program. This program is designed to provide financial incentives for the meaningful use of certified EHR technology. Other benefits that a covered entity will obtain from the use of EHR technology is reduction in errors, reminders and alerts, availability of data, support for clinical decisions, and prescription automation through e-prescribing and automated refills.

There are three main components of meaningful use. These include the use of certified EHR technology in a meaningful manner, for electronic health information exchanges, and for clinical quality submissions. Over the next 5 years, meaningful use will be implemented in three stages. Stage 1 baselines electronic data capture and information sharing and started in 2011 through 2012. Expected to

Table 1.2 NIST SP 800-53 Security Control Classes, Families, and Identifiers

Identifier	Family
Management Class	
CA	Security Assessment and Authorization
PL	Planning
PM	Program Management
RA	Risk Assessment
SA	System and Services Acquisition
Operational Class	
AT	Awareness and Training
CM	Configuration Management
CP	Contingency Planning
IR	Incident Response
MA	Maintenance
MP	Media Protection
PE	Physical and Environmental Protection
PS	Personnel Security
SI	System and Information Integrity
Technical Class	
AC	Access Control
AU	Audit and Accountability
IA	Identification and Authentication
SC	System and Communications Protection

be implemented in 2014 and 2015, stage 2 and stage 3, respectively, will expand on the initial baseline along with expected future rule makings yet to be determined.

As of the writing of this book, over 2,000 hospitals and 41,000 doctors have received a total of $3.12 billion in incentive payments for adopting meaningful use. Under the Medicare Electronic Health Record Incentive Program, an eligible entity could receive as much as $44,000, and under the Medicaid Electronic Health Record Incentive Program, an eligible entity could receive as much as $63,750 (Clark 2012).

1.12 Breach Notification Rule Overview

Increased breach notification requirements came about as part of the HITECH Act enacted under the American Recovery and Reinvestment Act (ARRA) on February 17, 2009. These breach notification provisions apply to HIPAA-covered entities and business associates that access, maintain, retain, modify, record, store, destroy, or otherwise hold, use, or disclose unsecured protected health information. In short, if a covered entity discovers a breach of unsecured protected health information, it is required to promptly notify the affected individuals and the Secretary of Health and Human Services. If a business associate of a covered entity discovers that it had a breach, it must notify the covered entity of the breach. In some cases, the media must also be notified of such a breach, and for any breach involving more than 500 individuals, the Secretary of Health and Human Services is required to post a list of covered entities on the HHS Web site. As of the beginning of February 2012, there were 392 organizations reporting data breaches of more than 500 records since September 2009. A list of these organizations can be found at http://www.hhs.gov/ocr/privacy/hipaa/administrative/breachnotificationrule/breachtool.html.

1.13 Enforcement Rule Overview

The HHS strengthened HIPAA enforcement as a response to the HITECH Act that was enacted as part of the American Recovery and Reinvestment Act of 2009. New, stricter monetary penalties were enacted for violations of HIPAA occurring after February 18, 2009. The revisions included four categories of violations along with four different, incrementing tiers of monetary amounts. The modifications capped each violation at $50,000 per violation with an aggregate limit for identical violations set at $1.5 million per calendar year. As a note of reference, an organization could get assessed penalties for different kinds of violations so it could face total fines in excess of $1.5 million. The new requirements also provided an affirmative defense, waiver, and notice of proposed determination. Finally, the new HITECH Act provided for the enforcement of HIPAA Privacy or Security Rule violations by states' attorney generals.

Recently, the director of the Office for Civil Rights (OCR), Leon Rodriguez, emphasized a new era of "monetary enforcement" rather than the long-standing approach of "hand-holding" to assist covered entities (and business associates) in compliance efforts. In an interview conducted by *Report on Patient Privacy*, Rodriguez discussed OCR's plans to refocus on "high-impact cases." He emphasized "covered entities (CEs) and business associates (BAs), in the future, will face sanctions on all lapses discovered during an investigation regardless of whether they are directly related to the incident that sparked OCR's attention in the first place" ("'Monetary Enforcement'" 2012).

Rodriguez also warned that OCR will be going after a covered entity along with its business associate for sanctions resulting from a breach or violation when they are jointly responsible. Systemic issues underlying an incident will be a big consideration when determining an assessed monetary amount. In cases, from years past, where corrective actions would have been taken to fix issues, a greater priority will now be focused on high-impact areas of concern. These investigations will be done more quickly and will emphasize enforcement efforts. Once the Omnibus Rule is implemented, OCR will also be focusing attention on business associates. "There are going to be cases where culpability is shared equally between the CE and BA and in other cases where it might be more heavily found on one side or the other," Rodriguez indicated ("'Monetary Enforcement'" 2012).

1.14 Anti-Kickback Statute

Certain enumerations for reimbursable services are subject to criminal penalties under 42 USC § 1320A-7B, amending the Medicare and Medicaid Patient Protection Act of 1987. Although this "Anti-Kickback Statute" does not necessarily apply to HIPAA regulations, it does fall under compliance related to possible agreements with third-party organizations. Violation of this law is a felony level offense with fines not to exceed $25,000 or imprisonment not to exceed 5 years, or both. The law makes it illegal for anyone that "knowingly and willfully [solicits, receives, offers, or pays] any remuneration (including any kickback, bribe, or rebate), directly or indirectly, overtly or covertly, in cash or in kind, or [to induce such person]" for the following:

■ "In return for referring [or to refer] an individual to a person for the furnishing or arranging for the furnishing of any item or service for which payment may be made in whole or in part under a Federal health care program"; or
■ "[In return for] to purchase, lease, order, or arrange for or recommend purchasing, leasing, or ordering any good, facility, service, or item for which payment may be made in whole or in part under a Federal health care program."

An analysis of this statute and through other case law such as *United States v. Greber*, 760 F. 2d 68, 71 (3d Cir), the *reasons* behind an inducement is irrelevant, suffice it to say, if the purpose is to induce referrals, then the law is violated (Manning 1996). It does not matter if there are other reasons for inducement or if the inducement actually causes a referral, suffice it to say, if the purpose is to induce referrals, then the law is violated (Manning 1996).

There are several "safe harbor" exceptions to this anti-kickback statute summarized next, but they are narrowly focused:

1. A discount in price is exempted by a provider of service or other entity as long as it is properly disclosed and reflected in costs claims or charges made by the provider.
2. Any amounts paid by an employer to an employee of the employer are exempted for covered items or services.
3. Any amounts paid to a purchasing agent are exempt as long as the following are met:
    a. A written contract with the agent for each individual or entity that specifies the amount to be paid to the agent. This could be a fixed amount or on a percentage of the value of the purchases made.
    b. In the case of an entity that is a provider of services (as defined in section 1395x (u)), the agent discloses the amount received to the entity and upon the request of the Secretary of HHS with respect to purchases made by or behalf of the entity.
4. A waiver of any coinsurance may be exempted if the individual qualifies for subsidized services.
5. Any payment practice that is promulgated through regulations specified by the Secretary of HHS may be exempted.
6. Enumerations pursuant to a written agreement between the organization and the individual or entity if the organization is an eligible organization under section 1395mm or through a risk-sharing written agreement placing the individual or entity at substantial financial risk for the cost or utilization of the items or services which the individual or entity must provide may be exempted.
7. A waiver of reduction by pharmacies that meet other specific conditions specified in this statute may be exempted.
8. Any remuneration between a federally qualified health center and a Medicare Advantage (MA) organization pursuant to a written agreement may be exempted if other conditions are met as per this statute.
9. Any remuneration between a health center entity and any individual or entity providing goods, items, services, donations, loans, or a combination of these to the health center pursuant to a contract, lease, grant, loan, or other agreement as long as the agreement contributes to the enhancement of the health center servicing an underserved area may be exempted along with other conditions that are met as per this statute.

1.15 Patient Safety and Quality Improvement Act of 2005 (PSQIA)

To enhance the data available to assess and resolve patient safety and healthcare quality issues, a voluntary reporting system was established through the Patient Safety and Quality Improvement Act of 2005 (PSQIA). PSQIA, although not specifically part of HIPAA, provides federal privilege and confidentiality protection for patient safety information. This *patient safety information* is known as patient safety work product and these federal privileges are meant to encourage the reporting and analysis of medical errors. The Agency for Healthcare Research and Quality (AHRQ) is authorized to list patient safety organizations (PSOs), external experts that collect and review patient safety information. In addition, HHS is authorized to impose civil monetary penalties for violations of confidentiality to the patient safety work product.

The implementation specification for the PSQIA is known as the Patient Safety Rule. This regulation was published on November 21, 2008, and became effective January 19, 2009, under 42 CFR Part 3. There are four subparts to the Patient Safety Rule as follows:

- Subpart A—Defines terms related to the Patient Safety Rule.
- Subpart B—Provides for the requirement of AHRQ to list PSOs. The PSOs are designated experts that provide recommendations and feedback to healthcare providers after analyzing patient safety events or other collected information.
- Subpart C—Describes the patient safety work product privileges and confidentiality protections along with exceptions to these protections.
- Subpart D—Establishes the framework for HHS to ensure compliance with this rule by providing monitoring activities, enforcement actions, and hearing procedures.

As is the case for voluntary compliance with the HIPAA Privacy and Security Rule, the Office for Civil Rights (OCR) wants compliance with the Patient Safety Rule. OCR may conduct investigations into any complaints leveled as it pertains to violations of the Patient Safety Rule. In addition, OCR may conduct compliance reviews. If OCR determines a violation was committed, it has the authority to impose a penalty of up to $11,000 per violation.

Additional information on the Patient Safety Rule can be found at http://edocket.access.gpo.gov/2008/pdf/E8-27475.pdf.

1.16 Consumer Privacy Bill of Rights

On February 23, 2012, President Barack Obama's administration introduced a new Consumer Privacy Bill of Rights "as a blueprint for privacy in the information age" (Whitehouse 2012). Although this "bill of rights" is not directly related to HIPAA/HITECH, it could definitely increase the oversight with respect to privacy and security. This framework follows seven principles or "rights" that consumers should have over the control of their personal data (defined as any data, including aggregations of data, that is linkable to a specific individual, computers, or other devices) and how it should be used by companies. Here is a summarized version of the principles of the Consumer Privacy Bill of Rights:

1. "Individual Control: Consumers have a right to exercise control over what personal data companies collect from them and how they use it."
   a. Companies should provide consumers such control over personal data shared and how this information is collected, used, or disclosed.
   b. Companies should enable easily used and accessible mechanisms of choices, based on the personal data collected, on how personal data is collected, used, or disclosed.
   c. At times and where it allows consumers to make meaningful decisions, companies should offer consumers clear and simple choices about the collection, use, and disclosure of their personal data.
   d. Companies should offer accessible and easily used methods to withdraw or limit consent.
2. "Transparency: Consumers have a right to easily understandable and accessible information about privacy and security practices."
   a. Companies should clearly describe the following to consumers at times to provide for the meaningful understanding of privacy risks and to exercise controls over:
      i. What personal data is collected
      ii. Why the data needs to be collected
      iii. How the data will be used
      iv. When the data will be deleted or de-identified
      v. Whether the information will be shared with third parties
      vi. What the rationale or reasons the information will be shared with third parties
3. "Respect for Context: Consumers have a right to expect that companies will collect, use, and disclose personal data in ways that are consistent with the context in which consumers provide the data."
   a. Companies should limit use and disclosure for purposes consistent with the relationship, unless required by law to do otherwise.
   b. Companies should disclose in a manner that is easily actionable by consumers for what purpose personal data may be used or disclosed that is not consistent with the original context of the use or disclosure.
   c. Companies should adjust transparency based on the context of obtaining the information that in based on the consumer's age or familiarity with the technology the consumer utilizes.

    d. Companies may need to require greater protection for children and teenagers when obtaining personal data.

4. "Security: Consumers have a right to secure and responsible handling of personal data."

    a. Companies should conduct risks assessment on the privacy and security of personal data.

    b. Companies should maintain reasonable safeguards to control:

       i. Risks of loss

       ii. Unauthorized access, use, destruction, or modification

       iii. Improper disclosure

5. "Access and Accuracy: Consumers have a right to access and correct personal data in usable formats, in a manner that is appropriate to the sensitivity of the data and the risk of adverse consequences to consumers if the data is inaccurate."

    a. Companies should maintain accurate personal data.

    b. Companies should provide consumers with reasonable access to their personal data and provide appropriate means and opportunity to correct, request deletion, or request limitation of use.

    c. Companies should follow the principles of freedom of expression and freedom of the press when handling personal data.

    d. Companies should consider scale, scope, and sensitivity of personal data collected and likelihood that unauthorized use or disclosure of this information can cause financial, physical, or other material harm to consumers when determining measures to use to maintain accuracy and provide access, correction, deletion, or suppression capabilities.

6. "Focused Collection: Consumers have a right to reasonable limits on the personal data that companies collect and retain."

    a. Companies should follow the Respect for Context principle.

    b. Companies should dispose of in a secure fashion or de-identify personal data when it is no longer needed, unless otherwise under legal obligations.

7. "Accountability: Consumers have a right to have personal data handled by companies with appropriate measures in place to assure they adhere to the Consumer Privacy Bill of Rights."

    a. Companies should be accountable to enforcement authorities and consumers.

    b. Companies should hold employees responsible.

       i. Companies should train their employees on these principles.

       ii. Companies should regularly evaluate employees' adherence.

    c. Companies should conduct full audits.

    d. Companies and third parties that are disclosed personal data should maintain enforceable contracts to adhere to these principles, unless otherwise required by law.

There are four key elements to the framework to achieve its goals:

- Consumer Privacy Bill of Rights—Based upon the U.S.-developed and globally recognized Fair Information Practice Principles (FIPPs)
- Enforceable codes of conduct—Form the basis of requirements in different business contexts that will be developed through a multistakeholder process
- Federal Trade Commission (FTC) enforcement—Provided for in its authority to prohibit unfair or deceptive acts or practices
- Increasing global interoperability—Through mutual recognition, development of codes of conduct, and enforcement cooperation

To avoid duplicate regulations, since covered entities and other business associates are already subject to existing federal data privacy laws, "the Administration supports exempting companies from consumer data privacy legislation … however, activities within these companies that do not fall under an existing data privacy law would be covered by the legislation that the Administration proposes" (Whitehouse 2012).

One of the important notes to mention about this framework is enforcement actions. "Enforcement actions by the [Federal Trade Commission] FTC (and State Attorneys General) have established that companies' failure to adhere to voluntary privacy commitments, such as those stated in privacy policies, are actionable under the FTC Act's (and State analogues) prohibition on unfair or deceptive acts or practices. [FTC Act § 5, 15 U.S.C. § 45]" The administration indicates that the same authority that allows the FTC to take the aforementioned enforcement actions will justify their taking the same actions under the adherence to a multistakeholder code of conduct. This code of conduct, once adopted, will become "legally enforceable under existing laws." "Although companies may choose to adopt multiple codes of conduct to cover different lines of business," the Consumer Privacy Bill of Rights should help to establish a common baseline.

1.17 Federal Rules of Civil Procedures

A major regulation that affects just about every single U.S. entity was the new amendments to the Federal Rules of Civil Procedures (FRCP) that became effective December 1, 2006. These rules provided for enhanced handling of electronic information, including e-mail, instant messaging chats, documents, accounting databases, Web sites, and other electronic stored information (ESI) as it relates to lawsuits that cross state lines and court cases that involve federal regulations. The FRCP amendments put organizations on notice that no matter how small or large, no matter how many staff members or the limitation of resources an organization may have, information contained in electronic form must be retained and able to be retrieved in a readable format during litigation proceedings.

Although a covered entity may have policies or procedures in place to handle electronic retention, such as e-mail retention, a covered entity must be able to demonstrate or prove that its policies are being followed and it is in compliance. For instance, if a covered entity's policy is to destroy all e-mail after 6 years, then the covered entity had better have appropriate procedures in place to demonstrate that e-mail is being destroyed as per their policy. Unfortunately, there is currently no set time indicated for the retention and it is recommended that a covered entity obtain an opinion from its legal staff regarding retention periods. In addition, when "litigation holds" are placed on certain information, a covered entity should have strict procedures in place to handle this information accordingly.

Per FRCP Rule 26(f)(3), ESI should be produced in its original form. One of the considerations that a covered entity should cover is how is e-mail archived and can it be retrieved as required in its original form. This archiving system has to be secured so that information cannot be modified in an unauthorized manner. Covered entities that do not consider these items in their document storage solutions or cannot provide ESI in a timely fashion could be severely penalized in court. Covered entities could also face summary judgments, sanctions, evidence spoliation, or other adverse actions. Due to the complexity and wide range of information systems, expert advice should be sought when encountered by e-discovery litigation issues.

1.18 Summary

This chapter was intended to provide an overview of the HIPAA/HITECH Privacy and Security Rule standards and implementations. Terms, as they are defined throughout the HIPAA regulations, were explained and emphasis was placed on the qualifiers for a covered entity. As discussed, other entities, such as business associates working with covered entities and using electronic protected health information, must also secure this information. In addition, some financial incentives regarding the use of electronic medical records and substantiating meaningful use of these records were discussed. This chapter further discussed requirements of a covered entity if a breach occurs and described some penalties that could be enforced if complaints are received or compliance is not met.

A summary of the Anti-Kickback Statute was provided. Although this somewhat falls out of the scope of the HIPAA/HITECH regulations, it was thought best to include a brief discussion of the subject matter since it deals with compliance and agreements with other parties. The Patient Safety and Quality Improvement Act of 2005 (PSQIA), better known as the Patient Safety Rule, was also discussed.

The chapter continued with a summary of the new Consumer Privacy Bill of Rights. How this framework will affect the healthcare industry is still up for debate; however, it is important to note that Washington has taken a serious look at privacy and security issues. These issues have become a primary concern for the administration and although the government strives for voluntary compliance, the framework definitely includes enforcement actions.

The chapter ended with an overview of the Federal Rules of Civil Procedures. Covered entities should be aware of their requirements to produce electronically stored information as it pertains to lawsuits or other litigation holds. Expert legal and technical advice should be sought to assist the covered entity in these matters.

Chapter 2

Relevance of HIPAA/HITECH to Healthcare Organizations

Objectives

The objectives of this chapter are as follows:

- Explain the importance of security and the financial impact it has on the covered entity, individuals, entire industries, and around the world.
- Understand the importance of security on healthcare organizations.
- Understand the impact of crimes related to medical identity theft.
- Understand items related to information security that should be taken under consideration over the next year and into the future.
- Understand why Internet criminals go unpunished and why Internet crime is a profitable venture.
- Understand social engineering and the affect it can have on the covered entity.
- Determine some of the workplace threats that the covered entity may face.
- Understand the importance of compliance and securing electronic protected health information.
- Determine some of the impediments that the covered entity may be facing in complying with Health Insurance Portability and Accountability

Act (HIPAA)/Health Information Technology for Economic and Clinical Health (HITECH) Act regulations.
■ Determine possible solutions to protect the covered entity from becoming a victim.

2.1 Why Is Security Important?

In January 2012, Federal Bureau of Investigation (FBI) Director Robert Mueller testified before the Senate Select Committee on Intelligence explaining that cyberthreats would surpass terrorism as the nation's top concern. At the RSA Conference in San Francisco held on March 1, 2012, speaking to a crowd of 20,000 cybersecurity professionals, Mueller stated, "We are losing data, we are losing money, we are losing ideas and we are losing innovation. Together we must find a way to stop the bleeding" (Fox News 2012).

A study performed by Norton, an antivirus software development company, determined that there are 141 victims of cybercrime per minute in the United States. The study suggests that over the last year, the total bill for cybercrime topped $139 billion in the United States with over $388 billion being assessed globally. The top three types of cybercrimes, according to the report, were viruses or malware, online credit card fraud, and e-mail phishing scams (Weigel 2011).

Another survey, conducted by Check Point of over 850 information technology (IT) and security professionals around the world, provides further evidence that 48% of enterprises have been victims of social engineering attacks with the more common threat sources being phishing e-mails and social networking sites. The survey emphasizes that new employees and contractors are more susceptible to these types of social-engineering techniques. Terry Greer-King, UK managing director for Check Point, said: "Although the survey shows that nearly half of enterprises know they have experienced social engineering attacks, 41% said they were unsure whether they had been targeted or not. Because these types of attacks are intended to stay below an organization's security radar, the actual number of organizations that have been attacked could be much higher. Yet 44% of UK companies surveyed are not currently doing anything to educate their employees about the risks, which [are] higher than the global average" (Help Net Security 2011).

The Ponemon Institute, a privacy and information management research firm, along with PGP Corporation, a global leader in enterprise data protection, have reported annually for over the last 5 years the U.S. Cost of a Data Breach Study. The study takes a detailed look at 45 data breach cases that affected 5,000 to 101,000 records over 15 different industries. "According to the study, data breach incidents cost U.S. companies $204 per compromised customer record in 2009, compared to $202 in 2008. Despite an overall drop in the number of reported breaches (498 in

2009 vs. 657 in 2008 according to the Identity Theft Resource Center) the average total per-incident costs in 2009 were $6.75 million, compared to an average per-incident cost of $6.65 million in 2008" (Ponemon Institute 2011).

"The state of technology security overall is so weak that intelligence officials see hacking as one of the largest threats to western powers" (Menn 2011). According to the technology research firm Gartner, law enforcement officials arrest less than 1% of the cybercriminals. Although most law enforcement agencies concentrate their efforts on nation-backed cyberattacks, a new wave of "hacktivism" (the combination of computer hacking with political activism) has sprung up, blurring the lines between protesters, criminals, and spies. Law enforcement does not have the resources or expertise to handle this problem since the best cyberexperts usually work for higher paying private security companies.

Not only are there huge financial losses due to the lack of security, but also entire companies along with people's careers have been ruined. In February 2010, an article was published citing the chief executive officer of HBGary Federal, Aaron Barr, regarding the names of the individuals in a hacktivist group known as Anonymous. An all-out hacking campaign was conducted on HBGary Federal's servers to find out what Barr knew about the group. It took a weekend to gain access to the company's e-mails that were then publicly released. Unfortunately, the names of the individuals that Barr thought were involved in the hacktivist group were not correct and the repercussions of the hack devastated the security company along with forcing Barr's resignation.

After a hack was discovered in July 2011 and made public in August, the Dutch certificate authority DigiNotar, a subsidiary of VASCO, filed for bankruptcy protection. Approximately 531 fake certificates were issued as a result of the breach. Digital certificates are used as the authentication backbone of secure transactions over the Internet. If one of these certificates is compromised, any transmission thought to be secured using the certificate could ultimately be intercepted and deciphered. Other companies such as CloudNine and Blue Frog were also forced to be shut down due to online attacks (Kingsley-Hughes 2011).

Gary S. Miliefsky, founder and chief technology officer of NetClarity, a leading provider of patented network access control products, made some rather disturbing predictions for 2012 related to cybercrime and cyberwar. One of the top predictions is that small and medium sized businesses (SMBs) will be the top target for cybercriminals in 2012. Miliefsky advises that the effects on these businesses will be huge and as a result cause a lot of them to go out of business (PRWEB 2012).

All companies that conduct business over the Internet or in some way connect their systems to the Internet are at risk. To estimate the risk exposure an organization may face, go to the data breach risk calculator provided by Symantec and the Ponemon Institute at databreachcalculator.com. Based on the information provided, this calculator can determine the cost that the organization may face if a breach occurs to its information systems.

2.2 Are Healthcare Organizations Immune to Security Concerns?

According to a report from PricewaterhouseCoopers, LLP (PwC), "Electronic health data breaches are increasingly carried out by 'knowledgeable insiders' bent on identity theft or access to prescription drugs" (Eisenberg 2011). Since September 2009, more than 385 incidents affecting more than 19 million individuals have been reported to the Office for Civil Rights in which medical information was stolen or inappropriately disclosed. Out of these incidents affecting 500 or more records, roughly 55% involved an unencrypted electronic device or media being lost or stolen and about 22% involved business associates (Anderson 2012).

The most frequently reported issue is an internal party improperly using the protected health information. The problem will only increase and become more serious as more health information is put into cyberspace. James Koenig, co-lead of PwC's Health Information Privacy and Security Practice, said that the information target at hospitals "is either health insurance information, to be able to resell access to people who don't have insurance or, most often, access to prescription drugs which are a commodity that can be sold on the street" (Eisenberg 2011). A report that analyzed data from a survey of 600 executives from the healthcare industry indicated that half of the organizations reported a privacy or security-related issue over the last 2 years. Three-quarters of these executives indicated that they were already sharing or would be sharing patient data in clinical studies, postmarket surveillance of drugs, or the development of new medical programs. Unfortunately, only half of the executives are advising that they are addressing privacy and security related issues within their organizations.

These statistics are also supported by a survey conducted by HIMSS, which found that only 53% of healthcare organizations were conducting the mandatory annual risk assessments. Fifty-eight percent of these organizations had no dedicated staff for security efforts and half of the respondents spend less than 3% of their organizational resources on security (Painter 2011).

Healthcare providers are not immune to security breaches. A massive security breach affecting the protected health information of 4.9 million individuals in 10 states was reported by TRICARE, the U.S. military health program. It appears as though a contractor, Science Applications International Corporation (SAIC), on September 14, 2011, advised TRICARE that it lost a backup tape containing data on patients that were treated in San Antonio's military facilities between 1992 and September 7, 2011. The data included such items as names, Social Security numbers, addresses, phone numbers, clinical notes, laboratory tests, and prescriptions (Goedert 2011).

Micky Tripathi, president and CEO of Massachusetts eHealth Collaborative, an organization supported by 34 nonprofit healthcare organizations in Massachusetts, attests to the fact that a breach of electronic protected health information can be costly. After a laptop containing approximately 14,000 unencrypted patient records was stolen from an employee's car, the organization spent close to $300,000 to handle this breach. Tripathi did a really good job in explaining his first-hand account of the incident and how his organization responded to the breach in his blog post at http://www.histalkpractice.com/2011/12/03/first-hand-experience-with-a-patient-data-security-breach-12311/. One of the more interesting points of the article was how the organization determined "significant risk of harm" as is the requirement for notification. After conducting an analysis of the information stolen, it utilized a simple formula that any patient record containing a name along with a Social Security number or date of birth would render this patient at significant risk of harm and required notification to be made to the individual about the breach. Out of 14,000 records, only 1,000 met these criteria. The article further notes eight items that the organization learned from its experience with this breach (Tripathi 2011). These items are summarized as

1. Determine what type of security posture the organization currently has.
2. Assume all portable devices contain sensitive information, no matter what may have been said to the contrary.
3. Set expectations of contractors from the start as to who will have access to information and how this information will be handled.
4. Appropriately handle a security incident and make it a priority.
5. Do not underestimate the burden that an incident may have on the organization.
6. Keep logs.
7. Individuals involved in the incident should take responsibility for their actions.
8. The organization, as a whole, should take responsibility for its actions.

In October 2011, Sutter Health reported that a desktop computer was stolen from the administrative offices of Sutter Medical Foundation, a physician network in Sacramento, California. The unencrypted desktop contained two databases with patient information. One of the databases held information on 3.3 million individuals from 1995 through January 2011 for Sutter Physician Services, which provides billing and other administrative services for 21 Sutter units. The other database contained 943,000 records (944,000 upon another count) on Sutter Medical Foundation patients dated January 2005 to January 2011 (Anderson, "Computer Theft" 2011). Sutter is facing two class-action lawsuits related to this incident. One of the lawsuits seeks $1,000 for each of the 4.2 million patients affected, totaling more than $4.2 billion in damages. The other lawsuit seeks another $1,000 for each of the 944,000 records, totaling in excess of $944 million (Anderson, "More Breach" 2011).

2.3 Suffering from Data Breaches

During a recent survey conducted in February 2012 by the Ponemon Institute of 700 healthcare practitioners, 91% of participants with 250 workforce members or less indicated that they suffered from at least one data breach over the past year. In addition, 23% of these respondents experienced at least one patient medical identity theft within their organization during the same time period (Bowman 2012).

Major contributing factors for these breaches included workforce member negligence and noncompliance issues. Areas of particular concern involved mobile device use and social media activity. What is probably more disconcerting, however, is that 75% of these organizations lacked adequate funding to prevent the breaches in the first place and almost half (48%) of them indicated that their organization spends less than 10% of their annual budget to secure their data. This is indicative of the fact that executive officers do not see information security as an important priority in their organization. Unfortunately, as indicated in previous surveys, data security breaches cost the U.S. healthcare industry roughly $6.5 billion annually (Bowman 2012).

The cost of a breach can be split into five main categories:

1. Legal/Regulatory
2. Financial
3. Operational
4. Clinical
5. Reputational

The following are the losses that could be incurred under each category (American National Standards Institute 2012):

- Legal/regulatory
  - Fines and penalties assessed at the federal level (by the Office for Civil Rights [OCR]) or at the state level to include cost of corrective action plans
  - Lawsuit costs include legal, settlement, payments to individuals, or insurance deductibles
  - Loss (or reinstatement) of accreditation
- Financial
  - Business distraction costs
  - Remediation costs that include investigation or forensic costs, corrective action costs, workforce sanctions, or identity theft monitoring
  - Communication costs that include costs associated with notifying individuals or media, and public or investor relation campaigns
  - Insurance deductible or increase costs that include broker costs or cost of resources in negotiations with another agency
  - Changing vendors (in cases of a business associate breach) that includes due diligence costs, transition costs, and increased cost of services from a new vendor
- Operational
  - Recruiting and training new hires costs
  - Reorganizational costs

- Clinical
  - Diagnosis delays or inaccuracies
  - Processing fraudulent claims
  - Research results containing inaccurate data
- Reputational
  - Loss of current or future patients
  - Losing business partners
  - Staff losses

One of the most important aspects of any patient and healthcare provider relationship is *trust*. Every medical record contains a personal history of the individual that demonstrates the trust the individual has in his or her provider. The longevity of any covered entity will be greatly diminished if this trust is broken by a breach of personal health information. A covered entity cannot ignore the consequences of a data breach.

2.4 Rise of Medical Identity Theft

In the *Second Annual Survey on Medical Identity Theft*, published March 2011, the Ponemon Institute found that nearly 1.5 million Americans are victims of medical identity theft. The extrapolated cost per victim was up by about $500 from the previous year to an astounding $20,663 to resolve a case of medical identity theft. The national impact of medical identity theft crimes is close to $31 billion a year (Ponemon Institute, LLC 2011).

Some of the key factors identified in this study were as follows:

- Many people are unaware of the seriousness of medical identity theft crimes and the affects that it can have on them, such as negatively affecting credit scores. Primary consequences of these types of crimes are the financial harm that it could cause to the victim or the loss of health coverage.
- Committing medical identity theft is fairly easy, such as utilizing a name to obtain healthcare services, treatment, pharmaceuticals, equipment, or other benefits.
- Medical identity theft victims tend to be older.
- Victims have a hard time determining when the crime may have occurred.
- Since most victims share their medical information with family, these family members become the most likely individuals to steal identity.

Larry Ponemon, chairman and founder of the Ponemon Institute, stated, "Our study shows that the risk and high cost of medical identity theft are not resonating with the public, revealing a serious need for greater education and awareness." He further opines that "these results put an even greater onus on healthcare organizations to make the security of sensitive personal health information a priority in order to protect patient privacy" (Millard 2011). Some experts are claiming that cyber espionage and privacy violations are going to be some of the biggest security threats in 2012 (b.p 2012).

To help organizations and consumers prevent or protect themselves from identity theft, the Federal Trade Commission's (FTC's) Bureau of Consumer Protection has established a campaign, "AvoID Theft: Deter. Detect. Defend." Through this effort, a repository of ID theft information has been developed, including the FTC's Consumer Education Tool Kit, to assist individuals. The tool kit includes a how-to guide, video, brochure, CD-ROM, and an in-depth guide to identity theft. This kit along with other information can be obtained by going to the FTC's Web site at http://business.ftc.gov/documents/taking-lead-prevent-identity-theft.

2.5 Internet Crimes Go Unpunished

As opposed to other crimes, the chances of being caught or punished as a result of conducting Internet crime is significantly lower than for other crimes. In addition, the payout for conducting Internet crimes is more lucrative than for other crimes. For comparison, according to statistics from the FBI, there were 5,628 bank robberies in 2010 with $43 million stolen. On average, this is $7,643 per heist with about 22% of these funds recovered. Perpetrators of these crimes tend to face long jail times or injuries, up to and including death, depending on the circumstances of the event. For Internet crimes, there were approximately 300,000 victims with a financial loss of $1.1 billion. Although this averages out to only $3,666 per victim, some perpetrators are never caught and can rack up thousands to hundreds of thousands of dollars committing these types of crimes (Grimes 2012).

When talking about identity theft, which comprises only 9.8% of all types of Internet crime, the FBI was only able to arrest 1,600 individuals from 2003 to 2006 (from which trend data is available); however, only a third of these cases resulted in jail time. This jail time, of course, was a lot less than what would be handed down in the case of a bank robbery. Considering that about 4% of the adult population of the United States was affected by identity theft, this 8.3 million-victim count is pretty astonishing. This comes out to about 1 convicted cybercriminal for every 20,750 identity theft victims. Fast forward a few years, and the prosecution rates are not getting any better. According to the FBI's 2010 Internet Crime Report, out of the 1,420 prepared cases, there were only 6 convictions related to identity theft alone. This was out of a reported 303,809 complaints. Given these numbers, only 1 convicted cybercriminal was put behind bars for every 50,635 victims. If the entirety of Internet crime or cybercrime is taken into perspective, the conviction rates only get worse, as can be imagined (Grimes 2012).

2.6 Social Engineering and HIPAA

Note: The following section on social engineering is provided with permission by Chris Hadnagy, a subject matter expert on social engineering and the author of *Social Engineering: The Art of Human Hacking*.

A young man walks into the hospital office building dressed in a nice polo shirt and a pair of khakis. He is carrying a laptop bag and a clipboard. Determined, he walks pass the nurses and to the elevator. Hitting a button to go to the top floor, when he exists the elevator, he approaches the "gatekeeper's" desk and says, "Hi, I am Paul. I have a repair ticket for a Mr. ... um ... wow this is embarrassing. I can't read the writing here, all I know is he is on vacation and was complaining about a slow computer ..." A short pause and the secretary says, "Mr. Kalipi?"

"Yes! That's it," the young man exclaims.

"Oh, yes he was saying his computer is slow. His office is on the right, third door down."

"Thank you."

Fortunately in this case, the "tech" was a hired security professional that was paid to test the people network of this healthcare facility, but had it been a malicious attacker, the whole network would have been infiltrated.

As far as vectors go, there may be none easier than social engineering. What is social engineering? How is it used? Why does your healthcare facility need to be tested for it? These and many more questions will be answered throughout this section.

2.6.1 Social Engineering: What Is It?

I define *social engineering* as "any act that influences a person to take an action that may or may not be against their best interest." It is a broad definition because I do not view social engineering as always a negative. Marketers, teachers, priests, therapists, your spouse, kids, and friends all use social engineering to get you to take action, but these same principles, applied in a negative manner, can make it feasible to influence you and make you do, say, or not do something that can lead to a compromise of your sensitive information.

Studying what makes up the psychological and physical aspects of a social engineer can help you to remain secure. To do this, the following sections cover six steps to mitigating social engineering attacks and tie them specifically to the healthcare industry. These six tips are in the book *Social Engineering: The Art of Human Hacking,* but have been slightly adapted for the healthcare industry in this section.

2.6.2 Tip 1: Learn to Identify Social Engineering Attacks

Healthcare is all about "caring" and helping others. That mindset is important to keep, but it is also what malicious social engineers will use to attack a healthcare facility. If workforce members are aware that malicious people use *USB drops* (i.e., USB keys loaded with malicious files to get workforce members to load them into their computers) or phone calls to elicit personal details out of them, then they can be more alert to these types of attacks.

This does not mean that each healthcare professional needs to spend countless hours scouring the Internet for these stories. I encourage the tech staff of the healthcare facilities to have a newsletter or bulletin that can warn the workforce members of these attacks.

2.6.3 Tip 2: Security Awareness Should Be Personal and Interactive

When asked what most employees thought about security awareness training, an overwhelming majority said they felt it was boring, did not work, and was a waste of valuable time. The industry responds with making shorter, less personal, and more boring training. Why?

Compliance regulations force healthcare providers to have training for its workforce members but does not enforce the quality of the training. It is proven that if the training is personal to the workforce member's own life, then it can make a change to how they view security. How do you do that as a healthcare provider?

Once you have your third-party audits, use that information to tailor specific training that is personal to workforce members. If your staff is weak on passwords, demonstrate how easy it is to crack five-character passwords. If your staff was duped by the USB drop attack, show how easy it is to gain remote access using this method. When we (1) tell, (2) show, then (3) tell again, we help the workforce member make it personal and retain the information.

2.6.4 Tip 3: Understand the Value of the Information They Possess

This is probably an understatement when it comes to healthcare. The information on patients is damaging enough. Despite any ailments or other information they possess, the details on each patient such as name, address, date of birth, payment information, Social Security number and next of kin is a malicious social engineer's dream. Most healthcare professionals will definitely be leery of handing out any information to anyone just because they ask, but what about other forms of information leakage?

If a social engineer can breach the network using a ruse, they can gain access to all that information and more. In one audit, we found the name of one of the accounts payable people online. We called "Michelle" pretending to be a local waste management sales representative that wanted to give her company a new quote for waste management services. After some quick rapport building, I simply asked,

"Michelle, I am going to send you this quote this afternoon, and I am not asking your price point now, but since I want to make sure I can give you the best I can, would you tell me who you presently use?"

"XYZ Waste, but you didn't hear that from me."

"OK, I will send this over your way today or tomorrow AM, ok?"

After hanging up, I called back and asked for the security desk. I got "Richard" on the phone. "Richard, this is Paul from XYZ Waste. Michelle called me and said there is a report about a damaged dumpster on the lot. I am going to send Jim out tomorrow AM to take a look at it to see if we need to replace it."

The next day, I showed up with an XYZ shirt and my trusty clipboard. I walked up to the security booth, "Hey, my name is Jim from XYZ. I was sent to check a dumpster with some damage ..."

"Jim ... Jim ..." he repeated my name as he searched his list, "JIM! OK, I see you here."

"Ah, great. So I have a note here, it is one of the paper dumpsters. Can you point me in the right direction?"

"Sure, go down, follow the fence, then take a left behind that building and it is the fourth group on the right."

Driving down, midday to do a fully "authorized" dumpster dive gave me bags and bags of paper trash. Much of the trash was unshredded patient files and notes from doctors along with a couple of USB keys. We discovered a treasure trove of valuable information in the dumpster.

What does this story prove? Small, seemingly non-valuable pieces of information are what lead to big breaches. Healthcare professionals need to be aware that these small pieces of data can be what a hacker will use to further any attack.

2.6.5 Tip 4: Updates Are Essential

One great way to potentially stop a hacker is to make sure software and technology are updated and secure. What do I mean by that?

During one test, sitting in the lobby of the office building with a high-powered antenna, we found an executive with a wireless access point. Not only was a *rogue* access point against the rules, but he set it up running WEP encryption, which meant that anyone with BackTrack (i.e., a hacking software platform) and a few minutes could crack the password and gain wireless access to the network.

That is exactly what happened, giving access to all the databases, patient files, network folders, and more that the executive had access to.

WEP technology is very old, out of date, and insecure. When a healthcare facility does not update their technology, or software, it can leave them vulnerable to attack via outdated browsers, PDF reading software, or other software that has security flaws.

This is not uncommon; unfortunately, driving around one major city with a fellow security professional, he pointed out to me a hospital that uses a WEP network to transmit important data between buildings. These types of practices are screaming for a hacker to exploit. All we can hope for is that a security professional is the one to find the holes first and help his client get patched before a malicious hacker does.

2.6.6 Tip 5: Develop Scripts

When I speak on this topic, many people feel I am talking about scripts in the sense of writing out what to say and when to say it. That cannot be further from the truth. I think anytime a script, in that sense, is used, it frustrates the listener and the user. It also leaves the user at a greater disadvantage when something not on the script is thrown in.

What I mean about scripts is to prepare what you will do when (notice not if) someone tries to social engineer information from you. If you have never thought through the scenarios then you may find yourself unprepared when it does occur.

During one security awareness training, we spoke to some of the employees as we were prepping the information. When I asked some employees, "Why do you think it is important to be secure at work?" here are some of the answers I got:

- "What do I care, it's not my data."
- "Because I need my job."
- "I don't want to get fired."
- "I don't want to be the one causing the breach."

How would you feel if your employees answered that way? I can tell you this is not what you want to hear. These same employees were asked what they would have done if they felt they clicked a link they should not have or if they answered questions they should not have. Answers I got:

- "Don't tell anyone, or you can get canned."
- "Hope to God that you didn't give up too much."
- "Shut the computer down and go home till tomorrow."

What was overwhelming to me is that not one employee knew what to do in these situations. As bad as that is, what was even worse was that the companies had no procedures in place to handle these situations. Employees should know whom they should call, where they should forward e-mails, and how they should handle every situation they feel could be a threat. Does the company have an "abuse" department to forward e-mails to? Is there a team of people that your healthcare staff can call to help if they feel that someone was asking questions they shouldn't have?

Help workforce members come up with methods of handling and deferring these types of prying questions to someone else. Help workforce members understand how to handle an e-mail they feel is a phish. Help them be prepared so that they do not fall victim to these types of attacks.

2.6.7 Tip 6: Have and Learn from Social Engineering Assessments

Probably the most important tip in the list is this one. Having social engineering assessments is essential to remaining secure and complying with HIPAA. Healthcare professionals have to interact with people all day, every day. This means there is a greater likelihood that they will become targets of malicious social engineers.

Assessments can find where you are strong and where your facility is weak. Once you have your social engineering assessment, you can prepare effective and personalized security awareness training. In addition, this assessment can help you prepare scripts to combat attacks. You can see where you need updates and you can help train your staff to identify these attacks. All of this starts with assessments.

2.6.8 Wrapping It Up

Making a plan to stay secure from malicious social engineering is not easy. I won't pretend to say that it is, but it is possible to not be the low hanging fruit, to be the company that is not easy pickings for the hackers. These six steps cannot guarantee 100% security, nothing can, but they can give you a leg up on the battle to keep your healthcare facility secure.

2.7 Threats in the Workplace

According to the *Cisco Annual Security Report* published at the end of 2011, there appears to be an increase in vulnerabilities along with more focused or targeted attacks. It is predicted that mobile devices along with hacking cloud infrastructure will be on the rise in 2012. Cybercrime will also focus on money laundering. It was noted that security threats are being ignored in the workplace. IT policies are frequently ignored by 7 out of 10 young employees, and 1 in 4 individuals age 30 and younger have fallen victim to identity theft, according to the *Cisco Connected World Technology Report* (Akwaja 2012).

Some of the most important items recommended by security experts for securing the enterprise are the following (Akwaja 2012):

1. Assess the totality of the network. Know where the boundaries are and identify normal activity so that suspicious activity can be easily recognized.
2. Focus on acceptable use items that can be enforced and those behavioral items related to proper business conduct.

3. Assess the data that must be protected. Know where the data is located and implement a data loss prevention (DLP) program. Determine individuals that are authorized to access the data.
4. Determine how data is being secured. Follow up on third-party vendors to ensure that they are protecting the information.
5. Re-evaluate the security awareness training program. Younger workforce members may be more receptive to shorter training sessions than older workforce members.
6. Develop a monitoring program. Determine what information is being sent out, by whom, and to whom. Block items that are not authorized.
7. Be prepared. Plan for technology advancements.
8. Have an incident response plan ready. The plan should cover a multitude of events and should be initiated quickly and effectively.
9. Implement adequate security controls.
10. The technology landscape is always changing, keep informed.

2.8 Enforcement Activities

According to Leon Rodriguez, the director of Health and Human Services' Office for Civil Rights, he "'absolutely' plans to continue the office's ongoing efforts to ramp up enforcement of HIPAA with resolution agreements, civil monetary penalties and other enforcement actions" (Anderson, "Interview" 2011). Rodriguez went on in an interview to say that it was not the first objective of his office to penalize covered entities but rather to work with them to find ways to improve their compliance efforts. He indicated that the HIPAA Privacy and Security Rules help ensure that patients feel confident that their information is secure. Rodriguez said, "Very often a patient who does not have confidence in the security of their information, and, by the way, in their access to that information, may not seek care in situations where they absolutely should" (Anderson, "Interview" 2011). Rodriguez also alluded to the fact that he will be making sure his staff is properly trained in enforcement activities and emphasized how important privacy and security are to him and the Secretary of Health and Human Services. "So we're going to be serious about our enforcement work and no less serious about making sure that we educate everybody out there, both covered entities and patients, about what the requirements are for health information privacy," Rodriguez stated (Anderson, "Interview" 2011).

To assist in enforcement, the Department of Health and Human Services awarded a $9.2 million contract to the consulting firm of KPMG, LLP, to launch the audit program as mandated by the HITECH Act. The first step, as explained by Susan McAndrew, deputy director of the federal agency overseeing the audit program, is to create a comprehensive set of protocols for conducting an audit and setting up measures of compliance. There are plans to have as many as 150 on-site audits conducted through the end of 2012. "McAndrew encourages healthcare organizations to prepare for the audits by taking several steps, including reviewing their privacy and security policies and procedures; ensuring that they've documented patient information safeguards; completing an updated risk assessment; and developing a breach incident response plan" (Anderson, "McAndrew Explains" 2011).

One example of the enforcement actions that the OCR can apply against covered entities, the first civil monetary penalty (CMP) for violations of the HIPAA Privacy Rule was imposed against Cigna Health of Prince George's County, Maryland, for $4.3 million. On "October 20, 2010, OCR found that Cigna violated the rights of 41 patients by denying them access to their medical records when requested between September 2008 and October 2009" (Department of Health and Human Services Press Office 2011). The CMP for these violations was $1.3 million. Cigna refused to respond to OCR's demands during the investigation. For the willful neglect to comply with the HIPAA Privacy Rule and failure to cooperate with OCR, Cigna was additionally fined $3 million.

Another example of enforcement actions is the following: On February 14, 2011, Massachusetts General Physicians Organization, Inc. (Mass General) settled with a $1 million agreement for potential violations of the HIPAA Privacy and Security Rules. In addition, Mass General had to comply with a corrective action plan (CAP) to implement safeguards for the privacy of patient information. The incident arose from the loss of 192 patient records (including patients with HIV/AIDS) of the Mass General's Infections Disease Associates outpatient practice (Department of Health and Human Services Office for Civil Rights 2011).

One of the first enforcement actions under the HITECH security breach notification requirements was against BlueCross and BlueShield of Tennessee. The company agreed to a $1.5 million settlement for the theft of 57 hard drives in 2009 containing over 1 million BlueCross customers' information such as names, Social Security numbers, dates of birth, plan numbers, and diagnosis codes. OCR determined that the company failed to implement appropriate and adequate administrative safeguards along with adequate access control for the facility that initially stored the drives. In addition to the settlement, BlueCross and Blue Shield of Tennessee has reportedly spent nearly $17 million in its breach notification efforts since the theft. Being the state's largest health insurer with more than 3 million members, the company has agreed to a 450-day corrective action plan to review and address gaps in its HIPAA privacy and security policies and procedures (Sells 2012).

Not only does OCR have enforcement authority over HIPAA, but the HITECH Act gave the attorney generals of each state new authority to enforce penalties for HIPAA violations. In the first week of July 2010, a $250,000 settlement agreement was reached by Health Net, a health insurer, regarding a loss of a computer disk drive that contained unencrypted protected health information of approximately 1.5 million health plan participants. This was the first action by an attorney general across the nation under the enactment of the HITECH Act in February 2009. Health Net also had to provide 2 years of credit monitoring for the participants, obtain identity theft insurance in the amount of $1 million, and reimburse any affected participant for security freezes. In addition, there is a contingent payment of $500,000 that will need to be paid if it is discovered that the information lost was actually accessed or misused. Health Net agreed to implement corrective actions such as the use of encryption and improving security awareness training of its personnel (Proskauer Rose, LLP 2010).

In another, more recent incident, the attorney general of Minnesota sued a consulting firm, Accretive Health Inc., hired by two hospitals to compile individual medical checklists, over a lost laptop with unencrypted medical data on 23,500 individuals. The lawsuit alleges that the loss of information violates federal health privacy regulations and state consumer protection laws (Kennedy 2012).

2.9 Impediments to HIPAA/HITECH Compliance

There are several reasons why an organization may not be in compliance with HIPAA/HITECH requirements. One of the main reasons could just be a lack of knowledge or understanding about what is required by the regulations. The regulations may be difficult to understand or address and guidance may be limited. Technology, although prevalent for a while, has caused some nuisances with regulations. The regulators are trying to catch up with technology and are making good strides; however, new threats are always being introduced that need to be addressed. There are going to be some growing pains in dealing with these new or modified HIPAA/HITECH requirements, but it will be essential to try to get in front of these regulations and become proactive in securing patient information.

Another reason for noncompliance is that there may be no single individual responsible for compliance activities or the individual involved in compliance may have other job duties that are completely different than compliance-related activities. This may relate to the lack of knowledge issue since it has normally been the job of healthcare providers to take care of patients and not necessarily function in the security realm.

Systemic issues in the organization brought on by the indifference that upper management may have toward compliance are definitely an impediment. Some organizations may feel that it is an acceptable risk to be in noncompliance and will pay any fines accordingly when caught. These executives may feel that it is good business in that it may be less expensive to pay fines than to spend money and resources on becoming compliant. Unfortunately, this may be a fatal thought process and could put the organization out of business. As was discussed earlier, fines and civil liability are increasing and if a small organization is hit with a multimillion-dollar lawsuit, it could be ruined. Besides the financial penalties, the reputational risks that an organization faces, especially in the healthcare industry where reputations are very important, could bankrupt an organization or cause irreversible harm.

The lack of resources to include financial support, people, and time are major factors that may lead to noncompliance. There may not be a budget set aside for HIPAA/HITECH compliance along with subject matter experts to handle the organization's compliance needs. There may be policies and procedures in place; however, these policies and procedures may not be implemented or workforce members may not follow them due to the policies and procedures hindering functionality. The very first step to implementing an information security program is conducting a risk assessment. Without the appropriate resources assigned to this activity, the risk assessment will not be performed and an adequate information security program will never get started.

2.10 God Complex

Being in the healthcare industry and saving people's lives may cause certain individuals to have what is known in psychology as the "God complex." This is basically the concept that certain things do not apply to the individual since the individual knows better. This principle also applies to information security. Ask yourself, do you follow every single rule on the list of security policies all the time? The answer will probably be that a few rules are broken, at least some of the time. This, unfortunately, creates a weak security environment. The individuals having the most privileges on an information system are usually the ones who are most targeted. Since privileged users are normally the ones who think they know best, they may not follow the same rules that are in place for everyone else. They may utilize another antivirus software program as opposed to the assigned antivirus package. They may even turn off local firewalls since this control may cause issues when running certain programs. In addition, these programs are probably not authorized to be used on the corporate systems in the first place.

No one wants to be told what to do and those who make the rules should be the first to follow the rules. Unfortunately, the superiority complex is probably one of the hardest behaviors to break. The truth of the matter is that if the enforcers follow the same policies, the security posture across the entire organization will be increased. Don't be a person who says "Do as I say, not as I do"; instead, set the example for the rest of the team to follow. It would be better to have the attitude that you would not ask anyone in your organization to do something that you are not willing to do yourself (Los 2012).

2.11 Recommendations

The point of this section is to emphasize the importance of information security. Using statistics and specific examples is sometimes the best way to get the point across. What can be done to prevent these items discussed earlier from happening to the organization? There are three straightforward recommendations that will increase the security posture of the organization tremendously.

First, elevate information security to the top of the organization. Just as a company may have a chief financial officer, a chief executive officer, and/or a chief information officer, the company should also have a chief information security officer. This individual should be well versed in all aspects of information security and have the necessary authority to carry out their assignments and responsibilities. As is demonstrated throughout this book, information security is complex and interweaves within many areas of the organization. (See Figure 2.1.) It encompasses multiple disciplines and every component works together to create an adequate security posture within the covered entity.

Second, one of the weakest links in security is people. No matter how much is spent on technology, how many technical controls are in place, or how secure a covered entity attempts to be, people that are ignorant or lazy become a serious

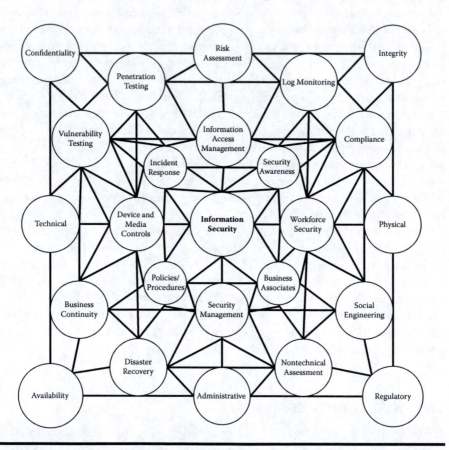

Figure 2.1   The information security web.

security threat. Note: When utilizing the word *ignorant*, the author does not mean people are stupid, but rather individuals may not be aware of or taught certain things that can make them and ultimately the organization more secure. Hopefully by demonstrating the importance of security and making it a major commitment at the organization, emphasis will be made on secure behaviors. Demonstrating the importance of security should also change unacceptable behavior in workforce members. Providing security awareness training and enforcing proper security procedures should contribute to the increase of the security posture of the covered entity. An appropriate combination of rewards and sanctions should enforce the importance of security.

Third, understand that security is an ongoing process. There is no one-time fix, and it takes time and resources to develop an effective information security program. There should be no qualms about hiring outside experts to assist in developing or testing the information security program. Internal workforce members may not have the appropriate skills or knowledge to design a program as intricate as required by information security. Just as it may have taken years of education, training, and practice to become a brain surgeon, it has also taken a lot of time and effort to become a highly qualified information security practitioner. "Information security professionals make up just over one percent (1%) of all IT professionals tracked by the U.S. Bureau of Labor Statistics," as noted in a study conducted by Information Security Media Group (Wilson 2012). Make information security a priority by setting up the necessary resources and funding.

2.12 Critical Infrastructure Implications

While this book was being written, some important legislation was introduced to the U.S. Congress. Specifically, the legislature has recognized the importance of cybersecurity and as FBI Director Robert Mueller explains, "The danger of cyberattacks will equal or surpass the danger of terrorism 'in the foreseeable future'" (Washington Post editorial 2012). For this reason, the Cybersecurity Act of 2012 is under debate. One of the major components of this new legislation is the authority provided to the Department of Homeland Security to supervise systems that could cause a mass casualty event, the interruption of life-sustaining services, mass evacuations, or catastrophic economic damage to the United States. These systems are normally referred to as "critical infrastructure" systems, and according to the Homeland Security Presidential Directive (HSPD) 7, the following 17 sectors are identified (Homeland Security 2008):

1. Agriculture and food
2. Banking and finance
3. Chemical
4. Commercial facilities

5. Communications
6. Critical manufacturing
7. Dams
8. Defense industrial base
9. Education facilities
10. Emergency services
11. Energy
12. Healthcare and public health
13. Information technology
14. National monuments and icons
15. Nuclear reactors, materials, and waste
16. Transportation systems
17. Water

The new legislation will require organizations' operating systems within these critical sectors to work with Homeland Security on protection plans and to submit to audits to validate effectiveness of these plans. For any firms failing to comply with these requirements, fines could be levied. Unfortunately, the lack of resolve to protect these systems in the private sector has resulted in enforcement efforts by the government. With the introduction of these new regulations, the status quo has become an unacceptable risk to U.S. national security (Washington Post editorial 2012).

With respect to the healthcare industry, "The Healthcare and Public Sector constitutes approximately fifteen percent (15%) of the gross national product with roughly eight-five percent (85%) of the sector's assets privately owned and operated. … The Healthcare and Public Health Sector plays a significant role in response and recovery across all other sectors in the event of a natural or manmade disaster" (Homeland Security 2008).

2.13 What the Future Holds

As regulations strengthen and regulators begin more stringent enforcement of these regulations, it will become more apparent to healthcare providers that steps need to be taken to strengthen their compliance posture. There will be several changes in the upcoming years as HIPAA and HITECH regulation enforcement becomes more prevalent. Compliance programs will become essential for healthcare providers and business associates. Additional resources will be needed in the development of policies, procedures, and reviews associated with conforming to new regulations and requirements. As the need for compliance programs increases, so will the demand for compliance professionals to assist in developing and managing these programs.

One area of the healthcare field that will see increased enforcement activities is home care providers. Home care providers, in particular, will face greater scrutiny as the federal government pressures states into taking more enforcement actions.

As word spreads for rewards to report compliance issues, home care providers will become more of a target. Home care providers will see an increase in penalties.

It is no surprise that the healthcare industry has seen an increase in fraud. From medical identity theft to Medicaid and Medicare fraud, penalties will increase and providers will no longer be excluded from protecting against fraud. More enforcement of the anti-kickback laws will also take place. As Medicaid and Medicare adopt new requirements for obtaining provider numbers, it will be harder for new providers to obtain these numbers and existing providers that have not shown a lot of growth may lose their eligibility (Maynard 2011).

In addition to enforcement and fraud, covered entities need to be concerned with other security matters. Malware has been on the rise and trends show that these types of programs are not going away anytime soon. A half dozen of the top malware trends to watch for in 2012 are the following (Mediati 2012):

1. *Secure Socket Layer (SSL)* may not be safe anymore. Sites protected by SSL security have been assumed to be safe to use, but unfortunately new malware has been designed to alert when users go to sites protected by SSL. Before the encryption technology starts, the malware is capturing username and password combinations.
2. *Targeted malware* is on the rise. This software accesses the user's browser history and only activates upon seeing certain sites visited. Related to online medical records, if a patient obtains his medical record from an online source, this malware will note the browsing history and activate to capture credentials of this site.
3. *Malware becoming stronger.* As malware becomes more advanced, it can infect systems without being noticed or bypass antivirus (and other) protective solutions.
4. *Ransomware* is on the rise. This type of software, although not new, may come in the form of fake antivirus software. Once installed, it will take control of the system until a ransom is paid.
5. *Bots* make a comeback. This is an older issue, but may reemerge in the future and target very specific companies or individuals.
6. *Mobile malware* is on the rise. With the ever-increasing use of mobile technology, it only makes sense that criminals will design malware for mobile devices.

2.14 Summary

In this chapter, the importance of information security was revealed. Healthcare organizations are not immune to security breaches or to becoming victims of cybercrime. In fact, due to the information that healthcare organizations maintain, they are at a much higher risk of being targeted than possibly other organizations in other industries. For this reason, emphasis needs to be placed on protecting organizations' assets, including the information that they create or maintain.

Multiple sources of statistics and examples of major breaches were provided. These examples were to demonstrate the importance of information security for a covered entity. Some explanation as to the reasons for the rise in cybercrime and, more specifically, medical identity theft were discussed. Workforce members were disclosed as being one of the major weaknesses in any security framework within an organization. Related to this was a discussion of social engineering that specifically targets these weaknesses in workforce members, primarily when it comes to helping others. Being aware of this potential threat could prevent the organization from becoming a victim. Additional high-level recommendations, along with the other recommendations provided throughout this book, should assist in making the covered entity more secure.

This book will discuss several different regulations to enforce compliance with information security standards, but a covered entity should want to protect its clients' personal information even without these requirements. In fact, one of the tenets in a modern version of the traditional Hippocratic Oath that most physicians swear to, as penned by Dr. Louis Lasagna in 1964, is: "I will respect the privacy of my patients, for their problems are not disclosed to me that the world may know" (Wikipedia 2010). This is the basic concept of the HIPAA/HITECH Privacy and Security Rules.

Chapter 3

Compliance Overview

Objectives

The objectives of this chapter are as follows:

- Understand that regulations are requirements that need to be met by the covered entity.
- Understand regulations assist in the development of policies.
- Understand procedures utilize standards to implement policies.
- Understand guidelines are set by procedures.
- Determine what is meant by reasonable safeguards to secure electronic protected health information.
- Determine what the covered entity should concentrate on in regard to becoming compliant.
- Understand the importance of conducting a risk assessment.
- Understand the importance of security awareness training.
- Determine if the covered entities' current business associate agreements contain the required elements.
- Understand what will be expected from the audit pilot program designed by the Office for Civil Rights (OCR) to conduct compliance assessments on covered entities.
- Understand the differences between the SAS 70 and SSAE 16 audits.

3.1 Interrelationship among Regulations, Policies, Standards, Procedures, and Guidelines

There is sometimes a misconception that regulations, policies, procedures, standards, and guidelines are interchangeable or synonymous with one another. This could not be further from the truth. To understand their differences, these terms need to be fully defined as they relate to compliance. These terms will also be defined as it relates to the Health Insurance Portability and Accountability Act (HIPAA)/Health Information Technology for Economic and Clinical Health (HITECH) Act subject matter.

HIPAA/HITECH defines regulations that are mandated by law. These regulations must be implemented and compliance must be met, or there could be severe consequences. These *regulations* form the basis for the covered entities' policies. *Policies* are the intentions of management to come into compliance with the regulations. Policies are high-level requirements that are documented and approved by management to direct employees in the process of complying with the stated objectives.

Standards are set by policies that help produce the *procedures* that will be followed to carry out the objectives of the policies. *Standards* attempt to tie the procedures with their policies. Procedures are more detailed than policies and normally provide step-by-step instructions to follow in complying with the policy. Normally, there is one policy statement and several procedures on what the covered entity should do to carry out the policy. Once the procedures have been developed, guidelines are usually established. *Guidelines* are common practices that are followed by employees of a covered entity and are normally the real-life practices that are in place as established by a given procedure. See Figure 3.1.

3.2 Reasonable Safeguards

As discussed earlier, a covered entity must have in place appropriate administrative, technical, and physical safeguards that protect against the unauthorized use or disclosure of protected health information. This does not mean that the covered entity's safeguards will guarantee that such use or disclosure will not happen, but rather the potential risk of such activities is acceptable. Of course the safeguards implemented will vary from one covered entity to another based upon several factors, such as the covered entity's size or nature of work. It is imperative that every covered entity conduct a risk assessment to determine what safeguards should be implemented based on their distinct requirements. A covered entity may be limited by resources, such as finances or administration; however, there are several examples of safeguards that do not require a lot of effort. Related to administrative controls, providing security awareness training to employees can provide a huge return by increasing the security posture of the covered entity. One technical control that is probably already in place is the use of passwords on

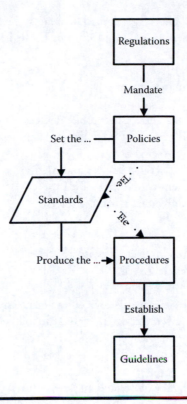

Figure 3.1 **Interrelationship of regulations, policies, standards, procedures, and guidelines.**

computer systems or programs that store protected health information. A physical control that could be implemented immediately is the practice of speaking quietly when discussing a patient's condition or not using a patient's name when walking through public areas.

3.3 Centers for Medicare and Medicaid Services Compliance Review

During 2009, five covered entities were reviewed for compliance with the Security Rule by the Office of E-Health Standards and Services (OESS) of the Centers for Medicare & Medicaid Services (CMS). Historically, these reviews were conducted after complaints were "filed against entities" (FAEs). However, covered entities were also reviewed during this year that had no complaints filed. The reason to take a little time to discuss the results of this review is that it gives the covered entity some insight as to areas of compliance that need improvements.

It appears that the following particular areas were focused on (Centers for Medicare & Medicaid Services [CMS] Office of E-Health Standards and Services [OESS] 2009):

- Risk analysis and management
- Security training
- Physical security of facilities and mobile devices
- Off-site access and use of EPHI (electronic protected health information) from remote locations
- Storage of EPHI on portable devices and media
- Disposal of equipment containing EPHI
- Business associate agreements and contracts
- Data encryption
- Virus protection
- Technical safeguards in place to protect EPHI
- Monitoring of access to EPHI

Although the sample size for this review was rather small (only five individual covered entities were reviewed), CMS indicated the following areas of concern over all of them:

1. Risk analysis
2. Currency and adequacy of policies and procedures
3. Security training
4. Business associate agreements

Three other areas (workforce clearance, workstation security, and encryption) appeared to be issues from previous year (i.e., 2008) reviews, but CMS did not note these issues in the current review. Through the next several sections, areas of concern along with common pitfalls of the covered entities that CMS noted will be discussed.

3.3.1 Risk Analysis

The 2009 HIPAA Security Compliance Review indicated that covered entities are not performing the required risk assessments. The risk assessments are not reviewed on an annual basis or they were outdated based upon significant changes in the covered entities' environment. It appears that the covered entities did not understand the process of conducting a risk assessment. The assessments reviewed were not formally documented or fully developed to cover all necessary steps in the risk assessment process. For instance, the risk assessments appeared to have skipped the first step in identifying systems that store, process, or transmit electronic protected health information. These risk assessments failed to have a complete inventory of systems and locations where these systems are stored.

To mitigate these shortcomings, it is recommended that risk assessments be completed every 18 months or upon a significant change in the technical environment. A significant change in the environment can be brought on by introducing new systems such as electronic medical records solutions. Significantly upgrading existing systems or disposing of retired systems can alter the technical environment of the covered entity. Physically moving electronic assets to different locations can require additional physical controls be implemented. Any reorganization of the covered entity's management or introducing new service offerings can require a change in the environment of the covered entity.

The risk assessments need to address all risks of the covered entity and establish an effective risk assessment process. This risk assessment process, described in detail in Chapter 12, includes identifying where data is stored and what systems are considered critical. Identifying threats and vulnerabilities to these systems along with analyzing the controls implemented to protect these systems can be determined by conducting vulnerability/penetration tests of these systems by experienced individuals. Exploiting these vulnerabilities will provide insight into the impact on the covered entity and assist in assessing the level of risks. By conducting these types of tests or exercises, the covered entity can determine additional controls that should be implemented. As previously discussed, the risk assessment should be formally documented and shared with executive level management to determine corrective actions for any deficiencies identified.

3.3.2 Currency and Adequacy of Policies and Procedures

According to the CMS, out of the five covered entities reviewed, only one had adequate policies and procedures implemented. Conditions of the review indicated that covered entities only had a few policies and procedures in place and most did not address the HIPAA/HITECH Security Standards and Implementation Specifications. In addition, actual guidelines followed were not consistent with the documented procedures or procedures did not follow the documented policies.

One of the recommended solutions is for covered entities to develop formally documented policies that are approved by management and reviewed on a periodic basis. In addition, the workforce member that is responsible for developing these policies and procedures must be one of the covered entity's designated HIPAA security officers. The process for reviewing policies and procedures should include the following:

- Identify the management personnel responsible for the review
- The ability for workforce members to obtain the most recent version of the policies/procedures

■ Assess against current operational and regulatory requirements
■ Update as necessary
■ Document that the review was conducted
■ Communicate any updates to the other workforce members as necessary

Developing a standard policy and procedure format will enable consistency across relevant business units. To disseminate policies and procedures, the covered entity should look at a centrally managed repository solution that could automatically notify workforce members when updates occur. For example, this could be performed through an intranet site to inform workforce members of changes or through another type of shared portal that can notify workforce members of updates to policies and procedures. Posting changes in common areas could also provide notification to workforce members of updates. Security awareness training should reiterate any updates to policies and procedures and how these updates are made public to workforce members along with expectations of workforce members to keep abreast of these changes.

In regard to conducting periodic evaluations of policies and procedures, the individuals conducting these reviews should not be the same individuals responsible for the processes under review. These individuals should also have expertise or a reasonable level of competence when conducting these assessments. There are several methods that can be utilized to carry out these reviews such as walkthroughs of the process, interviews of workforce members, assessment of results, or actual testing of controls to determine effectiveness of the policy or procedure in place. For larger covered entities the internal audit team may be utilized to conduct the review as long as they have an appropriate level of separations of duties and competencies to conduct such audits. For smaller covered entities or in larger entities that may not have the expertise in-house, an independent third-party service provider should be contracted to assist the covered entity in determining their level of compliance.

3.3.3 Security Training

CMS determined that covered entities do not have policies and procedures in place to address the HIPAA/HITECH Security Rule provisions for security awareness training. For those covered entities that did have policies and procedures in place, they inadequately address the Security Rule requirements. When training was conducted, covered entities did not document or retain evidence of the training as required. In addition, security awareness training was not conducted prior to workforce members being granted access to systems containing electronic protected health information and refresher training was not provided on a regular basis.

Recommendations for these deficiencies are probably self-explanatory. However, as a point of reference, the covered entity needs to develop formal documented security awareness training policies that require new workforce members to receive training prior to gaining access to electronic protected health information. Security awareness training should be provided to all workforce members as a refresher on an annual basis and training material should be updated at least on an annual basis or when necessary. Furthermore, any identified threats through the risk assessment process should be incorporated into the security awareness training. One example of such risk that may be identified is that posed by workforce members working remotely to access electronic protected health information. Finally, attendance of security awareness training needs to be documented, retained, and there should be predetermined sanctions for any workforce member failing to complete this mandatory training or managers that fail to have their members provided with this training.

3.3.4 Business Associate Agreements

There appear to be many deficiencies noted by CMS when it comes to the agreements between business associates and the covered entity. First, the covered entities reviewed had business associates, but there were no business associate agreements (BAAs) between them. Second, there may have been a BAA, but it was not signed by both parties as required. Finally, the BAAs did not address certain requirements dictated by the regulation such as addressing the HIPAA/HITECH Security Rule, developing a comprehensive risk management program, reporting vulnerabilities, reporting breaches, performing activities, and the right of the covered entity to perform an audit on the business associate or require corrections to any deficiencies discovered during the assessment.

It is recommended that covered entities develop a comprehensive process to define the requirements and selection criteria for a business associate. A covered entity should focus on the business processes of the business associate and vet these categories accordingly. A covered entity should develop a standardized template and process of review to document the completion, date, and signatures of both the covered entity and business associate entering into the agreement. The review of the agreements should be conducted at least annually and the procedures should be standardized to document the preamble, body, terms/conditions, and penalties of all business associate agreements.

A contractual document should be developed to describe the business relationship, the services provided, the flow of HIPAA/HITECH Security Rule Standards and Implementation Specifications, and the flow of the specification for the Minimum Necessary Rule regarding electronic protected health information. The business associate contract should have:

- A start and end date
- Full service description
- Delivery terms/conditions
- Delivery specifications
- Requirements for conducting a periodic risk assessment and reporting results to the covered entity

- Provision for covered entity to conduct audits on the business associate
- Any other provision regarding vulnerabilities discovered by the business associate's risk assessment to mitigate such risks as applicable

This contractual template should be attached to the business associate template.

3.4 HIPAA/HITECH Privacy and Security Audit Program

To ensure compliance with the HIPAA/HITECH Privacy Rule, Security Rule, and the Breach Notification Standards, the Department of Health and Human Services (HHS) is required under Section 13411 of the HITECH Act to conduct periodic audits of covered entities and business associates. The Office for Civil Rights (OCR) established a pilot program that would perform these mandated audits on up to 150 covered entities between November 2011 and December 2012. The program's objectives are to identify compliance opportunities, best practices, and new risks or vulnerabilities that were not discovered through OCR's complaint investigation and compliance reviews. This program is a new part of OCR's overall health information privacy and security compliance program.

There were three steps in the process of this pilot audit program. First, starting around July 2011, there was the development of the audit protocol. Just as discussed earlier, this was the test plan development phase. To make sure the testing protocols will work, a small sample of about 20 audits would be conducted. Covered entities were selected, notified, and the audits were performed utilizing the developed testing protocols in phase 2. A review was conducted and changes were made, as necessary, to the testing protocols so that they could be implemented in a standardized manner to the rest of the covered entities chosen. Phase 3 would consist of completing the remaining audits by December 2012.

Of course, every covered entity and business associate could be eligible for an audit. In this first round of auditing, only covered entities such as health services, health plans, and healthcare clearinghouses were chosen. OCR is responsible for selecting the entities that would provide a broad and diverse assessment base. Related to the enforcement authority of the OCR, the covered entity should comply with the audit and cooperate fully with the auditor throughout this process. As of this writing, KPMG, LLP, was selected as the OCR auditor for this pilot program.

The audit will include a site visit along with an audit report. Utilizing an interview and observation process, the auditor will determine compliance with the privacy and security standards. The auditor will share the results with the covered entity allowing the covered entity to respond to any findings. A final report, with issues identified along with resolution actions of the covered entity, will be submitted to OCR. The audit could take up to 30 business days to complete. Once the covered entity receives the notification letter that it was chosen for the audit, it has a limited number of days (i.e., 10 business days) to supply all requested documentation. This notification will commence between 30 and 90 days prior to the expected site visit. Onsite work could take between 3 and 10 business days with a draft of the audit report to follow around 20 business days thereafter. The covered entity will have an opportunity to respond to the findings within 10 business days and the final audit report will be submitted to OCR within 30 business days after the responses are received from the covered entity. These audits are primarily utilized for compliance improvement; however, serious violations could come under compliance review by OCR to address these issues.

The final audit report will include (Lamkin 2012):

- Covered entity's name and description
- Methodology and timeframe
- Best practice observations
- Other related documentation such as data, interview notes, and checklists
- A listing of the following for each finding
  - *Condition*—The evidence to back up any notation of noncompliance
  - *Criteria*—Citation of the potential violation of the HIPAA/HITECH Privacy or Security Rule the finding presents
  - *Cause*—Supporting documentation to substantiate the reason a finding exists
  - *Effect*—The risk presented by the finding
  - Recommendations to mitigate the finding
  - Any corrective actions taken by the covered entity
- Conclusion
- Corrective action plan
- Recommendations to HHS (i.e., continued corrective action or future oversight recommendation)

3.5 SAS 70/SSAE 16 Debate

The American Institute of Certified Public Accountants (AICPA) developed the Statement on Auditing Standards number 70 (SAS 70) to focus on controls around internal financial reporting. Since data centers and colocations (COLOs) companies house systems that maintained financial reporting applications, users of these companies needed an objective opinion about these data centers. These users started to use the SAS 70 as a requirement before they would utilize the data center (or COLO) companies. The data center owners went out and conducted these audits, but it was not long before marketing got involved and claimed that their businesses were "SAS 70 certified" to validate their data centers. Unfortunately, the SAS 70 had no objective criteria. Some audit reports may have as little or as many control objectives as the operators of the data center wanted to include on the report. In addition, these companies may claim to be audited even if they did not pass the audit. "The end result is that a SAS 70 audit means nothing without reading the details of the audit report" (Klein 2012). French Caldwell, research vice president at Gartner, concurs with this point by saying, "SAS 70 is basically an expensive auditing process to support compliance with financial reporting rules like the Sarbanes-Oxley Act (SOX). Chief Information Security Officers (CISOs), compliance and risk managers, vendor managers, procurement professionals, and others involved in the purchase or sale of IT services and software need to recognize that SAS 70 is not a security, continuity or privacy compliance standard" (Gartner 2010).

In an attempt to fix some of these issues with the SAS 70 audit, AICPA created a new standard known as the Statement on Standards for Attestation Engagements No. 16 (SSAE 16). The SSAE 16 now requires "the auditor to obtain a written assertion from management regarding the design and operating effectiveness of the controls being reviewed" (Klein 2012). The company can still choose its own controls, but as long as management attests to the fact that they follow these controls, they can claim to be SSAE 16 audited. It is still up to the report reader to decide the worth of the audit.

Since the SSAE 16 still focused on internal financial audits, the AICPA developed the Service Organization Controls 2 (SOC 2) audit specifically for data centers. To make things a little more confusing, however, they also developed the following (Klein 2012):

■ Service Organization Controls 1 (SOC1) (also known as SSAE 16)—Type 1 and Type 2 that can be delivered from a SSAE 16 audit
■ Service Organization Controls 2 (SOC 2)—Type 1 and Type 2 but can use up to five different control objectives as follows:
  – Security
  – Availability
  – Processing integrity
  – Confidentiality
  – Privacy of systems/information
■ Service Organization Controls 3 (SOC 3)—Only audit that has a public seal that provides the same level of assurance as SOC 2 but does not provide a detailed description of tests performed. SOC 3 is intended for general release.

As a special note of reference, some companies are now claiming to be "SSAE 16 SOC 2 Certified"; however, there is no such certification available. "As long as users only look for the SSAE 16 audit checkbox, operators will be tempted to use the least rigorous audit criteria to simply pass the audit" (Klein 2012). This is synonymous with claiming to be "Certified HIPAA Compliant"; there is no such certification available as well. Per the HHS, "There is no standard or implementation specification that requires a covered entity to 'certify' compliance" (Department of Health and Human Services Office for Civil Rights n.d.). Although 45 CFR § 164.308(a)(8) requires a covered entity to perform "a periodic technical and non-technical evaluation that establishes the extent to which an entity's security policies and procedures meet the security requirements," this evaluation can be performed by either internal or external organizations that provide evaluations or "certification" services. "It is important to note that HHS does not endorse or otherwise recognize private organizations' 'certifications' regarding the Security Rule, and such certifications do not absolve covered entities of their legal obligations under the Security Rule" (Department of Health and Human Services Office for Civil Rights n.d.). Just because a covered entity conducted "certification" by an external organization does not mean that HHS will not subsequently find a security violation for which the covered entity will be held responsible.

As Caldwell states, "To ensure that vendor controls are effective for security, privacy compliance and vendor risk management, SAS 70, its successor Statements on Standards for Attestation Engagements (SSAE) 16, and other national audit standards equivalents should be supplemented with self-assessments and agreed-upon audit procedures" (Gartner 2010). Some of these other national audit standards include the following (Gartner 2010):

■ Internal Organization for Standardization (ISO) standard certifications
■ BITS Shared Assessments—Provided by a consortium of service providers, their customers, audit firms, and other third-party assessors
■ SysTrust and WebTrust—Sponsored by AICPA and performed by qualified CPA auditors
■ AT Section 101—Sponsored by AICPA and performed by qualified CPA auditors but a more flexible attestation procedure

3.6 Corporate Governance

Compliance along with information security is an enterprise-wide, corporate governance issue. Major decisions related to the way that compliance is handled in an organization need to be made at the highest level. With limits in budgets and resources, some covered entities have resorted to implementing a multitier approach to governance. This approach includes the following:

■ *An executive-level steering committee*—Normally chaired by the chief information security officer. This committee is responsible for providing the overall broad strategy and commitment to information security efforts including compliance-related matters. This committee will establish budget limitations, goals, priorities, and actions that should be carried out by participants.

■ *Advisory groups*—These groups could be organized by projects or functions within the covered entity. These teams can provide detailed insights that can then be reported or recommended back to the steering committee.
■ *Subcommittees*—These subcommittees should include representation from across all areas of the covered entity.

Along with setting up an organizational structure, certain rules should be applied. For instance, certain proposals should come from certain responsible parties within the covered entity. These proposals require sponsorship from executive management and each one should have a business case to justify the need. Reviews should be conducted on the effect the proposals it may have on existing systems. Finally, the process developed needs to be adhered to and there should be no opportunity for bypassing by the decision makers.

The following are some additional rules that should be implemented to handle the corporate governance process (Morrissey 2012):

1. *Chain the committees*—The chairperson for one committee should be on the committee of the next upper level. For instance, the chairperson of one of the subcommittees should be on the executive-level committee that will make the decisions that the subcommittee is handling.
2. *Set authority*—Clear lines of authority should be drawn so that each committee is aware of the level of authority they have over certain decisions.
3. *Make time worthwhile*—Do not have meetings just to have them. For instance, if meetings are only providing status reports, e-mail these reports to responsible workforce members rather than having a meeting. Use meetings to make important decisions and discuss matters that could not be handled in other ways.
4. *Use governance accordingly*—Some covered entities are not at the level to implement this process. Know when the likelihood of success for such a method is appropriate.
5. *Leaders should take a stand*—Individuals in charge of the committees need to have the proper authority and can take a stand. If real change will take place, these leaders must be able to articulate their decisions and have the proper authority to carry them out.

3.7 Summary

This chapter explains the differences between regulations, policies, procedures, standards, and guidelines. A lot of individuals believe that these terms are interchangeable, but they have very different and specific meanings. An understanding of these differences is necessary to better comprehend the overall compliance process. Safeguards are the result of analyzing the necessary resources that must be implemented to adequately satisfy compliance. These safeguards must be reasonably implemented based on several factors including financial, technical, and personnel resources available to the covered entity. Specific areas of concern were noted through the Centers for Medicare & Medicaid Services' compliance review. These issues were published so that other covered entities can benefit from this insight to strengthen their own compliance efforts. As part of the HITECH enforcement requirements, the Office for Civil Rights hired KPMG, LLP, to conduct audits on 150 covered entities by the end of 2012. Although this audit is intended to assist in compliance efforts, severe violations may come under additional investigations. As discussed in Chapter 2, civil penalties can be severe and covered entities should take the appropriate actions to limit their risks of liability.

This chapter ended with a discussion on SAS 70 and SSAE 16 reporting. A lot of specific information was provided on the audits themselves, but one of the most important tips is that the reports, no matter what type, should be read and a determination should be made as to how well the organization under audit is conducting business.

Chapter 4

Privacy Rule Detailed

Objectives

The objectives of this chapter are as follows:

- Understand the meaning of "minimum necessary."
- Understand what consent an individual may provide regarding his or her own personal health information.
- Determine what is permitted use and disclosure of protected health information.
- Understand the permitted use and disclosure as it relates to: individuals; treatment, payment, and healthcare operations; and the opportunity to agree or object to the use and disclosure of protected health information.
- Understand what is meant by incidental use and disclosure of protected health information.
- Understand the 12 exemptions as they relate to public interest and benefit activities related to the use or disclosure of protected health information without an individual's authorization.
- Determine what makes up a limited data set.
- Understand what is considered authorized use and disclosure of protected health information.
- Understand the nuances of psychotherapy notes and marketing related to the use and disclosure of protected health information.
- Determine what types of privacy practice notices are required.
- Understand the content required for these notices, requirements for providing the notice, and the receipt of the acknowledgment of these notices.

- Determine what types of organizational options are available related to the release of protected health information, revocation of consent, and filing a privacy compliant.
- Understand the rights of an individual: to access protected health information; amend protected health information; receive an accounting of disclosure of protected health information; request restriction on the disclosure of protected health information; and options for confidential communications of protected health information.
- Understand the administrative requirements of the HIPAA Privacy Regulation related to the following: privacy policies and procedures; personnel privacy; workforce training and management; mitigation efforts; data safeguards; complaint resolution; retaliation and waiver process; documentation and record retention; and specific exceptions for fully insured group health plans.
- Understand the different organizational options available to the covered entity and determine what, if any, options may apply to the covered entity related to complying with the HIPAA Privacy Rule.
- Understand special circumstances involving authorized personal representatives and minors related to the disclosure of protected health information.
- Determine if any other state laws applicable to the covered entity supersede federal requirements.
- Understand actions that can be enforced for violation of the HIPAA Privacy regulations.
- Determine if the covered entity has met compliance dates.

Background

As of this book's writing, the National Institute of Standards and Technology (NIST) put out a draft of an updated special publication 800-53, Recommended Security Controls for Federal Information Systems, Revision 4 (February 2012) that now includes an entire control set for privacy controls. These controls were designed to be utilized at the organization or department level by privacy officials in coordination with the security official. Throughout the next section, references will be provided in related areas to this privacy control guidance. The following are the major sections of the control set:

- AP—Authority and Purpose
- AR—Accountability, Audit, and Risk Management
- DI—Data Quality and Integrity
- DM—Data Minimization and Retention
- IP—Individual Participation and Redress

- SE—Security
- TR—Transparency
- UL—Use Limitation

4.1 Minimum Necessary

Except for treatment purposes, a covered entity must develop policies and procedures to reasonably limit, the *minimum necessary*, its disclosures and requests for protected health information for payment and healthcare operations. A covered entity should apply the least amount of privileges to their individual employees based upon the roles of their employees. These restrictions should be applied through policies and procedures to restrict access to protected health information as need-to-know or to perform their job functions. There are several different examples to demonstrate how the minimum necessary standards can be applied, but there may be an easier example of what not to do. It would be a violation of the minimum necessary standard if a hospital employee is allowed routine, unimpeded access to patients' medical records if that employee does not need this access to do his or her job.

The covered entity should refer to the following reference for further details related to the minimum necessary standard:

- NIST SP 800-53 DM-1 Minimization of Personally Identifiable Information

4.1.1 Sample of Minimum Necessary Standard Policy

PURPOSE OF POLICY

To ensure compliance with the HIPAA Privacy Rules regarding the minimum necessary requirements for the use or disclosure of protected health information.

POLICY DETAIL

The minimum necessary requirements will be met when using or disclosing protected health information or when requesting such information. [The covered entity] will not use, disclose, or request the entire medical record of an individual unless this entire record is necessary to accomplish the use, disclosure, or request.

[The covered entity] will provide for classes of workforce members that need access to protected health information as part of their job responsibilities in respect to treatment, payment, or healthcare operations. In addition, [the covered entity] will determine access rights as needed and any other appropriate condition for such access by those classes of workforce members. Finally, [the covered entity] will make every reasonable effort to limit the access required by those classes of workforce members.

Routine Disclosures: There are some instances where disclosures are made on a recurring basis as part of [the covered entity's] business operations. These types of disclosures are limited to the least amount that is reasonable necessary for the activity of the disclosure. Some examples of these types of disclosures are:

- Claims processing
- Services for pharmaceuticals
- Clinical operations
- Continuity of care from outside providers
- Patient transfers to other facilities
- Consultation
- Specialty services, both on-site and off-site
- Diagnostic services
- Emergency transport
- Case management
- Consultants
- Agency accreditation

MINIMUM NECESSARY STANDARD DISCLOSURES APPLY

The covered entity will apply the minimum necessary standard by:

- Utilizing a limited data set
- Utilizing criteria designed to limit the disclosure of protected health information to the minimum necessary to accomplish the purpose of the disclosure
- Reviewing requests for disclosures based on these criteria

Under reasonable circumstances, [the covered entity] may rely on the minimum necessary standard when:

- Disclosing protected health information to public officials (as permitted by the HIPAA Privacy Rule)
- Requested by another covered entity
- Requested by a workforce member or business associate
- Requested for research purposes after documentation or representation has complied with the applicable Privacy Rules pertaining to research

MINIMUM NECESSARY STANDARD DISCLOSURES DO NOT APPLY

The following types of disclosures do not apply the minimum necessary standards:

- Disclosure to or requests by a healthcare provider for treatment
- Disclosures to the individual whose protected health information is being disclosed upon their request
- HIPAA-compliant authorization disclosures
- Disclosures made to the Secretary of the Department of Health and Human Services
- Disclosures required by law
- Disclosures necessary to comply with the Privacy Rule requirements

4.2 Individual Consent

A covered entity may choose to obtain the individual's consent to use and disclose their information; however, a "consent" document does not release a covered entity from the requirements under the Health Insurance Portability and Accountability Act (HIPAA) Privacy Rule to get an individual's "authorization" where those requirements exist to use or disclose protected health information. An example of the requirement to obtain an authorization from an individual would be in the case to obtain psychotherapy notes under 45 CFR § 164.508.

4.3 Permitted Uses and Disclosures Detailed

As mentioned earlier, there are some purposes or situations where a covered entity is permitted to use and disclose protected health information without specific authorization from an individual. These situations will be specifically addressed in the next sections.

4.3.1 To the Individual

It more or less goes without saying that a covered entity can provide protected health information to the individual that is the subject of that information. When patients request information contained in their medical records, the doctor is permitted to disclose this information to the patient. An individual is paying for healthcare services rendered by the healthcare provider and therefore is entitled to obtain information related to these services. The Privacy Rule has always provided for the right of individuals to have access to their own records. With the number of individuals retiring and the rise of electronic health records making it easier to access information, requests for this information will increase. Covered entities will have to prepare themselves for these requests.

The covered entity should refer to the following reference for further details related to individual access:

■ NIST SP 800-53 IP-2 Individual Access

4.3.2 Treatment, Payment, Healthcare Operations

Protected health information can be used or disclosed for the purposes of treatment, payment, and other healthcare operations. These are the core healthcare activities as defined in 45 CFR § 164.501:

■ *Treatment*—"The provision, coordination, or management of healthcare and related services among healthcare providers or by a healthcare provider with a third party, consultation between healthcare providers regarding a patient, or the referral of a patient from one healthcare provider to another."

■ *Payment*—Encompasses the various activities of healthcare providers to obtain payment or reimbursement for services rendered. In the case of a health plan, it is the ability to obtain premiums and to fulfill their obligations under the plan. The HIPAA Privacy Rule provides several examples of common payment activities that include the following:

– Determining eligibility or coverage under a plan and adjudicating claims
– Risk adjustments
– Billing and collection activities
– Reviewing healthcare services for medical necessity, coverage, justification of charges, and the like;
– Utilization review activities
– Disclosures to consumer reporting agencies (limited to specified identifying information about the individual, his or her payment history, and identifying information about the covered entity)

■ *Healthcare operations*—These are the core business and support functions for the treatment and payment of health services such as administrative, financial, legal, and quality improvement activities of a covered entity. As defined in 45 CFR § 164.501, healthcare operations are limited to the following activities:

– "Conducting quality assessment and improvement activities, population-based activities relating to improving health or reducing healthcare costs, and case management and care coordination;
– Reviewing the competence or qualifications of healthcare professionals, evaluating provider and health plan performance, training healthcare and non-healthcare professionals, accreditation, certification, licensing, or credentialing activities;
– Underwriting and other activities relating to the creation, renewal, or replacement of a contract of health insurance or health benefits, and ceding, securing, or placing a contract for reinsurance of risk relating to healthcare claims;
– Conducting or arranging for medical review, legal, and auditing services, including fraud and abuse detection and compliance programs;
– Business planning and development, such as conducting cost-management and planning analyses related to managing and operating the entity; and
– Business management and general administrative activities, including those related to implementing and complying with the Privacy Rule and other Administrative Simplification Rules, customer service, resolution of internal grievances, sale or transfer of assets, creating de-identified health information or a limited data set, and fundraising for the benefit of the covered entity. General Provisions at 45 CFR § 164.506."

A covered entity may, without the individual's authorization, use or disclose protected health information as follows:

- For the covered entity's own treatment, payment, and healthcare operations activities.
- For the treatment activities of any healthcare provider, including those providers that may not be covered by the HIPAA Privacy Rule.
- To another covered entity or a healthcare provider, including those providers that may not be covered by the HIPAA Privacy Rule for the payment activities of the entity that receives the information.
- To another covered entity for certain healthcare operation activities of the entity that receives the information if there is (or was) a relationship between the entities in regard to the individual that is the subject of the information and the protected health information pertains to that relationship. In addition, the disclosure of such information is for a quality-related healthcare operations activity or for the purpose of healthcare fraud and abuse detection or compliance.
- If the covered entity is a participant in an organized healthcare arrangement (OHCA), it may disclose the protected health information about an individual to another covered entity that participates in the OHCA for any joint healthcare operations of the OHCA.

4.3.3 Uses and Disclosures with Opportunity to Agree or Object

An individual can provide informal permission to the covered entity by being asked to disclose such information or in a situation where the individual is clearly given the opportunity to agree or object to the disclosure. Exigent circumstances may arise in cases where the professional judgment of the healthcare provider comes into play when an individual is incapacitated and the use or disclosure of such information about an individual is believed to be in the best interest of that individual.

A covered entity may rely on an individual's informal permission to list the individual's name, general condition, religious affiliation, and location in a provider's facility in the facilities' patient directory. The covered entity may also rely on informal permission to disclose information to relatives, friends, or other persons that the individual identifies related to the individual's care or payment for care. For notification purposes, the covered entity may disclose the individual's location, general condition, or death to family members, personal representatives, or others responsible for the individual's care. This type of information may also be disclosed to public or private entities authorized by law (or charter) to assist in disaster relief efforts.

4.3.4 Incidental Use and Disclosure

Incidental use or disclosure is permitted if it is a by-product of another permissible or required use or disclosure. As long as the covered entity has applied reasonable safeguards and minimum necessary standards described earlier, this incidental use or disclosure is allowed. An example of unlawful use or disclosure would be if an employee overheard a conversion about a patient that was being discussed by other employees who may not be authorized to possess such information. A covered entity is required to impose minimum necessary standards limiting only those individuals requiring access to a patient's information to have access to this information in accordance with the employee's roles or job functions.

If an employee that may not be required to have such access, has unimpeded access to all patient files the HIPAA Privacy Rule has been violated. If a discussion of patient information was overheard as a result of this access, the covered entity would be in further violation of the HIPAA Privacy Rule. For instance, a receptionist has access to full patient medical records. This receptionist may not have a job duty that requires having full access to these records. Through the course of this access, the receptionist was talking to a fellow workforce member about a patient's condition and another patient overheard this discussion. The discussion included specific treatment details, patient names, and other protected health information. The workforce members are violating the HIPAA Privacy Rule requirements throughout this scenario and placing the covered entity at risk for liability of this use and disclosure violation.

4.3.5 Public Interest and Benefit Activities

For certain activities related to the public interest or benefit, a covered entity can release protected health information without an individual's authorization. There are 12 public policy reasons that the HIPAA Privacy Rule permits the covered entity to use or disclose protected health information without an individual's authorization or permission.

- *Required by law*—As was defined earlier related to the HIPAA/HITECH regulations.
- *Public health activities*—Covered entities may disclose protected health information to public health authorities to prevent or control disease, injury, or disability. A *public health authority* as defined in 45 CFR § 164.501 is "an agency or authority of the United States government, a State, a territory, a political subdivision of a State or territory, or Indian tribe that is responsible for public health matters as part of its official mandate, as well as a person or entity acting under a grant of authority from, or under a contract with, a public health agency." Examples of public health authorities include: state and local health departments, the Food and Drug Administration (FDA), the Centers for Disease Control and Prevention (CDC), and the Occupational

Safety and Health Administration (OSHA). As a general rule of thumb, these agencies are only supposed to use the information in accordance with the minimum necessary standards and reasonably limit the use of such information for public health purposes. Other public health activities are included in permissible disclosure as follows:

- Reporting known or suspected child abuse or neglect.
- Reporting to the Food and Drug Administration (FDA) for public health purposes related quality, safety, or effectiveness of a product or activity regulated by FDA.
- Reporting information on a person at risk of contracting or spreading a disease as necessary to carry out public health interventions or investigations.
- Reporting information to an individual's employer as it relates to complying with the Occupational Safety and Health Administration (OSHA), the Mine Safety and Health Administration (MSHA), or the requirements of state laws having a similar purpose at the request of the employer. Per 45 CFR § 164.512 (b)(1), the covered healthcare provider must provide the individual with written notice that the information will be disclosed to their employer.

■ *Victims of abuse, neglect, or domestic violence*—Covered entities may disclose protected health information to government authorities in reference to victims of abuse, neglect, or domestic violence.

■ *Health oversight activities*—For purposes of authorized health oversight activities such as audits and investigations necessitated by oversight of healthcare or government benefit programs, a covered entity may disclose protected health information to health oversight agencies. One of these health oversight agencies is the Office for Civil Rights (OCR) of the Department of Health and Human Services (HHS). This could also include any entity hired on the behalf of these health oversight agencies to perform oversight activities as in the case of KPMG, LLP be contracted by OCR to perform audit work.

■ *Judicial and administrative proceedings*—Through an order from a court, administrative tribunal, response to a subpoena, or other lawful process, a covered entity may disclose protected health information in a judicial or administrative proceeding.

■ *Law enforcement purposes*—A covered entity may disclose protected health information to law enforcement officials for law enforcement purposes under the following six conditions:

- Of course, as required by law as previously described
- To identify or locate a suspect, fugitive, material witness, or missing person
- In response to a law enforcement official's request for information about a victim or suspected victim of a crime
- If the covered entity suspects criminal activity as the cause of death or to alert law enforcement of the death

- If the covered entity believes the protected health information is evidence of a crime that occurred on its premises
- When necessary to inform law enforcement about the commission and nature of a crime, the location of the crime or crime victims, and the perpetrator of the crime
■ *Decedents*—Covered entities may disclose protected health information to funeral directors, as needed, and to coroners or medical examiners to identify a deceased person, determine the cause of death, and perform other functions authorized by law.
■ *Cadaveric organ, eye, or tissue donation*—covered entities may use or disclose protected health information to facilitate the donation and transplant of cadaveric organs, eyes, and tissue.
■ *Research use*—Covered entities may use or disclose protected health information without authorization by the research participant under one of the following conditions:
  - Pursuant to a waiver authorized by an Institutional Review Board (IRB) or Privacy Board as defined in 45 CFR § 164.512 (i)(1)(i). Approval of a waiver of authorization must meet the following three criteria:
    • "The use or disclosure of protected health information involves no more than a minimal risk to the privacy of individuals, based on, at least the presence of the following elements:
      ■ an adequate plan to protect the identifiers from improper use and disclosure;
      ■ an adequate plan to destroy the identifiers at the earliest opportunity consistent with conduct of the research, unless there is a health or research justification for retaining the identifiers or such retention is otherwise required by law; and
      ■ adequate written assurances that the protected health information will not be reused or disclosed to any other person or entity, except as required by law, for authorized oversight of the research project, or for other research for which the user or disclosure of protected health information would be permitted by this subpart;
    • The research could not practicably be conducted without the waiver or alteration; and
    • The research could not practicably be conducted without access to and use of the protected health information."
  - Preparation of a research protocol or for similar purposes upon representation from the researcher, either in writing or orally, that the researcher will not remove any protected health information from the covered entity and the information is necessary for research purposes.
  - Research of decedents upon representation from the researcher, either in writing or orally, that the researcher will not remove any protected health

information from the covered entity and the information is necessary for research purposes.

- Data use agreement between the covered entity and researcher for a limited data set. A limited data set excludes specific identifiers of the individual or of relatives, employers, or household members of the individual. As defined in 45 CFR § 164.514(e), the data use agreement must:
  - "Establish the permitted uses and disclosures of the limited data set by the recipient, consistent with the purposes of the research, and which may not include any use or disclosure that would violate the Rule if done by the covered entity;
  - Limit who can use or receive the data; and
  - Require the recipient to agree to the following:
    - Not to use or disclose the information other than as permitted by the data use agreement or as otherwise required by law;
    - Use appropriate safeguards to prevent the use or disclosure of the information other than as provided for in the data use agreement;
    - Report to the covered entity any use or disclosure of the information not provided for by the data use agreement of which the recipient becomes aware;
    - Ensure that any agents, including a subcontractor, to whom the recipient provides the limited data set agrees to the same restrictions and conditions that apply to the recipient with respect to the limited data set; and
    - Not to identify the information or contact the individual."
- Research use/disclosure with individual authorization—If an individual provides an authorization to disclose protected health information to a research project, then the covered entity is permitted to share this information. There are a couple of special provisions that apply to research authorizations. First, the authorization may state that it does not expire or have an expiration date and may continue until the end of the research study (unlike other authorizations). Second, the authorization may be combined with consent to participate in the research or with any other legal permission related to the research study.
- Accounting for research disclosures—If an individual requests to know to whom their protected health information was disclosed, the covered entity is required to provide an accounting of this disclosure during the 6 years prior to the individual's request or since the applicable compliance date (whichever is sooner). This accounting must include specific information about each disclosure. If the same person or entity requested multiple disclosures for a single purpose, then a more general accounting is permitted. There are two exemptions on this accounting requirement: an individual's authorization for research disclosure and a data use agreement for disclosures of the limited data set. For disclosure of protected

health information for research purposes without an individual's authorization that involves at least 50 records, the covered entity, under a simplified accounting rule, can provide individuals with a list of the protocols as well as the researcher's name and contact information related to the disclosure of the individual's protected health information.

- Transition provision—If a covered entity obtained any one of the following prior to the compliance date of the HIPAA Privacy Rule, a covered entity may use and disclose protected health information for research: an authorization or other express legal permission to use or disclose; the informed consent of the individual; and a waiver of informed consent by an IRB or exception under FDA's human subject protection regulations at 21 CFR § 50.24 (Exception from informed consent requirements for emergency research). (Note: If an informed consent waiver was obtained prior to the compliance date but is subsequently sought after, then the covered entity must obtain the individual's authorization.)

■ *Serious threat to health or safety*—A covered entity can disclose protected health information to someone it believes can prevent or lessen a serious and imminent threat to a person or the public. This could include disclosing information to law enforcement as needed to identify or apprehend an escapee or violent criminal.

■ *Essential government functions*—Certain essential government functions do not require authorization to use or disclose protected health information. Such functions include: "assuring proper execution of a military mission, conducting intelligence and national security activities that are authorized by law, providing protective services to the President, making medical suitability determinations for U.S. State Department employees, protecting the health and safety of inmates or employees in a correctional institution, and determining eligibility for or conducting enrollment in certain government benefit programs."

■ *Workers' compensation*—Workers' compensation laws or other similar programs providing work-related injury or illness benefits may obtain protected health information. Disclosure is permitted without individual authorization to the extent necessary to comply with laws (state or other) and to obtain payment for healthcare provided to the injured or ill worker. If the individual has provided an individual authorization for disclosure, such information will be permitted to be disclosed accordingly.

4.3.6 Limited Data Set

Limited data set is protected health information where specified direct identifiers of individuals, their relatives, household members, and employers have been removed. If a recipient enters into a data use agreement with a covered entity specifying safeguards will be implemented to secure the protected health information within the limited data set, then the information may be used or disclosed for research, healthcare operations, and public health purposes.

4.4 Authorized Use and Disclosure

If protected health information is not being used or disclosed for treatment, payment, healthcare operations, or otherwise permitted or required by the HIPAA Privacy Rule, then the covered entity must obtain the individual's written authorization. A written authorization has certain core elements, statements, and conditions that are required to be included. The next couple of sections will explain these specific terms.

The covered entity should refer to the following reference for further details related to authorization:

■ NIST SP 800-53 IP-1 Consent

4.4.1 Valid Authorization Core Elements

The implementation specifications under 45 CFR § 164.508 (c) state the following in regard to the elements that must be contained within a valid authorization to allow covered entities to disclose an individual's protected health information:

■ A specific and meaningful *description* of the information to be used or disclosed.
■ Authorized *requestor's name* or other specific identification of requestor.
■ Authorized *recipient's name* or other specific identification of covered entity that may make the request for use or disclosure.
■ *Purpose* of the request. If the individual does not want to provide a statement of purpose, he or she may use the statement "at the request of the individual."
■ An *expiration date*. As discussed earlier under "Research use/disclosure with individual authorization" and under "Limited Data Set," an individual may use the statements "end of the research study" or "none" under these circumstances.
■ The individual's *signature and date*. In the case of a personal representative, a description of the representative's authority to act on the individual's behalf must be provided.

These six elements must be present on all valid written individual authorizations.

4.4.2 Valid Authorization Required Statements

The implementation specifications under 45 CFR § 164.508 (c) also state the following regarding the required statements that must be contained within a valid authorization to adequately place the individual on notice regarding the disclosure of an individual's protected health information:

■ A statement providing a description of how the individual may *revoke* the authorization
■ A statement that either states the *ability or inability* to provide treatment, payment, enrollment, or eligibility for benefits, or, the results of the consequences of not signing the authorization
■ The potential that the information authorized to be disclosed may possibly be *redisclosed* by the recipient of the information and no longer protected under the authorization.

In addition to the core elements and required statements, the authorization should be in plain language. Once an individual signs an authorization, a copy should be maintained in the individual's records and a signed copy of the authorization must be provided back to the individual for his or her own records.

4.4.3 Psychotherapy Notes

Psychotherapy notes are special protected health information that requires an individual's authorization to disclose under any circumstances. The only exceptions to the special treatment of psychotherapy notes are as follows:

■ A covered entity that originated the notes may use them for treatment of the individual
■ A covered entity that originated the notes may use the notes for its own training
■ A covered entity may use the notes to defend itself in legal proceedings brought by the individual
■ The Department of Health and Human Services (HHS) may require them for investigation or compliance related matters
■ Use them in cases of imminent threat to public health or safety
■ Provide them to a health oversight agency for lawful oversight of the covered entity that originated the notes
■ Provide them to a coroner or medical examiner in performing their lawful duties
■ As required by law

4.4.4 Marketing

Marketing is defined by the HIPAA Privacy Rule as making "a communication about a product or service that encourages recipients of the communication to purchase or use the product or service." There are a few exceptions that are specifically addressed for this definition of marketing. For the most part, however, a covered entity must obtain an individual's authorization to disclose protected health information as already discussed. Furthermore, HITECH Section 13405 (d) requires an individual's authorization if the covered entity sells protected health information.

Marketing is also defined as "an arrangement between a covered entity and any other entity whereby the covered entity discloses protected health information to the other entity, in exchange for direct or indirect remuneration, for the other entity or its affiliate to make a communication about its own product or service that encourages recipients of the communication to purchase or use that product or service." There are no exceptions to this definition of marketing. If a certain activity does not fall under the specific definition of marketing, this activity is not considered to be marketing and therefore is not exempt from any of the requirements for use or disclosure of protected health information.

The first marketing exception is that a covered entity, such as a health plan, may communicate its own products and services to its enrollees. These types of communications could alert the individual of the health plan regarding replacements, enhancements, or value-added services of the plan.

A second marketing exception exists when communication is made for the treatment of the individual. This could include a pharmacy sending reminders about refilling an individual's prescription as part of providing treatment to the patient.

The third and final marketing exception is made for case management or coordination of care for an individual. For instance, a physician could share a patient's medical record with different alternative treatment, therapy, healthcare providers, or settings of care to determine the best treatment available for the individual. In any of these cases, the activity should be otherwise permissible under the HIPAA Privacy Rule.

Face-to-face communication made by the covered entity to an individual or a promotional gift of nominal value provided to the individual by the covered entity does not require an individual's authorization. In any other case where the communication does not meet the aforementioned definition of marketing, the covered entity is required to obtain an individual's authorization for use or disclosure of their information.

4.5 Privacy Practices Notice

As expected, individuals have the right to know how a covered entity may use or disclose protected health information about them. This requires a covered entity to develop a notice of the covered entity's privacy practices. This also requires the covered entity to provide such notice to the individual. There are a few exempted covered entities that are not required to provide a privacy notice to an individual. The following covered entities are exempted from providing privacy practice notices:

■ Healthcare clearinghouses that create or receive protected health information as a business associate to another covered entity

- A correctional institution that has a covered healthcare provider component
- A group health plant that provides benefits through contract with health insurance issuers or health maintenance organizations (HMOs) as long as they do not create or receive protected health information (other than summary health information) or enrollment/disenrollment information

The covered entity should refer to the following references for further details related to privacy notices:

- NIST SP 800-53 TR-1 Privacy Notice
- NIST SP 800-53 TR-2 System of Records Notices and Privacy Act Statements
- NIST SP 800-53 TR-3 Dissemination of Privacy Program Information

4.5.1 Content of the Notice

There are several elements that must be contained in the notice of privacy practices of a covered entity provided to an individual. First, the notice must be in "plain language" and describe how the covered entity may use and disclose protected health information about the individual. This means that the notice must be easy to read and easy to understand by an average individual. The covered entity should detail how it may use or disclose the individual's information along with examples of this use and disclosure.

Second, the notice must include the rights of the individual with respect to their information and how the individual should exercise their rights. Again, the individual should have a right to the privacy of his or her health information. If an individual wants to review their medical records, for instance, the individual should be provided information on the process that they will be able to follow to get this information.

Third, the notice should include details on filing a complaint with the covered entity for any suspected violation of an individual's privacy rights or violations of the HIPAA Privacy Rules. These details should include contact information and a process of making a compliant. In addition, any retaliation against an individual making a complaint is unlawful.

Fourth, the notice should contain a statement that the covered entity is required by law to maintain the privacy of the protected health information. Since the notice describes examples of how a covered entity will use or disclose protected health information, any use or disclosure of such information (without a written authorization) is against HIPAA Privacy Rules. The covered entity could describe the steps they take to protect the privacy of an individual's protected health information.

Fifth, the notice should include contact information on whom the individual could contact to get further information about the privacy policies of the covered entity. Although the privacy notice is written to be understood by the majority of the individuals, some individuals still may have questions on their rights or how the covered entity protects their information. For this reason, a workforce member or a group of workforce members should be designated by the covered entity to provide this information to individuals upon request. The notice should provide the steps to take to contact the workforce member (or group) to answer their questions or concerns.

Finally, the notice must include an effective date. This should be the date that all terms of the privacy notice went into effect. Any material changes to the privacy policy should be promptly revised and distributed accordingly to the affected individuals. There are certain requirements regarding the verification of receipt of these notices that will be discussed later.

4.5.1.1 Sample of a Privacy Practice Notice

This notice describes how medical information about you may be used and disclosed.

[The covered entity] is required by law to maintain the privacy of an individual's protected health information. [The covered entity] reserves the right to change privacy practices and the terms of this notice at any time, allowed or required by law. This includes the right to make changes in privacy practices and the revised terms of this notice effective for all personal and health information [the covered entity] maintains. This also includes information created or received before the changes occurred. Any material changes to [the covered entity's] privacy policy will be promptly revised and distributed to the individual.

Definition of protected health information: Individually identifiable health information transmitted by electronic media, maintained in electronic media, or transmitted or maintained in any other form or medium, whether electronic, paper, or oral. *Health information* is broadly defined as any information, in any form or medium, that relates to the past, present, or future physical or mental health, condition, provision of healthcare, or future payment for the provision of healthcare of or to an individual. Individually identifiable health information includes many common identifiers such as name, address, birth date, and Social Security number.

Safeguards [the covered entity] implements: There are several safeguards [the covered entity] implements to protect the individual's protected health information. Examples include, but are not limited to:

- Restricting access to the individual's protected health information
- Limiting the use and disclosure of the individual's protected health information
- Notifying the individual of their rights on protected health information
- Training employees and associates about [the covered entity's] privacy policies and procedures
- [Insert other specific steps taken to safeguard protected health information]

Use and disclosure of protected health information: Where as required by law, [the covered entity] must use and disclose protected health information to the individual or someone who has the legal right to act on the individual's behalf and to the Secretary of the Department of Health and Human Services.

[The covered entity] has the right to use and disclose protected health information as follows:

■ To a doctor, a hospital, or other healthcare provider as part of the individual's medical care;
■ For payment activities for healthcare services;
■ For healthcare operation activities to include enrollment processing, inquiries response/request services, care coordination, dispute resolution, medical management, quality improvements, competence review, and premium determinations;
■ For underwriting activities [if applicable];
■ For plan sponsorship [if applicable];
■ For communicating with the individual about services, appointment reminders, or treatment alternatives that relate to the individual;
■ In cases of emergency, to the individual's family or friends if the individual is not available;
■ To the individual's family or friends that the individual identifies as having direct involvement with the individual's healthcare or payment of care;
■ To substantiate payment information to subscriber for the Internal Revenue Service
■ In case of serious health or safety threat, to public health agencies
■ In case of abuse, neglect, or domestic violence, to the appropriate authorities
■ In response to a court or administrative order, subpoena, discovery request, or other lawful process
■ For law enforcement purposes, to military authorities, and as otherwise required by law
■ To assist in disaster relief efforts
■ For compliance programs and other health oversight activities
■ To fulfill workers' compensation law requirements
■ In cases of serious or imminent threat to the individual's health or safety or the health or safety of others
■ In limited circumstances, for research purposes
■ In cases of organ transplants
■ To a coroner, medical examiner, or funeral director

Use of protected health information not described in this notice: [The covered entity] will request written permission from the individual before using or disclosing the individual's protected health information in all situations that are not described in this notice. The individual has the right to revoke permission granted at any time by written notification. [The covered entity] will not use or disclose protected health information for any reason not described in this notice without an individual's permission.

An individual's protected health information may continue to be used or disclosed for purposes described in this notice even if the individual is no longer a patient or plan member [as applicable]. Once the legal retention period has been met, the protected health information will be destroyed.

Individual's rights to protected health information:

■ The individual has the right to review and obtain copies of their own protected health information or a summary of this information. [The covered entity may charge a reasonable fee for the cost of copying and postage.]

- The individual has the right to notification of denial or adverse decisions concerning healthcare coverage [if applicable].
- Upon request, the individual has the right to receive a written copy of this privacy notice at any time.
- The individual has the right to restrict use or disclosure of the individual's protected health information. [The covered entity] is not required to agree to these restrictions; however, if agreed to, [the covered entity] will comply with these restrictions. The individual can terminate these restrictions at any time.
- The individual has the right to request an amendment of protected health information if they believe that the information is inaccurate or incomplete. [The covered entity] may deny such request if the information was not created or maintained by [the covered entity] or if it is believed to be correct and complete. The individual has the right to response with a written explanation that will be included with the protected health information.
- The individual has the right to an accounting of the disclosures of the individual's protected health information in cases other than treatment, payment, health plan operations, and other certain activities. [The covered entity] will maintain this information for 6 years. [The covered entity may charge a reasonable fee for the cost of copying and postage.]
- The individual has the right to receive confidential communications of protected health information in a different manner or at a different place to avoid life-threatening situations. [The covered entity] will make every reasonable attempt to accommodate this request.

[Describe how the individual may receive a copy of the privacy notice.]

Information collected: [The covered entity] collects information on an individual through applications and forms the individual completes.

Information received: [The covered entity] may receive other information through the use of [the covered entity's] Web site or through other medical benefit or health plans, contract service providers, or business associates.

Affiliated companies or nonaffiliated third parties: [The covered entity] may share information with these companies and third parties as permitted by law. If there is a joint marketing agreement in place between another organization and [the covered entity], we may share information in order to communicate other product and service offerings. The individual has the right to opt-out of receiving notification on these products and services. [Describe the process the individual may follow to opt-out of these offerings.]

Include details on filing a complaint with the covered entity. [The covered entity may also include the information on submitting a written complaint to the U.S. Department of Health and Human Services, Office of Civil Rights (OCR).]

[Provide a list of companies, affiliates, or subsidiaries that adhere to the covered entity's privacy policies and procedures.]

Special note: As of this writing, a proposed rule change (dated July 14, 2010) may be approved that will require the following three items be added to the Notice of Privacy Policy:

1. "The addition of the sale of protected health information as a use or disclosure that requires the express written authorization of the individual";
2. [A] separate statement that provides advance notice to the individual if the healthcare provider receives financial remuneration from a third party to

send treatment communications to the individual about that party's products or services, and the right of the individual to elect not to receive such communications"; and

3. [The] right of the individual to restrict disclosures of protected health information to a health plan with respect to treatment services for which the individual has paid out of pocket in full."

4.5.2 Providing the Notice

Upon request, the covered entity must make its privacy notice available. The covered entity must prominently display its notice on its Web site. If an individual elects to receive electronic notices, a covered entity may e-mail the notice to the individual. In cases of emergencies, the notice must be provided to the individual as promptly as practically acceptable.

Specifically for health plans, as of April 14, 2003 (as of April 14, 2004, for small health plans), the privacy policy must be provided to all enrollees or to new enrollees at the time of enrollment.

4.5.3 Acknowledgment of Notice Receipt

Covered entities that provide direct treatment must obtain an individual's written acknowledgement of receipt of the privacy notice except in cases of emergency treatment situations. Again, this notice is required after April 14, 2003, or no later than the date of the first service provided. If, for any reason, the acknowledgment cannot be obtained, the provider must document the efforts to obtain and the reason why an acknowledgment was not obtained.

If the privacy notice was delivered electronically, as over the Internet or through e-mail, the provider must automatically and contemporaneously send an electronic response notice to validate that the notice was received. A good-faith effort must be made to obtain a return receipt or other transmission to verify receipt of the notice.

4.5.4 Organizational Options

Covered entities that fall under an organized healthcare arrangement (OHCA) may use a joint privacy practice notice as long as each agrees to abide by the notice's requirements to protect health information. The notice distribution obligation is satisfied for other participants at the first point that an OHCA member satisfies this requirement.

4.5.4.1 Sample of Consent for Release of Protected Health Information

[The covered entity] is required by law to maintain the privacy of an individual's protected health information. Any material changes to [the covered entity's] privacy policy will be promptly revised and distributed to the individual.

[Person whose information will be released: include name, date of birth, address, member or patient number, phone number, etc.]

I understand that this authorization will allow [the covered entity] and its affiliates to use or disclose the protected health information as described. This could include any and all protected health information or specific information related to a condition, injury, or other information.

[Person to whom this information can be disclosed to or used by: include name, date of birth, address, relationship to requestor, etc.]

[Provide an explanation statement for the reason of the consent.]

I understand that I have the right to revoke this authorization at any time by sending written revocation to [the covered entity]. Unless otherwise revoked, the authorization will expire in [number of months or specific date].

I understand the revocation will not apply to information that has been released in response to this authorization and could be re-disclosed by the recipient. If this occurs, the information may not be protected by federal privacy regulations.

I understand that I sign this consent by my own free will and that the covered entity will not base any treatment or payment decision on signing of this authorization.

[Signature of individual and date signed.] (Note: If a legal representative is signing the consent then the covered entity should request a power of attorney or other copy of authorization.)

[Explain how the form should be submitted.]

[Include details on filing a complaint with the covered entity.]

[Contact information on whom the individual could contact to get further information about the privacy policies of the covered entity.]

4.5.4.2 Sample of Revocation of Consent of Protected Health Information

[The covered entity] is required by law to maintain the privacy of the individual's protected health information. Any material changes to [the covered entity's] privacy policy will be promptly revised and distributed to the individual.

[Person whose information will no longer be released: include name, date of birth, address, member or patient number, phone number, etc.]

I no longer authorize [the covered entity] to use or disclose the protected health information as described: this could include any and all protected health information or specific information related to a condition, injury, or other information.

[Person to whom this information can no longer be disclosed to or used by: include name, date of birth, address, relationship to requestor, etc.]

I understand that this revocation will not apply to information that has been released in response to the previous authorization.

[Signature of individual and date signed.] (Note: If a legal representative is signing the consent then the covered entity should request a power of attorney or other copy of authorization.)

[Explain how the form should be submitted.]

[Include details on filing a complaint with the covered entity.]

[Contact information on whom the individual could contact to get further information about the privacy policies of the covered entity.]

4.5.4.3 Sample of Privacy Complaint Form

[The covered entity] is required by law to maintain the privacy of the individual's protected health information. Any material changes to [the covered entity's] privacy policy will be promptly revised and distributed to the individual.

Use this form to submit a complaint about [the covered entity's] privacy practices as well as compliance with [the covered entity's] Notice of Privacy Practices or state and federal privacy laws and regulations. [The covered entity] will not retaliate in any way and it will not influence your treatment, payment, enrollment, or eligibility for benefits.

After receiving this form, [the covered entity] will conduct a timely and impartial investigation of the complaint and provide a written response to you.

Provide all details related to the privacy complaint and attach additional documentation to support the allegations as needed.

[Person filing complaint: include name, date of birth, address, relationship to requestor, etc.]

[Signature of individual and date signed.] (Note: If a legal representative is signing the consent then the covered entity should request a power of attorney or other copy of authorization.)

[Explain how the form should be submitted.]

[Contact information on whom the individual could contact to get further information about the privacy policies of the covered entity.]

4.5.5 Access

An individual has the right to review and obtain a copy of his or her protected health information in a designated record set maintained by the covered entity. Per 45 CFR § 164.501, a *designated record set* is defined as "a group of records maintained by or for a covered entity that is: the medical records and billing records about individuals maintained by or for a covered healthcare provider; the enrollment, payment, claims adjudication, and case or medical management record systems maintained by or for a health plan; or used, in whole or in part by or for the covered entity to make decisions about individuals." In general, the designated record set "means any item, collection, or grouping of information that includes protected health information and is maintained, collected, used, or disseminated by or for a covered entity."

The following are some exceptions of protected health information that the individual does not have the right to review and obtain a copy of:

■ Psychotherapy notes
■ Information compiled for legal proceedings
■ Laboratory results to which the Clinical Laboratory Improvement Act (CLIA) prohibits access
■ Information held by certain research laboratories

Under special circumstances, a covered entity may deny an individual access to protected health information such as when a healthcare professional believes access to this information may cause harm to the individual or others. An individual does have the right to have a second opinion conducted by another licensed healthcare professional.

Reasonable, cost-based fees may be assessed by the covered entity for the cost of copying and postage for any individual request. This fee could be a reasonable amount charged for the time for a medical records clerk to copy the information requested, the supplies (i.e., toner, paper, envelopes) for copying the information, and, of course, the postage (if applicable) for sending the material to the individual.

4.5.5.1 Sample of Request to Access Protected Health Information

[The covered entity] is required by law to maintain the privacy of the individual's protected health information. Any material changes to [the covered entity's] privacy policy will be promptly revised and distributed to the individual.

I hereby request access to my protected health information that [the covered entity] maintains in a set of specific record(s). [The covered entity] will notify me within [number of] days with the determination of my request. If it should take longer to fulfill this request, I will receive notice at that time. If the request is denied, I will receive a written explanation of the reason for denial.

[Describe the protected health information requested along with time periods.]

[Describe the method by which this request should be met: mail or in person.]

[The covered entity] may charge a reasonable cost-based fee for the copying and mailing of the request.

[Person requesting access: include name, date of birth, address, member or patient number, phone number, etc.]

[Signature of individual and date signed.] (Note: If a legal representative is signing the consent then the covered entity should request a power of attorney or other copy of authorization.)

[Explain how the form should be submitted.]

[Include details on filing a complaint with the covered entity.]

[Contact information on whom the individual could contact to get further information about the privacy policies of the covered entity.]

4.5.6 Amendment

When an individual feels that his or her protected health information is inaccurate or incomplete, the individual has a right to have the covered entity amend this information. A covered entity could accept or deny the amendment. If it is accepted, the covered entity has to make a reasonable effort to provide this amended information to individuals that may need it or to individuals that the covered entity is aware of that may rely on this information from the individual. If it is denied, the individual has the right to submit a statement of disagreement to include in the record. If another covered entity makes an amendment request, then the record must be updated accordingly.

4.5.6.1 Sample of Request for Amendment of Protected Health Information

[The covered entity] is required by law to maintain the privacy of the individual's protected health information. Any material changes to [the covered entity's] privacy policy will be promptly revised and distributed to the individual.

I hereby request to amend my protected health information that [the covered entity] created and maintained; however, I understand that [the covered entity] may deny my request if [the covered entity] did not create or maintain the information, or the information provided is not correct or complete. If the request is denied, I will receive a written explanation and have the right to file a written disagreement statement to include with my protected health information.

[Describe the protected health information that is believed to be inaccurate or incomplete.]

[Include contact information on anyone that should receive notice of this amendment.]

[The covered entity] will notify me within [number of] days with the determination of my request. If it should take longer to fulfill this request, I will receive notice at that time.

[Person requesting amendment: include name, date of birth, address, member or patient number, phone number, etc.]

[Signature of individual and date signed.] (Note: If a legal representative is signing the consent then the covered entity should request a power of attorney or other copy of authorization.)

[Explain how the form should be submitted.]

[Include details on filing a complaint with the covered entity.]

[Contact information on whom the individual could contact to get further information about the privacy policies of the covered entity.]

4.5.7 Disclosure Accounting

If an individual requests to know to whom their protected health information was disclosed, the covered entity is required to provide an accounting of this disclosure during the 6 years prior to the individual's request or since the applicable compliance date (whichever is sooner). This accounting must include specific information about each disclosure. If the same person or entity requested multiple disclosures for a single purpose, then a more general accounting is permitted.

Disclosure accounting is not required for the following:

■ Treatment, payment, or healthcare operations
■ To the individual or the individual's personal representative
■ Notification to persons involved in an individual's healthcare or payment for healthcare, for disaster relief, or for facility directories
■ Pursuant to an authorization
■ Of a limited data set

- National security or intelligence purposes
- To correctional institutions or law enforcement officials for certain purposes such as regarding inmates or individuals in lawful custody
- Incident to otherwise permitted or required uses or disclosures

Accounting disclosure may be temporarily suspended upon written request from a health oversight agency or law enforcement official in cases where the accounting of such disclosure would have an effect on their lawful duties. An example of temporarily suspending an accounting disclosure could be if a criminal investigation is ongoing related to healthcare fraud and the disclosure of accounting would jeopardize the investigation.

4.5.7.1 Sample of Request for Accounting of Disclosures

[The covered entity] is required by law to maintain the privacy of the individual's protected health information. Any material changes to [the covered entity's] privacy policy will be promptly revised and distributed to the individual.

I hereby request an accounting of disclosures that [the covered entity] has disclosed for reasons other than treatment, payment, health plan operations, and certain permitted activities as described in [the covered entity's] "Notice of Privacy Practices." [The covered entity] is not required to provide disclosures made before April 14, 2003 [or for small health plans, April 14, 2004].

I understand [the covered entity] has [number of] days from the receipt of this request to provide the information to me, including the following items:

- Date(s) of disclosure
- Name of entity receiving the protected health information, including the address, if known
- Brief description of the disclosed health information
- Brief description of the purpose of the disclosure

If [the covered entity] cannot provide this information within [number of] days, I understand that I will receive a written notice regarding the reason for the delay and an expected time for the completion of the request.

[The covered entity] may charge a reasonable cost-based fee for the copying and mailing of the request.

[Person whose information will be accounted for: include name, date of birth, address, member or patient number, phone number, etc.]

[Signature of individual and date signed.] (Note: If a legal representative is signing the consent then the covered entity should request a power of attorney or other copy of authorization.)

[Explain how the form should be submitted.]

[Include details on filing a complaint with the covered entity.]

[Contact information on whom the individual could contact to get further information about the privacy policies of the covered entity.]

4.5.8 Restriction Request

Although an individual has the right to request a covered entity to restrict use or disclosure of protected health information, the covered entity is not under any obligation to agree with the request. Except in cases of medical emergencies, a covered entity must comply with these restrictions, if agreed to.

4.5.8.1 Sample of Request for Restriction of Protected Health Information

[The covered entity] is required by law to maintain the privacy of the individual's protected health information. Any material changes to [the covered entity's] privacy policy will be promptly revised and distributed to the individual.

I hereby request restriction on the use and disclosure of my protected health information for treatment, payment, and health plan operations. I understand [the covered entity] is not required to agree to this restriction. I understand that if the request for restriction is honored, [the covered entity] is required to abide by the request except in an emergency situation or when the use or disclosure is permissible or required by law. I understand this restriction will remain in effect until I request termination of the restriction or until [the covered entity] notifies me they are terminating the restriction.

[Describe the protected health information that is requested to be restricted.]

[Person requesting restriction: include name, date of birth, address, member or patient number, phone number, etc.]

[Signature of individual and date signed.] (Note: If a legal representative is signing the consent then the covered entity should request a power of attorney or other copy of authorization.)

[Explain how the form should be submitted.]

[Include details on filing a complaint with the covered entity.]

[Contact information on whom the individual could contact to get further information about the privacy policies of the covered entity.]

4.5.8.2 Sample of Request for Restriction Termination

[The covered entity] is required by law to maintain the privacy of the individual's protected health information. Any material changes to [the covered entity's] privacy policy will be promptly revised and distributed to the individual.

I hereby request termination of the restrictions previously placed on my protected health information for treatment, payment, and health plan operations.

[Describe the protected health information that is requested to be terminated from restrictions.]

[Person requesting restriction: include name, date of birth, address, member or patient number, phone number, etc.]

[Signature of individual and date signed.] (Note: If a legal representative is signing the consent then the covered entity should request a power of attorney or other copy of authorization.)

[Explain how the form should be submitted.]
[Include details on filing a complaint with the covered entity.]
[Contact information on whom the individual could contact to get further information about the privacy policies of the covered entity.]

4.5.9 Confidential Communications Requirements

An individual can request an alternative means by which to communicate confidential information as opposed to the typical way in which the covered entity normally communicates with individuals. A covered entity must accommodate a reasonable request by the individual for this type of alternate mode of communication if the normal communication method will endanger the individual. A covered entity should not question such an endangerment statement; however, a covered entity could condition this compliance with a method of contact or explanation on how payments will be made for healthcare services in cases where an alternate address or method is employed.

4.5.9.1 Request for Alternative Communications

[The covered entity] is required by law to maintain the privacy of the individual's protected health information. Any material changes to [the covered entity's] privacy policy will be promptly revised and distributed to the individual.

I hereby request the protected health information detailed below be sent by alternative means or to an alternative location to avoid a life-threatening situation. I understand [the covered entity] may place conditions on the request based on payment arrangements and specific information about the alternative address or method of contact.

I understand that [the covered entity] will make a reasonable and good-faith effort to meet my request for delivery of information by an alternative means or method; however, [the covered entity] will continue to conduct normal healthcare operations with [specific information] still being disclosed on [specific notices].

[Describe the specific situation and the protected health information that requires an alternative communication method.]

[Describe the preferred method to accommodate this request and the length of time the request should last.]

[Person requesting alternative method: include name, date of birth, address, member or patient number, phone number, etc.]

[Signature of individual and date signed.] (Note: If a legal representative is signing the consent then the covered entity should request a power of attorney or other copy of authorization.)

[Explain how the form should be submitted.]

[Include details on filing a complaint with the covered entity.]

[Contact information on whom the individual could contact to get further information about the privacy policies of the covered entity.]

4.6 Administrative Requirements

The Department of Health and Human Services (HHS) has attempted to make the methods by which a covered entity can comply with the HIPAA Privacy Rules as flexible and scalable as possible. Since these rules cover a wide range of organizations with varied resources, HHS did not want to force any covered entity into specific solutions; however, there are some general rules that are mandated.

It is important that covered entities assign resources to maintaining compliance with the HIPAA Privacy Rules. These resources can be workforce members assigned the role of compliance or by contracting with expert third-party advisors to assist the covered entity in compliance efforts. As requirements and technology change, the covered entity needs to be prepared to keep current and emphasize compliance with these requirements.

The following are some of the HIPAA Administrative Requirements that will be discussed throughout the next sections:

- HIPAA privacy policies and procedures
- Privacy personnel
- Workforce training and management
- Mitigation
- Data safeguards
- Complaints
- Retaliation and waiver
- Documentation and record retention

In addition to these requirements, exceptions will be detailed for fully insured group health plans along with different organizational options to deal with HIPAA Privacy Rules.

4.6.1 HIPAA Privacy Policies and Procedures

As discussed, a covered entity must develop and implement written privacy policies and procedures. Of course, these policies and procedures must comply with the HIPAA Privacy Rules. These policies, along with their corresponding procedures, should be approved by management and disseminated to all workforce members. Formal reviews of these policies and procedures should be performed periodically and updated as new regulations take effect.

The covered entity should refer to the following references for further details related to HIPAA privacy policies and procedures:

- NIST SP 800-53 AP-1 Authority to Collect
- NIST SP 800-53 AP-2 Purpose Specification

- NIST SP 800-53 UL-1 Internal Use
- NIST SP 800-53 UL-2 Information Sharing with Third Parties

4.6.2 Privacy Personnel

A privacy official with responsibility over the development and implementation of a covered entity's privacy policies and procedures must be designated. This individual should be well versed in HIPAA/HITECH regulations and have the appropriate experience necessary to carry out his or her responsibilities. Furthermore, this individual should have the appropriate authority within the organization to fully implement the covered entity's privacy policies and procedures. A contact person or department must also be designated to receive complaints or to provide individual information on the covered entity's privacy policies and procedures. The privacy official may be the designated contact person (or the head of the department) that receives and handles complaints related to violations of the HIPAA Privacy Rules.

The covered entity should refer to the following references for further details related to the governance program:

- NIST SP 800-53 AR-1 Governance and Privacy Program
- NIST SP 800-53 AR-2 Privacy Impact and Risk Assessment
- NIST SP 800-53 AR-3 Privacy Requirements for Contractors and Service Providers
- NIST SP 800-53 AR-4 Privacy Monitoring and Auditing

4.6.3 Workforce Training and Management

A covered entity is required to train all workforce members on its privacy policies and procedures as appropriate for their job roles. A *workforce member* is defined as any employee, volunteer, trainee, or individual under direct control of the covered entity whether paid or not. Workforce members should be provided formal training that covers all aspects of the covered entity's privacy policies and procedures. These workforce members should also acknowledge that they attended this training by signing an acknowledgment form. This form should be retained within the workforce member's personnel file or tracked in some other manner. As changes are made to the policies and procedures, workforce members should be made aware of these changes.

A somewhat negative issue, but essential in the enforcement of policies and procedures, are disciplinary actions. To demonstrate the importance and the severity of consequences that the covered entity can face for failure to comply with the policies and procedures, actions to enforce compliance are a necessary evil. Disciplinary actions, for those who violate the policies or procedures, must be appropriately applied to all workforce members no matter their roles, responsibilities, or authority within the organization.

The covered entity should refer to the following reference for further details related to awareness training:

- NIST SP 800-53 AR-5 Privacy Awareness and Training

4.6.4 Mitigation

Mitigation is an important step for a covered entity to reduce the risk of liability. Mitigation efforts can begin prior to an incident occurring or after an incident occurs. A covered entity should be proactive in its attempts to lower perceived or actual risks it faces. If a covered entity knows of a violation of its privacy policies and procedures, the covered entity should be reactive and take practical steps to mitigate any harmful effects as a result of an incident. Violations of the covered entity's privacy policies and procedures could occur by the workforce member or its business associate. For either situation, the goal is to lessen the harm as a result of any unauthorized use or disclosure of protected health information.

The covered entity should refer to the following reference for further details related to mitigation efforts or response to an incident:

- NIST SP 800-53 SE-2 Privacy Incident Response

4.6.5 Data Safeguards

To prevent intentional or unintentional use or disclosure of protected health information, a covered entity must maintain appropriate and reasonable administrative, technical, and physical safeguards. Throughout this book, recommendations will be provided to assist the covered entity in maintaining reasonable safeguards to secure protected health information. One of the easiest and least expensive safeguards that a covered entity can implement is to limit incidental use and disclosure of protected health information as previously discussed.

The covered entity should refer to the following references for further details related to data safeguards:

- NIST SP 800-53 AR-7 Privacy-Enhanced System Design and Development
- NIST SP 800-53 DI-1 Data Quality
- NIST SP 800-53 DI-2 Data Integrity and Data Integrity Board
- NIST SP 800-53 DM-3 Minimization of PII Used in Testing, Training, and Research
- NIST SP 800-53 SE-1 Inventory of Personally Identifiable Information

4.6.6 Complaints

One of the elements required to be included in a covered entity's privacy practice notice is complaint procedures. A covered entity must have procedures in place for an individual to report a suspected violation of any HIPAA Privacy Rule violation or violation of the covered entity's own privacy policies and procedures. This procedure should be developed to include a contact person or department within the covered entity to whom an individual can make a complaint. This procedure may also include information on how the individual can submit a complaint to the Secretary of the Department of Health and Human Services regarding a violation of the HIPAA Privacy Rule.

The covered entity should refer to the following references for further details related to reporting complaints:

- NIST SP 800-53 AR-6 Privacy Reporting
- NIST SP 800-53 IP-3 Redress
- NIST SP 800-53 IP-4 Complaint Management

4.6.7 Retaliation and Waiver

A covered entity may not retaliate against a person that exercised his or her rights to report a violation of the HIPAA Privacy Rule. In addition, a covered entity may not require an individual to waive his or her rights as a condition for treatment, payment, enrollment, or benefits eligibility.

4.6.8 Documentation and Record Retention

A covered entity must retain its privacy policies and procedures; privacy practice notices; disposition of complaints; and other actions, activities, and designations that the HIPAA Privacy Rule requires to be documented for 6 years after the date of their creation or last effective date, whichever is later.

The covered entity should refer to the following references for further details related to documentation and record retention:

- NIST SP 800-53 AR-8 Accounting of Disclosures
- NIST SP 800-53 DM-2 Data Retention and Disposal

4.6.9 Fully Insured Group Health Plan Exception

If a fully insured group health plan maintains only the enrollment data and summary health information of individuals, then it is only obligated to comply with two HIPAA Privacy Rule administrative requirements. The first is that the fully insured group health plan cannot retaliate against an individual for making a complaint or require the individual to waive his or her rights as a condition of benefits. The second is that the fully insured group health plan must include an amendment in its documentation that provides for the disclosure of protected health information to the plan sponsor by a health insurance issuer or health maintenance organization (HMO) that services the group health plan.

4.7 Organizational Options

The HIPAA Privacy Rule attempts to address the privacy protections for a variety of organizational issues. Some of these organizational options are the following and will be discussed in the next sections:

- Hybrid entity
- Affiliated covered entity
- Organized healthcare arrangement
- Covered entities with multiple covered functions
- Group health plan disclosures to plan sponsors

To determine what types of options an organization may have in regards to complying with the HIPAA Privacy Rule, the specific functions of the organization need to be determined. A determination of the covered entity's status is determined by the covered function the organization performs.

4.7.1 Hybrid Entity

As discussed, covered functions determine the designation status of a person or organization as a covered entity. A *hybrid entity* is a single legal entity that conducts both covered and noncovered functions as it pertains to the HIPAA Privacy Rule. A covered entity must, in writing, designate the covered functions as one or more "healthcare component." Only the healthcare components of the entity are required to meet the HIPAA Privacy Rule. If a covered entity does not make such a designation, then the covered entity is subject to the HIPAA Privacy Rule in its entirety.

An example of a hybrid entity, as provided by the National Institutes of Health, is a university that has an academic medical center's hospital. The hospital conducts covered electronic transactions and is part of the university, which is a single legal entity. In this scenario, the entire university will be considered a covered entity; however, the university may decide to be a hybrid entity. The hospital can be designated as a healthcare component. If this occurs, the HIPAA Privacy Rule requirements would only apply to the hospital and not the university in its entirety. The HIPAA Privacy Rule would govern disclosure of protected health information to the rest of the university as it would any other outside entity.

4.7.2 Affiliated Covered Entity

As opposed to splitting up covered functions, as in the case of a hybrid entity, covered entities that are legally separated but maintain common ownership or control may elect to be covered under a single covered entity for purposes of HIPAA Privacy Rule compliance. This designation must be in writing. As a note of reference, if an affiliated covered entity performs multiple covered functions, then these functions must be in compliance with the HIPAA Privacy Rule as described later in Section 4.7.4. An example of an affiliated covered entity may be a managed healthcare provider that owns or operates different hospitals, physician centers, or managed practices under a single legal entity. A benefit of this designation allows the managed healthcare provider to share healthcare information between the different parties without having the need for business associate agreements between the different groups.

4.7.3 Organized Healthcare Arrangement

Covered entities that participate in an organized healthcare arrangement to manage and benefit their common enterprise can share protected health information with each other under this joint care operation arrangement. A common example of an organized healthcare arrangement is in a hospital setting where a physician with staff privileges provides healthcare services to patients of the hospital. There is a need to freely exchange information for the purposes of treatment, but there may also be a need to share health information related to the management or operations of the hospital.

4.7.4 Covered Entities with Multiple Covered Functions

A covered entity that performs multiple covered functions must operate its different covered functions in compliance with the applicable HIPAA Privacy Rule for that function. For example, a covered entity may not use or disclose an individual's protected health information that receives services from a healthcare provider for another health plan if the individual is not involved with the healthcare provider.

4.7.5 Group Health Plan Disclosures to Plan Sponsors

A group health plan may disclose enrollment or disenrollment information with the employer, union, or other employee organization that sponsors (i.e., plan sponsor) and maintains the group health plan. The group health plan includes the health insurer or HMO offered by the plan. In addition, a plan sponsor could request summary health information to obtain premium bids, or to modify, amend, or terminate the group health plan. *Summary health information* is information that summarizes claims history, claims expenses, or types of claims experience of the individuals of the plan and is stripped of all individual identifiers. (As a special note of reference, the five-digit zip code could remain within the data set and is not considered an individual identifier.)

A group health plan may provide protected health information of the enrollees to the plan sponsor for administrative functions. The plan sponsor must impose restrictions on the use and disclosure of the protected health information and certify to the group plan that the group health plan document has been amended to impose these restrictions. These documents must also include the restriction that the plan sponsor will not use or disclose the protected health information for any employment-related action or decision, or in connection with any other benefit plan.

4.8 Other Provisions: Personal Representatives and Minors

A *personal representative* is a person legally authorized to make healthcare decisions on an individual's behalf or to act for a deceased individual or the estate. With respect to use and disclosure of an individual's protected health information, a covered entity is required to treat a personal representative the same as it would the individual. The only exception is when there is a reasonable belief that the personal representative may be abusing or neglecting the individual or otherwise endangering the individual.

Parents are considered the personal representatives of their minor children. There may be certain situations in which state or other laws determine the rights of parents to access or control the minor child's protected health information. In cases where these laws may not determine the rights, licensed healthcare professionals, exercising their best professional judgment, may have discretion over providing or denying access to the parent. There are three circumstances specifically exempt in the HIPAA Privacy Rule when a parent is not considered a minor's personal representative:

■ When a minor consents to a healthcare service that, by state or other law, does not require the consent of a parent to obtain
■ When a court appoints or authorizes another individual, other than the parent, to make treatment decisions for a minor
■ If a parent agrees to a confidential relationship between the minor and the physician

4.9 State Laws

In most situations, federal requirements will be followed as opposed to state laws in cases where state laws are contrary to federal regulations. In this context, *contrary* means that it would be impossible for a covered entity to comply with both the state and federal requirements. There are a few exceptions to this preemptive clause. The first exception is that if a state's law provides greater privacy protection or privacy rights than the federal HIPAA Privacy Rule, the state law will be followed. The second exception is that if the state's law requires additional reporting of disease or injury, child abuse, birth, or death, or for public health surveillance, investigation, or intervention, it will be followed over the federal regulation. The final exception is that in cases of management or financial audits, the state could require additional health plan reporting requirements.

4.10 Enforcement

The Department of Health and Human Services (HHS) is responsible for the enforcement of compliance with the HIPAA Privacy Rule. HHS attempts to cooperate with covered entities in providing technical assistance to have them voluntarily comply with the regulations. The HIPAA Privacy Rule, as discussed, describes the process of filing complaints, providing reports or records to cooperate with compliance, and permitting HHS access to information to investigate or review compliance. As of October 20, 2009, there were new civil and criminal penalties enacted that the HHS can impose on individuals and covered entities to enforce the HIPAA Privacy Rule regulations.

4.11 Compliance Dates

Compliance to the HIPAA Privacy Rule is mandatory for all covered entities, except small health plans, as of April 14, 2003. Small health plans, generally those health plans reporting less than $5 million in annual receipts, had until April 14, 2004, to comply. As of the date of the publication for this book, all covered entities are required to comply with the HIPAA Privacy Rule, with no exceptions.

4.12 Summary

One of the first items discussed in this chapter is the level of access to protected health information being based on the "minimum necessary" principle. If workforce members' job roles or responsibilities do not require them to need certain information, then they should not have access to this information.

There are certain permitted uses and disclosures that are allowed, such as providing an individual's protected health information to the individual and for the treatment, payment, and other healthcare-related operations for the individual. There are also some incidental permitted uses and disclosures of protected health information if these uses or disclosures are by-products of other authorized uses or disclosures. There are 12 national priority purposes for which the HIPAA Privacy Rule permits the covered entity to use or disclose protected health information without an individual's authorization or permission.

Along with the permitted use or disclosure, authorized uses and disclosures were discussed. The core elements of valid authorization along with the required statements were provided. There are special circumstances involving psychotherapy notes and using certain guidelines to follow as it relates to marketing medical services or products to individuals. Also defined were limited data sets as protected health information where specified direct identifiers of individuals, their relatives, household members, and employers were removed.

A majority of this chapter was dedicated to providing samples of required notices. One of the most important notices is the privacy practice notice that informs the individual of the obligations of the covered entity in using or disclosing the individual's health information, the rights of the individual, and how to file a complaint if the individual feels that his or her information was utilized in an unauthorized manner. There are certain requirements for providing this notice and acknowledging receipt of this notice. Other samples of notices included in this chapter were those related to accessing, amending, or receiving an account of disclosure, and requesting restriction to, or requesting alternative communications for protected health information.

The HIPAA privacy regulations have multiple administrative requirements. These requirements start with having privacy policies and procedures implemented to provide the appropriate use and disclosure of protected health information. These policies and procedures should cover the assignment of a privacy official, workforce training, mitigating risk of unauthorized use or disclosure, and safeguarding data. There should be a complaint process developed for handling issues of any violations of the HIPAA Privacy Rule that also provides for protection against any retaliation for a complaint being received. Documentation and record retention should be covered as part of the administrative requirements and some exceptions pertaining to fully insured group health plans were discussed.

There are several options that a covered entity may exercise as part of its compliance with the HIPAA privacy requirements. The functions of the entity determine its requirement to comply with the regulations. For instance, a single entity may perform functions that are covered by the HIPAA Privacy Rule along with other functions that are not bound by these regulations. This entity may decide to be a hybrid entity with certain requirements regarding this split in functions. Another example may be that instead of splitting functions up within an entity, different entities having the same ownership may operate under the same HIPAA Privacy Rule as it relates to compliance to these requirements. There are other arrangements discussed related to organized healthcare arrangements as in hospitals and covered entities with multiple covered functions.

There are some special circumstances involving the use or disclosure of protected health information to authorized personal representatives of individuals and parents receiving protected health information on their minor children. States have varied ideas on the rights of parents over accessing their children's medical information. In certain situations, a licensed healthcare professional, exercising his or her best professional judgment, may have discretion over providing or denying access to the parent. It is normally the case where federal regulations trump states; however, some states have more restrictive privacy protection laws. In these cases, state laws supersede federal requirements.

This chapter ended by identifying the federal department that is responsible for enforcement of compliance with the HIPAA Privacy Rule, namely the Department of Health and Human Services. In addition, there are more severe civil and criminal penalties for violation of the HIPAA Privacy Rule implemented as of October 20, 2009. As of April 14, 2004, all covered entities were required to be compliant with the HIPAA Privacy Rule.

Chapter 5

Electronic Transactions and Code Set Rule Detailed

Objectives

The objectives of this chapter are as follows:

- Understand the meaning of the following terms as it relates to the Electronic Transactions and Code Set Rules: code set, code set maintaining organization, data condition, data content, data set, designated standard maintenance organization, direct data entry, electronic media, format, and standard transaction.
- Understand what the ASC X12 implementations specifications are and the specifications for retail pharmacies.
- Determine what ASC X12 specifications are utilized to conduct the following standard transactions: claims or encounters, remittance advice, eligibility inquiry and response, prior authorization and referral, and claim status inquiry and response.
- Determine the differences between the following medical code sets: ICD-9CM, NDC, CDT, HCPCS, and CPT-4.
- Understand that local codes are no longer authorized.
- Understand what are some of the other nonmedical code sets utilized in the healthcare industry, such as the following: provider taxonomy codes,

claim adjustment reason codes, remittance advice remark codes, claim status category codes, and other claim status codes.
■ Determine the requirements as they relate to Electronic Transactions and Code Set Rules for covered entities, health plans, and healthcare clearinghouses.
■ Understand some of the exceptions from the standards that may be in place to permit testing of proposed modifications to the Electronic Transactions and Code Set Rules.

Background

As previously discussed, one of the Health Insurance Portability and Accountability Act's (HIPAA's) goals was to standardize the way covered entities performed certain activities. One of the ways in which HIPAA implemented this goal was to set standard coding for electronic transactions. As of October 16, 2003, HIPAA required that all covered entities engaged in one or more types of electronic transactions must comply with the standard for that transaction. The Secretary of the Department of Health and Human Services (HHS) adopted eight different healthcare related transactions; five of them apply to healthcare providers. The American National Standards Institute (ANSI), assisted by several organizations such as the Accredited Standards Committee (ASC) X12N Subcommittee and the National Council for Prescription Drug Programs (NCPDP), specified the electronic standards for the healthcare industry. As required by HIPAA, healthcare organizations must use the ANSI ASC X12N and NCPDP standard formats for all HIPAA-defined transactions.

These standard organizations developed implementation guides to provide comprehensive technical details and other specific activities related to transactions, nonmedical standardized codes, and directions on how information is to be transmitted electronically. These instructions are used by healthcare software developers, health plans, payers, billing services, and healthcare clearinghouses to become compliant with the HIPAA requirements.

HIPAA does not require healthcare providers to conduct any standard transactions electronically. However, if these healthcare providers submit any standard transactions electronically then they must comply with the HIPAA regulations. If any of the transactions listed in the next sections are currently (or will be) submitted electronically, then they will have to meet the requirements. To increase efficiency, some health plans may only accept electronic transactions. To this end, the healthcare providers will have to meet the standard requirements if the healthcare provider wants to continue to do business with the health plans.

All covered entities, except small health plans, were required to comply with code sets and transaction standards by October 16, 2002. Small health plans had until October 16, 2003, to comply with these standards.

5.1 Definitions

The following are some definitions of terms used to explain standard transactions and code sets as defined in 45 CFR § 162.103 that have not been discussed as of yet:

Code set—"Any set of codes used to encode data elements [the smallest named unit of information in a transaction] such as tables of terms, medical concepts, medical diagnostic codes, or medical procedure codes. A code set includes the codes and the descriptors of the codes [or text defining a code]."

Code set maintaining organization (CSMO)—Organizations that maintain or create the code sets. "Maintain or maintenance refers to activities necessary to support the use of a standard adopted by the Secretary [of the Department of Health and Human Services], including technical corrections to an implementation specification, and enhancements or expansion of a code set. This excludes the activities related to the adoption of a new standard or implementation specification, or modification to an adopted standard or implementation specification."

Data condition—"The rule that describes the circumstances under which a covered entity must use a particular data element or segment" (or "a group of related data elements in a transaction").

Data content—"All the data elements and code sets inherent to a transaction, and not related to the format of the transaction. Data elements that are related to the format are not data content."

Data set—"A semantically meaningful unit of information exchanged between two parties to a transaction."

Designated standard maintenance organization (DSMO)—"An organization designed by the Secretary [of the Department of Health and Human Services] under [42 CFR] § 162.910(a)."

Direct data entry—"The direct entry of data that is immediately transmitted into a health plan's computer."

Electronic media—"The mode of electronic transmission. It includes the Internet (wide-open), Extranet (using Internet technology to link a business with information only accessible to collaborating parties), leased lines, dial-up lines, private networks, and those transmissions that are physically moved from one location to another using magnetic tape, disk, or compact disk media."

Format—"Refers to those data elements that provide or control the enveloping or hierarchical structure, or assist in identifying data content of, a transaction."

Standard transaction—"A transaction that complies with the applicable standard adopted under this part [45 CFR § 162]."

5.1.1 ASC X12 Implementation Specifications

The implementation specifications for ASC X12N standards may be obtained from the Washington Publishing Company (PMB 161, 5284 Randolph Road, Rockville,

MD 20852-2116; telephone: 301-949-9740, fax: 301-949-9742), or online at http://www.wpc-edi.com.

As indicated in 45 CFR § 162.920, the implementation specifications are as follows:

- "The ASC X12N 837—Healthcare Claim: Dental, Version 4010, May 2000, Washington Publishing Company, 004010X097, as referenced in §§162.1102 and 162.1802.
- The ASC X12N 837—Healthcare Claim: Professional, Volumes 1 and 2, Version 4010, May 2000, Washington Publishing Company, 004010X098, as referenced in §§162.1102 and 162.1802.
- The ASC X12N 837—Healthcare Claim: Institutional, Volumes 1 and 2, Version 4010, May 2000, Washington Publishing Company, 004010X096, as referenced in §§162.1102 and 162.1802.
- The ASC X12N 270/271—Healthcare Eligibility Benefit Inquiry and Response, Version 4010, May 2000, Washington Publishing Company, 004010X092, as referenced in §162.1202.
- The ASC X12N 278—Healthcare Services Review—Request for Review and Response, Version 4010, May 2000, Washington Publishing Company, 004010X094, as referenced in §162.1302.
- The ASC X12N 276/277 Healthcare Claim Status Request and Response, Version 4010, May 2000, Washington Publishing Company, 004010X093, as referenced in §162.1402.
- The ASC X12N 834—Benefit Enrollment and Maintenance, Version 4010, May 2000, Washington Publishing Company, 004010X095, as referenced in §162.1502.
- The ASC X12N 835—Healthcare Claim Payment/Advice, Version 4010, May 2000, Washington Publishing Company, 004010X091, as referenced in §162.1602.
- The ASC X12N 820—Payroll Deducted and Other Group Premium Payment for Insurance Products, Version 4010, May 2000, Washington Publishing Company, 004010X061, as referenced in §162.1702."

5.1.2 Retail Pharmacy Specifications

The implementation specifications for all retail pharmacy standards may be obtained from the National Council for Prescription Drug Programs (NCPDP), 94201 North 24th Street, Suite 365, Phoenix, AZ 85016; telephone 602-957-9105, fax 602-955-0749) or online at http://www.ncpdp.org.

As indicated in 45 CFR § 162.920, the implementation specifications are as follows:

- "The Telecommunication Standard Implementation Guide, Version 5 Release 1, September 1999, National Council for Prescription Drug Programs, as referenced in §§162.1102, 162.1202, 162.1602, and 162.1802.

- The Batch Standard Batch Implementation Guide, Version 1 Release 0, February 1, 1996, National Council for Prescription Drug Programs, as referenced in §§162.1102, 162.1202, 162.1602, and 162.1802."

5.2 Standard Transactions

Standard transactions include the following and will be explained in detail in the next sections:

- Claims or equivalent encounter information
- Payment and remittance advice
- Claim status inquiry and response
- Eligibility inquiry and response
- Referral certification and authorization inquiry and response
- Enrollment and disenrollment in a health plan
- Health plan premium payments
- Coordination of benefits

Note: Claims attachments and first report of injury are pending approval.

5.2.1 Claims or Encounters

Claims (or *encounters*) are a detailed, itemized record of healthcare services performed by a healthcare provider on an individual. These itemized records are known as healthcare service information that is provided by a healthcare provider to a health plan for service reimbursement. There are four different types of claims or encounters specified:

- The ASC X12N 837: Professional Implementation Guide (version 4010X097 and 4010X097A1)
- The ASC X12N 837: Institutional Implementation Guide (version 4010X091 and 4010X091A1)
- The ASC X12N 837: Dental Implementation Guide (version 4010X097 and 4010X097A1)
- The NCPDP: Retail Pharmacy Transactions (version 5.1 for telecommunications and version 1.1. for batch transactions)

Health plans have some flexibility in using these implementation guides. For instance, some health plans may require a healthcare provider to use the Institutional Implementation Guide to reimburse for home health services, whereas others may use the Professional Implementation Guide for the same types of services.

Healthcare providers will have to determine what guides their health plans are utilizing for reporting and reimbursement of specific services.

5.2.2 Remittance Advice

Remittance advice is an explanation of claim or encounter processing and/or payment sent by a health plan to a provider. It uses the ASC X12N 835: Healthcare Claim Payment/Advice Implementation Guide (version 4010X091 and 4010X091A1) and can also be used for electronic funds transfer (EFT) payments to a provider's bank.

5.2.3 Eligibility Inquiry and Response

An *eligibility inquiry and response* is an inquiry from a healthcare provider or the response from a health plan regarding an individual's eligibility for benefits (or coverage) under the plan. The ASC X12N 270-271: Healthcare Eligibility Benefit Inquiry and Response Implementation Guide (version 4010X092 and 4010X092A1) and the NCPDP: Retail Pharmacy Transactions (version 5.1 for telecommunications and version 1.1 for batch transactions) are used for eligibility inquiry and response.

5.2.4 Prior Authorization and Referral

The ASC X12N 278: Healthcare Services Review—Request for Review and Response Implementation Guide (version 4010X094 and 4010X094A1) and the NCPDP: Retail Pharmacy Transactions (version 5.1 for telecommunications and version 1.1 for batch transactions) are used for an inquiry from a provider and the response from a health plan about an individual's prior authorization or referral for services.

5.2.5 Claims Status Inquiry and Response

The ASC X12N 276-277 Healthcare Claim Status Request and Response Implementation Guide (version 4010X093 and 4010X093A1) and the NCPDP: Retail Pharmacy Transactions (version 5.1 for telecommunications and version 1.1 for batch transactions) are used for an inquiry from a provider and the response from a health plan about the processing status of a submitted claim or encounter.

5.3 Medical Code Sets

There are several medical code sets (or clinical codes) that have been approved for use by HIPAA. Medical code sets are usually maintained by external organizations such as professional societies and public health organization to characterize a medical condition or treatment. Medical code sets are used in transactions to identify procedures, services, and diagnoses pertaining to an individual's encounter with a healthcare provider. Nonmedical codes may be defined in implementation guides or maintained by other external organizations.

5.3.1 International Classification of Diseases (ICD)

For the conditions or causes of diseases, injuries, impairments, or other health problems, use International Classification of Diseases, 9th edition, Clinical Modification, Volumes 1 and 2 Procedures (including the Official ICD-9-CM Guidelines for Coding and Reporting). For the prevention, diagnosis, treatment, management, or other actions taken for diseases, injuries, and impairments on hospital inpatients, the International Classification of Diseases, 9th edition, Clinical Modification, Volume 3 Procedures (including the Official ICD-9-CM Guidelines for Coding and Reporting) are utilized.

5.3.2 National Drug Code (NDC)

For drugs and biologics on retail pharmacy drug transactions, the code set used is the National Drug Code (NDC). A standard has not been adopted for reporting drugs and biologics on nonretail pharmacy transactions.

5.3.3 Current Dental Terminology (CDT)

For dental services, the code set used is the Current Dental Terminology, Code on Dental Procedures and Nomenclature, version 3, as maintained by the American Dental Association.

5.3.4 Healthcare Common Procedural Coding System (HCPCS) and Current Procedural Terminology (CPT)

For physician services or other healthcare services to include, but not limited to, physician services, physical and occupational therapy services, radiological procedures, clinical laboratory tests, other medical diagnostic procedures, hearing and vision services, and transportation services including ambulance, the combination of the Healthcare Common Procedural Coding System (as maintained by HHS) and Current Procedural Terminology, 4th edition (as maintained by the American Medical Association) are utilized. HCPCS is also used for other substances, durable medical equipment, or other medical supplies such as orthotic and prosthetic devices.

5.4 Local Codes

Local codes are codes that different payer organizations, such as health plans including state Medicaid programs, devised to handle their own special circumstances.

Unfortunately, under HIPAA, these local codes are not allowed to be used, thus providers must replace these codes with the appropriate HCPCS and CPT-4 codes. Health plans are supposed to notify their providers with information to specify how the standard code sets will replace their local codes.

5.5 Nonmedical Code Sets

Nonmedical or *nonclinical code sets* are code sets that characterize a general administrative situation as opposed to a medical condition or service. Examples of general administrative nonmedical code sets are state abbreviations, zip codes, telephone area codes, and race or ethnicity codes. The following sections discuss other examples of specialized nonmedical code sets.

5.5.1 Provider Taxonomy Codes

To identify the provider's area of specialty, the provider taxonomy codes were utilized. These provider taxonomy codes were used to identify the specialty being billed on professional claims. This specialty information is no longer embedded into the provider identifier as adopted and the taxonomy codes have become a situational data element. Health plans may or may not require the taxonomy codes for both institutional and professional claims. However, taxonomy codes are required on claims where they are necessary for a health plan to adjudicate a claim.

5.5.2 Claim Adjustment Reason Codes

HIPAA requires that *local claim adjustment codes* that were sent by health plans to providers under their local explanation of benefits (EOB) be replaced with standard claim adjustment reason codes. The EOB codes were used to explain payment policies that impacted reimbursement such as why a claim or service line was adjusted. The Healthcare Claim Payment/Advice (835) should now be used by health plans to provide an explanation to the providers.

5.5.3 Remittance Advice Remark Codes

Remark codes add greater detail to an adjustment reason code.

5.5.4 Claim Status Category Codes

Claim status category codes describe the status of the claim such as whether it is received, pending, or paid. These codes are used in the Healthcare Claim Status Response (277) transaction.

5.5.5 Claim Status Codes

To add more detail than is provided in the Claim Status Category Codes, the Claim Status Codes are utilized. These codes are also used in the Healthcare Claim Status Response (277) transaction.

5.6 Requirements for Covered Entities

As a general rule, a covered entity, using electronic media, that conducts a transaction designated by the HHS Secretary as a standard transaction with another covered entity must follow the requirements of this standard transaction. If a health plan offers a direct data entry method to a healthcare provider to conduct a transaction for which a standard has been adopted, then the healthcare provider must use the applicable data content and data condition requirements of that standard. In this case, the healthcare provider is not required to use the format requirement of that standard. A business associate, including a healthcare clearinghouse, may be used to conduct a standard transaction on behalf of the covered entity and the covered entity must require the business associate (or subcontractor) to comply with all applicable standard transaction requirements.

5.7 Additional Requirements for Health Plans

A health plan must conduct a transaction as a standard transaction upon a request of a covered entity. If the transaction is a standard transaction, a health plan cannot delay or reject such a transaction or attempt to adversely affect the other entity or the transaction. If there are data elements that are not needed in a standard transaction, a health plan cannot reject this transaction on this basis alone.

In addition, a health plan may not offer an incentive for a healthcare provider to conduct a transaction under any direct data entry solution offered to the provider by the health plan.

Furthermore, a health plan may not charge fees (or costs) in excess of the fees (or costs) for normal telecommunications that the entity incurs when it directly transmits, or receives, a standard transaction to (or from) a health plan by requiring an entity to use a healthcare clearinghouse to receive, process, or transmit a standard transaction or when a health plan operates as a healthcare clearinghouse.

Finally, a health plan must accept and promptly process any standard transaction that contains valid codes and keep the code sets for the current billing period (and appeals period) still open to processing under the health plan's terms of coverage.

5.8 Additional Rules for Healthcare Clearinghouses

A healthcare clearinghouse, acting as a business associate for a covered entity, may receive a nonstandard (or standard) transaction and translate it into a standard (or nonstandard, respectively) transaction to transmit to (or on behalf of) the covered entity.

5.9 Exceptions from Standards to Permit Testing of Proposed Modifications

There are step-by-step instructions on the process by which a covered entity may request an exception to the standard transactions as described in 45 CFR § 162.940. In summary, an organization may request from the HHS Secretary an exception to the use of a standard if the organization meets certain requirements. For example, the organization must provide a detailed explanation comparing the recommended modification to the current standard. This explanation must demonstrate the following:

- An improvement in efficiency and effectiveness
- The needs of the modification
- The uniformity and consistency with other standards
- Costs
- Support by an ANSI-accredited standard setting organization (SSO) or other private/public organization
- Timely development, testing, implementation, and updating procedures
- Technology independence
- Be precise, unambiguous, and simple as possible
- Burden of paperwork or result in minimum data collected
- The flexibility to incorporate the modification.

The explanation must be less than 10 pages in length and also include specifications for the proposed modification, testing of the proposed modification, and written concurrences of trading partners that agree to participate in the test.

The HHS Secretary may grant an initial exception for a period not to exceed 3 years based on certain criteria such as whether the proposed modification demonstrates a significant improvement to the current standard, the extent of the exception, and after consulting with designated standard maintenance organizations (DSMOs). The HHS Secretary will notify the organization of an exception granted to include the length of time of the exception, the approved trading partners or geographical areas for testing, or any other conditions of the exception. The organization must submit a report within 90 days from the completion of the test to include the results of the testing along with a cost–benefit analysis. The HHS Secretary will also provide an explanation of the reasons for any exceptions denied.

5.10 Summary

One of the ways that HIPAA satisfied its goal of standardizing the way covered entities performed certain activities was to set standard coding for electronic transactions. Throughout this chapter, a detailed discussion took place on the five (out of the eight) different health transactions that apply to healthcare providers and the required code set for each. Under HIPAA, a provider is not required to conduct any standard transaction electronically. However, if a provider does perform any of these standard transactions electronically, then it must comply with the HIPAA Electronic Transactions and Code Set Rule requirements. As of October 16, 2003, all covered entities conducting electronic transactions must be compliant with the use of these code set standards.

Many terms, as they relate to the Electronic Transactions and Code Set Rules, along with providing details on the ASC X12 implementation specifications and how they apply to different standard transactions, were defined. The specifications utilized in the retail pharmacy industry were also discussed.

Each of the code sets utilized for the following standard transactions were explained: claims or encounters, remittance advice, eligibility inquiry and response, prior authorization and referral, and claim status inquiry and response. Some of the different medical code sets utilized in the healthcare industry such as ICD-9CM, NDC, CDT, HCPCS, and CPT-4 codes were also described. As a reminder, local codes are no longer authorized and must be replaced by the appropriate HCPCS and CPT-4 codes.

There are several other types of nonmedical code sets that were discussed throughout this chapter including provider taxonomy codes, claim adjustment reason codes, remittance advice remark codes, claim status category codes, and other claim status codes. Also described were some of the requirements pertaining to the covered entity, health plans, and healthcare clearinghouses as they relate to the use of the code sets for electronic transactions.

This chapter ended by discussing some exceptions that may be in place for testing purposes in regard to modifying the standards. As improvements are being made in the healthcare industry to maintain efficiency and expediency in providing health care services, modifications of the standard code sets may be practical. There are some ways that exceptions are made for the standards and some processes that need to be complied with for permitted testing of any proposed modifications.

Chapter 6

National Provider Identifier Requirements Detailed

Objectives

The objectives of this chapter are as follows:

- Understand the requirements behind the HIPAA National Provider Identifier Regulation.
- Determine if the organization is required to have a National Provider Identifier number assigned.
- Determine the dates of compliance, as applicable, to the covered entity.
- Understand the healthcare provider's unique health identifier.
- Understand the responsibilities of the National Provider System as it relates to assigning healthcare providers unique health identifiers.
- Determine what specifications of the healthcare providers' implementation requirement a covered entity must follow.
- Determine what specifications of the health plans' implementation requirement a covered entity must follow.
- Determine what specifications of the healthcare clearinghouses' implementation requirement a covered entity must follow.
- Understand what is involved in completing the National Provider Identifier Application.

Background

The National Provider Identifier (NPI), as previously discussed, is a unique 10-digit intelligence-free number assigned to all covered healthcare providers. In the next chapter, implementation specifications related to the NPI requirements will be discussed.

6.1 Definitions

As it relates to the requirements for the National Provider Identifier (NPI), any covered healthcare provider that meets the definition of a covered entity is required to have an NPI. See Chapter 1, Section 1.5 for further details and definitions.

6.2 Compliance Dates

The implementation specifications that will be discussed have a compliance date. This varied based on the category of the covered entity. For instance, healthcare providers and healthcare clearinghouses had to comply with this requirement no later than May 23, 2007. Small health plans had until May 23, 2008, but larger health plans had to comply by the same May 23, 2007, deadline.

6.3 Healthcare Provider's Unique Health Identifier

The NPI is the standard unique health identifier for healthcare providers in the United States. This number is a 10-digit identifier that does not provide any intelligent information about the provider. For instance, the identifier does not provide the location or name of the provider through the unique number sequence.

6.4 National Provider System

The National Provider System (NPS) was established to manage the assignment of NPIs to healthcare providers. This included the collection, maintenance, and update of information pertaining to the assignment of NPIs. The NPS is also responsible for deactivating or reactivating NPIs as necessary. NPIs will not be reassigned to another healthcare provider and NPS is responsible for upkeep of these records. Through the National Plan & Provider Enumeration System (NPPES), the NPI Registry can be searched and information about healthcare providers such as name, location, and telephone numbers can be queried. The NPI Registry can be searched at https://nppes.cms.hhs.gov/NPPES/NPIRegistryHome.do.

6.5 Implementation Specifications for Healthcare Providers

A covered entity that is a covered healthcare provider must obtain an NPI from the NPS for itself (or for any subpart of the entity that is a covered healthcare provider in cases where separate legal entities are involved). Healthcare providers that are not a covered entity may also obtain an NPI. The following are some requirements of the NPI:

- On all standard transactions requiring a healthcare provider identifier, the NPI must be utilized.
- When requested by another entity for a covered standard transaction, the NPI must be disclosed.
- If the covered healthcare provider makes any changes to the required data elements, within 30 days of the change, the healthcare provider should notify the NPS so that it can update the information.
- The NPI should be provided to business associates that conduct standard transactions on the covered healthcare provider's behalf.

6.6 Implementation Specifications for Health Plans

On all standard transactions where the healthcare provider's identifier is required, the health plan must use the healthcare provider's NPI. A health plan may not require an additional NPI from a healthcare provider that has already been assigned one.

6.7 Implementation Specifications for Healthcare Clearinghouses

On all standard transactions where the healthcare provider's identifier is required, the healthcare clearinghouse must use the healthcare provider's NPI.

6.8 National Provider Identifier (NPI) Application

Healthcare providers can apply for NPIs in the following ways:

1. Apply online at the National Plan & Provider Enumeration System (NPPES): https://nppes.cms.hhs.gov/NPPES/StaticForward.do?forward=static. instructions

2. Utilize an electronic file interchange organization (EFIO) as long as the EFIO has the healthcare provider's permission
3. Mail a completed, signed NPI Application/Update Form (CMS-10114) to NPI Enumerator, P.O. Box 6059, Fargo, ND 58108-6059. Application forms can be obtained online at https://www.cms.gov/cmsforms/downloads/CMS10114.pdf or requested through phone at 1-800-465-3203 or e-mail through customerservice@npienumerator.com.

The application requests some basic information, such as the reason for submitting the form (i.e., initial application, change of information, deactivation, or reactivation). The covered healthcare provider will have to provide entity type, identifying information, organization information, locations, other provider identification numbers, the provider taxonomy code, and license number. The application will also require a contact person's information and a certification, under penalty of law, that the information is accurate. The application includes instructions and a privacy statement as to what circumstances would allow for the disclosure of the information submitted.

6.9 Summary

In this chapter the requirement for all covered entities to obtain a National Provider Identifier (NPI) were discussed. The NPI is a unique 10-digit identifier that is ambiguous as to any identifiable information. The National Provider System (NPS) is assigned responsibility for the management of these healthcare providers' unique health identifiers. There are some implementation specifications that apply to the use of the NPI by the healthcare provider. For instance, the NPI will be utilized on all standard transactions requiring a healthcare provider identifier. The NPI will be disclosed when requested by another entity for the purpose of conducting a covered standard transaction. The healthcare provider will maintain up-to-date contact information with the NPS. If a business associate is conducting a standard transaction on behalf of a covered healthcare provider, the NPI should be provided for this transaction. In addition, there are implementation specifications for health plans and healthcare clearinghouses.

This chapter ended by explaining the qualifications of obtaining an NPI, the information required for the application, and by what method an NPI can be obtained. A list of all registered healthcare providers can be obtained by searching the National Plan & Provider Enumeration System (NPPES) at https://nppes.cms.hhs.gov/NPPES/NPIRegistryHome.do.

Chapter 7

Meaningful Use Detailed

Objectives

The objectives of this chapter are as follows:

- Understand what is meant by *meaningful use* as it relates to electronic health records.
- Determine the three main components of meaningful use.
- Understand the criteria to satisfy meaningful use.
- Understand the requirements surrounding meaningful use.
- For eligible professionals, understand the 25 meaningful use objectives, including the 15 core and 10 menu set objectives.
- For eligible hospitals and critical access hospitals, understand the 24 meaningful use objectives, including the 14 core and 10 menu set objectives.

Background

To achieve health and efficiency goals, the Centers for Medicare & Medicaid Services (CMS) have implemented an Electronic Health Records (EHR) Incentive Program. This program is designed to provide financial incentives for the "meaningful use" of certified EHR technology. Other benefits that a covered entity will obtain from the use of EHR technology is reduction in errors, reminders and alerts, availability of data, support for clinical decisions, and prescription automation through e-prescribing and automated refills.

7.1 Meaningful Use Defined

There are three main components of meaningful use specified in the American Recovery and Reinvestment Act of 2009. These include the use of certified electronic health record (EHR) technology in a meaningful manner such as e-prescribing, for electronic health information exchanges to improve healthcare quality, and for clinical quality submissions and other measures. Basically, to demonstrate meaningful use, healthcare providers are required to show that EHR technology is being utilized in ways that can be significantly measured in quantity and quality.

7.2 Meaningful Use Criteria

Over the next 5 years, meaningful use will be implemented in three stages. Stage 1 baselines electronic data capture and information sharing in 2011 and 2012. Expected to be implemented in 2013 and 2015, stage 2 and stage 3, respectively, will expand on the initial baseline along with expected future rule makings to be determined.

7.3 Meaningful Use Requirements

Meaningful use requirements must be met to qualify for incentive payments from CMS. The requirements can be met by eligible professionals, eligible hospitals, and critical access hospitals (CAHs) in the following ways:

- Medicare EHR Incentive Program—Successfully demonstrate meaningful use of certified electronic health record technology every year.
- Medicaid EHR Incentive Program—Demonstrate meaningful use in the first year of participation and every year following.
- Adopted—Showing evidence of acquiring and installing a certified EHR technology.
- Implemented—Demonstrating the use of certified EHR technology by entering data of patient demographic information into EHR or providing training to workforce members on EHR technology.
- Upgraded—Upgrade to EHR technology or provide additional functionality to existing technology to comply with the certification requirements of EHR technology.

7.4 Meaningful Use Stage 1 (2011 and 2012)

Eligible professionals or eligible hospitals and CAHs must meet a specific core and menu set of objectives, as described next:

■ Eligible professionals: There are a total of 25 meaningful use objectives to include 15 required core and 10 menu set objectives. To qualify, an eligible professional must meet all 15 required core and 5 of the 10 menu set objectives for a total of 20 objectives.

■ Eligible hospitals and CAHs: There are a total of 24 meaningful use objectives to include 14 required core and 10 menu set objectives. To qualify, an eligible hospital or CAH must meet all 14 required core and 5 of the 10 menu set objectives for a total of 19 objectives.

7.5 Clinical Quality Measures

To successfully demonstrate meaningful use, eligible professionals, eligible hospitals, and CAHs must report on clinical quality measures (CQMs). Quality measures are used to quantify healthcare processes in an effort to measure the quality of healthcare services. This Measures Management System (MMS) was developed by the collaborate effort of the Agency for Healthcare Research and Quality (AHRQ), the American Medical Association Physician Consortium for Performance Improvement (AMA PCPI), The Joint Commission, the National Committee for Quality Assurance (NCQA), the National Quality Forum (NQF), and other measure participants.

For eligible professionals, there are a total of 6 CQMs: 3 required core (or alternate core when necessary) and 3 additional selected from a set of 38 CQMs. For eligible hospitals and CAHs, all 15 of their CQMs must be satisfied. Additional information, specifications, and calculations for the numerator, denominator, and exclusions can be found at https://www.cms.gov/QualityMeasures/03_ElectronicSpecifications.asp.

7.5.1 Electronic Specifications

Electronic specifications are used to standardize the format of the data that is captured or stored in EHRs. Without a standard format, different EHR technologies may not be able to communicate with each other or be shared between entities. There are four components to each electronic specification:

1. Measure overview/description—Relevant information of a measure to include the title of the measure, description, number, period of measurement, and measure steward.

2. Measure logic—Contains the algorithm used to calculate performance that includes the population criteria and measure logic for the numerator, denominator, and exclusion categories.
3. Measure code lists—All codes pertaining to the measure.
4. Quality data set (QDS) elements—Model of information that contains the standard element, the quality data element, and the data flow attributes. QDS is used to describe clinical concepts in a standardized fashion so that there is no unambiguous interpretation of the data. The data can then be clearly located and clinical performance can be monitored.

It is important to note that the measure specification may assume a full calendar year for reporting; the calculation of the denominator and numerator are done on the first day of the 90-day reporting period to the last day of the 90-day reporting period continuously for the first payment year.

7.5.2 Clinical Quality Measures for Eligible Professionals

There are a total of 44 CQMs that include 3 core, 3 alternate core, and 38 additional CQMs. To meet the requirements, an eligible professional must report on 3 required core CQMs. If the denominator of 1 or more of the required core measures 0, the eligible professional must substitute an alternate core measure to report on. In addition, eligible professionals must report on a total of 6 CQMs that include the 3 required and 3 additional from the 38 additional CQMs. An eligible professional may report up to a maximum of 9 measures so as to attest to the 3 core, the 3 alternate core, and the 3 additional measures. Note that it may be acceptable to report a 0 denominator for the additional measures if there is no applicable population set for the measure. The Eligible Professionals Measure Specifications can be downloaded from https://www.cms.gov/apps/ama/license.asp?file=/QualityMeasures/Downloads/EP_MeasureSpecifications.zip.
    Table 7.1 provides a listing of the CQMs.

7.5.3 Clinical Quality Measures for Eligible Hospitals and Critical Access Hospitals

There is a total of 15 CQMs that eligible hospitals and CAHs must report. Table 7.2 provides a listing of the CQMs.

7.5.4 Alternative Reporting Mechanisms

The Center for Medicare and Medicaid Services will also accept quality measures extracted from a qualified EHR product through its Physician Quality Reporting System (PQRS). Additional information and details related to the PQRS can be viewed at https://www.cms.gov/PQRS//20_AlternativeReportingMechanisms.asp.

Table 7.1 CQMs for Eligible Professionals

	Measure Number	Title	Core/Alternate
1	NQF 0001	Asthma Assessment	
2	NQF 0002	Appropriate Testing for Children with Pharyngitis	
3	NQF 0004	Initiation and Engagement of Alcohol and Other Drug Dependence Treatment: (a) Imitation, (b) Engagement	
4	NQF 0012	Prenatal Screening for Human Immunodeficiency Virus (HIV)	
5	**NQF 0013**	**Blood Pressure Measurement**	**Core**
6	NQF 0014	Prenatal Anti-D Immune Globulin	
7	NQF 0018	Controlling High Blood Pressure	
8	*NQF 0024*	*Weight Assessment and Counseling for Children and Adolescents*	*Alternate*
9	NQF 0027	Preventive Care and Screening: Advising Smokers to Quit	
10	**NQF 0028**	**Preventive Care and Screening Measure Pair: (a) Tobacco Use Assessment, (b) Tobacco Cessation Intervention**	**Core**
11	NQF 0031	Preventive Care and Screening: Screening Mammography	
12	NQF 0032	Cervical Cancer Screening	
13	NQF 0033	Chlamydia Screening in Women	
14	NQF 0034	Preventive Care and Screening: Colorectal Cancer Screening	
15	NQF 0036	Use of Appropriate Medications for Asthma	
16	*NQF 0038*	*Childhood Immunization Status*	*Alternate*
17	*NQF 0041*	*Preventive Care and Screening: Influenza Immunization for Patients over 50 Years Old*	*Alternate*

Continued

Table 7.1 (*Continued*)   CQMs for Eligible Professionals

	Measure Number	Title	Core/Alternate
18	NQF 0043	Preventative Care and Screening: Pneumonia Vaccination for Patients 65 Years and Older	
19	NQF 0047	Asthma: Pharmacologic Therapy	
20	NQF 0052	Low Back Pain: Use of Imaging Studies	
21	NQF 0055	Diabetes Mellitus: Dilated Eye Exam in Diabetic Patient	
22	NQF 0056	Diabetes Mellitus: Foot Exam	
23	NQF 0059	Diabetes Mellitus: Hemoglobin Alc Poor Control in Diabetes Mellitus	
24	NQF 0061	Diabetes Mellitus: High Blood Pressure Control in Diabetes Mellitus	
25	NQF 0062	Diabetes Mellitus: Urine Screening for Microalbumin or Medical Attention for Nephropathy in Diabetic Patients	
26	NQF 0064	Diabetes Mellitus: Low Density Lipoprotein (LDL-C) Control in Diabetes Mellitus	
27	NQF 0067	Coronary Artery Disease (CAD): Oral Antiplatelet Therapy Prescribed for Patients with CAD	
28	NQF 0068	Ischemic Vascular Disease (IVD): Use of Aspirin or Another Antithrombotic	
29	NQF 0070	Coronary Artery Disease (CAD): Beta-Blocker Therapy for CAD Patients with Prior Myocardial Infarction (MI)	
30	NQF 0073	Ischemic Vascular Disease (IVD): Blood Pressure Management Control	
31	NQF 0074	Coronary Artery Disease (CAD): Drug Therapy for Lowering LDL-Cholesterol	
32	NQF 0075	Ischemic Vascular Disease (IVD): Complete Lipid Panel and LDL Control	

Table 7.1 (*Continued*)   CQMs for Eligible Professionals

	Measure Number	Title	Core/Alternate
33	NQF 0081	Heart Failure: Angiotensin-Converting Enzyme (ACE) Inhibitor or Angiotensis Receptor Blocker (ARB) Therapy for Left Ventricular Systolic Dysfunction (LVSD)	
34	NQF 0083	Heart Failure: Beta-Blocker Therapy for Left Ventricular Systolic Dysfunction (LVSD)	
35	NQF 0084	Heart Failure: Warfarin Therapy for Patients with Atrial Fibrillation	
36	NQF 0086	Primary Open Angle Glaucoma (POAG): Optic Nerve Evaluation	
37	NQF 0088	Diabetic Retinopathy: Documentation of Presence or Absence of Macular Edema and Level of Severity of Retinopathy	
38	NQF 0089	Diabetic Retinopathy: Communication with the Physician Managing Ongoing Diabetes Care	
39	NQF 0105	Major Depressive Disorder (MDD): Antidepressant Medication During Acute Phase for Patients with MDD	
40	NQF 0385	Colon Cancer: Chemotherapy for Stage III Colon Cancer Patients	
41	NQF 0387	Breast Cancer: Hormonal Therapy for Stage IC-IIC Estrogen Receptor/ Progesterone Receptor (ER/PR) Positive Breast Cancer	
42	NQF 0389	Prostate Cancer: Avoidance of Overuse of Bone Scan for Staging Low-Risk Prostate Cancer Patients	
43	**NQF 0421**	**Adult Weight Screening and Follow-Up**	**Core**
44	NQF 0575	Diabetes: Hemoglobin A1c Control (<8. 0%)	

Table 7.2   CQMs for Eligible Hospitals and CAHs

	Measure Number	Title
1	NQF 0495	Emergency Department Throughput—Admitted Patients Median Time from ED Arrival to ED Departure for Admitted Patients
2	NQF 0497	Emergency Department Throughput—Admitted Patients Admission Decision Time to ED Departure Time for Admitted Patients
3	NQF 0435	Ischemic Stroke—Discharge on Anti-Thrombotics
4	NQF 0436	Ischemic Stroke—Anticoagulation for A-Fib/Flutter
5	NQF 0437	Ischemic Stroke—Thrombolytic Therapy for Patients Arriving within 2 Hours of Symptom Onset
6	NQF 0438	Ischemic or Hemorrhagic Stroke—Anti-Thrombotic Therapy by Day 2
7	NQF 0438	Ischemic Stroke—Discharge on Statins
8	NQF 0440	Ischemic or Hemorrhagic Stroke—Stroke Education
9	NQF 0441	Ischemic or Hemorrhagic Stroke—Rehabilitation Assessment
10	NQF 0371	VTE Prophylaxis within Twenty-Four (24) Hours of Arrival
11	NQF 0372	Intensive Care Unit VTE Prophylaxis
12	NQF 0373	Anticoagulation Overlap Therapy
13	NQF 0374	Platelet Monitoring on Unfractionated Heparin
14	NQF 0375	VTE Discharge Instructions
15	NQF 0376	Incidence of Potentially Preventable VTE

7.6 Meaningful Use Specification Sheets

To qualify for incentive payments through the Medicare and Medicaid EHR Incentive Programs, a number of objectives must be met. These objectives are defined in the Meaningful Use Objectives Specification Sheets. Each specification sheet covers a single objective in detail to include what it takes to meet the objective, how to calculate the numerator or denominator if applicable, exclusion qualifications, definitions, and attestation requirements.

Remember, eligible professionals must meet 20 out of the 25 objectives to qualify for incentive payments. This includes satisfying the 15 required core objectives and 5 of the 10 menu set objectives. Eligible hospitals and CAHs must meet 24 objectives to include 14 required core and 5 of the 10 menu set objectives to qualify for incentive payments. The next sections will discuss these objectives.

7.6.1 Meaningful Use Core Measures for Eligible Professionals

The following are the 15 meaningful use required core objective measures for eligible professionals:

1. Use computerized provider order entry (CPOE) for medication orders directly entered by a licensed healthcare professional who can enter orders into the medical record per state, local, and professional guidelines. This measure determines if more than 30% of all unique patients during the reporting period have at least one medication entered into the CPOE from the patient's medication list. This objective excludes any eligible professional that wrote fewer than 100 prescriptions during the reporting period.

2. Checks are implemented for drug–drug and drug–allergy interactions. This measure determines if this functionality was enabled through the entire reporting period.

3. Problem lists of current and active diagnoses are kept up to date. This measure determines if more than 80% of all unique patients have at least one entry or indication that no problems are known as structured data in their patient records.

4. Permissible prescriptions are generated and transmitted electronically. This measure determines if more than 40% of the permissible prescriptions written are electronically transmitted using EHR technology. This objective excludes any eligible professional that wrote fewer than 100 prescriptions during the reporting period.

5. List of active medication is maintained. This measure determines if more than 80% of all unique patients seen by the eligible professional have at least one entry or note that the patient is not being prescribed any medication recorded as structured data in their EHR.

6. List of active medication allergies is maintained. This measure determines if more than 80% of all unique patients seen by the eligible professional have at least one entry or note that the patient is not known to have allergic reactions to medication recorded as structured data in their EHR.

7. All of the following demographic information is recorded: race, gender, ethnicity, date of birth, and preferred language. This measure determines if more than 50% of all unique patients seen by the eligible professional have this information recorded as structured data in their EHR.

8. Vital signs are recorded and changes charted. This includes height, weight, and blood pressure. Body mass index (BMI) is calculated and displayed, and growth charts (including BMI) for children 2 to 20 years of age are plotted and displayed. This measure determines if more than 50% of all unique patients over 2 years old seen by the eligible professional have this information recorded as structured data in their EHR.

9. Patients 13 years or older have their smoking status recorded. This measure determines if more than 50% of all unique patients over 13 years old seen by the eligible professional have their smoking status recorded as structured data in their EHR.

10. Ambulatory clinical quality measures are reported to CMS. This measure determines if the eligible professional is reporting ambulatory clinical quality measures to CMS as specified.

11. As related to specialty or high clinical priority, the eligible professional implements one clinical decision support rule along with the ability to track compliance with that rule.

12. Upon request, the eligible professional is able to provide patients with an electronic copy of their health information. This includes problem list, medication lists, diagnostic test results, and allergies to medication. This measure determines if more than 50% of all patient requests are satisfied within 3 business days. This objective excludes any eligible professional or their agents if there were no requests from patients during the EHR reporting period.

13. For each patient's office visit, a clinical summary is provided. This measure determines if more than 50% of all patients receive a clinical summary within 3 business days. This objective excludes any eligible professional that had no office visits during the EHR reporting period.

14. The eligible professional is able to electronically exchange key clinical information among care providers and authorized entities. This key clinical information may include, for example, problem list, diagnostic test results, medication list, and list of allergies to medication. This measure determines if at least one test of the certified EHR technology was performed in regard to electronically exchanging key clinical information.

15. Electronic health information created or maintained by the certified EHR technology is protected through the appropriate technical capabilities that are implemented. This measure determines if a security risk analysis was conducted or reviewed as required under 45 CFR § 164.308(a)(1). In addition, this measure determines as part of the eligible professional's risk management process if security updates are implemented as necessary and security deficiencies identified are corrected. The full requirements of a risk analysis are discussed in Chapter 12. As a note of reference, this is the only part of meaningful use that directly applies to the Health Insurance Portability and Accountability Act (HIPAA)/Health Information Technology for Economic and Clinical Health (HITECH) Act.

7.6.2 Meaningful Use Menu Measures for Eligible Professionals

The following are the 10 meaningful use menu measure objectives for eligible professionals. At least one of these objectives that is considered a public health measure must be met. A public health measure is marked with an asterisk (*):

*1. In accordance with applicable laws and practices, the eligible professional has the capability to submit electronic data and actual submissions to immunization registries or immunization information systems. This measure determines if at least one test of the certified EHR technology was performed in regard to submitting electronic data to immunization registries and is followed up to verify successful submission of such information. This objective excludes any eligible professional that did not perform any immunizations during the EHR reporting period or if the immunization registry does not have the capabilities to receive this information electronically.

*2. In accordance with applicable laws and practices, the eligible professional has the capability to submit electronic syndromic surveillance data and actual submissions to public health agencies. This measure determines if at least one test of the certified EHR technology was performed in regard to submitting electronic data to public health agencies and is followed up to verify successful submission of such information. This objective excludes any eligible professional that did not collect any reportable syndromic information during the EHR reporting period or if the public health agency does not have the capability to receive this information electronically.

3. Drug formulary checks are implemented. This measure determines if this functionality was enabled and access to at least one internal or external formulary was maintained through the entire reporting period. This objective excludes any eligible professional that wrote fewer than 100 prescriptions during the EHR reporting period.

4. Clinical lab tests are incorporated as structured data into the EHR technology. This measure determines if more than 40% of all clinical lab test results ordered by the eligible professional during the reporting period are incorporated into the certified EHR technology. These test results should include a positive or negative response or be in a numerical format. This objective excludes any eligible professional that has not ordered any lab tests that did not have results in a positive or negative or numerical format during the EHR reporting period.

5. For quality improvement, reduction of disparities, research, or outreach uses, specific conditions can be listed and reports generated. This measure determines if at least one report can be generated by the eligible professional that lists patients with a specific condition.

6. Reminders can be sent to patients, based on patient preference, for preventive or follow-up care. This measure determines if more than 20% of all patients

that are 65 years or older or those patients 5 years or younger were sent appropriate reminders during the reporting period. This objective excludes any eligible professional that has no patients older than 65 or younger than 5 with records maintained in the certified EHR technology.

7. The eligible professional is able to provide patients with an electronic copy of their health information within 4 business days of the information being available to the eligible professional. This includes problem list, medication lists, diagnostic test results, and allergies to medication. This measure determines if at least 10% of all unique patients seen by the eligible professional are provided timely (i.e., within 4 business days) electronic access to their health information. This objective excludes any eligible professional that did not order lab tests or create information that would be included in their electronic health information record.

8. The eligible professional is able to identify patient-specific educational resources and provides these resources to the patient as appropriate using the certified EHR technology. This measure determines if more than 10% of all unique patients seen by the eligible professional are provided patient-specific educational resources.

9. Medication reconciliation is performed by an eligible professional that believes an encounter is relevant or receives a patient from another care setting or provider. This measure determines if medication reconciliation is performed on more than 50% of transitional patients. This objective excludes eligible professionals that did not receive any patients from transitions in care during the EHR reporting period.

10. The eligible professional provides a summary care record for any patient that is referred or transitioned to another care setting or provider. This measure determines if a summary care record was provided for more than 50% of patients referred or transitioned to another care setting or provider. This objective excludes eligible professionals that did not refer or transition any patients to another care setting or provider during the EHR reporting period.

7.6.3 Meaningful Use Core Measures for Eligible Hospitals and Critical Access Hospitals

The following are the 14 meaningful use required core objective measures for eligible hospitals and CAHs:

1. Use computerized provider order entry (CPOE) for medication orders directly entered by a licensed healthcare professional who can enter orders into the medical record per state, local, and professional guidelines. This measure determines if more than 30% of all unique patients admitted to the eligible hospital's or CAH's inpatient or emergency department during the reporting

period have at least one medication entered into the CPOE from the patient's medication list.

2. Checks are implemented for drug–drug and drug–allergy interactions. This measure determines if this functionality was enabled by the eligible hospital or CAH through the entire reporting period.

3. Problem lists of current and active diagnoses are kept up to date. This measure determines if more than 80% of all unique patients admitted to the eligible hospital's or CAH's inpatient or emergency department have at least one entry or indication that no problems are known as structured data in their patient records.

4. List of active medication is maintained. This measure determines if more than 80% of all unique patients admitted to the eligible hospital's or CAH's inpatient or emergency department have at least one entry or note that the patient is not being prescribed any medication recorded as structured data in their EHR.

5. List of active medication allergies is maintained. This measure determines if more than 80% of all unique patients admitted to the eligible hospital's or CAH's inpatient or emergency department have at least one entry or note that the patient is not known to have allergic reactions to medication recorded as structured data in their EHR.

6. All of the following demographic information is recorded: race, gender, ethnicity, date of birth, preferred language, and preliminary cause of death in the event of mortality in the eligible hospital or CAH. This measure determines if more than 50% of all unique patients admitted to the eligible hospital's or CAH's inpatient or emergency department have this information recorded as structured data in their EHR.

7. Vital signs are recorded and changes charted. This includes height, weight, and blood pressure. Body mass index (BMI) is calculated and displayed, and growth charts (including BMI) for children 2 to 20 years of age are plotted and displayed. This measure determines if more than 50% of all unique patients over 2 years old admitted to the eligible hospital's or CAH's inpatient or emergency department have this information recorded as structured data in their EHR.

8. Patients 13 years or older have their smoking status recorded. This measure determines if more than 50% of all unique patients over 13 years old admitted to the eligible hospital's or CAH's inpatient or emergency department have their smoking status recorded as structured data in their EHR.

9. Hospital clinical quality measures are reported to CMS. This measure determines if the eligible hospital or CAH is providing aggregate numerator, denominator, and exclusions to CMS as specified.

10. The hospital or CAH must implement one clinical decision support rule related to a high priority hospital condition along with the ability to track compliance of that rule.

11. Upon request, the hospital or CAH is able to provide patients with an electronic copy of their health information. This includes problem list, medication lists, diagnostic test results, and allergies to medication. This measure determines if more than 50% of all patient requests are satisfied within 3 business days. This objective excludes any eligible hospital or CAH that had no requests from patients during the EHR reporting period.

12. Upon request and at the time of discharge, patients are provided an electronic copy of their discharge instructions. This measure determines if more than 50% of all patients receive discharge instructions upon request. This objective excludes any eligible hospital or CAH that had no requests for discharge instructions during the EHR reporting period.

13. The eligible hospital or CAH is able to electronically exchange key clinical information among care providers and authorized entities. This key clinical information may include, for example, problem list, diagnostic test results, medication list, list of allergies to medication, procedures, or discharge summary. This measure determines if at least one test of the certified EHR technology was performed in regard to electronically exchanging key clinical information.

14. Electronic health information created or maintained by the certified EHR technology is protected through the appropriate technical capabilities that are implemented. This measure determines if a security risk analysis was conducted or reviewed as required under 45 CFR § 164.308(a)(1). In addition, this measure determines as part of the eligible hospital's or CAH's risk management process if security updates are implemented as necessary and security deficiencies identified are corrected. The full requirements of a risk analysis are discussed in Chapter 12. As a note of reference, this is the only part of meaningful use that directly applies to HIPAA/HITECH.

7.6.4 Meaningful Use Menu Measures for Eligible Hospitals and Critical Access Hospitals

The following are the 10 meaningful use menu measure objectives for eligible hospitals and CAHs. At least one of these objectives must be met that is considered a public health measure. A public health measure is marked with an asterisk (*):

*1. In accordance with applicable laws and practices, the eligible hospital or CAH has the capability to submit electronic data and actual submissions to immunization registries or immunization information systems. This measure determines if at least one test of the certified EHR technology was performed in regard to submitting electronic data to immunization registries and is followed up to verify successful submission of such information. This objective excludes any eligible hospital or CAH that did not perform any immunizations during the EHR reporting period or if the immunization registry does not have the capabilities to receive this information electronically.

*2. In accordance with applicable laws and practices, the eligible professional has the capability to submit electronic reportable lab results data (as required by state or local law) and actual submissions to public health agencies. This measure determines if at least one test of the certified EHR technology was performed in regard to submitting electronic data to public health agencies and is followed up to verify successful submission of such information. This objective excludes any eligible hospital or CAH where a public health agency it reports to does not have the capability to receive this information electronically.

*3. In accordance with applicable laws and practices, the eligible hospital or CAH has the capability to submit electronic syndromic surveillance data and actual submissions to public health agencies. This measure determines if at least one test of the certified EHR technology was performed in regard to submitting electronic data to public health agencies and is followed up with verify successful submission of such information. This objective excludes any eligible hospital or CAH that did not collect any reportable syndromic information during the EHR reporting period or if the public health agency does not have the capability to receive this information electronically.

4. Drug formulary checks are implemented. This measure determines if this functionality was enabled and access to at least one internal or external formulary was maintained through the entire reporting period.

5. Advance directives for patients 65 and older are recorded. This measure determines if more than 50% of all unique patients older than 65 admitted to the eligible hospital's or CAH's inpatient unit have an indication of their advance directive status as structured data in their EHR. This objective excludes an eligible hospital or CAH that did not admit any patients 65 years or older during the EHR reporting period.

6. Clinical lab tests are incorporated as structured data into the EHR technology. This measure determines if more than 40% of all clinical lab test results ordered by an authorized provider of the eligible hospital or CAH during the reporting period are incorporated into the certified EHR technology. These test results should include a positive or negative response or be in a numerical format.

7. For quality improvement, reduction of disparities, research, or outreach uses, specific conditions can be listed and reports generated. This measure determines if at least one report can be generated by the eligible hospital or CAH that lists patients with a specific condition.

8. The eligible hospital or CAH is able to identify patient-specific educational resources and provides these resources to the patient as appropriate using the certified EHR technology. This measure determines if more than 10% of all unique patients admitted to the eligible hospital's or CAH's inpatient

or emergency department are provided patient-specific educational resources during the EHR reporting period.

9. Medication reconciliation is performed by an eligible hospital or CAH that believes an encounter is relevant or receives a patient from another care setting or provider. This measure determines if medication reconciliation is performed on more than 50% of transitional patients.

10. The eligible hospital or CAH provides a summary care record for any patient that is referred or transitioned to another care setting or provider. This measure determines if a summary care record was provided for more than 50% of patients referred or transitioned to another care setting or provider.

7.7 Proposed Changes to Stage 1 and Proposals for Stage 2

During the time of this writing, there have been some proposed changes to the meaningful use requirements. The proposal indicates that eligible professionals must meet (or qualify for an exclusion to) 17 core objectives and 3 of 5 menu objectives. Eligible hospitals and CAHs will have to meet (or qualify for an exclusion to) to 16 core objectives and 2 of 4 menu objectives. An overview of some of the changes to stage 1 objectives can be found next. Details to these changes can be found at http://www.gpo.gov/fdsys/pkg/FR-2012-03-07/pdf/2012-4443.pdf.

- Use computerized provider order entry (CPOE) for medication orders directly entered by any licensed healthcare professional that can enter orders into the medical record per state, local, and professional guidelines. Proposed changes are as follows: for year 2013, one additional alternative measure will be added and for year 2014 and beyond, it is proposed to replace this measure all together.
- Record and chart changes in vital signs. In 2013 only, proposed change to add alternative age limitations and alternative exclusions. From 2014 onward, proposed age limitations on growth charts and blood pressure changes.
- Capability to exchange key clinical information among providers of care and patient authorized entities electronically. For 2013 onward, the objective is no longer required.
- Report ambulatory clinical quality measures to CMS or the states. From 2103 onward, this objective will be incorporated into the definition of a meaningful EHR user and be eliminated as an objective under 42 CFR § 495.6.
- Objectives related to providing patients with an electronic copy of their health information (for the eligible professional), electronic copy of discharge instructions (for hospitals), and providing patients with timely electronic access to their health information (for the eligible professional), is proposed

to be replaced by three new objectives with the stage 2 objectives and one of the two stage 2 measures for 2014 onward. Since these are technical objectives, here are the details:

- Eligible professional objective—The ability for the patient to view online, download, and transmit their health information within 4 business days of the information being available to the eligible professional.
- Eligible professional measure—More than 50% of all unique patients seen by the eligible professional during the EHR reporting period are provided timely online access to their health information. (Note: Some exceptions may apply at the discretion of the eligible professional.)
- Hospital objective: the ability for the patient to view online, download, and transmit information about a hospital admission.
- Hospital measure—More than 50% of all patients who are discharged from the inpatient or emergency department of an eligible hospital or CAH have information available online within 36 hours of discharge.

■ Public health objectives. For 2013 onward, add "except where prohibited" to the objective regulation text for the public health objectives under 42 CFR § 495.6.

One of the other major technical changes is the emphasis that will be placed on addressing the encryption or security of data at rest. It will still be an objective to protect electronic health information created or maintained by the certified EHR technology. Conducting or reviewing a security risk analysis in accordance with the requirements under 45 CFR § 164.308(a)(1) will still be an important measure in protecting this information. In addition, emphasis will now be placed on the encryption or security of data at rest as required under 45 CFR § 164.312(a)(2)(iv) and 45 CFR § 164.306(d)(3). Security updates and correcting identified security deficiencies are a continued necessary part of the risk management process.

The new requirements for stage 2 are going to be known as the 2014 Edition, while the current meaningful use final rule is known as the 2011 Edition. In the 2011 Edition, a complete EHR system must be purchased. It did not matter if all of the functions in the EHR were used. In the 2014 Edition, it has become a little more flexible. The new proposal requires EHR technology to be certified to meet the definition of a Base EHR. The criteria for a Base EHR are as follows (Roberta 2012):

■ "Includes a patient demographic and clinical health information, such as medical history and problem lists;
■ Capacity to provide clinical decision support;
■ Capacity to support physician order entry;
■ Capacity to capture and query information relevant to health care quality;
■ Capacity to exchange electronic health information with, and integrate such information from other sources; [and]

■ Capacity to protect the confidentiality, integrity, and availability of health information stored and exchanged."

This new practical approach allows for the Base EHR and allows build out to meaningful use core objectives and meaningful use menu objectives. The EHR technology only has to be certified for the meaningful use state that is being reported and attested to.

There are three ways to meet the new certified EHR technology (CEHRT) definition:

1. Purchase a complete EHR
2. Purchase a combination of EHR modules as functionally required
3. Purchase a single EHR module

For calendar years 2012 and 2013, the EHR system has to be certified to the 2011 Edition requirements or equivalent 2014 Edition adoption. For stage 1 or 2 in 2014, the EHR must include a Base EHR and be certified to 2014 Edition standards along with supporting the meaningful use objectives and measures (Roberta 2012).

7.8 Summary

In this chapter, the incentives that can be provided to healthcare providers that utilize electronic health records that meet meaningful use criteria were discussed. The three main components of meaningful use are using electronic health records in a meaningful manner such as e-prescribing, for electronic health information exchanges to improve healthcare quality, and for clinical quality submissions and other measures.

There are several quality measures that eligible professionals, eligible hospitals, or critical access hospitals need to meet to demonstrate the requirements of meaningful use. For eligible professionals, there are a total of 25 meaningful use objectives to include 15 required core and 10 menu set objectives. To qualify, an eligible professional must meet all 15 required core and 5 of the 10 menu set objectives for a total of 20 objectives. For eligible hospitals and critical access hospitals, there are a total of 24 meaningful use objectives to include 14 required core and 10 menu set objectives. To qualify, an eligible hospital or CAH must meet all 14 required core and 5 of the 10 menu set objectives for a total of 19 objectives. These measures were described throughout the rest of this chapter.

One of the core objectives that is a little outside of the realm of actual measurements is the requirement for electronic health information created or maintained by the certified EHR technology be protected through the appropriate technical capabilities that are implemented. The importance of this measure is determined by a security risk analysis being conducted or reviewed as required under 45 CFR § 164.308(a)(1). In addition, this measure determines as part of the eligible hospital's or CAH's risk management process if security updates are implemented as necessary and security deficiencies identified are corrected. The full requirements of a risk analysis are discussed in Chapter 12.

Chapter 8

Breach Notification Detailed

Objectives

The objectives of this chapter are as follows:

- Understand what constitutes a breach under the HITECH Breach Notification Rule.
- Determine what is required as part of the notification process.
- Determine if media is supposed to be notified of a breach.
- Determine the requirements for notifying the Secretary of the Department of Health and Human Services.
- Understand what is required by a business associate that had a breach.
- Understand the burden of proof requirement in regard to making breach notifications.

Background

One of the provisions of the Health Information Technology for Economic and Clinical Health (HITECH) Act is the notification of individuals affected by a breach of their electronic protected health information. There are certain requirements that must be followed and thresholds that apply to the breach notification regulation.

To put the importance of protecting against breaches into perspective, the Ponemon Institute publishes an annual study of the cost of breaches to understand their financial impact on companies. For the 2009 Annual Study, some interesting facts surfaced regarding the healthcare industry in particular. The average cost for a company across all industries involved in a data breach is $204 per compromised record. For healthcare, the average cost is $294 and pharmaceutical is $310 per compromised record. "The most recent annual study of data loss by the Ponemon Institute—which took into account detection, notification, post-response and lost-business costs—puts the average full cost of a data breach at a whopping $7.2 million" (Voelker 2012).

In a couple of examples of how much a data breach can cost companies, as described earlier, BlueCross and BlueShield of Tennessee spent nearly $17 million dollars on breach notification efforts after losing 57 hard drives containing 1 million client records (Sells 2012). Impairment Resources LLC, a California company that reviewed medical records on workers' compensation and auto casualty claims for approximately 600 insurance companies and clients, filed for bankruptcy. The company indicated that "the cost of dealing with the breach was prohibitive" after the loss of detailed medical information (including addresses, Social Security numbers, and medical diagnosis) on 14,000 people when their San Diego headquarters' office was burglarized on New Year's Eve. The company indicated that after liquidating its assets, it would not have enough to pay lender Insurance Recovery Group and its other loans along with facing threats of lawsuits over the privacy breach (Stech 2012).

Not only are there direct costs and indirect costs related to the actual breach as seen in the previous examples, but the study shows that healthcare organizations experience attrition rates that are 62% higher than the average for postbreach clients. This indicates that healthcare organizations may be losing more clients after a breach than clients of other organizations in other industries. Patients want to trust their healthcare providers in providing quality healthcare-related services along with building trust that their protected health information is going to be secure.

Stolen or lost laptops accounted for 36% of all breaches and outside organizations (i.e., business associates) are responsible for 42% of all the breaches reported. It is amazing to note that 82% of the companies surveyed have had more than one data breach during 2009 that affected more than 1,000 individuals, containing protected health information.

The Ponemon Study implied some best practices or measures that should be taken to prevent breaches. A multilayer approach appears to be most effective, such as expanding the use of encryption, data and asset loss prevention solutions, identity and access management solutions, and end-to-end protection solutions. Since a large portion of breaches occurred from trusted vendors, conducting appropriate due diligence activities is necessary on these third-party providers (i.e., business associates). It is no longer sufficient to just have contracts in place but rather a more active approach in having third-party providers demonstrate compliance with the HIPAA Privacy and Security Rules. Although breaches can be mitigated to an acceptable level, they may not be prevented. It is important to be prepared and have

Table 8.1   Breach Methods

Breach Methods	2010	2009	2008	2007
Hacking	50%	40%	64%	59%
Malware	49%	38%	38%	31%
Physical theft	29%	15%	9%	15%
Privilege misuse	17%	48%	22%	22%
Social engineering	11%	28%	NI	NI
Significant errors	<1%	2%	1%	3%

Source: Verizon, 2008–2011 Data Breach *Investigations Reports*, USA.

Note: NI = no information related to this method provided for this year.

a comprehensive incident response plan implemented. This can assist the covered entity in mitigating damages caused by breaches when they occur.

It really is not a matter of whether a breach will occur, but rather when will the covered entity (or business associate) become a target of a breach. Even the auditors become victims at times. KPMG, LLP, the auditing company hired by the Office for Civil Rights (OCR) to conduct 150 HITECH required "periodic audits" on covered entities and business associates by December 31, 2012, reported a breach to the New Jersey healthcare system in June 2010. According to the report, an unencrypted flash drive containing over 4,500 patient records was misplaced around May 10, 2010. The patient records apparently did not include addresses, Social Security numbers, dates of birth, financial information, or any other personal identification numbers or identifiable information. Furthermore, KPMG indicated that it would be introducing additional training and improved flash drive encryption. KPMG was awarded the OCR's $9.2 million contract in June 2011 after meeting the technical proposals and qualifications set by predetermined evaluation criteria along with past performance on other audit compliance programs (Nicastro 2011).

Verizon conducts an annual Data Breach Investigative Report providing a statistical study of breaches. Table 8.1 provides some interesting figures for how some breaches have occurred during the last 4 years and their frequency of occurrences.

8.1 Definitions

To understand the requirements of this breach notification regulation, an understanding and definition of the elements that make up the rules must be covered. 45 CFR § 164.402 defines the following as it relates to this breach notification requirement:

■ *Breach* is defined as "the acquisition, access, use, or disclosure of protected health information in a manner not permitted under subpart E [45 CFR Subpart E —Privacy of Individually Identifiable Health Information] of this part which compromises the security or privacy of the protected health information [or poses a significant risk of financial, reputational, or other harm to the individual]."

If a breach occurs that affected the following *direct identifiers*, then a compromise of the security or privacy of the protected health information is said to have occurred:

1. Names
2. Postal address information, other than town or city, state, and zip code
3. Telephone numbers
4. Fax numbers
5. Electronic mail addresses
6. Social Security numbers
7. Medical record numbers
8. Health plan beneficiary numbers
9. Account numbers
10. Certificate/license numbers
11. Vehicle identifiers and serial numbers, including license plate numbers
12. Device identifiers and serial numbers
13. Web Universal Resource Locators (URLs)
14. Internet Protocol (IP) address numbers
15. Biometric identifiers, including finger and voice prints
16. Full-face photographic images and any comparable images

Note: For the purposes of breach notification, the use or disclosure of date of birth, zip codes, or any other information not listed above would not constitute a "compromise of the security or privacy of the protected health information."

■ *Breach exclusions*—The following three examples are not considered a breach:

1. A workforce member, person acting under the authority of a covered entity, or a business associate unintentionally acquires, accesses, or uses protected health information as long as it was done in good faith and within the scope of their authority. In addition, the further use or disclosures of the protected health information was in a manner permitted under subpart E [45 CFR Subpart E—Privacy of Individually Identifiable Health Information]. (Reference from 45 CFR § 164.402(2)(i))

2. "Any inadvertent disclosure by a person who is authorized to access protected health information at a covered entity or business associate to another person authorized to access protected health information at the same covered entity or business associate, or organized healthcare arrangement in which the covered entity participates, and the information received as a result of such disclosure is not further used or disclosed

in a manner not permitted under subpart E [45 CFR Subpart E—Privacy of Individually Identifiable Health Information] of this part." (Cited from 45 CFR § 164.402(2)(ii))

3. "A disclosure of protected health information where a covered entity or business associate has a good faith belief that an unauthorized person to whom the disclosure was made would not reasonably have been able to retain such information." (Cited from 45 CFR § 164.402(2)(iii))

■ *Unsecured protected health information* is defined as "protected health information that is not rendered unusable, unreadable, or indecipherable to unauthorized individuals through the use of a technology or methodology specified by the Secretary of Health and Human Services." The guidance provided by the Department of Health and Human Services is to encrypt or destroy (in paper or electronic form) protected health information so that it is unusable, unreadable, or indecipherable by unauthorized individuals.

As specified in the Security Rule under 45 CFR § 164.304, electronic protected health information has been encrypted by "the use of an algorithmic process to transform data into a form in which there is a low probability of assigning meaning without use of a confidential process or key." It may go without saying that the process or key must remain secure as well so as not to allow the ability to decipher the encrypted information. The encryption method utilized will depend on the state that the data is in. The following are the commonly recognized data states:

– Data in motion—Data traversing a network through a wired or wireless connection. Valid encryption processes for this state of data are referenced in the Federal Information Processing Standards (FIPS) 140-2 that includes standards described in the National Institute of Standards and Technology (NIST) Special Publication (SP) 800-52, Guidelines for the Selection and Use of Transport Layer Security (TLS) Implementations; NIST SP 800-77, Guide to IPsec VPNs; or NIST SP 800-113, Guide to SSL VPNs.

– Data at rest—Data being stored on a hard drive, tape, or other media storage device along with being saved in a database or file system. Valid encryption processes for this state of data are referenced in the National Institute of Standards and Technology (NIST) Special Publication (SP) 800-11, Guide to Storage Encryption Technologies for End User Devices.

– Data in use—Data that is being created, viewed, updated, deleted, or in general use. Note: Data in this state may not be encrypted due to the assumption that it is being used or disclosed in an authorized manner.

– Data disposed—Data that is being discarded on paper or electronic media. Protected health information is said to have been destroyed if one of the following processes were followed:

• Paper documents, films, or other hard copy media is shredded or physically destroyed in a manner that otherwise makes it impossible to read the protected health information contained on the media and this information could not be reconstructed.

- Protected health information cannot be retrieved on electronic media following the National Institute of Standards and Technology (NIST) Special Publication (SP) 800-88, and Guidelines for Media Sanitization has been followed to destroy, clear, or purge the data.

8.2 Individual Notification

As a general rule, a covered entity is required to notify any individual whose unsecured protected health information has been breached. This notification should also be made to each individual that a covered entity reasonably believes to be a subject of a breach. A covered entity is required to notify an individual of a breach in a reasonable time and in no case later than 60 days after discovery of a breach. A breach is determined to be discovered by a covered entity as of the first day in which the breach was known or, by exercising reasonable diligence, should have been known by the covered entity.

8.2.1 Content of Notification

The covered entity is required to include the following elements within the breach notification written in plain language:

- ■ The date of the breach or the date the breach was discovered along with a brief description of the nature of the breach.
- ■ The type of unsecured protected health information that was compromised.
- ■ Steps individuals could take to protect themselves from any damage that may result from the breach.
- ■ A brief description of the steps the covered entity is taking to investigate the breach, to assist individuals in mitigating any harm that may be caused by the breach, and an action plan that the covered entity will be following so as not to protect from any future breaches.
- ■ Contact information for individuals to follow up with the covered entity for further questions or information related to the breach. This contact information should include a toll-free telephone number, e-mail address, Web site, or postal address.

8.2.2 Written or Electronic Notification

The covered entity is required to notify an individual subject to a breach by first-class mail to the last known address on file for the individual. If the individual has agreed to electronic notification, then electronic mail complies with this requirement. If an individual is known to be deceased by a covered entity, then notification to either the next of kin or personal representative of the deceased individual should be made. As information becomes available about the breach, more than one notification may be provided.

If there is insufficient or out-of-date contact information on the individual, then a substitute form of notice shall be provided that is reasonably calculated to reach the individual. In the case of a deceased individual that had insufficient or out-of-date contact information that precludes written notification to the next of kin or personal representative, a substitute notice need not be provided. If there is insufficient or out-of-date information on fewer than 10 individuals, the substitute notice may be provided in an alternative written form, by telephone, or by some other means.

If there is insufficient or out-of-date contact information for 10 or more individuals, then the notice should be conspicuously posted on the covered entity's Web site's homepage for 90 days. The notice could also be conspicuously posted in major print or broadcast media in the geographic area where the individuals likely reside. For either notification method, a toll-free phone number must remain active for at least 90 days that can provide information to an individual regarding the breach of their unsecured protected health information.

If a covered entity deems the unsecured protected health information is subject to imminent misuse, the covered entity may urgently notify an individual by telephone or other means, as appropriate, in addition to providing a written notice.

8.3 Media Notification

If a covered entity experiences a breach of unsecured protected health information involving more than 500 residents of a state or jurisdiction, the covered entity shall report this breach to a media outlet serving the state or jurisdiction. As already discussed, a covered entity is required to notify the media outlet in a reasonable time and in no case later than 60 days after discovery of a breach. In addition, the notification should contain all required elements noted in Section 8.2.1. Final note: American Samoa and the Northern Mariana Islands are referenced as being included as a state for this standard.

8.4 Secretary Notification

A covered entity that discovers they have had a breach of unsecured protected health information affecting 500 or more individuals must notify the Secretary of the Department of Health and Human Services without unreasonable delays and in no case later than 60 days from the first day of discovery of the breach. If the breach involves less than 500 individuals, the covered entity must report the breach(es) annually. Notification of breaches must be submitted within 60 days of the end of the calendar year in which the breaches occurred for all breaches occurring within that calendar year. Each breach must be completed on a separate form. This breach notification form must be submitted electronically and the form can be found at http://ocrnofitications.hhs.gov.

If a breach occurs and the covered entity is not sure of the exact number of individuals affected, then the covered entity should provide an estimate of the number. A covered entity should also submit additional reports if new information was uncovered about the breach that should be reported to the HHS Secretary. For additional questions regarding the submission of the breach notification form to the HHS Secretary, e-mail OCR Breach@hhs.gov.

8.4.1 Sample Breach Notification Form

Breach Affecting: 500 or more individuals/less than 500 individuals
Report Type: Initial Breach Report/Addendum to Previous Report

Section 1—Covered Entity
Covered Entity Information: Name, Address, City, State, Zip Code along with Contact Information to include: Name, Phone Number, and E-mail.
Type of Covered Entity: Health Plan, Healthcare Provider, or Healthcare Clearing House.
Section 2—Business Associate
Business Associate Information (if applicable): Name, Address, City, State, Zip Code along with Contact Information to include: Name, Phone Number, and E-mail.
Section 3—Breach
Date of Breach and Date of Discovery.
Approximate Number of Affected Individuals.
Type of Breach: Theft, Loss, Improper Disposal, Unauthorized Access/Disclosure, Hacking/IT Incident, Unknown, or Other (provide description).
Breached Information Location: Laptop, Desktop Computer, Network Server, E-mail, Other Portable Electronic Device, Electronic Medical Record, Paper Document, or Other (provide description).
Protected Health Information Involved: Demographic, Financial, Clinical, or Other (provide description).
Breach Description: Provide location of breach, how the breach occurred, type of breach, type of media, type of protected health information, and any additional information about the breach.
Any Safeguards Implemented Prior to Breach: Firewalls, Packet Filtering (router-based), Secure Browser Sessions, Strong Authentication, Encrypted Wireless, Physical Security, Logical Access Control, Anti-Virus Software, Intrusion Detection, and/or Biometrics.
Section 4—Notice of Breach and Actions Taken
Date Individuals were Notified.
Was Substitute Notice Required? Was Media Notice Required?

Response Actions: Security and/or Privacy Safeguards, Mitigation, Sanctions, Policies and Procedures, or Other (provide description).
Section 5—Attestation
Name of workforce member submitting form and date of submission.

"Under the Freedom of Information Act (5 U.S.C. § 552) and HHS Regulations at 45 C.F.R. Part 5, OCR may be required to release information provided in your breach notification. For breaches affecting more than 500 individuals, some of the information provided on this form will be made publicly available by posting on the HHS web site pursuant to § 13402(e)(4) of the Health Information Technology for Economic and Clinical Health (HITECH) Act (Pub. L. 111-5). Additionally, OCR will use this information, pursuant to § 13402(i) of the HITECH Act, to provide an annual report to Congress regarding the number and nature of breaches that are reported each year and the actions taken to respond to such breaches. OCR will make every effort, as permitted by law, to protect information that identifies individuals or that, if released, could constitute a clearly unwarranted invasion of personal privacy."

8.5 Business Associate Notification

A business associate is required to notify the covered entity of a breach in a reasonable time and in no case later than 60 days after discovery of a breach. A breach is determined to be discovered by a business associate as of the first day in which the breach was known or, by exercising reasonable diligence, should have been known by the business associate. The business associate, to the extent reasonably possible, should provide the identification of each individual affected by the breach to the covered entity. The business associate should also provide any additional information that the covered entity may need as part of the breach notification requirement at the time of the notification or promptly thereafter as information becomes available.

8.6 Notification Delay Request of Law Enforcement

In some cases, notification of individuals affected by the breach may be delayed at the request of a law enforcement official. This may occur in cases of an ongoing investigation involving the breach or if it would cause damage to national security. If this type of incident were to occur, the covered entity or business associate should delay notification upon written notice from the law enforcement official requesting the delay and specifying the time period of the delay. A law enforcement official could also make an oral request for delay. If this occurs, a covered entity or business associate should document the statement of the request including the official making the request. An oral request should be honored for no more than 30 days from the date of the request unless a written notice from the law enforcement official follows with a specific time period to delay the breach notification.

8.7 Burden of Proof

The burden of proof falls on the covered entity and the business associate to demonstrate that all required notifications have been made in cases requiring breach notification. A covered entity or business associate must also document or prove that a use or disclosure of unsecured protected health information does not constitute a breach if such incident were to occur. Following the HIPAA Privacy Rule requirements with respect to breach notification, covered entities must have written policies and procedures in place regarding breach notification, covered entities must train employees on these policies and procedures, and covered entities must apply appropriate sanctions against workforce members who do not comply with the policies and procedures.

8.8 Sample of Breach Notification Policy

Purpose of Policy

[The covered entity] will comply with this policy to fulfill its obligations with the HITECH Act regarding the notification of individuals affected by a privacy and security breach of protected health information.

POLICY DETAIL

[The covered entity] will notify each individual affected by a breach if their protected health information has been compromised. A breach is defined as an unauthorized acquisition, access, use, or disclosure of protected health information which compromises the security of the information.

The Security Official [or Privacy Official] will be notified immediately once a breach has been discovered. The Security Official [or Privacy Official] will conduct an investigation into the breach that may require law enforcement based upon the type of breach that occurred. In situations involving law enforcement, notification of a breach may be delayed. If law enforcement requests a delay in notification, such request should be made in writing requesting the period of time such delay should take place. If a request for delay is made orally, the request should be documented and will be valid no longer than 30 days from the initial request unless a written request is submitted during that time.

Within 60 days of a breach, written notice should be sent to the last known address of the affected individual (or next of kin in cases of a deceased individual) via first class mail. If the individual has requested communication electronically, an e-mail notification will be sent.

If the breach involves more than 500 people in one state or jurisdiction, a notice must be provided to the prominent media outlet serving that state or jurisdiction. In addition, notice must be provided to the federal Department of Health and Human Services (HHS) immediately. If the breach involves less than 500 individuals, the breach must be logged and reported annually to HHS.

If the breach involves more than 10 individuals that do not have current available addresses, a notice will be placed on [the covered entity's] Web site or a notice will be provided to the major print or broadcast media in the geographic areas where the individuals affected by the breach likely reside.

A notice may be made by telephone in addition to the other required notices in urgent cases where the possibility of imminent misuse of the unsecured protected health information applies.

Other applicable state laws may apply for the breach of social security numbers, bank account numbers, or other similar personally identifiable information.

Breach documentation must be retained for 6 years.

Exceptions: An unintentional breach, made in good faith, and within the scope of the professional relationship between the entity maintaining the records and the individuals or entities involved in the incident is not considered a breach requiring notification. As long as the protected health information is not further acquired, accessed, used, or disclosed to any other person, no breach notification is required. For example, if a person authorized to access protected health information at [the covered entity] inadvertently discloses this information to another person also authorized to access the protected health information, this is not considered a breach. Similarly, disclosing information to an unauthorized person that [the covered entity] has a good-faith belief could not reasonably retain such information is not considered a breach. Finally, a breach has not occurred if a breach does not compromise the security or privacy of the protected health information or pose a significant risk of financial, reputational, or other harm to the individual.

8.9 Sample of Breach Notification to Individuals

[Letterhead]
[Date]
VIA FIRST CLASS MAIL
[Last known address of individual]

Dear [individual]:

A recent incident has occurred that may have involved your personal information. [The covered entity] has discovered that there is a possibility your protected health information may have been accessed/used/disclosed to an unauthorized person. On [date of breach], [describe what happened]. [Describe the type of data that may have been compromised.]

[Provide steps for the individual to mitigate any damage caused by the breach to include contacting the credit bureaus or placing fraud alert/monitoring on the individuals' credit files.]

[Describe the steps being taken by the covered entity in investigating this incident and what the covered entity will do in the future to prevent such a breach.] Law enforcement officials have been contacted and the breach is under investigation. Management has launched an investigation to determine the cause of the breach and will be taking steps to mitigate such breaches in the future based upon the results of the investigation. We are uncertain if your personal information was actually obtained through this incident; however, we wanted to bring this situation to your attention and suggest some steps that you can take to minimize any potential risks of identity theft.

As a result of this incident and our continued goal to safeguard your protected health information, we are increasing our security by taking the following measures: [insert measures here]

If you have any further questions or require additional information, please contact [the covered entity] at [include toll-free telephone number, an e-mail address, website, or postal address.]

We apologize for this occurrence and will notify you in the future if we receive any additional information on this matter.

Sincerely,

[contact information]

8.10 Summary

In this chapter, security breaches were defined that require notification under the HITECH Breach Notification Rule. This is probably one of the grayest areas when it comes to the HIPAA/HITECH Privacy and Security Rules implementations. There are a lot of judgment calls related to an incident actually being considered a breach under the definitions. It gets even more subjective when a determination has to be made of "significant harm to an individual" as a result of a breach affecting that individual. There is a good walkthrough of a security incident in Chapter 20 that demonstrates how the regulations should be applied. Since there may not be some clear answers, it is always important to have policies and procedures in place that have been carefully thought out involving all parties that may be involved in such an incident. By formally documenting the covered entity's response to a breach, the covered entity would be in a better position to be defended if any questions were to be raised on how an incident was handled.

In addition, the components required in a notification, the process by which a notification should be made, the requirements to notify media, and the requirements to notify the HHS Secretary were provided. Discussed were some specific requirements for notification by a business associate and circumstances that law enforcement officials may utilize to require a delay in notification. A covered entity has a burden to prove that it took all the necessary steps to notify individuals affected by a breach. Also provided were some sample breach notification policies, sample breach notification forms, and a sample of a breach notification letter to individuals.

Chapter 9

Enforcement Rule Detailed

Objectives

The objectives of this chapter are as follows:

- Understand that the Office of Civil Rights under the Department of Health and Human Services has the authority to take enforcement actions against violation of HIPAA rules.
- Understand the general penalties that could be assessed under enforcement actions.
- Determine what types of affirmative defenses a covered entity may have to allegations of potential violations.
- Understand the types of waivers that the Department of Health and Human Services Secretary could issue related to enforcement activities.
- Understand what a Notice of Proposed Determination is and what affect it can have on a covered entity.

Background

HIPAA Administrative Simplification: Enforcement, 45 CFR Part 160 defines the enforcement activity conducted by the Department of Health and Human Services (HHS), Office of Civil Rights (OCR). To strengthen enforcement of the Health Insurance Portability and Accountability Act (HIPAA) rules, section 13410(d) of the Health Information Technology for Economic and Clinical Health (HITECH) Act became effective February 18, 2009, revising section 1176 of the Act, 42 U.S.C. 1320d-5. These modifications established categories of violations with increasing levels of culpability. The modifications also require that penalties imposed be based on the nature of (and the extent of) harm caused by a violation. HHS will be implementing future rulemaking efforts for other enforcement provisions that have yet to become effective under the HITECH Act.

9.1 General Penalty

The following are some terms defined in 45 CFR § 160.401 as it relates to penalty enforcement:

"Reasonable cause means circumstances that would make it unreasonable for the covered entity, despite the exercise of ordinary business care and prudence, to comply with the administrative simplification provision violated."

"Reasonable diligence means the business care and prudence expected from a person seeking to satisfy a legal requirement under similar circumstances."

"Willful neglect means conscious, intentional failure or reckless indifference to the obligations to comply with the administrative simplification provision violated."

There are four categories of violations:

- A person did not know (and by exercising reasonable diligence would not have known) a violation occurred
- A person that had reasonable cause to know, but no willful neglect, that a violation occurred
- A person that caused a violation due to willful neglect but has corrected the violation within 30 days of finding out about the violation
- A person that caused a violation due to willful neglect and has not corrected the violation

There are four tiers of penalties based on the aforementioned categories for each violation capping the total amount for all identical violations in a calendar year at $1.5 million:

- Tier 1—$100 to $50,000
- Tier 2—$1,000 to $50,000
- Tier 3—$10,000 to $50,000
- Tier 4—$50,000

See Table 9.1.

Table 9.1 Categories of Violations and Respective Penalty Amounts

Violation Categories—Section 1176(a)(1) of the HITECH ACT	Each Violation	All Identical Violations within a Calendar Year
Person did not know of violation	$100–$50,000	max. $1,500,000
Person had reasonable cause to know of violation	$1,000–$50,000	max. $1,500,000
Person violated with willful neglect, but corrected violation	$10,000–$50,000	max. $1,500,000
Person violated with willful neglect, but did not correct violation	$50,000	max. $1,500,000

9.2 Affirmative Defenses

The Secretary of the Department of Health and Human Services may not impose civil monetary penalties on a covered entity that had a violation prior to February 18, 2009, if the covered entity establishes an affirmative defense with respect to the violation that includes:

- An act punishable under 42 USC 1320d-6
- Satisfactorily establishes to the Secretary of the Department of Health and Human Services that the covered entity did not have knowledge of the violation or, by exercising reasonable diligence, would not have knowledge of the violation
- The violation is:
  - Due to reasonable cause and not willful neglect
  - Corrected during the 30-day period of the first day that the covered entity knew of the violation or within such period as the Secretary of the Department of Health and Human Services deemed appropriate.

9.3 Waiver

The Secretary of the Department of Health and Human Services may provide a waiver for a violation due to reasonable cause and not willful neglect that is not corrected in a timely manner.

9.4 Notice of Proposed Determination

The Department of Health and Human Services (HHS) will provide a covered entity with additional notice and information regarding a violation. The Notice of

Proposed Determination is an attempt by HHS to provide a covered entity with an understanding of the violation findings.

9.5 Summary

In this chapter, the authority that the Office of Civil Rights (OCR) under the Department of Health and Human Services (HHS) has in enforcing HIPAA Privacy and Security requirements were discussed. Penalties for violating the Privacy and Security Rules can be severe and the HITECH Act now provides attorney generals of each state the ability to also bring enforcement actions against covered entities that violate these regulations.

The law maintains some affirmative defenses for covered entities to protect against possible violations. These are, however, pretty narrowly scoped and may not relieve the covered entity of all liability when it comes to complying with the regulations. The HHS Secretary can provide waivers and it is the goal of the HHS to assist in compliance rather than to proceed with harsh enforcement. If compliance is mandated, taking enforcement actions is one of the ways that OCR can force this compliance. The OCR will inform a covered entity of any actions through a Notice of Proposed Determination. As a note of reference, it appears that most covered entities come to an agreement with OCR and settle on a monetary sum for any alleged violations as opposed to the OCR taking actual enforcement actions. This is not to say that these settlements are not costly, but rather the incident does not necessarily get to the level where formal enforcement actions are taken.

Chapter 10

Security Rule Detailed

Objectives

The objectives of this chapter are as follows:

- Understand what the Security Rule is intended to accomplish.
- Understand the implementation specifications for the Security Rule.
- Determine what types of risk analysis and security analysis will be conducted.
- Understand the implementation process of the Security Rule.
- Understand the flexibility and scalability the covered entity has to implement the Security Rule.
- Understand the following terms as they relate to the Security Rule: access, administrative safeguards, authentication, availability, workstation, systems, malicious software, information system; users, confidentiality, encryption, facility, physical safeguards, security or security measures, security incident, and technical safeguards.
- Determine how policies and procedures are going to be drafted to address the Security Rule requirements.
- Understand the documentation requirements including time limits, availability, and updates of policies and procedures related to the Security Rule.
- Determine what components of a policy are required.

Background

As previously discussed, the Security Rule is a more comprehensive set of rules than those addressed in the Privacy Rule under 45 CFR § 164.530(c), one that requires a covered entity to implement appropriate administrative, technical, and physical safeguards to protect the privacy of protected health information. Per 45 CFR § 164.306, "Covered entities must do the following:

1. Ensure the confidentiality, integrity, and availability of all electronic protected health information the covered entity creates, receives, maintains, or transmits.
2. Protect against any reasonably anticipated threats or hazards to the security or integrity of such information.
3. Protect against any reasonably anticipated uses or disclosures of such information that are not permitted or required under subpart E [45 CFR Subpart E—Privacy of Individually Identifiable Health Information] of this part.
4. Ensure compliance with this subpart by its workforce."

To this end, the Health Insurance Portability and Accountability Act (HIPAA) Security Rule added the implementation specification.

10.1 Implementation Specifications

Implementation specifications are detailed instructions to implement a specific standard. The administrative, technical, and physical safeguards are comprised of a number of standards. Each of these standards may be comprised of a number of implementation specifications. An implementation specification may be required or addressable. As implied, if the implementation specification is *required*, then the HIPAA Security Rule mandates that the standard be complied with to meet the objective of the safeguard. If, on the other hand, the implementation specification is *addressable*, then the entity must determine if it is reasonable and appropriate for the covered entity. It is very important to note that addressable does not mean optional. A covered entity must analyze the specification as it relates to the likelihood of protecting the covered entity's electronic protected health information from reasonable threats. If a covered entity feels the specification is reasonable to apply, then the covered entity should implement the specification. If the covered entity believes the addressable specification is not reasonable and appropriate for its environment, then the covered entity must document the rationale supporting the decision and either implement an equivalent measure that would accomplish the same purpose or not implement the specification as long as the standard for which the specification applies can still be met.

There are a few factors that will determine the reasonableness of applying a specification. First, a covered entity is required to conduct a risk analysis. This should answer the question of what situations leave the entity open to risks associated with the unauthorized access or disclosure of electronic protected health information.

Second, a covered entity should perform a security analysis that measures the adequacy of the controls that are already being implemented or could be implemented to secure electronic protected health information. Finally, the covered entity should perform a financial analysis to decide how much implementing a specification is going to cost. For example, if the value of an asset is $1,000, then it would not make much sense to spend $10,000 on solutions to protect the asset; rather, a covered entity may accept the risk associated with the loss of this asset.

10.2 Implementation Process

A covered entity should follow the same basic processes described next in order to implement the HIPAA Security Rule requirements:

- Assess risks, security controls in place, and conduct a gap analysis to identify any inadequacies of the lack of controls
- Develop a plan for implementation to include:
  - Read and understand the requirements of the HIPAA Security Rule
  - Review both the required and addressable implementation specifications
  - Decide on the proper security measures to implement
- Solution implementation
- Decision documentation
- Conduct periodic reviews

10.3 Standards Are Flexible and Scalable

As has been previously discussed, the HIPAA Security Rule is designed to be scalable across small and large covered entities. Since each covered entity is different, the rules were not developed to be so specific that a covered entity does not have the latitude to decide how best to meet the requirements. Some factors, such as the size, complexity, and capabilities of the covered entity, will determine what solutions or methods will be implemented for compliance. In addition, costs to implement security measures will also vary depending on the resources available to a covered entity. Different covered entities face different types of threats and probability of occurrence, so the risks associated with protecting the covered entity's electronic protected health information will vary across the healthcare industry.

Every covered entity's technical infrastructure, to include its hardware, software, and personnel, will be different. The security standards do not specifically identify certain technology solutions to comply with the HIPAA Security Rule. Technology is always improving (and changing) and the security standards attempt to be technologically neutral.

10.4 Security Standards Defined

To comply with the security standards, the covered entity must understand what is required and the terminology used in meeting compliance. The following are several terms, as defined by 45 CFR § 164.304, that relate to security. These terms will be utilized throughout this book when discussing the HIPAA Security Standards:

Access—"The ability or the means necessary to read, write, modify, or communicate data/information or otherwise use any system resource." Similarly, access could be expressed in terms of the privileges or rights that an individual has as it relates to the type of information the individual can utilize. Access should be limited to the least privileges and based upon an individual's functional roles within the organization. For example, if an employee's role requires only access to information about an individual's health records for diagnostic purposes, then the employee probably will never need access to the individual's billing information. On the other hand, if the employee does billing for a covered entity, then the employee may not need to see the actual lab results of an individual.

Administrative safeguards—"Administrative actions, and policies and procedures, to manage the selection, development, implementation, and maintenance of security measures to protect electronic protected health information and to manage the conduct of the covered entity's workforce in relation to the protection of that information." These safeguards and the standards related to these safeguards will be discussed in detail in the upcoming sections.

Authentication—"The corroboration that a person is the one claimed." For example, if an individual identifies himself as an employee of a covered entity, the individual may have been issued a picture ID that was issued by the covered entity to identify this individual as an employee. *Passwords*, or "confidential authentication information composed of a string of characters," are the normal way in which individuals authenticate themselves to a networked computer or *workstation* ["an electronic computing device, for example, a laptop or desktop computer, or any other device that performs similar functions, and electronic media stored in its immediate environment"].

Availability—"The property that data or information is accessible and usable upon demand by an authorized person." As it relates to security, *systems* ["that normally include hardware, software, information, data, applications, communications, and people"] must be maintained and protected in such a fashion that individuals need to be able to access these systems when required. Denial of service type attacks, or *malicious software* [i.e., a virus designed to damage or disrupt a system] may target the availability of the *information system* [or "an interconnected set of information resources under the same direct management control that shares common functionality"] causing the system to crash or to be unavailable for the *users* ["persons or entities with authorized access"]. This loss of service can cause some financial hardship in cases where the loss of revenue due to system downtime occurs or reputational harm when systems are not available to allow the users to service their clients in a timely manner.

Confidentiality—"The property that data or information is not made available or disclosed to unauthorized persons or processes." If an unauthorized individual gains access to a person's electronic protected health information, then the confidentiality of this information has been breached.

Encryption—"The use of an algorithmic process to transform data into a form in which there is a low probability of assigning meaning without [the] use of a confidential process or key." Utilizing strong encryption is one way to ensure that information traversing a public electronic network is secure from devices that may listen in on this information. Encryption can also be utilized when sensitive data is being stored or what is known as when data is "at rest." An example of data at rest is when backups are conducted on databases. These backups may be conducted on tape media that should be encrypted if the tapes ever leave the *facility* [or "the physical premises and the interior and exterior of a building(s)"] where they were created.

Physical safeguards—"Physical measures, policies, and procedures to protect a covered entity's electronic information systems and related buildings and equipment, from natural and environmental hazards, and unauthorized intrusion." Physical safeguards are the first layers of defense, or protection, against unauthorized access to information or the systems housing this information.

Security or *security measures*—"Encompass all of the administrative, physical, and technical safeguards in an information system." Throughout this book, these terms may be interchangeable with controls or security controls.

Security incident—"The attempted or successful unauthorized access, use, disclosure, modification, or destruction of information or interference with system operations in an information system."

Technical safeguards—"The technology and the policy and procedures for its use that protect electronic protected heath information and control access to it." Although technical safeguards are important, most of the time these safeguards are only as good as the people that are using them.

10.5 Policy and Procedure Drafting

Under 45 CFR § 164.316, a covered entity must "implement reasonable and appropriate policies and procedures to comply with the standards, implementation specifications, or other requirement of" the HIPAA Security Rule. Following a flexible approach as provided for in the Security Rule 45 CFR § 164.306(b)(2), the covered entity should be able to determine reasonable and appropriate safeguards to implement and address in its policies and procedures. The factors to consider are the "size,

Table 10.1   Policies and Procedures and Documentation Requirements

Security Standards		
Policies and Procedures and Documentation Requirements		
164. 316(a)		**Policies and Procedures**
164. 316(b)(1)		**Documentation**
164.316(b)(2)(i)	R	Time Limit
164.316(b)(2)(ii)	R	Availability
164.316(b)(2)(iii)	R	Updates

Note: R = required.

complexity, and capabilities of the covered entity." In determining what technical controls to implement, the covered entity's "infrastructure, hardware, and software security capabilities" should be considered. The cost of any security measures implemented should be reasonable as it pertains to mitigating risks. These risks should be quantified by the probability of an incident occurring and the criticality of the incident if it were to occur as related to the unauthorized use or disclosure of electronic protected health information. There are a few specific requirements for the actual writing of the policies and procedures that will be covered in the next sections. See Table 10.1.

10.6 Documentation Requirements

Policies and procedures must be in written form and cover the following safeguards: administrative, physical, and technical. These policies and procedures, of course, can be in electronic form but must be documented accordingly. These policies and procedures must be appropriate and reasonable to comply with the HIPAA Security Rule standards and implementation specifications. If there are any actions, activities, or assessments required by the Security Rule, these documents must also be in written (electronic form). These actions, activities, or assessment documentation must be maintained to substantiate proof of compliance with the Security Rule requirements.

The security planning policy should cover at least the following components: the purpose, scope, responsibilities, management commitment, coordination among different departments, and compliance. These policies should be formally documented, disseminated, and reviewed and updated on a periodic basis (i.e., annually or upon any major changes that affect security planning). These policies should define the covered entity's overall objectives and include all areas where security is required. Remember, the goal of security planning and documentation is to implement formal policies and procedures that comply with the implementation of the HIPAA Security standards. Security policies and procedures should be maintained by a designated workforce member such as the security official or other responsible individual.

The security policy and procedure should consider the covered entity's provided services, and the complexity or size of its function. The complexity of the covered entity may come in the form of the technical capabilities including hardware and software that run the daily operations. The security policy and procedures should be designed to reflect the costs of the security measures implemented and cover the potential risks that the covered entity's environment may face. Security policies and procedures should be reviewed on a periodic basis (i.e., at least annually) and modified to reflect any changes within the environment. Documentation should be kept for any changes or new implementation of safeguards that require modification to these security policies and procedures, and that could be a response to security incidents, technology changes, or other similar situations. Documentation should also be kept for any decisions to mitigate risks related to management controls, security operations, and technical solutions implemented. The covered entity should also have a data retention policy and procedures in place that consider requirements for all HIPAA documentation and standards.

The covered entity should refer to the following references for further details related to documentation requirements:

- NIST SP 800-53 PL-1 Security Planning Policy and Procedures
- NIST SP 800-66 4.21 Policies and Procedures
- NIST SP 800-66 4.21.1 Create and Deploy Policies and Procedures
- NIST SP 800-66 4.21.2 Update Documentation of Policies and Procedures

10.6.1 Time Limit—Required—45CFR § 164.316(b)(2)(i)

A covered entity must retain policy and procedure documents and other actions, activities, or assessment documentation for 6 years from whichever is later, the date of creation or the date when the documentation was last in effect. These documentation retention requirements should align with other data retention policies.

The covered entity should refer to the following reference for further details related to documentation retention:

- NIST SP 800-66 4.22.2 Retain Documentation for at least 6 years

10.6.2 Availability—Required—45 CFR § 164.316(b)(2)(ii)

To those persons that are responsible for implementing the procedures to which the documented procedures pertain, a covered entity must make these documents available. Security awareness training should include awareness on the availability of the covered entity's security documents. Feedback should be welcomed from workforce members as to enhancing the implementations of the security policies and procedures.

The covered entity should refer to the following references for further details related to documentation availability:

- NIST SP 800-66 4.22.3 Assure that Documentation is Available to those Responsible for Implementation
- NIST SP 800-66 4.22.4 Update Documentation as required

10.6.3 Updates—Required—45 CFR § 164.316(b)(2)(iii)

Documentation should be reviewed periodically and updated as needed. These updates could be in response to operational or environmental changes that may affect the security of electronic protected health information. The covered entity should consider implementing a version control procedure or process to assist in recording a timeline of security policy and procedure updates or revisions.

The covered entity should refer to the following reference for further details related to documentation updates:

- NIST SP 800-66 4.22.4 Update Documentation as required

10.7 Components of Policies

A good policy usually consists of the following: a policy statement, scope of the policy, purpose of the policy, policy detail, policy authorization, and effective date of the policy. A policy statement is basically a statement describing the policy. It is a high-level overview describing the intent of management to ensure compliance with the objective that the policy is addressing. The scope of the policy describes the persons to whom the policy will apply. In most cases, the scope of the policy applies to the employees of the covered entity, but the policy could be applied to other individuals such as business associates or contractors that will be required to comply with the covered entities' policies as part of their contractual agreement.

The purpose of the policy describes what the policy is supposed to accomplish or the reasons behind the policy. The policy will start to get a little more detailed in the policy detail section of the policy to describe specifics of how the policy will be applied. Every policy should be authorized by an executive-level individual with authorization to enforce such policy, or in the case of a corporation, the board of directors should review and authorize the policies. Finally, the policy should have an effective date that is the date that the policy will be implemented and enforcement will begin.

10.7.1 Sample of General Information Applicable to All Privacy and Security Policies

POLICY STATEMENT

It is the policy of [the covered entity] to use and disclose protected health information (PHI) only for the purpose of treatment, payment, healthcare operations, or as otherwise allowed by law.

The covered entity will comply with applicable state laws and will consult with legal counsel when questions arise regarding the applicability of any state laws.

These policies are designed to comply with the Health Insurance Portability and Accountability Act of 1996 (HIPAA) and the Health Information Technology for Economic and Clinical Health Act of 2009 (HITECH Act).

SCOPE OF THESE PRIVACY AND SECURITY POLICIES

These policies apply to [the covered entity], business associates, contractors, subcontractors, or anyone working with or under the capacity of [the covered entity] with regard to PHI of individuals obtained in the course of [the covered entity's] business functions in administering and providing healthcare services.

APPLICABILITY OF THESE POLICIES

These policies are intended to guide [the covered entity's] workforce members on how to protect PHI of individuals while carrying out their job roles or functions.

Note: Applicable terms should be defined appropriately throughout the policies and procedures so that there is no misunderstanding and all affected individuals are given notification as to the meanings intended throughout the policies and procedures.

10.8 Summary

Throughout this chapter the HIPAA Security Rule was discussed in detail. The Security Rule is a more comprehensive set of rules than those addressed in the Privacy Rule, one that requires a covered entity to implement appropriate administrative, technical, and physical safeguards to protect the privacy of protected health information. To comply with the Security Rule, the regulation provides implementation specifications that are detailed instructions to implement a specific standard. An implementation specification may be required or addressable. Although a standard may be addressable, it does not mean that a covered entity does not have to comply with the standard, but rather the covered entity must analyze the specification as it relates to the likelihood of protecting its electronic protected health information from reasonable threats.

There is a process that can be followed to implement the Security Rule. This process starts with conducting a risk analysis and ends with conducting periodic reviews of the implementation process. The Security Rule is flexible and scalable, which allows the covered entity to appropriately implement safeguards or solutions that fit its needs and the resources available.

The Security Rule requires policies and procedures to be developed with certain time limits, availability, and update requirements. The chapter ended with a discussion of the components that make up a policy along with a sample of general applicable rules for all privacy and security policies.

Chapter 11

Security Rule: Administrative Safeguards

Objectives

The objectives of this chapter are as follows:

- Understand what standards make up the Administrative Safeguards related to the Security Rule regulations.
- Understand the security management process.
- Determine what is required by a risk analysis.
- Understand what is involved in risk management.
- Determine appropriate sanctions on workforce members for violations of policies and procedures.
- Understand what is required by an information system activity review.
- Determine which workforce member will be assigned security responsibilities.
- Understand workforce security requirements.
- Understand what is involved with authorization and supervision of workforce member access.
- Determine proper workforce clearance procedures.
- Determine appropriate termination procedures.
- Understand what is involved with management of information access.
- Determine if healthcare clearinghouse functions can be isolated.
- Determine how to address access authorization.
- Determine how to address access establishment and modification.
- Understand what is involved with security awareness training.

- Determine how to address security reminders.
- Determine what solutions will protect against malicious software.
- Determine what is necessary to monitor for log-ins.
- Understand the management of passwords.
- Determine what procedures are required to handle security incident.
- Understand how to respond to and report a security incident.
- Understand the requirement of a contingency plan.
- Determine what types of data backups are required.
- Understand what is involved in a disaster recovery plan.
- Determine when emergency mode operations go into effect.
- Determine how to address testing and revising disaster recovery plans.
- Understand how to conduct applications and data criticality analysis.
- Determine what types of evaluations are required.
- Understand business associate contracts and other arrangements.
- Determine what elements are required to be included in a written contract or other arrangement related to business associates.

Background

Over half of the Health Insurance Portability and Accountability Act (HIPAA) security requirements are covered under the Administrative Safeguards. As a reminder, the Security Rule defines administrative safeguards as, "administrative actions, and policies and procedures, to manage the selection, development, implementation, and maintenance of security measures to protect electronic protected health information and to manage the conduct of the covered entity's workforce in relation to the protection of that information." Some of these safeguards are required, while others are addressable. Compliance with the Security Rule will depend on several factors as defined in 45 § 164.306(b)(2) to include: the size of the covered entity; complexity of the covered entity; capabilities of the covered entity; the covered entity's technical resources to include hardware and software security capabilities; costs of controls; and the risk assessment based upon probability and criticality of potential risks to electronic protected health information. See Table 11.1.

11.1 Security Management Process

Under 45 CFR § 164.308(a)(1), a covered entity must "implement policies and procedures to prevent, detect, contain, and correct security violations." One of the first policies and procedures to be implemented involves conducting a risk assessment. A covered entity should develop and disseminate risk assessment policies and procedures so that all workforce members have an idea of this process. These risk assessment policies and procedures should be reviewed and updated as necessary.

Table 11.1 Administrative Safeguards

Security Standards		
Administrative Safeguards		
164.308(a)(1)		**Security Management Process**
164.308(a)(1)(ii)(A)	R	Risk Analysis
164.308(a)(1)(ii)(B)	R	Risk Management
164.308(a)(1)(ii)C	R	Sanction Policy
164.308(a)(1)(ii)C	R	Information System Activity Review
164.308(a)(2)	R	Assigned Security Responsibility
164.308(a)(3)		**Workforce Security**
164.308(a)(3)(ii)(A)	A	Authorization and/or Supervision
164.308(a)(3)(ii)(B)	A	Workforce Clearance Procedure
164.308(a)(3)(ii)C	A	Termination Procedures
164.308(a)(4)		**Information Access Management**
164.308(a)(4)(ii)(A)	R	Isolating Health Care Clearinghouse Functions
164.308(a)(4)(ii)(B)	A	Access Authorization
164.308(a)(4)(ii)C	A	Access Establishment and Modification
164.308(a)(5)		**Security Awareness and Training**
164.308(a)(5)(ii)(A)	A	Security Reminders
164.308(a)(5)(ii)(B)	A	Protection from Malicious Software
164.308(a)(5)(ii)C	A	Log-in Monitoring
164.308(a)(5)(ii)(D)	A	Password Management
164.308(a)(6)		**Security Incident Procedures**
164.308(a)(6)(ii)	R	Response and Reporting
164.308(a)(7)		**Contingency Plan**
164.308(a)(7)(ii)(A)	R	Data Backup Plan
164.308(a)(7)(ii)(B)	R	Disaster Recovery Plan
164.308(a)(7)(ii)C	R	Emergency Mode Operation Plan

Continued

Table 11.1 (*Continued*)   Administrative Safeguards

164.308(a)(7)(ii)(D)	A	Testing and Revision Procedures
164.308(a)(7)(ii)(E)	A	Applications and Data Criticality Analysis
164.308(a)(8)	R	Evaluation
164.308(b)(1)		**Business Associate Contracts and Other Arrangements**
164.308(b)(4)		Written Contract or Other Arrangement

Note: A = addressable, R = required.

In addition, workforce members that are affected or responsible for risk assessment activities should be trained accordingly.

At a minimum, the risk assessment policy should address the following: the purpose of the policy; the scope of the policy; high-level overview of the different roles and responsibilities of the workforce members; the commitment that management has towards the importance of a risk assessment; coordination between different departments or units within the covered entity; how workforce members are trained in risk assessment procedures; and how the covered entity will come into compliance with the risk assessment policies and procedures. The covered entity's risk assessment policy should also define the frequency with which the risk assessment is reviewed and updated.

In conducting the risk assessment, the covered entity should make sure to identify the types and uses of the information it creates, maintains, processes, stores, or transmits. This information should be classified based on its sensitivity levels. All information housing electronic protected health information should be identified. This inventory should be complete with all hardware including removable media, remote access, and mobile devices. Inventory should account for software including any types of reports, spreadsheets, databases, and so forth that may contain electronic protected health information. This inventory should also include all business functions of the covered entity along with verification of control over information systems. Inventory should be kept updated, current, and reviewed on a periodic basis to make sure that all information systems containing electronic protected health information are appropriately accounted for. Configurations for these information systems should also be documented including any connections to other systems within the internal network and external network.

The covered entity should refer to the following references for further details related to the security management process:

■ NIST SP 800-53 RA-1 Risk Assessment Policy and Procedures
■ NIST SP 800-53 SA-1 System and Services Acquisition Policy and Procedures
■ NIST SP 800-53 SA-2 Allocation of Resources

- NIST SP 800-53 SA-3 System Development Life Cycle
- NIST SP 800-53 SA-4 Acquisition Process
- NIST SP 800-53 SA-5 Information System Documentation
- NIST SP 800-53 SA-9 External Information System Services
- NIST SP 800-53 SA-10 Developer Configuration Management
- NIST SP 800-53 SA-11 Developer Security Testing
- NIST SP 800-53 SA-12 Supply Chain Protection
- NIST SP 800-53 SA-14 Critical Information System Components
- NIST SP 800-53 SA-15 Development Process, Standards, and Tools
- NIST SP 800-53 SA-16 Developer-Provided Training
- NIST SP 800-53 SA-17 Developer Security Architecture and Design
- NIST SP 800-53 SC-27 Operating System-Independent Applications
- NIST SP 800-53 SC-32 Information System Partitioning
- NIST SP 800-53 SC-34 Non-Modifiable Executable Programs
- NIST SP 800-53 SC-37 Distributed Processing and Storage
- NIST SP 800-53 SC-39 Out-of-Band Channels
- NIST SP 800-53 SC-40 Operations Security
- NIST SP 800-53 SC-41 Process Isolation
- NIST SP 800-53 PM-1 Information Security Program Plan
- NIST SP 800-53 PM-5 Information System Inventory
- NIST SP 800-53 PM-6 Information Security Measures of Performance
- NIST SP 800-53 PM-7 Enterprise Architecture
- NIST SP 800-53 PM-8 Critical Infrastructure Plan
- NIST SP 800-53 PM-11 Mission/Business Process Definition
- NIST SP 800-53 PM-12 Insider Threat Program
- NIST SP 800-53 PM-14 Operations Security Program
- NIST SP 800-53 PM-15 Testing, Training, and Monitoring
- NIST SP 800-60, Guide for Mapping Types of Information and Information Systems to Security Categories, March 2005
- NIST SP 800-66 4.1.1 Security Management Process: Identify Relevant Information Systems
- FIPS 199, Standards for Security Categorization of Federal Information and Information Systems, February 2004

11.1.1 Risk Analysis—Required—45 CFR § 164.308(a)(1)(ii)(A)

The covered entity is required to "conduct an accurate and thorough assessment of the potential risks and vulnerabilities to the confidentiality, integrity, and availability of electronic protected health information held by the covered entity." An entire section of this book was devoted to discussing the process of conducting a risk analysis. For the sake of simplification, a risk analysis must identify potential security risks. These risks can come from many different areas. The risk analysis must also determine the probability that an event will occur, and the magnitude of damage or loss of information that may occur from such an event if it were to occur. A security categorization should be determined for each information system along with the rationale behind such a ranking to be included in the covered entity's security plan. These security categorization decisions should be reviewed and approved by an official or delegated representative of the covered entity.

To assess the risk of electronic protected health information, a covered entity should determine how this information flows throughout the organization. This includes how electronic protected health information is created, received, maintained, or transmitted by the covered entity. See Figure 11.1 for an example on how information may flow through a covered entity and the areas that may be of concern regarding the protection of this health information.

The covered entity should also consider the less obvious sources of protected health information. This may include health plan forms, copies of insurance cards, medical history forms, specialty forms like labs or referral forms, or other forms that may be ancillary patient forms that contain protected health information that is required to be secured. Some covered entities may utilize answering services or electronic voice mail services. The messages left on these types of services may

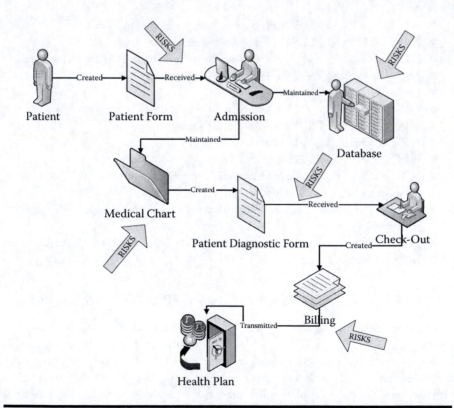

Figure 11.1   Sample information flow for a small healthcare provider.

contain electronic protected health information that is also required to be secure from unauthorized access. Other covered entities may use personal data assistants (PDAs), smart phones, or tablet devices. These organizations must consider the risks involved in using such devices and the controls implemented to secure any protected health information that may be created, received, stored, or transmitted from these devices.

Not only does the covered entity take into consideration internal sources of electronic protected health information, but the entity should identify the external sources of electronic protected health information. Some examples of external sources could include vendors or consultants that are working on behalf of the covered entity that create, receive, maintain, or transmit electronic protected health information.

Finally, a covered entity should consider all threats in the risk analysis to information systems that contain electronic protected health information. Threats may come from human sources such as burglary or espionage; natural sources such as earthquakes, floods, or fires; or environmental elements such as proximity to hazardous material factories or highways. Risks should be evaluated based on the likelihood and magnitude of harm from the unauthorized use or disclosure of electronic protected health information. The covered entity may also want to base its evaluation of risk on the confidentiality, integrity, availability, financial, regulatory, operational, or reputational losses of electronic protected health information.

The covered entity should document the risk assessment results as part of its security plan or within its own risk assessment report. As discussed earlier, the risk assessment results should be reviewed on a periodic basis and updated whenever significant changes have taken place within the information systems or the operational environment. Security states of systems continually change and new threats or vulnerabilities arise every day within these systems that need to be addressed. Covered entities should pay special attention to identified threats or vulnerabilities, and the recommended mitigation efforts to lower these risks to an acceptable level. Current and future risk mitigating controls should be formally documented, and the residual risks after these controls have been implemented should be tracked.

A covered entity should assign responsibility to a workforce member, group of workforce members, or a third-party service provider to verify that all selected security settings have been enabled on all hardware and software including remote access hardware and software solutions. These responsible parties should receive regular updates, information, or guidance from agencies such as the Office for Civil Rights (OCR), the Office of the Inspector General (OIG), the United States Computer Emergency Readiness Team (US-CERT), groups that alert on new viruses or malware, or other vendors or groups on security related matters.

The covered entity should refer to the following references for further details related to risk analysis:

- NIST SP 800-53 RA-2 Security Categorization
- NIST SP 800-53 RA-3 Risk Assessment

- NIST SP 800-66 4.1.2 Conduct a Risk Assessment
- Additions from the OCR 2010 Risk Analysis Guidance

11.1.1.1 Sample of Risk Analysis Policy

PURPOSE OF POLICY

To ensure that the individual's protected health information is used or disclosed in an appropriate manner and protected from unauthorized use or disclosure as set forth in the Privacy and Security Rules.

POLICY DETAIL

Risk analysis is a process that will be used to identify possible threats and vulnerabilities along with identifying possible ways to reduce risks. A comprehensive risk analysis will be performed by the security official working with the privacy official, legal, and other operational units to determine the status of the safeguards in place to protect electronic protected health information. These officials could get additional assistance in completing the risk assessment from outside independent assessors or consultants. The initial risk analysis will create a baseline for ongoing risk management activities including mitigation strategies. The risk assessment will be part of [the covered entity's] overall security plan. The risk assessment report will be reviewed on an annual basis or whenever significant changes have taken place within an information system or network environment. Testing of vulnerabilities or evaluations of new threats will be conducted on all information systems and network devices owned or operated by [the covered entity] on an annual basis in conjunction with the review of the risk assessment. This testing should be performed by a knowledgeable, experienced, and highly skilled individual assigned or hired by [the covered entity].

11.1.2 Risk Management—Required—45 CFR §164.308(a)(1)(ii)(B)

A covered entity is required to "implement security measures [that are] sufficient to reduce risks [to] vulnerabilities to a reasonable and appropriate level." A covered entity should have policies and procedures in place for security as part of its risk management process. To conduct proper risk management, the covered entity should identify the security measures or safeguards that are already in place to secure protected electronic health information. These safeguards should ensure the confidentiality, integrity, and availability of electronic protected health information. These safeguards should also protect against any reasonably anticipated threat or hazard to the unauthorized use or disclosure of electronic protected health information permitted under the HIPAA Privacy Rule.

Executive-level personnel should be directly involved in risk management and mitigation decisions. There should be a formally documented system security plan in place that details the covered entity's security practices. These security practices

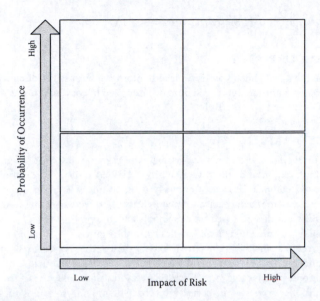

Figure 11.2   Risk analysis chart.

should be communicated throughout the entire organization through designated channels, such as documented procedures, training, e-mails, or other methods. In order to reduce the impact of the covered entity's operations, these security practices should detail the coordination of security-related activities that may affect information systems. In addition, these security practices should describe how new security controls are implemented into the existing environment along with providing a formally documented contingency plan for operations. Finally, the security plan should be reviewed and updated as necessary.

Some entities may decide to engage outside resources to assist them in risk management activities. If this occurs, an analysis should be conducted on these resources and the same adherence to protecting electronic health information need apply to these third-party service providers. Remember, risk analysis and the risk management process is an ongoing function and resources need to be assigned for these types of activities. A covered entity's workforce members should be properly trained in the risk management program (Figure 11.2).

The covered entity should refer to the following references for further details related to the security management process:

- NIST SP 800-53 PM-6 Risk Management Strategy
- NIST SP 800-66 4.1.3 Implement a Risk Management Program
- NIST SP 800-66 4.1.4 Acquire IT Systems and Services
- NIST SP 800-66 4.1.5 Create and Deploy Policies and Procedures

11.1.2.1 Sample of Risk Management Policy

PURPOSE OF POLICY

To ensure that individual's protected health information is used or disclosed in an appropriate manner and protected from unauthorized use or disclosure as set forth in the Privacy and Security Rules.

POLICY DETAIL

The security official will review and evaluate the risks to the security of protected health information and [the covered entity's] HIPAA policies to determine the adequacy of compliance at least annually or upon any relevant changes to the operational environment that impact the security of protected health information. Risks will be evaluated based on the impact and the probability of occurrence. Risks will be documented on a chart similar to the figure.

The security official will be responsible for performing ongoing risk management functions, as needed, to include periodic reviews and evaluations of technical solutions, policies and procedures, training, business associate agreements, and audit effectiveness. The security official will provide solutions to address any particular risk. These risk mitigation strategies will depend on [the covered entity's] size, complexity, capabilities, technical infrastructure, and the probability along with the criticality of the impact that a potential risk presents to [the covered entity's] protected health information. Risks can be accepted if the potential impact is reasonably low and the cost to mitigate such risk is extremely high. Risks can also be mitigated to an acceptable level, be transferred to another entity, or covered by insurance.

11.1.3 Sanction Policy—Required—45 CFR §164.308(a)(1)(ii)(C)

A covered entity is required to "apply appropriate sanctions against workforce members who fail to comply with the security policies and procedures of the covered entity." A covered entity must have an existing sanction policy and procedure to meet this requirement. If a covered entity does not have an existing sanction policy, the covered entity should modify its policy to include language relating to violations of the security policies and procedures. In addition, the covered entity is required to have workforce members sign a statement of adherence to security policies and procedures as a prerequisite for employment. Compliance with this requirement could come in the form of signing a statement as part of employees' initial hire and when they receive the covered entity's employee handbook or as part of a signed confidentiality statement.

The security policies and procedures statement of adherence should state that the workforce member acknowledges that violations of security policies and procedures may lead to disciplinary action up to and including termination. The sanction policy should provide examples of potential violations of the policy and procedures, and the disciplinary actions should be adjusted based on the severity of the violation. Examples of potential violations could include system misuse or any fraudulent activity involving the covered entity's electronic protected health information. The covered entity's policies and procedures should provide for the process of reporting possible inappropriate activities to management.

The covered entity should refer to the following references for further details related to the sanction policy:

- NIST SP 800-53 PS-8 Personnel Sanctions
- NIST SP 800-66 4.1.6 Develop and Implement a Sanction Policy

11.1.3.1 Sample of Sanction Policy

PURPOSE OF POLICY

To set forth the appropriate disciplinary procedures for workforce members who fail to comply with [the covered entity's] privacy and security policies and procedures and to ensure compliance with the HIPAA Privacy Rule and Security Rule.

POLICY DETAIL

[The covered entity] will apply the same progressive disciplinary procedure to workforce members who fail to comply with [the covered entity's] privacy and security policies and procedures, up to and including termination for serious and/ or repetitive violations, as it applies to all other instances of workforce misconduct. [Note: This could be addressed in the employee's handbook or the disciplinary actions could be detailed here.]

In the opinion of the privacy official (the security official), if the violation of a workforce member is deemed to be serious or a willful disregard of these policies is demonstrated through repeated violations, the privacy official (the security official) may impose an appropriate sanction outside of the progressive disciplinary levels.

The sanction policy does not apply to:

1. Workforce members covered by the conditions met for the disclosures by whistleblowers
2. Disclosures by workforce members who are victims of a crime
3. Workforce members exercising any of their rights under the HIPAA Privacy Rule

[The covered entity] will document all sanctions that are applied to the workforce member and retain this documentation for 6 years from the date the document was created or the date the sanction was implemented, whichever is later.

A workforce member is required to sign a statement of adherence to the security policies and procedures as [part of receiving an employee's handbook or part of a confidentiality statement] as a prerequisite to employment. This statement of adherence will state that the workforce member acknowledges that violations of security policies and procedures may lead to disciplinary action, up to and including termination.

EXAMPLES OF VIOLATIONS

[Provide some examples of potential violations of the privacy and security policy and procedure as previously discussed.]

11.1.4 Information System Activity Review— Required—45 CFR § 164.308(a)(1)(ii)(D)

A covered entity must have procedures in place to "regularly review records of information system activities." These information system activities may include audit logs, access reports, and security incident tracking reports. First, the covered entity should identify what types of auditing and activity reviewing functions the current information system is capable of providing. The covered entity should determine the types of logs or reports the information systems can generate. Second, the covered entity should determine whether these functions are adequately used and monitor appropriate activity to promote continual awareness of the information systems. Finally, there should be policies in place to establish the reviews that will be conducted on the information system activities and procedures to describe specifics of the reviews.

The formally documented systems activity process or procedure should detail the workforce member or department within the covered entity that is responsible for these processes. These procedures should also detail how often the information systems activities are reviewed and if there are any exceptions that may change the reporting process. The purpose for these systems activity processes is to demonstrate that there is an established continuous monitoring strategy implemented.

As part of this monitoring activity, a configuration management process needs to be in place. This configuration management process should determine if there are any security impacts that may affect the operational environment when changes are made to the information systems. These security issues may be identified through ongoing security controls assessments in accordance with the covered entity's information systems activity review. The covered entity's executive team should be kept updated on the security state of the information systems by making a report of such posture on a periodic basis.

The objective of this monitoring activity should be to identify or detect suspicious activities. Certain types of suspicious activities could indicate that an information system attack is occurring. For instance, a large amount of port scanning traffic could indicate that someone may be probing the information systems for vulnerabilities. Monitoring activity should also identify any unauthorized use of a system. This could be discovered by monitoring access to privileged accounts or directories that may contain electronic protected health information. Therefore, it is important to deploy monitoring devices strategically throughout the information systems to gather essential information and track interesting activity. In addition, monitoring activity should be increased whenever there is information received from credible sources that indicate the potential for increased risks to the covered entity's operations.

A general rule of thumb regarding monitoring activities is that a covered entity would be allowed to monitor activity on all information systems that they own. Common practice is to provide a notice of such monitoring to workforce members that are authorized (or unauthorized) to access these information systems. A sample notice can be found in Chapter 17, Section 17.2.1. A covered entity may want to consider obtaining a legal opinion as it relates to information system monitoring activities relevant to appropriate local laws, regulations, or other requirements.

Normal information system behaviors need to be baselined prior to determining what activity may be out of the norm. A covered entity needs to be able to manage its information systems in a manner that provides verification that any authorized devices or users accessing the network are authorized. One point of weakness in any information system is the initial setup of a new user or device on the network. At the start, these devices or users are foreign to the network making this a good place for a malicious person to target in an attempt to circumvent authentication controls that may be in place. The procedures for this initial authentication process need to be strong enough to counter any attempt to gain unauthorized access to the information systems or network.

These procedures need to address any loss, compromise, damage, or revocation of the authenticators. In most cases, these authenticators are a username and password combination to authenticate the identity of the individual or device gaining access to the network resources or information systems. Default settings or authenticators for new devices should be changed to reflect the standards that the covered entity has implemented. In addition, authenticators should be configured for minimum/ maximum and reuse restrictions. For instance, passwords should be changed every 30 days and a workforce member should not be able to use 1 of the last 10 passwords they used in the past. For specific network devices such as routers or switches, access credentials should also be changed on a periodic basis (i.e., quarterly).

It may go without saying, but passwords should not be shared between work-force members or kept written down in an unsecured fashion. If a list must be kept, it is imperative that special precautions be taken to protect these lists. For instance, there are several password storage software programs that utilize strong encryption to store credentials or these lists could be kept in paper form in a secured location like a fireproof safe.

Sanctions should be brought against any workforce member that violates the protection governing credentials. If any compromise of such credentials is sus-pected, it should be brought to the attention of the security official immediately and proper steps should be followed that are covered in the covered entity's incident response plan related to such activity.

The covered entity should refer to the following references for further details related to information system activity review:

- NIST SP 800-53 AC-25 Reference Monitor Function
- NIST SP 800-53 AU-13 Monitoring for Information Disclosure
- NIST SP 800-53 CA-7 Continuous Monitoring
- NIST SP 800-53 SI-4 Information System Monitoring
- NIST SP 800-53 IR-5 Authentication Management
- NIST SP 800-53 IR-6 Incident Reporting
- NIST SP 800-53 SC-35 Technical Surveillance Countermeasures Survey
- NIST SP 800-66 4.1.7 Develop and Deploy the Information System Activity Review Process
- NIST SP 800-66 4.1.8 Develop Appropriate Standard Operating Procedures
- NIST SP 800-66 4.1.9 Implement the Information System Activity Review and Audit Process

11.1.4.1 Sample of Information System Activity Review Policy

PURPOSE OF POLICY

To ensure that the individual's protected health information is used or disclosed in an appropriate manner and protected from unauthorized use or disclosure as set forth in the Privacy and Security Rule.

POLICY DETAIL

Personnel in [the covered entity's] Information Technology Department will be assigned responsibility to review access logs for information systems by each workforce member on a daily basis. Audit logs and security incident tracking reports will be reviewed periodically to identify any unauthorized access or attempted access to [the covered entity's] information systems. These reports will be run at least weekly, or when an incident is suspected of occurring, utilizing [insert software or monitoring solution].

All suspicious activities will be reported to the security official. Reports documenting suspicious activities will be maintained and will be made accessible to the security official.

11.1.5 Assigned Security Responsibility— Required—45 CFR §164.308(a)(2)

A security official will be designated. The security official is "responsible for the development and implementation of the [security] policies and procedures required by [the Security Rule]." The covered entity should clearly identify and document the responsibilities of the security official. The security official should also have the appropriate authority to carry out responsibilities within the covered entity. This means that a senior-level executive or manager should be assigned the security official role. Depending on the size, complexity, and technical capabilities of the covered entity, the roles and responsibilities of the security official should be

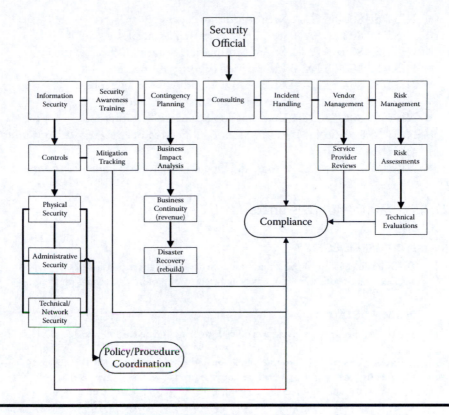

Figure 11.3   Security official's roles and responsibilities.

developed appropriately. The security official should be provided a complete job description that accurately reflects his or her security duties and responsibilities. In some instances, the security official may also be designated as the privacy official.

As part of the security official's roles and responsibilities, information systems for processing should initially be authorized prior to commencing operations and before any components are added. This security authorization should be periodically updated. In addition, the security official should be responsible for overseeing the development and communication of the covered entity's security policies and procedures. The security official is also responsible for constructing the covered entity's risk assessment and tracking the covered entity's periodic security evaluation results along with continuous monitoring. The security official may be the individual within the covered entity that can authorize the acceptance of information system risk items. Finally, the security official is responsible to ensure that security concerns of system implementations have been addressed along with directing any security purchases or security-related investments. See Figure 11.3.

The covered entity should refer to the following references for further details related to assigned security responsibilities:

- NIST SP 800-53 CA-6 Security Authorization
- NIST SP 800-53 SA-8 Security Engineering Principles
- NIST SP 800-53 PM-2 Senior Information Security Officer
- NIST SP 800-53 PM-3 Information Security Resources
- NIST SP 800-53 PM-4 Plan of Action and Milestones Process
- NIST SP 800-53 PM-10 Security Authorization Process
- NIST SP 800-53 PM-13 Information Security Workforce
- NIST SP 800-66 4.2.1 Select a Security Official to Be Assigned Responsibility for HIPAA Security
- NIST SP 800-66 4.2.2 Assign and Document the Individual's Responsibility

11.1.5.1 Sample of Designated Personnel Policy

PURPOSE OF POLICY

To ensure that appropriate personnel have been designated the responsibilities to carry out specific functions related to privacy and security of protected health information.

POLICY DETAIL

The HIPAA Security Rule requires officials to be designated as follows:

Privacy official—[Insert title of designated individual] [Note: The covered entity may want to use titles as opposed to individual names so that policies are not required to be changed if the person leaves employment] is designated as [the covered entity's] privacy official responsible for the policies, procedures, and the federal privacy regulations related to the HIPAA Privacy Rule. The privacy official may designate duties, roles, or assignments to workforce members as needed.

Responsibilities of the privacy official [not a complete list]
  - Responsible for the development and implementation of the policies and procedures related to compliance with the HIPAA Privacy Rules.
  - Development and maintenance of all forms or document requests related to protected health information.
  - Responsible for receiving and processing requests for amendments to individual's protected health information records.
  - Responsible for receiving and processing requests for accounting of protected health information.
  - Provide approval for any request of disclosure of protected health information.
  - Responsible for determining the seriousness of a Privacy Rule violation as it pertains to sanctions against a workforce member.
  - Responsible for determining the appropriate access levels to workforce members, contractors, business associates, and any other individual that may need access to protected health information.
  - Contact person for and determining proper guidance for any subpoenas, discovery requests, or other lawful process such as a judicial or administrative order.

- Contact person for any breach notifications and responsible for determining the proper course of action related to any confirmed or possible security breaches.
- Contact person for any complaints, for both internal and external individuals, regarding the violation of any HIPAA Privacy Rule.
- Conduct investigations into any complaints regarding the violation of any HIPAA Privacy Rule.
- Conducting appropriate Privacy Rule training for workforce members.
- Responsible for conducting risk analysis related to compliance with the HIPAA Privacy Rule.

Security official—[Insert title of designated individual] is designated as [the covered entity's] security official responsible for the policies, procedures, and the federal security regulations related to the HIPAA Security Rule.

Responsibilities of the security official [not a complete list]

- Responsible for the development and implementation of the policies and procedures related to compliance with the HIPAA Security Rule.
- Responsible for determining the seriousness of a Security Rule violation as it pertains to sanctions against a workforce member.
- Contact person for any breach notifications, or security incident, and responsible for determining the proper course of action related to any confirmed or possible security breaches.
- Conduct investigations into any complaints regarding the violation of any HIPAA Security Rule.
- Conduct appropriate Security Rule training for workforce members.
- Conduct audit reviews of information systems.
- Responsible for conducting risk analysis related to compliance with the HIPAA Security Rule.
- Responsible for assuring the appropriate levels of security and minimizing any problems associated with critical business functions.
- Responsible for assuring appropriate backups are conducted on the information system's data.
- Responsible for password management.

11.2 Workforce Security

A covered entity must "implement [adequate] policies and procedures to ensure that all members of its workforce have appropriate access to electronic protected health information." [Note: This is provided for under the Information Access Management standard.] In addition, covered entities must implement adequate policies and procedures to prevent those workforce members who do not have access under the Information Access Management standard from obtaining access to electronic protected health information.

A covered entity should have a formally documented personnel security policy in place. This policy should be well developed, disseminated, and reviewed or updated on a periodic basis. It should at least address the following: purpose, scope, roles, responsibilities, management commitment, coordination among departments of the covered entity, and compliance. In addition to this policy, a formally documented procedure should be developed for the implementation of the personnel security policy and associated controls.

The covered entity should refer to the following reference for further details related to workforce security:

■ NIST SP 800-66 4.3 Workforce Security

11.2.1 Authorization and/or Supervision— Addressable—45 CFR § 164.308(a)(3)(ii)(A)

There should be adequate implementation of "procedures for the authorization and/ or supervision of workforce members who work with electronic protected health information." This also includes implementation of procedures in locations where electronic protected health information may be accessed. Identifying the roles and responsibilities of each function within the covered entity is one way in which appropriate access levels could be determined. Based upon the job description, appropriate access levels to electronic protected health information should be provided to the workforce member. In addition, a covered entity should determine the individual, whether a supervisor or manager, who is authorized to provide access to electronic protected health information to a workforce member. So as not to create additional work, a covered entity should look at existing processes involving paper records to assist in determining the appropriate levels of access to electronic protected health information.

A covered entity should have a written list detailing the workforce members who have a business need to view, alter, retrieve, or store electronic protected health information. In addition to this need, the person granting the workforce member authorization should be noted along with the times, circumstances, and purposes that this workforce member is entitled to such information.

Job descriptions should detail the roles and set of qualifications of each workforce member as it relates to the appropriate levels of access to electronic protected health information. It may go without saying that an individual should be determined capable and qualified for the position that he or she is in relevant to the job description of that position. Each position should report to one and only one supervisor or manager in an effort to establish clear lines of authority. Workforce members should be provided a copy of their job descriptions that should lay out their conditions of access to certain protected health information along with making them aware of the specific individual that supervises them. Along with the job description, workforce members should sign an appropriate access agreement before allowing them access to any covered entity's information systems. These access agreements should be reviewed and updated on a periodic basis.

A covered entity needs to address all roles within the organization including maintenance personnel. Since these personnel may have access to protected health information after hours or perform technical maintenance duties as needed, it is imperative that a process is established for providing them authorization and that a current list of these individuals is maintained.

Along with maintenance personnel, security roles and responsibilities should be established for third-party service providers. Certain security requirements should be established for these providers in accordance with the covered entity's security policies. These service providers should also be monitored by the covered entity for compliance with these requirements.

The covered entity should refer to the following references for further details related to authorization and supervision:

- NIST SP 800-53 MA-5 Maintenance Personnel
- NIST SP 800-53 PS-6 Access Agreements
- NIST SP 800-53 PS-7 Third-Party Personnel Security
- NIST SP 800-66 4.3.1 Implement Procedures for Authorization and/or Supervision
- NIST SP 800-66 4.3.2 Establish Clear Job Descriptions and Responsibilities
- NIST SP 800-66 4.3.3 Establish Criteria and Procedures for Hiring and Assigning Tasks

11.2.2 Workforce Clearance Procedure—Addressable—45 CFR § 164.308(a)(3)(ii)(B)

A covered entity should have procedures in place for determining the appropriate access levels workforce members have to necessary information. These procedures should be standard across the entire organization when determining access of related workforce job functions. As discussed earlier, a workforce member's job function or role should determine what access level that individual has to protected health information. Job roles and functions will also determine if the individual is not required to have and should be prevented from accessing protected health information. These access levels should follow the minimum necessary standards.

Each workforce member's position should be assigned a risk designation. As previously discussed, individuals filling these positions should be properly screened in accordance with established criteria. In addition, these risk designations should be reviewed on a periodic basis and revised as necessary as part of the covered entity's periodic rescreening process. Prior to filling any position, prospective workforce members should be properly screened. Background checks should be conducted to ensure that an individual does not have a criminal record and that educational and employment references are validated as is reasonably appropriate for the position to be filled. A covered entity should have a formally documented procedure in place to obtain sign-offs to grant and terminate access to electronic protected health information.

The covered entity should refer to the following references for further details related to workforce clearance:

- NIST SP 800-53 PS-2 Position Categorization
- NIST SP 800-53 PS-3 Personnel Screening
- NIST SP 800-66 4.3.4 Establish a Workforce Clearance Procedure

11.2.3 Termination Procedures—Addressable—45 CFR § 164.308(a)(3)(ii)(C)

If a workforce member leaves the employment of a covered entity, there needs to be a termination policy and procedure in place. This policy, or procedure, should assign an individual, or department, responsibility for removing the workforce member from access to an information system. The workforce member also needs to be denied physical access to the facility. The communication of such termination needs to be conducted in a timely manner so that actions can be immediately taken to prevent any unauthorized access of a terminated workforce member. To verify compliance with policies and procedures implemented to handle terminated workforce members, active and disabled account lists should be reviewed on the information system to ensure only authorized workforce members have access to these systems. In cases of workforce members such as system administrators that may have elevated privileges, a review of these privileged groups should be conducted to ensure that all access has been disabled for these workforce members.

Covered entities need to address different types of separations or terminations of their workforce members. For instance, there could be voluntary termination that may include voluntary separation where a workforce member changes employment or a workforce member may retire. There could also be changes within the organization that require elevated or de-escalation of privileges for such events as promotions, transfers, or internal changes in employment. There may be cases of involuntary termination to include criminal or disciplinary actions against workforce members, reduction in workforce, involuntary transfers, or termination with cause. A covered entity should have separate procedures to handle these different termination events.

Covered entities should consider having a standard termination checklist. This list should include certain activities that are required to occur when a workforce member leaves employment. The list may include returning physical access control devices such as keys, badges, cards, and fobs. The list should include terminating access to information systems such as deactivating user accounts for the network and all applications, remote access, and returning any electronic assets that may be assigned to the workforce member such as laptops, PDAs, and cell phones. The list should request the return of all data or information that may be in possession or under control of the workforce member. Finally, a covered entity should have an exit interview with the terminated workforce member to cover all terms or conditions of the termination.

The covered entity should refer to the following references for further details related to workforce termination procedures:

- NIST SP 800-53 PS-4 Personnel Termination
- NIST SP 800-53 PS-5 Personnel Transfer
- NIST SP 800-66 4.3.5 Establish Termination Procedures

11.2.4 Sample of Workforce Security Policy

PURPOSE OF POLICY

To ensure that the individual's protected health information is used or disclosed in an appropriate manner and protected from unauthorized use or disclosure as set forth in the Privacy and Security Rules.

POLICY DETAIL

[The covered entity's] classes of workforce members and appropriate access profiles are described in the Information Access Management policy. At times, changes to access levels of an individual workforce member may be necessary for promotions, demotions, or changes in job functions. The IT Department will receive such requests via the [Employee Access Profile Authorization Form] signed by the workforce member's supervisor. Upon termination of any workforce member, human resources will notify the IT Department immediately via e-mail or by phone to disable any access privileges that the workforce member has to protected health information. The human resources department will follow up with [an Employee Termination Access Form] as documentation for the removal of access of the workforce member. The IT Department will review access privileges on a weekly basis to ensure that only current workforce members have appropriate access rights to the information systems and report any changes to the security official.

11.3 Information Access Management

Per 45 CFR § 164.308(a)(4)(i), a covered entity should "implement [adequate] policies and procedures for access authorization to electronic protected health information that are consistent with the applicable [Privacy Rule requirements]." To start the implementation process, a covered entity should set up different types of classes (or groups) based on the different job functions or roles of the members of the workforce. In addition, different classifications should be developed for the types of information that the covered entity creates, maintains, or transmits. This information may include protected health information, business-related sensitive or confidential information, and public information. Protected health information has already been discussed; however, a covered entity is normally in the business to continue operations and will generally have information that is specific to its own business. Confidential or proprietary information could include information that is owned, licensed, or possessed by the covered entity that must be protected. This information could be trade secrets or other information regarding the covered entity's business relationships. Public information is information that is available to the public. Examples of public information include marketing and advertising information that may be available on the covered entity's Web site. The covered entity could utilize other types of classifications of information as it may apply to its environment. Table 11.2 shows an example of different classes and access profiles to information based on the workforce job roles.

The covered entity should refer to the following references for further details related to information access management:

■ NIST SP 800-53 AC-21 Collaboration and Information Sharing
■ NIST SP 800-53 AC-22 Publicly Accessible Content
■ NIST SP 800-53 AC-23 Data Mining Protection
■ NIST SP 800-53 SC-7 Boundary Protection
■ NIST SP 800-66 4.4 Information Access Management

11.3.1 Isolating Healthcare Clearinghouse Functions— Required—45 CFR § 164.308(a)(4)(ii)(A)

As discussed, a healthcare clearinghouse, acting as a business associate for a covered entity, may receive a nonstandard (or standard) transaction and translate it into a standard (or nonstandard, respectively) transaction to transmit to (or on behalf of) the covered entity. A covered entity is required to isolate healthcare clearinghouse functions. To comply with this requirement, the covered entity should determine if a healthcare clearinghouse is part of a larger organization. If it is, the covered entity should determine if the clearinghouse implements "policies and procedures that protect the electronic protected health information of the clearinghouse from unauthorized access by the larger organization." In addition, it should be identified whether the larger organization performs healthcare clearinghouse functions.

Once the determination has been made on these healthcare clearinghouse functions, the covered entity should identify and determine whether additional technical safeguards are necessary to separate electronic protected health information between the larger organization and the healthcare clearinghouse functions. Remember that the goal of this determination is to make sure that electronic protected health information used by the healthcare clearinghouse is protected against unauthorized access by the larger organization.

The covered entity should refer to the following reference for further details related to isolating healthcare clearinghouse functions:

■ NIST SP 800-66 4.4.1 Isolate Healthcare Clearinghouse Functions

11.3.2 Access Authorization—Addressable—45 CFR § 164.308(a)(4)(ii)(B)

The covered entity should "implement policies and procedures for granting access to electronic protected health information." Although this section is addressable, as

Table 11.2 Job Classes and Access Profiles

Job Title, Job Group, or Job Description	Description of the Type (or Category) of Information that Requires Access	Access Profile (Physical or Logical)
Chief Executive Officer	PHI, Business Sensitive, Confidential, Public	Unlimited Access to all PHI; Unlimited Access to All Business Sensitive, Confidential, and Public Information
Chief Financial Officer	PHI, Business Sensitive, Confidential, Public	Limited Access to PHI as it relates to accounting functions; Unlimited Access to All Business Sensitive, Confidential, and Public Information
Chief Medical Officer	PHI and Public	Unlimited Access to all PHI and Public Information
Chief Operating Officer	PHI, Business Sensitive, Confidential, Public	Limited Access to PHI as it relates to the operational functions; Unlimited Access to All Business Sensitive, Confidential, and Public Information
Chief Administrative Officer	PHI, Business Sensitive, Confidential, Public	Limited Access to PHI as it relates to the operational functions; Unlimited Access to All Business Sensitive, Confidential, and Public Information
Privacy Official or Security Official	PHI, Business Sensitive, Confidential, Public	Unlimited access to all information
Legal Counsel	Determined by Privacy Officer	Limited access to information to provide legal advice to the covered entity; determined on a case-by-case basis

Continued

Table 11.2 (*Continued*)   Job Classes and Access Profiles

Job Title, Job Group, or Job Description	Description of the Type (or Category) of Information that Requires Access	Access Profile (Physical or Logical)
IT Group	PHI, Business Sensitive, Confidential, Public	Unlimited access to all information for setup and maintaining security of information
Human Resource Group	PHI, Business Sensitive, Confidential, Public	Limited access to employee PHI and access to other information as required by job functions
Accounting Group	PHI, Business Sensitive, Confidential, Public	Limited access to employee PHI and access to other information as required by job functions
Marketing Group	Business Sensitive, Confidential, Public	Limited Access based on job functions
Physician Group	PHI, Confidential, Public	Full access to PHI; limited access to other information based on job functions
Nursing Group	PHI, Confidential, Public	Full access to PHI; limited access to other information based on job functions
Medical Records Group	PHI, Confidential, Public	Full access to PHI; limited access to other information based on job functions
Medical Billing Group	PHI, Confidential, Public	Full access to PHI; limited access to other information based on job functions

Note: PHI = protected health information.

discussed earlier, this does not mean that a covered entity should not comply with this standard. The covered entity should take into consideration different factors on how it will comply with this standard. For instance, the covered entity should determine how access to the following is granted and maintained: workstations, transactions, programs, processes, and other mechanisms related to electronic protected health information. The covered entity should document this authorization in such a way that it can easily determine how access is granted and by whose authority this access is authorized.

The policies and procedures granting access should be consistent with applicable requirements of the HIPAA Privacy Rule. These policies and procedures should also include appropriate authorization and clearance procedures prior to granting access that is in line with the workforce security procedures. Again, these procedures should be formally documented, auditable, and approved by a manager or supervisor. There should also be specific access rules to applications and systems based on a workforce member's job functions. In addition, there should be stronger controls over the access of data that is considered more sensitive.

Related to access authorization, the covered entity should take into consideration the formal verification process that is in place prior to resetting a workforce member's account. Most information systems will lock an account out after a certain number of failed log-on attempts. Since it is recommended that account passwords be changed on a routine basis, workforce members will have a tendency to forget or type in their passwords wrong. This leads to their accounts being locked and access restricted. For this reason, there should be procedures in place to validate the identity of a workforce member requesting an account reset. In small organizations, all workforce members will personally know each other so a phone call to the IT help desk with caller ID and voice verification will suffice. In larger organizations, workforce members may not know one another. In this case, an "out-of-bounds" validation should be used. For instance, the IT help desk could have another database with secret questions or personal identification numbers (PINs). If a workforce member calls in to reset their account, the help desk personnel could ask them a secret question (or request a PIN) and validate the answer (or PIN) in the out-of-bounds database. Once this validation is made, the account can be reset or a password can be changed on the account.

Another possible solution to comply with access authorization at the network level consists of implementing a media access control (MAC) filtering or port security solution. This is more of a technical safeguard whereby devices are authorized to connect to the network on top of authorizing users. This is an additional level of security that is very effective in preventing unauthorized devices from connecting to the network. In addition, this type of solution also provides monitoring and alerting functions to identify any devices that immediately try to communicate on the network.

A covered entity may decide to authorize remote access to certain workforce members to allow them access to data or applications housed on a covered entity's internal network from external remote locations. Although there are some very effective solutions that can be implemented to protect the data while in transit and that could make remote access just as safe as if a workforce member was connected to the internal network while on site, special considerations and procedures should be developed to address remote access users. For instance, does the covered entity require remote users to utilize only assigned laptops that have been configured by the covered entity's IT staff? Does the remote access solution require multifactor authentication such as a username–password combination along with a hardware or software token? Does the remote device have security controls configured such as antivirus software installed, restrictions on access, encryption of data while in transit or while being stored, firewall protection, and so forth?

A covered entity may utilize several different types of business associates that may require certain access to data or information controlled by the covered entity. A covered entity should have policies and procedures in place to address or determine if direct access will be provided to these third-party providers. These third-party providers could include health plans, business associates, or other healthcare providers. Furthermore, a covered entity may decide to provide certain access to patients. If a covered entity allows for its patients to access their electronic protected health information, special considerations and security controls need to be implemented so that patients can only view their own information and not any other patient's information. In addition, there needs to be an appropriate validation method to verify that the patient requesting the information is the identified individual authorized to obtain this information.

The covered entity should refer to the following references for further details related to access authorization:

- NIST SP 800-53 PS-3 Access Agreements
- NIST SP 800-53 PS-7 Third-Party Personnel Security
- NIST SP 800-66 4.4.2 Implement Policies and Procedures for Authorizing Access

11.3.2.1 Sample of Access Authorization Policy

PURPOSE OF POLICY

To ensure that the individual's protected health information is used or disclosed in an appropriate manner and protected from unauthorized use or disclosure as set forth in the Privacy and Security Rules.

POLICY DETAIL

[The covered entity] must implement facility and device access controls to protect devices that store electronic protected health information through the use of, but not limited to, the following: safeguards built into the construction of the facility; theft prevention devices; intrusion prevention/detection solutions; metal keys; badge access; cipher locks; enhanced security mechanical locks; escorting visitors; fire alerting and extinguishing solutions; and the development of access profiles for workforce members. Once the need or usefulness of any data is stored on any device or media, there should be controls in place for the proper sanitation and destruction of these devices or media so that the electronic protected health information cannot be used. To corroborate a workforce member's identity, authentication controls will be implemented. To prevent the unauthorized alteration or destruction of electronic protected health information, validation controls will be implemented. [Describe any other physical or technical access controls that the covered entity may have in place.]

The security official, or the designated workforce member, will be responsible for maintaining and monitoring the above physical and technical access controls implemented. The security official will also be responsible for recommending and implementing additional safeguards, when necessary, to decrease the risk of unauthorized access to protected health information to an acceptable level.

The security official, or the designated workforce member, will be responsible for maintaining this policy and documenting the effectives of all physical and technical controls implemented.

11.3.3 Access Establishment and Modification— Addressable—45 § CFR 164.308 (a)(4)(ii)(C)

This standard addresses the policies and procedures in place for establishing access and modifying access to electronic protected health information. The covered entity should have policies and procedures that document system access and these policies and procedures should be updated as necessary. Furthermore, management, or other assigned workforce members, should periodically review the list of workforce members that have access to electronic protected health information to ensure these workforce members have authorized access. Only valid users, consistent with the covered entity's policies and procedures, should have access as appropriate to electronic protected health information. Management should be required to sign off on such access and workforce members should be granted the minimum amount of privileges necessary to perform their assigned job duties.

In addition to workforce member access, all software upgrades, hardware replacement, or other network changes or modifications should be formally documented. There should be procedures in place to cover these types of modifications that could have an effect on access to electronic protected health information. These change management processes should require approval and authorization from management and include "back-out" procedures. Back-out procedures are detailed instructions on how to get the information system, software, or network back to its original condition before a modification to these systems occurs. Before any major changes that could affect the confidentiality, integrity, or availability of protected health information takes place, these modifications should be tested. Testing of modifications could occur within a specified network or system utilized for such testing or it could be done on a small sample of systems prior to deploying the changes to all the systems that are in the production environment.

It is important that security access controls align with other technical or operational areas. For instance, a workforce member having the authority to access electronic assets in the server room for maintenance should, of course, have physical access to this area. Furthermore, audit trails of this workforce member accessing these assets should be reviewed and aligned with the member's assigned privileges. Systems in place to monitor and identify the authorization of this workforce member should align with the policies and procedures that were implemented to allow this member access to the server room in the first place. In this demonstration, a simple event such as someone entering the area where critical electronic assets are stored can become very complex in terms of securing these assets. All the administrative, physical, and technical controls must be aligned to allow for a simple operational event such as maintenance to a server.

The covered entity should refer to the following references for further details related to access establishment and modification:

- NIST SP 800-66 4.4.3 Implement Policies and Procedures for Access Establishment and Modification
- NIST SP 800-66 4.4.4 Evaluate Existing Security Measures Related to Access Controls

11.3.3.1 Sample of Access Establishment and Modification Policy

PURPOSE OF POLICY

To ensure that the individual's protected health information is used or disclosed in an appropriate manner and protected from unauthorized use or disclosure as set forth in the Privacy and Security Rules.

POLICY DETAIL

[The covered entity] will implement procedures to establish appropriate access levels of workforce members to electronic protected health information based on the workforce member's roles, responsibilities, and functions in the organization related to minimum necessary standards of access to this information. [The covered entity] will modify these access levels of the workforce members in cases of promotions, demotions, transfers, or when access to electronic protected health information is no longer required. When a workforce member leaves or is terminated for any reason, access to electronic protected health information will be immediately prevented.

11.4 Security Awareness Training

A covered entity should provide adequate security awareness training to all members of its workforce including management or executive level personnel. Although the next few security awareness training sections are addressable, this does not mean that a covered entity is not required to provide this type of training to its workforce; rather, a covered entity has discretion on how it will comply with these standards. A covered entity should have a formally documented security awareness training policy that addresses at least the following elements: purpose, scope, roles and responsibilities, commitment from management, unit coordination, and, of course, compliance. This policy should be reviewed on a regular basis and updated accordingly along with being disseminated to workforce members as applicable.

Along with a formally documented policy, a covered entity should have a formally documented procedure to implement the security awareness training policy. This procedure should assist in the implementation of security controls. This procedure should include providing security awareness training as part of a new workforce member's initial training. This procedure should also include management level members and contractors as appropriate. When there are major system changes that may affect the security of the system, new training procedures should be developed and disseminated to workforce members. Like the policy, the procedure for security awareness training should be updated periodically.

To stay current on security trends, it is important that a covered entity seek out and participate in security-related groups and associations. There are several such groups throughout the security community. An Internet search will reveal several well-known and reputable groups. These groups should be able to assist a covered entity in providing ongoing security awareness education for workforce members along with sharing current security-related information such as new threats and vulnerabilities. These groups should also be able to keep a covered entity up to date with the latest security technologies, practices, and techniques.

When developing security awareness training material, it is important to determine the covered entity's security training needs. Key workforce members should assist in the development of these security training needs. These security training needs should take into consideration security around sensitive data and of course, electronic protected health information. An analysis should be conducted to determine the needs related to security awareness training and what programs may be available to fulfill those needs. A training strategy and plan should be developed and approved along with appropriate awareness and training content, materials, and methods. To show compliance with the security awareness training requirements, proper documentation should be maintained and workforce members' training should be tracked accordingly.

The covered entity should refer to the following references for further details related to security awareness training:

- NIST SP 800-53 AT-1 Security Awareness and Training Policies and Procedures
- NIST SP 800-53 AT-2 Security Awareness
- NIST SP 800-53 AT-3 Security Training
- NIST SP 800-53 AT-4 Security Training Records
- NIST SP 800-53 AT-5 Contacts with Security Groups and Associations
- NIST SP 800-66 4.5 Security Awareness and Training
- NIST SP 800-66 4.5.1 Conduct a Training Needs Assessment
- NIST SP 800-66 4.5.2 Develop and Approve a Training Strategy and Plan
- NIST SP 800-66 4.5.4 Develop Appropriate Awareness and Training Content, Materials and Methods
- NIST SP 800-66 4.5.5 Implement the Training
- NIST SP 800-66 4.5.7 Monitor and Evaluate Training Plan

11.4.1 Sample of Security Awareness Training Policy

POLICY STATEMENT

It is the policy of [the covered entity] to train all of its workforce members, including management and executive-level officers, on the HIPAA Privacy Rule and Security Rules policies and procedures. This training will be aligned and appropriate to the workforce member's functions within the organization when it comes to the use and disclosure of protected health information.

POLICY SCOPE

This policy applies to all workforce members of [the covered entity].

PURPOSE OF POLICY

This policy sets forth the type of training that workforce members will receive as required by the HIPAA Privacy Rule and Security Rule.

POLICY DETAIL

[The covered entity] will provide HIPAA Privacy and Security Rule training to each workforce member within 30 days of their initial hire date and at least annually thereafter. In addition, upon a material change to these policies and procedures, all workforce members will receive training on these modifications as it pertains to their roles dealing with protected health information within a reasonable period of time.

Training will contain:

- Security awareness in the form of live lecture or video-based training
- Policies and procedure training
- Training reminders through e-mails, bulletin boards, pamphlets, workforce meetings, newsletters, Web site, etc.
- Formal policy and procedure training memos
- Details on sanctions

[The covered entity] will document all training provided by maintaining the policies and procedures in written or electronic form. All workforce members will document attendance by signing an attendance list if in a classroom session, through completing a quiz as proof of completion of training, or by logging attendance if participating in a video-based training seminar. These training documents will be retained for 6 years from the date of its creation or the date it was last in effect, whichever is later.

11.4.2 Security Reminders—Addressable—45 CFR § 164.308(a)(5)(ii)A)

As seen in the preceding sample policy, covered entities should develop "periodic security updates." Security is an ongoing process and workforce members tend to become complacent about security over time. It is common practice to provide updates, or security reminders, through printed flyers or in electronic form such as e-mail. Workforce meetings can be a practical place to provide security tips as agenda items or discuss specific topics related to security issues. Postings in common areas such as the lunchroom or where workforce members pick up their mail can be good locations to post security reminders. Of course, nothing could be better than formal training or retraining on security.

The covered entity should refer to the following references for further details related to security reminders:

- ■ NIST SP 800-53 SI-5 Security Alerts, Advisories, and Directives
- ■ NIST SP 800-66 4.6 Implement Security Reminders

11.4.3 Protection from Malicious Software—Addressable—45 CFR § 164.308(a)(5)(ii)(B)

An enterprise-level antivirus solution should be installed on all workstations and servers. There should be adequate procedures in place for "guarding against" malicious software. This solution should also *detect* and *report* on types of malware, viruses, spyware, Trojans, back doors, suspicious programs, open ports, and so on. There are several different credible software vendors that produce good antivirus solutions. Each one of these solutions comes with its own pros and cons along with different pricing structures. A discussion will not take place on all the different brands of antivirus here; suffice it to say that any solution chosen should come from a reputable source and the covered entity should conduct its own due diligence in choosing the right solution to meet its needs. The antivirus solution should be controlled from a central console that can provide a report of all the systems that have been updated with new virus definitions and report on any possible viruses that were detected.

Consideration should be made for multiple levels of virus detection when dealing with e-mail. Since e-mail is one of the most common ways that systems get infected, there should be at least three different layers of protection. First, before the e-mail even enters any internal systems, it should be scanned by an external device or third-party service provider. This device, or provider, should be utilizing a different antivirus engine than what is installed inside of the organization. Any executable files should be extracted or filtered at this level prior to entering the internal network. Second, once the e-mail arrives inside of the network, to an internal e-mail server, for instance, the e-mail server should have its own antivirus solution. Again, this antivirus engine should be different than the antivirus engine installed on the workstations. Finally, each workstation receiving e-mail for an end user should have a different antivirus engine than those already installed on the e-mail server or at the perimeter e-mail device. This comes out to three different antivirus engines scanning e-mail before it is opened or read by the end user.

Recently, an Indiana hospital was a victim of an unidentified malware attack that compromised a server used to collect data from Web forms such as names, addresses, and Social Security numbers. Most of the 12,000 individuals affected were applying for jobs at Goshen Hospital. However, there appeared to be some outpatient information as well. The malware was described as "relatively common" but "malicious," which begs the question of why it was not discovered sooner? The moral of this story is to make sure that the antivirus solution implemented is working appropriately and kept up to date (Dunn 2012).

A specific person or group, such as the IT Department, should be responsible for conducting vulnerability management efforts. This person, or group, should receive regular notification of new vulnerabilities that software vendors have made public for their applications. Mitigating strategies, especially for high or critical-type vulnerabilities, should be implemented within a reasonable amount of time. Normally, software vendors will put out patches to correct these vulnerabilities. These patches should be deployed to applicable systems within 30 days of their official release. Of course, these patches should be tested since it has been the case that patches may cause issues with a specific system. Since every network is configured differently and has different programs installed, a patch that works just fine on one system may cause major issues with another system.

To deploy and manage patches, it is recommended that an automated patch management solution be implemented. This automated patch management solution should be able to deploy patches to several systems concurrently. The patch management solution should be able to report on the status of the patches for each system.

A vulnerability assessment should be conducted on the entire network at least annually, or when there are any major changes to the network, to validate and verify that critical or security-related patches are being deployed appropriately. Although a patch management system may be implemented, it has been the author's experience that on occasion these solutions may falsely report the status of updates and leave certain systems vulnerable to attack. *Trust but validate* is a good rule to follow.

As part of the security awareness training, workforce members should be trained on the proper procedures regarding the use of software. Malicious software can be a big problem and workforce members need to be trained on how to handle encounters with these types of programs. Although technical controls can assist in guarding against the installation and detection of malicious software, the end users need to know that they should not attempt to download, install, or click on any links that may allow downloading or installation of unauthorized software programs. Workforce members need to be aware of the procedures for reporting such attempts to the appropriate security official or designated IT personnel.

The covered entity should refer to the following references for further details related to protection from malicious software:

- NIST SP 800-53 SC-38 Malware Analysis
- NIST SP 800-66 4.5.3 Protection from Malicious Software, Log-in Monitoring, and Password Management

11.4.4 Log-In Monitoring—Addressable—45 CFR § 164.308(a)(5)(ii)(C)

To verify that appropriate access is being maintained, the covered entity should have adequate procedures in place to monitor any log-in attempts. These procedures should also report any discrepancies between those accesses that are permitted and those that should be denied. The following are some recommendations for logging parameters:

- Account logon—Success and failure auditing
- Account management—Success and failure auditing
- Directory service access—Failure auditing
- Logon events—Success and failure auditing
- Object access—Success and failure auditing
- Policy change—Success and failure auditing
- Privilege use—Success and failure auditing
- Process tracking—Failure auditing
- System events—Success and failure auditing

A covered entity should implement a system log (or syslog) server that can collect all the audit logs from different sources such as internal servers and routers. This syslog server will allow the aggregation of information and should be able to produce reports to show suspicious activity or behavior. The syslog should allow writing of logs from the different sources but allow read-only access to the user to prevent any unauthorized manipulation of the log events. These logs should be reviewed on at least a weekly basis or when unusual activity is suspected. There should be a specific individual, or group of individuals, assigned the responsibility of reviewing these logs. These logs should be kept for 6 years to maintain consistency with other requirements of the HIPAA Security Rule.

These logs can become large in size and take up a considerable amount of hard drive space depending on the activity that occurs on the network. Special considerations should be made to monitor resources dedicated for log monitoring. It is recommended to maintain at least 30 days of network logs readily available on logging systems with the ability to archive these logs on other media such as tapes or larger hard drives.

As part of security awareness training, workforce members need to be aware that their activity is monitored. Any suspicious activity or discrepancies outside of normal activities should be investigated.

The covered entity should refer to the following reference for further details related to log-in monitoring:

■ NIST SP 800-66 4.5.3 Protection from Malicious Software, Log-in Monitoring, and Password Management

11.4.5 Password Management—Addressable—45 CFR § 164.308(a)(5)(ii)(D)

A covered entity should have procedures in place for "creating, changing, and safeguarding passwords." Since passwords are one of the most common ways to validate access to an information system, it goes without saying that these passwords need to be protected. As a way to protect against individuals performing particular actions as another individual, policies should state that workforce members under no circumstances should share their passwords with others. In addition, the workforce member should commit their password to memory and not write their passwords down in a notebook. From experiences, this author has found passwords written on sticky notes taped to the underside of keyboards, taped to monitors, or written in a Rolodex under *P* for passwords. An emphasis should be made through security awareness training that a common sense approach should be used to maintain the security over workforce members' passwords.

As a note of reference, usernames are the first half of the username–password combination utilized in most information systems. The covered entity should consider making usernames unique just like the passwords to make it more difficult for brute force password-type attacks. Since it is common practice to use a part of the workforce member's name, it is pretty easy to figure out the username. In a brute force attack, once the username is known, the attacker can run through a list of passwords to see if a common password was used. If a lockout parameter was not set, it is just a matter of time before an account is compromised.

It is recommended that all initial passwords for new accounts be unique. Passwords should never be left blank, be the same as the username, the name of the covered entity, or a hybrid (i.e., combination) of these items. Passwords should be complex utilizing lowercase and uppercase letters, numbers, and special symbols. A good password is one that is at least 8 characters for a limited user type account and at least 15 characters for an administrative level account. A user should use a password for at least 3 days before they are allowed to change it. [An exception for this minimum password age setting would be to set this to 1 day as long as the last 20 passwords or more are remembered.] Passwords should be changed every 30 days and the system should remember at least the last 10 passwords. Accounts should lock out after three failed attempts and stay locked out until an administrator unlocks them. A group policy, if applicable, should be set so that the systems lock with a password protected screen saver after 15 minutes of inactivity.

As part of the security awareness training, workforce members need to be trained on password management. This includes creating strong passwords, routinely changing these passwords, and making sure to secure these passwords.

The covered entity should refer to the following reference for further details related to password management:

■ NIST SP 800-66 4.5.3 Protection from Malicious Software, Log-in Monitoring, and Password Management

11.4.5.1 Sample of Password Policy

PURPOSE OF POLICY

To ensure that the individual's protected health information is used or disclosed in an appropriate manner and protected from unauthorized use or disclosure as set forth in the Privacy and Security Rules.

POLICY DETAIL

The Security Official, or designated workforce member, is responsible for password management. This will include designing procedures related to the required length, complexity, number of log-in attempts, monitoring, terminating, and session inactivity.

[Note: Procedures should be developed to outline the specifics of this policy. A covered entity may choose to place these specifics in the policy, but if the parameters change, these policies may need to go to the board for their approval. Procedures may be a little easier to change when needed.]

11.5 Security Incident Procedures

Security incidents are those situations where it is believed that protected health information has been used or disclosed in an unauthorized fashion. A security incident can also be the actual unauthorized access, use, or disclosure of such information or the modification or destruction of this information. Any interference with system operations of an information system can also be considered a security incident. Several different examples of security incidents will be provided in the following section and Chapter 14 is devoted to how to appropriately handle these types of security violations.

The covered entity should refer to the following reference for further details related to security incidents:

■ NIST SP 800-66 4.6 Security Incident Procedures

11.5.1 Response and Reporting—Required—45 CFR § 164.308(a)(6)(ii)

Covered entities must implement adequate policies and procedures to address security incidents. This includes identifying and responding to suspected or known security issues or breaches. As required in other standards, a covered entity should have monitoring solutions implemented and capable of alerting workforce members when suspicious activity occurs on the network. Workforce members should be auditing and reviewing higher risk activities to ensure that policies and procedures are being followed. To a reasonable extent, the covered entity should implement mitigation strategies against known vulnerabilities that will protect them from any harmful effects from a security incident. For instance, critical severity patches issued by software vendors should be installed on production systems within 30 days of release. In addition, malicious code protection software, such as antivirus solutions, should run real-time scanning activities and be kept up to date on a continuous basis.

Some of the known vulnerabilities that a covered entity should be prepared for and have policies or procedures in place to handle are the following:

- Passwords that may be stolen or accounts that may be used in an unauthorized manner to obtain access to electronic protected health information
- Backup solutions that do not work or tapes that become corrupted, which does not allow the restoration of electronic protected health information
- Information systems that contain electronic protected health information that get infected with viruses or malware
- Burglaries that lead to the theft of media or devices containing electronic protected health information
- Failure to follow policies and procedures such as those involving the deletion of accounts utilized by former employees that may be used by another individual for the unauthorized access to electronic protected health information
- Allowing unauthorized users to utilize laptops, hard drives, removable drives, or other media that contains electronic protected health information
- Any potential physical or technical events that have been discovered through the HIPAA-required security risk assessment

Policies and procedures should identify the individual workforce member responsible for handling security incidents and to whom these incidents should be reported. Normally, the security official is the designated individual for making a report and handling of security incidents. However, the covered entity may decide to designate this role to another workforce member under the direction of the security official.

As already discussed, the covered entity should have a formal incident management policy in place for reporting information security events. This policy should address the establishment of an incident response team that should include IT, security, audit, legal, public relations, or other workforce members that may be affected by the event. The policy (or procedure) should address specific responsibilities of each of the assigned incident response team members and those workforce members that should react to any type of security incident.

The documented incident response procedures should provide the covered entity with a single point of reference as a guide for the daily operations of the incident response team. Based on a myriad of known or expected scenarios identified through the covered entity's risk assessment, specific actions in certain timeframes should be defined in the policies and procedures. There should also be a formal escalation procedure to follow. Notification and the proper communication of a security incident are essential so that all relevant workforce members can react appropriately. Procedures for notifying workforce members, legal, law enforcement, insurance companies, forensic experts, regulators, the media, and individuals that may be affected by the security incident should be developed. This procedure may name a specific individual or group of individuals that will be authorized to speak on the covered entities' behalf to the media, law enforcement, clients, business associates, or others.

It should go without saying that policies and procedures should require workforce members (or business associates) to report any suspected or observed security violation. If a workforce member or business associate becomes aware of a possible vulnerability that threatens the security of the covered entity's protected health information, these situations should also be reported. The covered entity should develop a mechanism for tracking security incidents that include quantifying and monitoring types of incidents, volumes of activity, and the costs associated with any security incident. The covered entity may find it helpful to develop a standard incident reporting template to ensure that all necessary information is obtained. IT staff should be knowledgeable in the ways to properly handle a security incident including the proper steps to collect any digital evidence. If resources are not available in-house, then an outside expert, such as a forensic expert or law enforcement, should be brought in to handle these situations.

The incident response policy, like other policies, should cover at least the following components: purpose, scope, responsibilities, management commitment, coordination among different departments, and, of course, compliance. These policies should be formally documented, disseminated, and reviewed and updated on a periodic basis (i.e., annually or upon any major changes that affect incident handling). Remember, the goal of incident management is to reduce the risks inherent in securing protected health information and to mitigate any harmful events from the possible exploitation of vulnerabilities.

Throughout Chapter 14, the implementation of an incident response plan that will be capable of preparing the covered entity to handle security incidents will be detailed. This plan will also detail the detection and analysis of a security incident along with the containment, eradication, and recovery if an incident occurs.

Incident handling activities need to be coordinated with contingency planning activities. Several elements that cause disruptions, especially when dealing with electronic information systems, may derive from a security incident. There is no reason why two separate plans need to address the same issues, but rather one concise procedure could cover multiple situations. To do this, the covered entity will want to look at the underlying general framework rather than specific elements. For instance, if a system was brought down due to malicious software, the recovery procedure could be reinstalling the system from known good media. Although incident response could lead to further investigation on how the malicious software was introduced to the system to verify that no other vulnerabilities were present, the continuity procedure will dictate that the system needs to come back online as soon as possible. There does not necessarily have to be two separate procedures for recovering a system from known good media. In addition, the business continuity and disaster recovery plan should be utilized to determine what critical functions should be restored first in cases of a system disruption.

The incident response plan should be tested on a regular basis and lessons learned through ongoing incident handling activities should be incorporated into the incident response procedures. Any applicable changes resulting from testing exercises should be identified and handled accordingly. It is important that individuals responsible for the incident response plan are appropriately trained in their roles. There should also be periodic incident response refresher training provided.

The covered entity should refer to the following references for further details related to security incident response and reporting:

- NIST SP 800-53 IA-5 Authentication Management
- NIST SP 800-53 IA-6 Authenticator Feedback
- NIST SP 800-53 IA-7 Cryptographic Module Authentication
- NIST SP 800-53 IR-1 Incident Response Policy and Procedures
- NIST SP 800-53 IR-2 Incident Response Training
- NIST SP 800-53 IR-3 Incident Response Testing
- NIST SP 800-53 IR-4 Incident Handling
- NIST SP 800-53 IR-5 Incident Monitoring
- NIST SP 800-53 IR-7 Incident Response Assistance
- NIST SP 800-53 IR-8 Incident Response Plan
- NIST SP 800-53 IR-9 Information Spillage Response
- NIST SP 800-53 SI-3 Malicious Code Protection
- NIST SP 800-53 SI-8 Spam Protection
- NIST SP 800-66 4.5.3 Protection from Malicious Software, Log-in Monitoring, and Password Management
- NIST SP 800-66 4.6.1 Determine Goals for Incident Response
- NIST SP 800-66 4.6.2 Develop and Deploy an Incident Response Team or Other Reasonable and Appropriate Response Mechanism

- NIST SP 800-66 4.6.3 Develop and Implement Procedures to Respond to and Report Security Incidents
- NIST SP 800-66 4.6.4 Incorporate Post-Incident Analysis into Updates and Revisions

11.5.1.1 Sample of Security Incident Policy

PURPOSE OF POLICY

To minimize, to the extent possible, the adverse effect of any inadvertent or intentional disclosure of individual protected health information and to comply with the requirements of the HIPAA Privacy and Security Rules related to security incident handling.

POLICY DETAIL

[The covered entity] will prevent, detect, contain, and correct security violations or security incidents to provide for a reasonable level of assurance that protected health information is secure. [Procedures should be developed to provide details of the exact steps or solutions the covered entity uses to implement this policy.] In addition, [the covered entity] will conduct vulnerability/penetration testing on at least an annual basis or when there are any major changes that can affect the security of protected health information. Any findings noted in these tests will be mitigated to a reasonable level, tracked, and reported to management. Finally, any reported security incident or violation will be monitored and handled in accordance with [the covered entity's] security incident handling procedures.

Workforce members, or any business associate of [the covered entity], will immediately notify the security official of any known, suspected, or possible security violations or incidents that are contrary to the security of protected health information.

Once the report is made, the security official will investigate the incident to determine the appropriate course of action. To mitigate any circumstances arising from the unauthorized disclosure or the reported security incident, the security official may take the following course of action:

- Contact the workforce member or entity to which disclosure was made to determine if any further disclosure of the information may have occurred
- If possible, attempt to stop any further use or disclosure of the protected health information
- If appropriate, correct any wrong or inaccurate information that was disclosed
- Attempt to retrieve the information that was inappropriately disclosed
- Conduct sanction activities against any workforce member or business associate responsible for the disclosure
- Obtaining additional expert resources in cases where this expertise is required to prevent further disclosure or collection of evidence
- Reporting of the incident to legal counsel or law enforcement, if necessary

11.6 Contingency Plan

A covered entity needs to be able to sustain or resume business during or after an emergency. To this end, covered entities must implement adequate policies and procedures, as needed, to respond to emergency or other situations that could cause damage to systems that contain electronic protected health information. Some of the emergency situations that should be considered are fire, vandalism, system failures, and natural disasters. Preventative measures or steps that the covered entity can take immediately for each scenario should be outlined throughout the contingency plan. Costs of these preventive measures should also be considered. Entire books have been written on business continuity and disaster recovery. A comprehensive process will be discussed that can be utilized to develop the business continuity and disaster recovery plan in Chapter 15, but here are some specific elements that are either required or addressable under the HIPAA Security Standards.

The business continuity and disaster recovery policies, like other policies, should cover at least the following components: the purpose, scope, responsibilities, management commitment, coordination among different departments, and, of course, compliance. These policies should be formally documented, disseminated, and reviewed and updated on a periodic basis (i.e., annually or upon any major changes that affect business continuity). These policies should define the covered entity's overall objectives and include all areas where resumption of business processes is required. Remember, the goal of business continuity is to continue serving the clients through an emergency situation, whereas disaster recovery is to get critical systems working as quickly as possible when they go down.

Along with the aforementioned components, the contingency policy, or plan, should address resources required to continue business operations during an emergency. The plan should address training and testing of the procedures developed to restore or continue operations. The plan must be maintained and should be assigned to a workforce member responsible for the maintenance of the plan. This workforce member may call on several different individuals throughout the covered entity to assist in the development and writing of the plan; however, it is best to have one member coordinating all of this activity. The plan would not be complete without the requirement for the procedures regarding backup of data. Since information is one of the most valuable assets any covered entity holds, it is imperative that an efficient, robust backup solution is implemented.

As discussed in full detail in Chapter 15, the plan should outline critical services that must be operational within a specific timeframe either during or after an emergency situation occurs. This outline should also cover the dependencies of one system on another. For instance, if e-mail is considered a critical service, then the server that houses the e-mail needs to be operational for this service to continue. In addition, the data housed on this server may need to be recreated from backups in situations where the entire e-mail database was lost or corrupted.

The plan should outline alternative operational contingencies when there is a loss of critical functions. Physical resources such as office space should also be considered in these alternate contingency plans. For each critical function, the question of how this function will continue to operate without a critical resource should be asked. For instance, if human resources is considered a critical function within the covered entity, how will these workforce members continue to work if there is a loss of power and their computers are inoperable? Maybe this will be a situation where a manual process will need to be developed for all the critical functions that human resources performs. Once power is restored and computers are operational, the manual functions may then need to be entered into the electronic systems. The plan should account for this transfer.

The plan needs to include a determination of when contingency actions need to be activated and who are the individuals that are authorized to activate these contingency plans. This needs to be determined up front and not during an emergency situation. Triggers should be developed based on criteria such as loss of capabilities, impact to service delivery, or the duration of an outage. The plan should identify these trigger points. For example, if there is a loss of power for more than 4 hours, then the contingency actions may be to set up main operations at another office or set up emergency generators to run critical systems. Based upon certain criteria, an assigned workforce member may have the authority to make the decision to activate the contingency plan and place the covered entity in *emergency operation mode.* The workforce members should then be fluent in these procedures and act in accordance with the emergency mode of operation's directives.

Once the emergency has subsided, a decision should be made to return to normal operations. There should be formal documented recovery procedures in place to recover from an emergency or restore systems back to their normal operational state. Again, there should be someone assigned with the responsibility to make the determination of switching from recovery mode back to normal operations.

The covered entity should refer to the following references for further details related to contingency planning:

- NIST SP 800-53 CP-1 Contingency Planning Policy and Procedures
- NIST SP 800-66 4.7 Contingency Plan
- NIST SP 800-66 4.7.1 Develop Contingency Planning Policy
- NIST SP 800-66 4.7.3 Identify Preventive Measures
- NIST SP 800-66 4.7.4 Develop Recovery Strategy

11.6.1 Data Backup Plan—Required—45 CFR § 164.308(a)(7)(ii)(A)

An important element of any disaster recovery plan is the ability to reconstitute an information system with the exact data at the point that an emergency situation occurs. A covered entity must have adequate procedures in place to create an exact copy of electronic protected health information. It must also have adequate procedures to maintain this data and retrieve it when necessary. This recovery plan needs to address the objectives, priorities, and metrics by which recovery is to take place. To back up all data contained in the information systems may be unrealistic or cost prohibitive. A covered entity needs to identify the specific electronic protected health information that is critical for continued operations and make sure that there is a solution in place to protect this information in emergencies. Some of the data sources that may be critical to a covered entity include:

- Patient accounting systems
- Electronic medical records
- Health maintenance and case management information
- Digitized diagnostic images
- Electronic test results
- Other digital documents maintained

Remember that these systems may also be important under incident handling activities and coordination should be made between the disaster recovery and incident handling procedures.

The covered entity needs to assign individuals specific roles and responsibilities in the contingency plan. There may be certain individuals responsible for actually backing up data and others responsible for transporting these backups off-site. There may be other individuals responsible for hardware that may be different than those responsible for software. The contingency plan should cover all of these different roles and identify the workforce members responsible for each. The contingency plan should also be reviewed for each information system and approved by the covered entity's designated official. Each of the designated workforce members responsible for contingency activities should receive a copy of the contingency plan or a portion of this plan that they are responsible to recover or the information system that they are responsible for. Furthermore, any changes to these procedures also need to be communicated to the contingency plan workforce member.

There are several different types of digital backup methods. This could include online backups, disk-to-disk backups, removable media, tape, CD/DVD, or other solutions. The covered entity's backup plan should consider how these backup media are stored. This storage could be on-site or off-site, but a procedure needs to be implemented to make sure this media is secure and protected from unauthorized use, lost, or damage. It is recommended that an alternative secure storage site be established in case a total loss occurs at the primary location that protects the confidentiality and integrity of the backup information.

The covered entity needs to develop a backup strategy that covers updates to the electronic protected health information on a regular basis. Some organizations will conduct a full weekly backup of the data with differential (or incremental) backups daily.

Differential backups only back up the files that have been modified (or changed) since the last full backup. It is much quicker to restore a differential backup; however, the amount of data backed up increases until the next full backup is conducted.

Incremental backups also only back up files that have changed, but incremental backups only back up changes since the last backup (either full or incremental). Although incremental backups are extremely fast and can be done at closer intervals, restoring these types of backups can take longer. To restore incremental backups, the systems have to be reconstituted from the full backup and every existing incremental backup that was completed.

A reliable backup solution (or software) should be researched that includes encryption capabilities. Backup data should be encrypted on media especially if the backup media is taken off-site at another location from where it was originally created. All backup media need to be accounted for and proper documented inventory sheets should be maintained. Recovery of backup data should be conducted on a routine basis to make sure that the backup solution is working properly. Nothing is worse than finding out the backup solution is not working properly or the backup data is corrupted when a restoration of an information system takes place during an emergency situation. When restoring systems, security measures need to be addressed so that there is no deterioration of the security state from the original to the backup. For example, if a compromise were to occur, the procedures to recover the systems should include restoration from known good media.

As part of the contingency plan, the covered entity may want to establish an alternate work site. This would include the necessary arrangements to permit the general restoration of operations for critical functions in a specified period of time consistent with the covered entity's restoration objectives. This would also include any equipment or supplies needed to resume temporary operations at this alternative site. It is imperative that alternative telecommunication services be included within the contingency plan such as alternative telephone services, wireless, satellite, radio, or other form of communication that is essential during emergency operations.

The covered entity should refer to the following references for further details related to data backup planning:

- NIST SP 800-53 CP-2 Contingency Plan
- NIST SP 800-53 CP-6 Alternate Storage Site
- NIST SP 800-53 CP-7 Alternate Processing Site
- NIST SP 800-53 CP-8 Telecommunications Services
- NIST SP 800-53 CP-9 Information System Backup
- NIST SP 800-53 CP-10 Information System Recovery and Reconstitution
- NIST SP 800-53 CP-12 Alternate Communications Protocols
- NIST SP 800-53 SC-5 Denial of Service Protection
- NIST SP 800-53 SC-6 Resource Availability

11.6.2 Disaster Recovery Plan—Required—45 CFR § 164.308(a)(7)(ii)(B)

In developing the required disaster recovery procedures, the covered entity needs to make sure that adequate procedures are implemented to restore any lost data. The recovery of this data needs to take into consideration any issues specific to the operating environment. As stated earlier, the plan needs to address the specific data that should be restored and a copy of the plan needs to be available when an emergency arises. Keeping a copy of the plan in more than one location is a good idea. Some covered entities have decided to place their plans online so that they can be accessible from any location where Internet service is available. Although this may work in most emergency situations, it could create other issues if Internet service is unavailable as may be the case in a natural disaster.

The business continuity or disaster recovery plan should contain, at a minimum, the following elements:

- A business impact analysis (BIA)
- Identify the covered entity's business functions and their priorities in the resumption process
- Time metrics of essential systems to be recovered to include maximum tolerable downtimes (MTDs) and recovery point objectives (RPOs)
- Updated contact information for critical personnel, command centers, alternate command centers, and critical vendors along with roles each of the workforce members or vendors will have during an emergency

Chapter 15 will discuss these items in detail.

The covered entity should also refer to the following references for further details related to disaster recovery planning:

- NIST SP 800-53 CP-2 Contingency Plan
- NIST SP 800-53 CP-11 Predictable Failure Prevention
- NIST SP 800-66 4.7.5 Develop Backup Plan and Disaster Recovery Plan

11.6.3 Emergency Mode Operation Plan— Required—45 CFR § 164.308(a)(7)(ii)(C)

A business continuity plan or disaster recovery plan needs to include the criteria for declaring a disaster or emergency mode operations. The plan should also assign authority to individuals that can make the decision to declare such operations. Once an emergency has been declared, a covered entity is required to have procedures established for the continued operations of critical business functions and to protect the security of electronic protected health information while conducting operations in emergency mode. The covered entity will have to balance the need for the security of electronic protected health information over the need to access this information. The covered entity may need to establish alternate security measures for the protection of electronic protected health information in cases of emergency.

Remember, in certain emergency situations, electronic systems may not be functional. In these cases, the emergency mode operation plan needs to include possible manual procedures that also include security precautions for the creation or maintenance of these paper documents. Once information systems are brought back online, there needs to be procedures in place to synchronize manual procedures with electronic procedures.

The covered entity should refer to the following references for further details related to emergency mode operations:

- NIST SP 800-53 Safe Mode
- NIST SP 800-53 SC-24 Fail in Known State
- NIST SP 800-53 SC-25 Thin Nodes
- NIST SP 800-66 4.7.6 Develop and Implement Emergency Mode Operations Plan

11.6.4 Testing and Revision Procedures— Addressable—45 CFR § 164.308(a)(7)(ii)(D)

A covered entity should have procedures adequately implemented to conduct periodic tests and updated to the contingency plans. Contingency plans are recommended to be tested at least annually and kept up to date on a concurrent basis. Testing should be performed on all critical systems throughout the entire enterprise. This can be done by conducting tabletop exercises, scenarios, full-blown recovery tests, or through actual real-life events. Testing may include external vendors, alternate sites, and other service providers that assist the covered entity in its contingency plan. Testing could also be phased in by testing the critical systems first based on the risk assessment and gradually rolling the testing out to the entire enterprise. A determination will have to be made whether testing will be conducted during normal business hours or after hours. A word of caution: Testing should not compromise the ability to continue normal service operations in either case.

The contingency plan should be modified to address any issues identified from the results of testing. Processes for restoring data, disaster recovery, and emergency mode operations should also be well documented. Workforce members responsible for performing disaster recovery tasks should have a good understanding of their responsibilities and be trained in these procedures accordingly. Refresher training should be provided to these workforce members on a periodic basis (i.e., at least annually).

The covered entity should refer to the following references for further details related to testing and revision procedures:

- NIST SP 800-53 CP-3 Contingency Training
- NIST SP 800-53 CP-4 Contingency Plan Testing
- NIST SP 800-66 4.7.7 Testing and Revision Procedures

11.6.5 Applications and Data Criticality Analysis— Addressable—45 CFR § 164.308(a)(7)(ii)(E)

As mentioned earlier, the business continuity and disaster recovery plan should contain a prioritized list of specific applications and data that must be immediately restored in cases of emergency and that must be available at all times. This list should reflect the relative criticality of the specific application and data that supports other components of the contingency plan. This analysis should also determine the hardware, software, and workforce members that are critical to the day-to-day operations of the covered entity. Based upon the desired service levels that the covered entity wants to maintain, a determination must be made on the nature and the degree of impact in the event that any of these critical assets are unavailable. The covered entity needs to outline the amount of time it is willing to tolerate any disruption in services and figure out at what point a significant outage would cause detrimental and unrecoverable harm to the covered entity. Support from external providers such as utility companies or other contractors should be sought to mitigate damages that could be caused by outages. The most cost effective solution should be sought to recover critical services and obtain the resources necessary for the recovery process. These items will be fleshed out as part of the steps that will be discussed in Chapter 15.

The covered entity should refer to the following reference for further details related to applications and data criticality analysis:

- NIST SP 800-66 4.7.2 Conduct an Applications and Data Criticality Analysis

11.7 Evaluation—Required—45 CFR § 164.308(a)(8)

One of the most important requirements of the HIPAA Security Rule is reflected in 45 CFR § 164.308(a)(8), which states that a covered entity is required to "perform a periodic technical and nontechnical evaluation, based initially upon the standards implemented under this rule [the HIPAA Security Rule] and subsequently, in response to environmental or operational changes affecting the security of electronic protected health information, that establishes the extent to which an entity's security policies and procedures meet the requirements [of the HIPAA Security Rule]."

The only way to prove that solutions implemented as part of policies and procedures are meeting the requirements of the HIPAA Security Rule standards is to perform testing on these measures. It is recommended that an annual technical and nontechnical evaluation be performed on the covered entity. This should be performed by an experienced and reputable third-party provider to maintain independence. Although there may be a lot of highly skilled resources on staff, the unfortunate part of an evaluation is that they may not have enough separation of duties or be independent enough to provide value to the review. Normalcy or the possibility of being shortsighted in conducting these types of evaluations points to the support of getting an outside party to conduct such reviews. Furthermore, internal staff may not have the appropriate experience or training necessary to conduct a thorough technical and nontechnical evaluation.

When choosing an external vendor to perform this assessment, the covered entity should consider the credentials and experience of these vendors. The vendor conducting this type of security assessment should be well versed in the HIPAA regulations and have the technical expertise to ensure that critical systems will not be affected during testing operations. The covered entity should have a budget for internal and external resources participating in the evaluation. The security program budget should establish priorities and goals for continuous improvement.

Technical reviews should be performed both internally and externally on the covered entity's network. External tests should be performed a little more frequently such as semiannually as opposed to internal testing that is recommended to be performed at least annually. These tests should include both vulnerability and penetration testing along with the nontechnical compliance side that covers all of the HIPAA Security Rule. As a special note of reference, prior to any penetration testing being conducted, management approval should be required. All reports, evaluations, and supporting material that are considered in any of the analyses, recommendations, or changes made based on these recommendations should be thoroughly documented and approved by management. Furthermore, if there were any identified security incidents, modifications to the covered entity's network, or new technology that was implemented, an additional evaluation should be performed to substantiate any changes within the covered entity's security posture as a result of these items.

The security assessment and authorization policies should cover at least the following components: purpose, scope, responsibilities, management commitment, coordination among different departments, and compliance. These policies should be formally documented, disseminated, and reviewed and updated on a periodic basis (i.e., annually or upon any major changes that affect the security assessment). These policies should define the covered entity's overall objectives and include the associated security assessment and authorization controls. Remember, the goal of the security assessment is to determine the security posture of the covered entity, the effectiveness of current controls in place, the determination of the requirement of additional controls, and overall compliance with the HIPAA Privacy and Security Rules. When it comes to security evaluations, it is crucial to have senior management level support and the need for all workforce members to support the security evaluation process. The security assessment should not be reviewed as a negative process, but rather an important process to strengthen the security posture of the covered entity.

Since security is an ongoing process, previous reports or any other documentation related to compliance, security controls, integration, or other solutions deployed to protect electronic protected health information should be provided during the assessment. This will enable the assessor to gather a baseline of the overall security posture of the covered entity. Upon additional testing of these controls, a determination can be made whether these controls are effective or in need of improvement to secure electronic protected health information. A covered entity may choose to have certain workforce members responsible for the security of electronic protected health information along with corporate, legal, and regulatory compliance workforce members participating in the evaluation.

The security assessment plan should be developed to describe the scope of the assessment including any controls under review. The plan should include procedures that will be utilized to determine the effectiveness of the security controls implemented. The security assessment plan should also specify the environment and team that will be involved in performing the assessment. Security controls under review should be assessed to determine if they are operating as intended to include proper configurations and desired outputs in regard to meeting the security requirements. In addition to security controls, administrative, technical, and operational matters related to security should be reviewed. The security assessment plan should specify that a report will be documented for the results of the assessment along with documenting all work papers that were utilized in result determination. This report should be disseminated to the appropriate authorized security official or other designated workforce member. Remember, information in this report may be of a sensitive nature and it should be treated in accordance with other confidential information along with allowing access only to authorized individuals.

Recommended actions should be considered for implementation to mitigate any shortcomings that may have been discovered. The decision to take any remediation actions should be documented and tracked. Acceptance of risk should be appropriately justified.

The covered entity should refer to the following references for further details related to evaluations and security assessments:

- NIST SP 800-53 CA-1 Security Assessment and Authorization Policies and Procedures
- NIST SP 800-53 CA-2 Security Assessments
- NIST SP 800-53 SI-2 Flaw Remediation
- NIST SP 800-53 SI-6 Security Function Verification
- NIST SP 800-66 4.8 Evaluation
- NIST SP 800-66 4.8.1 Determine Whether Internal or External Evaluation is Most Appropriate

- NIST SP 800-66 4.8.2 Develop Standards and Measurements for Reviewing All Standards and Implementation Specifications of the Security Rule
- NIST SP 800-66 4.8.3 Conduct Evaluation
- NIST SP 800-66 4.8.4 Document Results
- NIST SP 800-66 4.8.5 Repeat Evaluations Periodically

11.7.1 Vulnerability/Penetration Testing

An important note should be provided in this section. Although this author strongly recommends a vulnerability/penetration test be performed to assist in the evaluation of the security in the covered entity, be aware that not all service providers that perform this type of service are qualified to conduct this service.

In addition, there are a few important differentiators between a good and a great vulnerability/penetration test. The first differentiator is the quality of the analysis performed on the findings and demonstration of how these findings affect the covered entity's environment in reality. Although many service providers will run commercial-grade tools to perform the vulnerability and penetration testing activities, without having the experience to go through this excessive amount of information and determine what are the real risks, the covered entity will get nothing more than a ton of meaningless information on a report.

This carries over to the next differentiator where the report explains the importance of these findings. A professional report will be able to explain the findings in terms that executives will understand and provide realistic recommendations to mitigate the threats. A great report can provide the rationale and justification for any expenditure that may be required.

The covered entity should refer to the following references for further details related to vulnerability and penetration testing:

- NIST SP 800-53 RA-5 Vulnerability Scanning
- NIST SP 800-53 SC-26 Honeypots
- NIST SP 800-53 SC-30 Concealment and Misdirection
- NIST SP 800-53 SC-31 Covert Channel Analysis
- NIST SP 800-53 SC-36 Honeyclients

11.8 Business Associate Contracts and Other Arrangements

As required by 45 CFR § 164.308(b)(1), a covered entity should obtain "satisfactory assurance" that its business associates will "appropriately safeguard the electronic protected health information created, received, maintained, or transmitted on the covered entity's behalf." The Organizational Requirements under 45 CFR

§ 164.314 govern the elements related to the components required in the contracts of business associates, and the Security Standards: General Rules under 45 CFR § 164.306 define the appropriate safeguards surrounding the security of the electronic protected health information required to be met by the business associate of the covered entity.

Although satisfactory assurance is met through a written contract or other arrangement, it is recommended that the same level of due diligence met by the covered entity to secure electronic protected health information is being met by the business associate. One way in which this assurance can be satisfied would be to obtain a review or evaluation from an independent third party providing an opinion or detailing the level of security in place by the business associate. This review should be periodically performed on all business associates to ensure compliance and to evaluate the effectiveness of the security controls implemented by the business associates.

A SAS 70 review of third-party providers was an industry standard for auditing service providers' internal security controls. As of June 2011, the SAS 70 has been replaced with the Standards for Attestation Engagements (SSAE) No. 16. The reason for this replacement was that U.S. organizations reporting standards would match the international reporting standards (ISAE 3402). A covered entity is recommended to obtain an SSAE No. 16, or some other documented review, of a business associate to ensure that it is meeting and implementing the appropriate safeguards required by the Security Rule.

The covered entity should designate a workforce member or a department responsible for coordinating vendor due diligence activities such as vetting, execution, and review of business associate agreements. This designated party should monitor all vendors that require a business associate agreement to be completed and evaluate each vendor for satisfactory assurance to complying with the HIPAA Security Rule.

The designated workforce member or department should review the list of business associates and reevaluate on a periodic basis whether these business associates have access to electronic protected health information. In addition, the tracking mechanism in place should detail the information systems or functions that are utilized by the vendor and are covered under the business associate agreement. When updates to the business associate agreement are necessary due to changes in regulations or for other matters, the tracking solution should monitor updates as necessary. Criteria should be established to measure the contract performance of each business associate.

Special considerations should be made involving service providers of external information systems. Specifically, these providers should comply with the covered entity's information security requirements and implement security controls in accordance with the HIPAA Security Rule, other regulations, or industry guidance. In addition, the covered entity should document and define all users' roles or responsibilities with regard to accessing external information systems. The covered entity should be monitoring, for compliance, the security controls implemented by service providers especially for those related to external systems.

As described in detail in Chapter 19, Section 19.1, the business associate contract requires certain elements be included. The contract must include security requirements that address confidentiality, integrity, and availability of electronic protected health information including security requirements that meet all of the HIPAA Security Rule regulations per the Health Information Technology for Economic and Clinical Health (HITECH) Act. The contract must also include that any subcontractors of the business associate must comply with the HIPAA Security Rule. Furthermore, the contract must specify that if a business associate discovers a breach, it must report the breach to the covered entity.

The business associate contract should include what type of services are being offered by the business associate and what are the business associate's roles and responsibilities over electronic protected health information. The contract should also include an expected outcome of the business associate's services. In addition, the contract should include that appropriate training, as required by the Security Rule, will be provided to the business associate's employees regarding the security over electronic protected health information.

The contract should specify how electronic protected health information is transmitted between the business associate and the covered entity and specify necessary security controls over the electronic protected health information. The contract should allow for the termination of services if it is discovered that a business associate is not complying with the requirements of the contract; however, the business associate should be provided the opportunity to correct its actions.

Another type of arrangement that may take place is an interconnection security agreement. This type of agreement authorizes connections from the covered entity's information systems to another information system outside of the normal control of the covered entity. In these types of agreements, the covered entity should document at least the following for each connection: the interface characteristics, security requirements, and type of information transmitted through the connection. These types of connections should be monitored and enforcement of security requirements maintained.

A memorandum of understanding (MOU) may be another arrangement if the business associate is a federal, state, or local government entity. The MOU could be utilized in place of a business associate agreement for the sharing of electronic protected health information, but it should state all required safeguards for the protection of this electronic protected health information being shared. Note: The covered entity should be well versed in any additional laws or regulations that govern the use of electronic protected health information by a business associate that is a government entity.

The covered entity should refer to the following references for further details related to business associate contracts and other arrangements:

- NIST SP 800-53 CA-3 Information System Connections
- NIST SP 800-53 SA-9 External Information System Services
- NIST SP 800-66 4.9 Business Associate Contracts and Other Arrangements
- NIST SP 800-66 4.9.1 Identify Entities that Are Business Associates under the HIPAA Security Rule
- NIST SP 800-66 4.9.3 Establish Process for Measuring Contract Performance and Terminating Contract if Security Requirements Are Not Being Met
- NIST SP 800-66 4.9.4 Implement an Arrangement Other Than a Business Associate Contract if Reasonable and Appropriate

11.8.1 Written Contract or Other Arrangement— Required—45 CFR § 164.308(b)(4)

A covered entity is required to document the satisfactory assurances required by the Business Associate Contracts and Other Arrangements standards through a written contract or other arrangement with the business associate that meets the Organizational Requirements under 45 CFR § 164.314(a). This means that a covered entity should identify all business associates that include the following:

- Clearinghouses
- Medical billing services
- Vendors of hardware/software
- External consultants
- Lawyers
- Transcription Contractors
- Other business associates that may have access to electronic protected health information

All of these business associates must have contracts signed and in place to comply with the HIPAA Privacy Rule. In addition, these contracts should also address the HIPAA Security Rule requirements. After reviewing these contracts, if they do not cover the HIPAA Security Rule requirements, it should be determined whether the existing contracts could be modified to include coverage for the HIPAA Security Rule standards. If not, new contracts may be necessary to satisfy these requirements.

11.9 Summary

This chapter is dedicated to a detailed overview of the administrative safeguards under the HIPAA Security Rule requirements. These administrative safeguards make up over half of all of the requirements defined under the HIPAA Security

Rule. This chapter begins with details on the process behind security management. This process includes conducting a risk assessment and analyzing the results. This will assist in developing solutions to manage risks. To enforce policies and procedures designed to mitigate risks, sanctions may be required and all workforce members should be aware of these sanction policies. To verify that controls in place are working as expected on information systems, activity reviews need to be conducted. Finally, there should be specific workforce members assigned certain responsibilities related to security management.

One of the first lines of defense for any information security program is the security surrounding workforce members. There needs to be proper authorization or supervision procedures in place to only allow those workforce members access to the information they require to carry out their responsibilities. Each workforce member should be appropriately cleared or vetted before allowing them access to this information. In addition, when a workforce member changes position or is terminated for any reason, procedures need to be in place to handle these modifications in access levels.

The procedures in place to address access fall under information access management. To assist in this management, a covered entity may decide to isolate certain healthcare clearinghouse functions, if applicable. As discussed, all access requires authorization. Procedures need to be implemented to establish this initial access and any modification of this access through the term of the workforce members' employment with the covered entity.

Having a strong security awareness program is essential to maintaining a strong security posture. Workforce members need to know what expectations are regarding security and reminders of such expectations are essential to maintain security. Since people can make mistakes, some technical solutions should be implemented such as malicious software protection and monitoring capabilities for log-ins. Malicious software protection can assist in preventing unauthorized software from being loaded onto information systems along with preventing software that may be infected with viruses or spyware from being installed on these systems. Monitoring log-ins provides a way to analyze behaviors and detect suspicious activity. For instance, if a workforce member is logging in after normal work hours, this may be indicative of the workforce member's account being compromised or the workforce member may be accessing information systems in an unauthorized fashion. Since username and password combinations are the standard authorization mechanism, it is important that security awareness training includes details on how to manage these account passwords. This training could include steps to take to protect passwords and how to design strong passphrases.

It is usually the situation that security professionals are not asking if a security incident will occur, but rather when a security incident will occur. For this reason, a covered entity needs to have appropriate security incident procedures in place to respond and report to such matters. These policies and procedures will define what a security incident is, what workforce members will be responsible for handling it, the proper course of action to follow, and what needs to be done to resolve a security incident.

When a security incident occurs, it may involve disruption of information services. For this reason, a covered entity needs to have appropriate contingency plans in place. These plans should include regular backups of data so that systems can be restored to a current state. The disaster recovery plan is required to be developed along with plans on operating in an emergency mode of operations. This emergency mode may include manual processes to critical business functions that will need to be performed while automated information systems are down. Once the information systems are brought back to an operating state, these manual processes will need to be converted or data entered back into the information systems.

No contingency plan will be complete without testing to make sure that the procedures will work as expected. There also needs to be a process to modify or revise these contingency plans to encompass items that may be an issue. Throughout the contingency planning process, special emphasis should be placed on critical applications and data. An analysis of these critical items should take place and solutions should be developed to mitigate harm that may occur to these systems.

Not only will the contingency plan be tested, but the overall information security program needs to be evaluated. This is probably one of the most important standards of all of the HIPAA Security Rule requirements. A technical and nontechnical evaluation is required to be performed to evaluate the efficiency of the safeguards that are implemented. This technical and nontechnical evaluation should be performed by independent and highly qualified individuals. The better the evaluation is performed, the better the issues can be addressed or risks mitigated. Since these evaluations are important, companies or individuals conducting these types of tasks should be well vetted.

This chapter ended with a discussion on business associates and the contracts required to be fulfilled between them and the covered entity. New proposals will enhance the requirements of the business associates to take more responsibility over electronic protected health information. Even though an agreement may be made between the two organizations, it will not relieve a covered entity from liability if one of their business associates has a breach involving the covered entity's protected health information. It has become imperative that covered entities validate how well their business associates are protecting their information.

Chapter 12

Security Rule: Risk Assessments

Objectives

The objectives of this chapter are as follows:

- Understand what is involved in conducting a risk assessment.
- Determine the characteristics of an information system.
- Determine the threats related to a specific information system.
- Determine the vulnerabilities of an information system.
- Understand how to conduct a control analysis.
- Understand the likelihood of an event occurring.
- Understand the impact of an event occurring.
- Determine risks.
- Determine risk mitigation solutions.
- Understand the risk management process.
- Understand the elements of a risk assessment report.

12.1 Risk Assessment Overview

The National Institute of Standards and Technology (NIST) 800 Series of Special Publications (SP), specifically, SP 800-30—Risk Management Guide for Information Technology Systems, discusses in detail how a covered entity should perform a risk assessment. Although there is no requirement to follow this exact process, the information presented in this publication can definitely be used as a guide in conducting a risk assessment. It is the author's intention to take this information and provide a roadmap that can be followed to conduct a HIPAA required risk assessment under 45 CFR § 164.308(a)(1)(ii).

Risk is the impact that a certain event may cause on the covered entity based on the probability or likelihood that this event will take place. Changing this definition just slightly to utilize some other terms such as threats and vulnerabilities, risk is analyzed based upon the probability that a *threat* will be exploited for a specific *vulnerability* and to determine the impact that occurs. Risks arise from the liability (such as financial, legal, or reputational) or the loss of use due to an event occurring. Such events could be the unauthorized use or disclosure of electronic protected health information, errors or omissions of specific information in a patient's medical records, destruction of information, disruption of necessary services (i.e., electrical, technical, etc.) that impacts business operations, or failure to conduct due diligence or due care that leads to a breach of electronic protected health information either by the covered entity itself or by a business associate of the covered entity.

Here are a couple of terms that must be understood related to risk before proceeding any further. *Vulnerability* is defined in NIST SP 800-30 as "[a] flaw or weakness in system security procedures, design, implementation, or internal controls that could be exercised (accidentally triggered or intentionally exploited) and result in a security breach or a violation of the system's security policy." Vulnerabilities could exist in an information system based on the hardware or software configured for the system or present just by the pure nature of the functions performed by the information system.

An adapted definition of *threat*, from NIST SP 800-30, is "[t]he potential for a person or thing to exercise (accidentally trigger or intentionally exploit) a specific vulnerability." There are numerous sources of threats, but classifying threats into the following five broad categories is a good starting point:

1. Human threats
2. Environmental threats
3. Software/hardware threats
4. Regulatory threats
5. Future threats

In a risk assessment, systems or processes are identified within the covered entity that pose a significant risk to the operations based on the possibilities of threats exploiting vulnerabilities and the resulting impact of these events taking place. *Risk mitigation* is the process of implementing solutions or performing actions to ultimately reach the goal of decreasing the risk level or the impact of the event to an acceptable level.

Since there is some understanding of why risk assessments are performed, take a look at the steps that will be followed in performing this assessment. The following are the eight steps that will be followed to perform the risk assessment:

1. System characterization
2. Threat identification
3. Vulnerability identification and categorization
4. Control analysis
5. Likelihood rating
6. Impact rating
7. Risk determination
8. Risk mitigation or recommendations

See Figure 12.1 for further details.

12.2 System Characterization

The first step of the risk assessment is to identify the systems that are under review. The systems could be hardware, software, processes, or other types of business functions. Concentration may be made on the technology base that makes up the systems or processes. This technology base may be broken up into the system boundaries, the system elements, the system users, or the network infrastructure that makes up the system.

During this step, the purpose of the assessment on this system should be identified. In addition, a description of the technology base that makes up the system under review needs to be addressed. System boundaries should also be identified such as whether the systems under review are internal or external. What types of network devices are installed to serve or separate the systems? For instance, if a file server is under review. This file server may operate internally and have a firewall device installed to protect it from external access. The file server may utilize switches or routers to allow authorized devices to connect to it. The file server may also require username and password authentication to gain access to its resources.

All components or assets assigned to this system should be identified. A system inventory should be taken to specify the type of host device, applications installed, location, internal or external, type of operating system, asset tag, system group, department assigned, or any other details that may describe the system in detail. Each system should be classified based on the type of information the system may process, store, or transmit. The information could be classified as public, private, or protected health information. A determination of the information classification and a definition of each classification should be designated within the covered entity's risk assessment policies and procedures.

The systems should be ranked on the functions that they perform such as public-related functions, private-related functions concerning the covered entity itself, or if the system performs transactions on electronic protected health information. Again, these rankings should be defined in the risk assessment procedures. Along with system rankings, classifying the systems on their criticality may also be

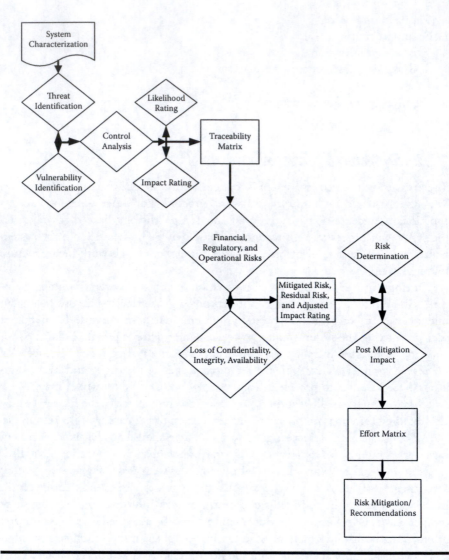

Figure 12.1   Risk assessment steps.

performed. This criticality ranking could be determined by the impact that would result to the covered entity if the system was down for an extended period of time. Some examples of criticality rankings are: not critical, semicritical, or a priority system that is crucial to the covered entity's operations.

Each system should then be reviewed for the specific controls that the system currently implements. The control set that used in this assessment is NIST 800-53, Recommended Security Controls for Federal Information Systems, Revision 4 February 2012 (National Institute of Standards and Technology 2012). All of the controls are listed within the set to see what controls apply to the specific system under review. All of the planned controls are also listed that may be implemented in the future or may be under discussion for implementation. This may be a tedious process; however, it is important to identify these items so that proper risk calculations can be made later. Along with controls, any known vulnerabilities should be identified for each system. These vulnerabilities could be identified through testing or could be possible issues that are discovered through the analysis of controls.

The final component of system characterization is the users or groups of users that have access to this system. The access levels should be determined and the rights that are granted to these users or groups should be described. Here, a rationale of all system access can be made and a determination of the proper roles of each user or group of users should be identified.

12.3 Threat Identification

As discussed earlier, a *threat* is the potential of a *threat source* to *exploit* a specific *vulnerability*. Some vulnerabilities will be discussed in the next section, but for now, know that a threat source is the intent or method by which an exploitation of a vulnerability occurs. A threat source could also be a situation or method by which vulnerabilities are triggered by accident.

As mentioned, threat sources are classified into five broad categories: human threats, environmental threats, software/hardware threats, regulatory threats, or future threats. Each of these categories can be broken into subcategories such as accidental, criminal, internal, and external. The following is more details regarding each of these broad categories of threats.

Human threats can consist of two subcategories: accidental or premeditated threats. Accidental human threats are those threats that may cause loss or damage to the covered entity's assets. The sources of these accidental human threats can come from internal sources like untrained workforce members or external sources such as business associates. These types of threats may include errors or omissions by workforce members or business associates. If a threat is not accidental then it may be premeditated or intentional. Threats of this type include criminal, malicious, or possibly conducted with political motives. Examples of these threats include terrorist acts, theft, fraud, sabotage, kidnapping, ransom, and espionage. These premeditated or intentional threats can also come from internal sources like disgruntled workforce members or external sources such as hackers or cyberterrorists.

Environmental threats are related to the loss of physical or infrastructure support. These types of losses normally come from natural threats, man-made threats, or system support threats. Natural threats may include hurricanes, floods, tornadoes, earthquakes, fires, or snow storms. Man-made threats may include intentional attacks, wars, environmental accidents, hazardous spills, and arson. System support threats could include any disruption in utility services such as electricity, water, or temperature control systems like heating or air-conditioning.

Software/hardware threats are those dealing with specific technology issues such as hardware component failures, data corruption, or error operations from programming issues. Vendor updates for software packages can also be sources of threats since there have been several past examples of updates causing systems to become unstable or fail. One of the other major issues in this category of threats is malicious code. This includes viruses, malware, worms, spyware, and Trojans.

Regulatory threats come from regulatory entities dealing with laws and regulations. In the healthcare industry, failing to meet the requirements of HIPAA regulations could cost the covered entity financially with civil fines or other sanctions. Regulations can be found internally through policies and procedures or externally through laws. This regulatory threat could also include the threat of loss of reputation. In the healthcare industry where potential clients normally become patients through word of mouth, the loss of a covered entity's reputation could produce a huge negative impact on the organization.

Future threats are those threats that may arise due to technology advancement. An example of this threat could be a "zero-day" vulnerability that was just discovered with an exploit for the vulnerability spreading around public forums on the Internet. These threats could also include items that may not be an issue currently but could become one in the future. For instance, several years back, not a lot of individuals cared about their personal, private information. With the increase of identity theft and increased regulations to protect personally identifiable information, privacy has become a serious matter and securing electronic protected health information is a major concern for all covered entities.

Here is a list of threat sources that could be utilized within the risk assessment:

- Human—Accidental—Internal
- Human—Accidental—External
- Human—Malicious—Internal
- Human—Malicious—External
- Environmental—Accidental—Internal
- Environmental—Accidental—External
- Environmental—Malicious—Internal
- Environmental—Malicious—External
- Software—Accidental—Internal

- Software—Accidental—External
- Regulatory—Internal
- Regulatory—External
- Emerging—Accidental—Internal
- Emerging—Accidental—External
- Emerging—Malicious—Internal
- Emerging—Malicious—External
- Hardware—Accidental—Internal
- Hardware—Accidental—External
- Software—Malicious—Internal
- Software—Malicious—External
- Hardware—Malicious—Internal
- Hardware—Malicious – External

Here is a list of possible actions that could take place provided a threat source creates an accidental or intentional event:

- Accident (in transit)
- Administration
- Arson
- Assault on employee
- Blackmail
- Bomb/terrorism
- Browsing of proprietary information
- Capture/decryption of electronic protected health information while in transit
- Chemical spill
- Civil liability
- Collusion
- Computer abuse
- Database corruption
- Destruction of data
- Destruction of equipment
- DNS/Web site spoofing
- Dormant user accounts
- Downloading infected software from Internet
- Earthquake
- Economic exploitation
- Electrical service failure
- E-mail viruses
- Equipment damage
- Expandability
- Explosion
- Extreme humidity

- Extreme temperatures
- Fees
- Financial cost to upgrade
- Fire
- Flood
- Fraud and theft
- Fraudulent data entry
- Fraudulent transactions
- General system attack (denial of service)
- Hardware failure of workstations/laptops
- Hardware failure of network devices
- Hardware failure of servers
- Hurricane
- Improper data processing
- Incomplete/nonexistent backups
- Infected software or disks on clients
- Infected software or disks on servers
- Infected software or disks on Web servers
- Information theft
- Information warfare
- Injection of malicious code
- Input of falsified information
- Internet denial of service attack
- Intrusion of personal privacy
- Invalid data entry
- IP spoofing
- Listening services/open ports on internal systems
- Listening services/open ports on Web servers
- Loss or destruction of data
- MAC address spoofing
- Malicious employee
- No access to system
- OS/software install/patch corrupts data
- Pandemic
- Password guessing/cracking
- Password sniffing—Private network
- Password sniffing—Internet
- Pharming
- Physical access to unsecured logged in terminal
- Point of failure
- Power failure
- Privacy act
- Regulatory

- Reputation risk
- Sale of personal information
- Snow/ice
- Spyware
- System crash
- System damage
- System failure
- System instability
- System intrusion
- System penetration
- System sabotage
- System tampering
- Targeted system attack
- Telephone outages
- Telephone service
- Theft of data
- Theft of equipment
- Tornado
- Unable to obtain security patches
- Unauthorized access
- Unauthorized deletion
- Unauthorized monitoring
- Unauthorized system access
- Unauthorized system/process stoppage
- Unprotected shares/resources
- UPS/generator failure
- Victim of social engineering
- Vulnerable CGI programs
- Weak passwords
- Website defacement of DMZ servers
- Website defacement of Internet servers
- Wireless
- Wireless access compromise
- Worm or other self-propagating virus

12.4 Vulnerability Identification

The next step is to identify vulnerabilities for a system that could be exploited by a threat source. As a reminder, *vulnerability* is defined in NIST SP 800-30 as "[a] flaw or weakness in system security procedures, design, implementation, or internal controls that could be exercised (accidentally triggered or intentionally exploited) and result in a security breach or a violation of the system's security policy." The vulnerabilities may be identified from interviewing subject-matter experts, observing weaknesses in security policies or procedures, or by performing tests on the system or components of the system to validate the presence of vulnerabilities within the system.

The vulnerability should be detailed along with providing possible threat sources and a description of the potential harm that could be caused if the vulnerability was exploited. In this step, a mapping or correlation between the vulnerability discovered, the source of the threat that could coincide with the vulnerability, and the threat action that could be caused by the exploitation of the vulnerability should be performed. For example, if the room that stored servers did not have a fire alarm nearby, the vulnerability would be that a fire could start in this room without any notification. The source of the threat for this vulnerability could come from multiple sources such as someone setting a fire in this room (i.e., human—malicious—internal) or an electrical plug could have been frayed and caused a fire (i.e., environmental—accidental—internal). Multiple actions could take place caused by this event such as a fire, of course, and equipment damage. Additional actions could take place such as data damage, no access to the system, reputational risk, or possibly civil or regulatory fines depending on the extent of the situation. A table or spreadsheet may be utilized to demonstrate these correlations.

12.5 Control Analysis

An analysis should be performed on the specific controls that the system under review currently has in place or will have in place. The NIST SP 800-30—Risk Management Guide for Information Technology Systems defines three broad classes of controls: management, operational, and technical. Each class has several families of controls. Several specific controls are identified for each family. These control references are noted throughout this book and here are what the 18 control families are:

1. AC—Access Control
2. AT—Awareness and Training
3. AU—Audit and Accountability
4. CA—Security Assessment and Authorization
5. CM—Configuration Management
6. CP—Contingency Planning
7. IA—Identification and Authentication
8. IR—Incident Response
9. MA—Maintenance
10. MP—Media Protection
11. PE—Physical and Environment Protection
12. PL—Planning

13. PS—Personnel Security
14. RA—Risk Assessment
15. SA—System and Services Acquisition
16. SC—System and Communications Protection
17. SI—System and Information Integrity
18. PM—Program Management

Each control should be assessed to validate if they are covered by policy, the procedure, and then implemented, tested, or integrated into the system under review. For this step, a gap analysis, discussed in Chapter 16, may be a good place to start.

12.6 Likelihood Rating

In this section, rating the possibility, probability, or the likelihood that the vulnerability could (or will) occur will be discussed. Since these ratings may be a little subjective, it is important that a defined rating scheme is developed. Consider utilizing a low, medium, or high rating scale, or one that is a little more granular such as no credible chance of occurring to an inevitable chance of occurrence along with the steps to likely and unlikely changes in between. Whatever rating is decided upon, it basically comes down to understanding what each rating is trying to describe along with examples of each. It is also very important to be consistent and have a reasonable explanation for choosing one rating over another.

For example, a high probability of occurrence could be defined as the extremely likely event of a threat being triggered or vulnerability being exploited. For instance, if the facility is located near the beach in Florida, there may be a high probability that a hurricane may cause extreme weather conditions that may affect the business during hurricane season. On a 10-point scale, this rating would be between 7 and 10.

In addition, a medium probability of occurrence may be defined as a moderate likelihood of a threat being triggered or vulnerability being exploited. For instance, the lack of keeping systems up to date may lead to the possibility of a system being compromised by malicious software that may exploit a known vulnerability in the system. On a 10-point scale, this rating would be between 4 and 6.

Finally, a low likelihood of occurrence may be defined as a very unlikely chance that a threat will be triggered or a single vulnerability will be exploited; however, there still may be an opportunity for such an event to occur. Someone conducting a risk assessment may be remiss if they did not mention these types of events and some discussion is not made to determine if mitigation efforts are necessary. For instance, a system could have improper configuration settings, and although it would not necessarily create an immediate threat, the settings may be modified to increase the security of the system. On a 10-point scale, this rating would be between 0 and 3.

12.7 Impact Rating

In the impact rating step, the impact or the realized effect that an exploited vulnerability will have on the covered entity will be determined. Impact will be defined on a 10-point scale where 1 is the lowest and 10 is the highest impact as follows:

1. No real impact on the covered entity
2. Very little impact on the covered entity
3. Little impact on the covered entity
4. Some impact on the covered entity
5. Midlevel impact on the covered entity
6. Significant impact on the covered entity
7. Serious impact on the covered entity
8. Severe impact on the covered entity
9. Crippling impact on the covered entity
10. Covered entity can no longer operate

There are five areas that will be rated when it comes to the impact on the covered entity. Each of these areas can also be weighted as will be seen in Section 12.8 as it applies to the impact that each may have on the covered entity. The following are the five areas along with their corresponding definitions:

1. Financial—The actual monetary cost of an event occurring. A covered entity can quantify this loss from low to high based on an actual figure. For instance, a low financial impact could be any impact up to $10,000. A mid-level financial impact could be a cost from $10,001 to $49,999. A high-level financial impact could be a cost over $50,000. A covered entity could then redefine this into a 10-point scale to maintain consistency throughout the risk assessment process.
2. Regulatory—Primarily based on audits conducted by regulatory enforcement agencies or those items set by regulations. A low regulatory rating item could be a recommendation that relates to a policy or procedure mandated by regulation that needs to be strengthened. A medium regulatory rating item could be a policy or procedure that is not fully implemented that could leave a covered entity open to civil liability. A high regulatory rating item is an audit finding that needs to be corrected immediately or a violation of a regulatory requirement. A covered entity should redefine this rating into a 10-point scale.
3. Confidentiality—This is defined as the unauthorized use or disclosure of protected health information. An impact rating scale can be used to rate each vulnerability as to the impact it would have on the confidentiality of protected health information.
4. Integrity—This is defined as protected health information being modified in an unauthorized fashion or being corrupted accidentally. An impact rating

scale can be utilized to rate each vulnerability as to the impact it would have, if any, on the modification of protected health information.

5. Availability—The amount of time the operations will be disrupted due to an event that has occurred. This item can be quantified in terms of the number of hours that operations will be disrupted. For instance, a low rating could define a disruption lasting less than 1 hour. A medium rating could be more than an hour but less than 3 hours. A high rating could be anything lasting more than 3 hours. Again, these ratings will be defined differently for each covered entity based on their own levels of sensitivity to an event. This rating should be redefined, for consistency, to a 10-point scale based upon the aforementioned impact rating scale.

An analysis will be conducted of impact separately for each of the vulnerabilities identified in Section 12.4.

12.8 Risk Determination

Risks can be determined in two ways: qualitative and quantitative. Management or executive-level workforce members may like the qualitative method since it is easier to understand and clearly identifies the specific nature of the risk in terms of the covered entity's resources. For instance, a high qualitative measure can be described as the doors closing on the facility and no business occurring. In a quantitative evaluation, a high measure would be described as the loss of $100,000 per day in revenues based upon 8 hours of time that the covered entity will be conducting business. Throughout this process, measures were quantified utilizing qualitative means. As expressed, it was very important to specifically define measures and be consistent across each area under review.

In this step, a determination of the actual risk perceived will be determined for each of the vulnerabilities identified. Consideration will be taken for the controls in place and the probability of occurrence of each event taking place. This will assist in making a final determination of the impact rating. Some calculations will be performed in this step, but if using a preconfigured spreadsheet or table, this risk determination can be easily completed.

There are a couple of additional items that need to be covered to tie the control analysis conducted in Section 12.5 to the risk determination. Risk mitigated factor is the percentage of risk perceived to be mitigated by controls that are currently implemented to protect against a certain vulnerability. Residual risk factor is the percentage of risk left over that needs to be mitigated. For example, if a vulnerability is believed to be 75% risk mitigated from controls in place, the residual risk will obviously be 25% (100% − 75% = 25%). Realize, all risks can never be mitigated so there will always be some sort of residual risk; however, depending on the controls in place, this residual risk may be very low.

As explained earlier, the five areas of risk analyzed can be weighted as well. For instance, the unauthorized use or disclosure of protected health information (i.e., confidentiality) may be considered twice as important to the covered entity as the other areas. Availability, on the other hand, may be considered half as important as the other areas. In the calculation, this weighted perspective will be accounted for through the weighted impact rating. The weighted impact rating is an average of all impact ratings across the five areas of concern. In this example, the weighted impact rating will be calculated as follows:

Weighted Impact Rating = [(Financial Impact Rating + Regulatory Impact Rating) + (2 × Confidentiality Impact Rating) + Integrity Impact Rating + (0.5 × Availability Impact Rating)]/5.5

Remember, this is an average of the five areas of concern with an emphasis on one of these areas along with a de-emphasis on another area. The number 5.5 is calculated as follows:

Financial + Regulatory + Integrity + (2 × Confidentiality) + (0.5 × Availability)

or

$$1 + 1 + 1 + 2 + 0.5 = 5.5$$

To continue on with the risk determination, the final impact rating will be calculated as follows:

Final Impact Rating = [(Possibility of Occurrence + Weighted Impact Rating)/2] × Residual Risk Factor

The result will be rounded to the nearest whole number for simplicity purposes.

Again, the goal of this risk determination is to explain or quantify the real world threats of any vulnerability being exploited, the impact of these events occurring, taking into consideration mitigating controls that are currently in place, and the possibility of these events occurring. Taking all of these factors into consideration, the result will be a final impact rating that can be utilized to justify expenditures to mitigate, accept, transfer, or ignore the risks. These terms will be discussed in the next section.

12.9 Risk Mitigation

Now that a final impact rating has been calculated for the identified vulnerabilities, a decision must be made on how these findings will be mitigated. As an organization, management should decide an acceptable level of risk. Based upon the current calculations, this acceptable level of risk may be any final impact rating less than 4 (i.e., low-level rating). Anything higher than 5 (i.e., medium to high rating levels) must be mitigated as per the covered entity's risk assessment policy.

Recommendations should be applied to all identified vulnerabilities. A benefit–effort analysis should be conducted. This benefit–effort analysis will rank the effort involved to implement a recommendation along with the benefit it will supply. Here is where caveats apply. In some situations, the effort involved, which may include resources and finances, will be considered way above the benefit of the implemented solution. This benefit–effort analysis will assist in making a risk mitigation decision.

The risk mitigation decisions are as follows:

- *Mitigated*—Risks that are believed to be at an unacceptable level and should be considered for mitigation efforts. Recommendations in this area should be considered and resources will be assigned to correct these issues, bringing the risks to an acceptable level.
- *Transfer*—Risks that are believed to be at an unacceptable level, but the covered entity feels that it would be less expensive to buy insurance for these risks as opposed to other solutions to mitigate the risks. The risk is then transferred to another organization such as an insurance company.
- *Accepted*—Risks that are believed to be at an unacceptable level. However, based upon the benefit–effort analysis, mitigating the risk is out of the question. Although the risk may be unacceptable, management will accept this risk as part of conducting business and make the risk acceptable. The covered entity has documented the rationale behind accepting these risks and can justify why they may deem the risk to be acceptable.
- *Ignore*—Although it would not be recommend to ignore risks, this is a legitimate option. Many individuals may be of the opinion that what they don't know about, won't hurt them. It is recommended to rethink this position especially if documentation to these items are stated otherwise. Ignoring risks could leave a covered entity in a liable situation and it may be playing a game of roulette. Although the covered entity may be lucky and win, it is usually the case that it will lose and depending on what is at stake, it may lose big time.

12.10 Risk Management

The risk determination has been performed, recommendations have been accepted, and now it is time to manage or track these mitigation items. Conducting a risk assessment is an ongoing process since the environment is always changing. A covered entity must be able to manage risks effectively. This involves tracking solutions and verifying that these solutions are meeting their intended purposes. A covered entity must also not forget that these mitigation efforts could divulge other risks. Mitigation efforts require that evaluations and re-evaluations be performed on responses and actions to obtain the proper balance of risks. When solutions are implemented, changes to the risk evaluations should be made related to these mitigation efforts and reassessment of the level of risks using the steps described earlier. The status of certain solutions to confirm that these projects are progressing as expected should also be tracked.

In regard to tracking, a list of recommendations accepted should be kept. This list should document the following:

- The area of concern identified
- The workforce member responsible for its implementation
- Any review that needs to be performed
- Actions taken
- Controls to be validated
- Any further testing to confirm that the implementation of the recommended solution brought the risk to an acceptable level

Any other additional notations should be kept as to the rationale behind recommendations for documentation purposes.

12.11 Risk Assessment Report

The result of all these steps within this chapter is to finalize a *risk assessment report*. Within this report, the following will be provided: an executive summary, highlighted risks, and a summation of the effective controls in place as they relate to the 18 control categories that were discussed in Section 12.5.

The first part of the risk assessment should be the *executive summary*. This summary page should contain the background or purpose of the risk assessment being performed. For instance, if risks assessments are performed on individual systems, this paragraph would be intended to provide the reader the details around the system analyzed. If this is an overall risk assessment, this section should provide the entire scope that was under review. This background area may also provide the authority by which this risk assessment was performed. Remember that under 45 CFR § 164.308 (a)(1)(ii)(A), a covered entity is required to "conduct an accurate and thorough assessment of the potential risks and vulnerabilities to the confidentiality, integrity, and availability of electronic protected health information held by the covered entity."

In the next section, an overview or an opinion should be provided by the individual conducting the risk assessment as to the state of security within the covered entity. Both good and bad notations should be made within this summary. The summary should include notation about the controls being adequate to provide a strong security posture with evidence that they are implemented from a top-down governance approach. This summary could also include the number of identified findings as they relate to risk levels.

This leads into the next section that relates to identifying the more notable risks. Since this is a summary of risks and the rest of the report will provide details to these findings, this section should be of a high-level overview so that the executives can get a basic understanding of what the report will discuss.

The next sections of the report are split into three broad categories: administrative, technical, and physical. This is similar to the HIPAA Security standards. This is, of course, intentional since the covered entity will find that to have a secure posture related to information security, multiple areas must be addressed.

12.11.1 Administrative Controls

This is one of the major areas since most information security governance starts with policies and procedures. To remain consistent with the 18 broad categories under the NIST framework, these control sets will be distributed accordingly. Notice that some of these control sets could fit under multiple areas, but for simplicity, these areas are sorted accordingly to the majority of the subject matter covered in these areas. For each control area, write one or two paragraphs that summarize the controls analyzed specific to this risk assessment.

- Access Control (AC)—The logical and administrative access controls such as the policies and procedures reviewed during this assessment will be discussed in this section. A determination will be made whether these policies and procedures are appropriately implemented or in need of improvement as it relates to the specific systems under review.
- Security Awareness Training (AT)—This section will summarize what types of training are provided to the workforce members of the covered entity. Again, a determination will be made in regard to the adequacy of the training or if there were any violations to the security training policies and procedures identified during this assessment.
- Audit and Accountability (AU)—This section will mostly cover the adequacy of the information security risk management process in place and compliance with policies and procedures. This section will detail how audits are conducted, who is responsible for conducting these audits, what may occur as a result of the audit, and how compliance is achieved through the use of the information provided in this risk assessment report.
- Security Assessment and Authorization (CA)—On the same level as Audit and Accountability (AU), the risk assessment should describe the types of security assessment and under whose authority these tests were performed. The information provided by these assessments is utilized to make decisions based on the level of risks determined in this risk assessment. The information provided in the report is only as good as the data utilized to make the

determinations on risk. If the security assessments were not performed by experienced individuals, the risk determinations could be inaccurate and could cause the covered entity to make business decisions based on bad information. The purpose of the risk assessment is to provide accurate information to guide the covered entity into making rational decisions to increase the security posture of the organization.

■ Contingency Planning (CP)—This section discusses the ability for the covered entity to continue business if certain disruptive events were to take place. This section summarizes the adequacy of the business continuity and disaster recovery plan to address the continuation of functions during emergency mode operations.

■ Risk Assessment (RA)—This section may be redundant since this entire report is being written to cover this requirement. However, this section could be used to describe how and when the risk assessments are conducted, by whom and under what methodology they are conducted, and describe the steps that are taken to maintain the adequacy of the risk assessment program.

■ Program Management (PM)—This section could be utilized to address any third-party service providers or business associates that may play a significant role in the mitigation of risks identified throughout this assessment. A summary of how these business associates are managed, what types of agreements are in place, and what types of assurances are made to the security of protected health information may be addressed in this area.

■ Personnel Security (PS)—This section summarizes the policies and procedures in place for hiring workforce members such as conducting background checks along with the process for authorizing their respective access levels to protected health information. This section could also address specific policies and procedures designed for the personal welfare of workforce members, such as security provided after hours or first aid kits being stationed throughout common areas of the facility.

■ Planning (PL), System and Services Acquisition (SA), and Maintenance (MA)—This section describes three different but related control sets. First, there is the planning stage of any systems. This section should describe how solutions are recommended and the steps implemented prior to putting solutions into place. Second, this section should detail how systems are acquired and by what method these systems are chosen. Some of this may be covered under Program Management (PM) as well. Finally, this section should describe how maintenance is performed and systems are kept functional throughout their life cycle.

12.11.2 Physical Controls

The first layer of defense to secure protected health information is through physical controls. There may only be two broad categories under this section, however, these categories will contain several elements that, if appropriately implemented, could provide a high level of security for the covered entity.

- Physical and Environmental Protection (PE) —This section should summarize the physical controls implemented by the covered entity. For instance, some of these controls could include: lighting, locks or badge access, designated data center, designated records room, surveillance equipment, alarms, and security guards. The location and surroundings of the facility should also be described in this section.
- Media Protection (MP)—This section will include the handling of electronic media and paper-based media. This section should describe how and where this media is stored, who handles the media, how the is media tracked or inventoried, and what happens to the media once it is no longer needed.

12.11.3 *Technical Controls*

The final control set is related to technical controls. Since it is normally the case that most of the intellectual assets or data of a business is stored in electronic form, it is imperative that adequate technical controls are implemented.

- Configuration Management (CM)—This section summarizes the processes in place to manage system configurations. This section should describe what types of configurations are made, what or who determines these configurations, and how modifications are managed throughout the life cycle of the system. A covered entity should have a formal change management policy and procedure in place that includes an authorized individual that approves changes along with back-out procedures to return systems back to original settings in cases where issues arise from a system modification.
- Identification and Authentication (IA)—This section describes the method used to authenticate workforce members such as the use of unique user IDs along with passwords. This section also includes a description of logging capabilities, the rationale behind logging, review of these logs, and how exceptions are handled.
- Incident Response (IR)—Leading from a description of exception handling, this section will discuss specifics on what procedures the covered entity has in place to deal with incident detection and response. This section should summarize the capabilities that the covered entity has in place to detect suspicious activity and the resources that it may utilize to handle a major incident such as vetting a digital forensic expert.
- System and Communications Protection (SC)—This section describes the technical controls in place for the communication between systems. This could include how systems are segregated from each other, what type of malicious code protection is in place such as antivirus, what type of network access

control is in place such as firewalls or routers, and other mechanisms in place to protect electronic protected health information in transmission mode.

■ **System and Information Integrity (SI)**—Along the same lines of communication protection, this section deals with the integrity of the information that systems collect or store. This section may describe the encryption that is utilized on data while in transit or being stored along with error handling checkers to prevent corruption of data. These error handlers could be installed within the application or within the systems to prevent or make notifications of possible suspicious activity.

12.12 Summary

This chapter details how to conduct a risk assessment. Following this step-by-step process will bring together all of the necessary elements to conduct a thorough assessment and determine the critical systems of the covered entity. Characterizing each system or function by the type of information and processes that the system relates to will assist the covered entity in prioritizing its criticality. Determining the types of threats along with the different vulnerabilities that systems are susceptible to will provide the basics to complete the risk analysis. Analyzing the different controls that are implemented or may be implemented in the future is needed to assist in the determination of the likelihood and the impact that a certain situation will have on a particular system. Once all of this information is gathered, a determination of risk can be assessed along with any other mitigating controls.

These steps will assist in the risk management process where one of the final outputs is a completed risk assessment report. This risk assessment report should cover administrative, physical, and technical controls, and provide a clear understanding of what steps are required to increase the security posture of the covered entity. Many findings may become apparent when conducting this assessment. These findings should be formally tracked and documented so that risks or the impact of harm can be mitigated. Executive management should approve the risk assessment report and solutions should be developed to decrease risks to acceptable levels.

Chapter 13

Security Rule: Security Awareness Training

Objectives

The objectives of this chapter are as follows:

- Understand how to set up a training strategy and plan.
- Determine what type of content, materials, or methods to provide in security awareness training.
- Determine how to implement security awareness training.
- Understand what is involved with monitoring and evaluating the security awareness training plan.
- Determine how to develop an outline for security awareness training to include all necessary elements.

Background

Under 45 § CFR 164.308(a)(5), security awareness training needs to be addressed as part of the Security Rule requirements. It is completely up to the covered entity how this security awareness training occurs. In the following sections, some important considerations when developing the covered entity's security awareness training will be discussed. Since the front line workforce members are usually the gatekeepers and the first line of defense in security, the author thought it was important to devote an entire chapter of this book to cover specifics on security awareness training.

As discussed in Chapter 11, Section 11.4, a covered entity should have formal policies and procedures regarding security awareness training and education. This is all well and good, but now the covered entity needs to decide what is actually going to be trained. First, the covered entity needs to conduct a training gap analysis. This will determine the security awareness needs and what needs to be covered to satisfy these needs. The covered entity should interview key workforce members to determine some of these needs. If the covered entity has a security awareness program already established, the covered entity should evaluate what is being taught and if it currently covers the needs of the organization. The covered entity may need to modify this training accordingly, but it may be easier than starting from scratch.

Second, once the covered entity has conducted the gap analysis, the covered entity should outline specific content that should be covered in the training. The covered entity also needs to take into account the audience in which this training will occur. For example, if the need is to train on specific details of security as it relates to a specific application being utilized, the covered entity probably does not need to give this type of training to executive level members who are not necessarily doing this specific type of work. The covered entity needs to develop training specific to the audience. If this is the first time the covered entity is developing a security awareness program, the covered entity needs to set priorities as to the content and audience members in an effort to gradually roll out the program to all workforce members. By initially pushing out the training to a smaller group, the covered entity can identify any gaps it may have and update the training materials as it is pushed out to all members.

The covered entity should refer to the following references for further details related to security awareness training:

- NIST SP 800-53 PS-1 Personnel Security Policy and Procedures
- NIST SP 800-66 4.5.1 Conduct a Training Needs Assessment

13.1 Training Strategy and Plan

The training strategy and plan should include an outline of the specific policies and procedures. Of course, the plan should include the scope and breadth of content being covered considering the audience. It needs to have a goal in mind and the audience needs to know the purpose of the security awareness program. The learning objectives should be clear and easily understood by the target audience. The covered entity also needs to determine by what method the security awareness training will be deployed. For example, will the covered entity have a live trainer conducting multiple training sessions at set times or will the covered entity use technology to have its workforce members utilize computer-based training? Just as a point of reference, this author has always felt that training in a live environment was better than letting workforce members train on their own. If the covered entity has a good speaker with interesting topics, live training can go a long way.

As part of the training strategy, the covered entity needs to be able to evaluate the effectiveness of its security awareness training program. The covered entity will be spending a lot of time and effort in developing this program, and the covered entity needs to make sure that the program is working as planned. Developing measurement techniques can be difficult but is necessary. Testing the workforce member's knowledge on the subject matter may be an appropriate technique. This testing method could also provide an insight into any gaps in training that may be present. Real-world exercises could be another measurement technique. For instance, if the security awareness training includes topics on social engineering, the covered entity may hire a company to conduct social-engineering-type activity to see how its workforce members react. Again, the covered entity should be able to determine the effectiveness of its training program.

As already may be noticed, the author is calling this security awareness training a "security awareness program." This is intentional since it will not suffice just to have initial training for new hires and training on an annual basis. Although policies and procedures should include such verbiage, workforce members need constant reminders on the importance of security. Conducing continuous and routine security awareness demonstrates a commitment by management. Designating security awareness as a program is proper. In addition, since there have been several updates to the Health Information Technology for Economic and Clinical Health (HITECH) Act and other Health Insurance Portability and Accountability Act (HIPAA) Privacy and Security Rules, it is important that workforce members are kept abreast of these changes throughout the security awareness program. The security awareness program should have dedicated staff responsible for its implementation and resources, such as funds, to properly carry out its mission.

As mentioned, it is important to design the training around the audience. Specific technical topics should be addressed to workforce members based upon their job roles, duties, and responsibilities. The covered entity also needs to address training for nonemployees. This could include third-party providers, volunteers, interns, or anyone else that may have access to protected health information. The covered entity cannot forget that under 45 CFR § 164.530(b) a covered entity is required to provide training to all workforce members on their privacy policies and procedures including the disciplinary actions for those who violate these policies/procedures. Read Chapter 4, Section 4.6.3 for additional information.

The covered entity should refer to the following references for further details related to the training strategy plan:

- NIST SP 800-53 AT-3 Security Training
- NIST SP 800-66 4.5.2 Develop and Approve a Training Strategy and Plan
- NIST SP 800-66 4.5 Security Awareness and Training

13.2 Training Content, Materials, and Methods

Once the covered entity has developed its training strategy and plan and management has approved it, now the covered entity needs to select specific topics to be included in the training content. The covered entity has already outlined the objectives and goals, so it needs to develop material that will satisfy these items. Of course the Internet has a wealth of information that can be used to develop the material. One word of caution: Make sure the information utilized in the training material is from a reputable source. Do not forget about e-mail advisories, news sources, magazines, or sources other than the Internet.

In preparing this book, the author kept track of interesting items that crossed his desk in an effort to keep this information current and relevant. Nothing hits home more than something happening to a related organization in the local community. Most individuals think that bad things cannot happen to them, but it becomes surreal when it does or when it happens to someone close to them. News items can be an effective tool in getting the point across.

One of the first items that should be covered in the training material is the covered entity's security policies and procedures. Every workforce member should have a copy of these policies and procedures. Workforce members should also know where the master copies of these policies and procedures are kept. Special emphasis should be placed on making every workforce member aware of the individual in the organization who should be contacted to handle a security-related incident. It should also go without saying that security-related incidences should be defined so that workforce members know what type of events to report. Although it may not be a pleasant topic, training needs to cover the covered entity's sanction policy or the consequences that workforce members can face if they do not comply with the security policies and procedures.

New technology brings new areas of concern. For instance, mobile devices such as laptops, PDAs, tablets, and smart phones have become accepted tools in most organizations. These devices have become more powerful and technologically advanced over the years. Training should include the policies and procedures around the control over these mobile devices and the acceptable use of these devices. As technology advances and security issues arise, the security training materials need to be updated.

To demonstrate compliance, the covered entity needs to document and track all workforce members and their security training activities. This documentation needs to include the workforce members' initial new hire training and specific periodic training. These records should be kept for a specific time period in accordance with the covered entity's retention policy.

The covered entity should refer to the following references for further details related to training content, materials, and methods:

■ NIST SP 800-53 AT-4 Security Training Records

■ NIST SP 800-66 4.5.4 Develop Appropriate Awareness and Training Content, Materials, and Methods

13.3 Implement Security Awareness Training

All aspects of the security awareness program have been discussed, short of actually conducting the training itself. As indicated before, the author prefers the live instructor method of training over other methods and if the covered entity agrees, it should now be ready to schedule the training for its workforce members. Depending on the size of the organization and the resources available, the covered entity may be able to cover all of its workforce members in one session. Of course, this security awareness training may have to be scheduled over several sessions, thereby ensuring all members, including management, attend. As discussed, all new hires should go through this training when they are initially hired and all members of the workforce should have formal refresher training at least annually. The covered entity will still want to schedule and plan for mini-sessions throughout the year that may cover specific topics related to security to keep security awareness fresh in the workforce member's mind.

In addition to these mini-sessions, the covered entity may decide to publish a monthly newsletter with a specific section dedicated to security to assist in disseminating the security message to the workforce members. Through the use of technology that the covered entity probably already has in place, the covered entity could provide security tips through implemented screensavers or provide computer alerts that could instantly give information to the workforce members. The covered entity could also consider producing short videos that could be streamed out to the workforce members throughout the year. Do not forget that e-mail has become an effective form of communication and could easily provide a way to get the security message out. To save on the cost of travel, the covered entity may consider having live training through teleconferencing or Web meeting solutions. Finally, the covered entity could leverage prescheduled existing staff meetings to take a few minutes to discuss security matters and reinforce the importance of security.

The security awareness program is designed to ensure that all workforce members receive the necessary training as required by their job roles and responsibilities. All workforce members should be required to attend security awareness training. The workforce members are expected to retain and utilize the information presented throughout the program to make the organization more secure. The workforce members are expected to follow policies and procedures regarding the HIPAA Privacy and Security Rule. If a workforce member is not abiding by these rules, it is expected that sanctions will be imposed on the workforce member. Violations of the organization's policies and procedures should not be tolerated and should be dealt with in accordance with the organization's sanction policy.

The covered entity should refer to the following reference for further details related to implementing security awareness training:

■ NIST SP 800-66 4.5.5 Implement the Training

13.4 Monitor and Evaluate Training Plan

Security awareness training material should be kept current and updated periodically. Since new threats, vulnerabilities, and risks to the organization change, it may be necessary to change the material frequently to stay up with the current security trends. As changes are made to technology or procedures, it is imperative that additional training or dissemination of this information is made to all workforce members. Good documentation should be kept on the security awareness program and a corrective action plan should be in place to handle any problems that may arise within this program.

The covered entity should refer to the following reference for further details related to monitoring and evaluating the training plan:

■ NIST SP 800-66 4.5.7 Monitor and Evaluate Training Plan

13.5 Sample Outline of Security Awareness Training

The following is a sample outline of topics that should be covered in security awareness training.

■ HIPAA/HITECH Privacy and Security Rule
  – Security awareness training
■ Overview/objectives
  – What are HIPAA and the HITECH Act?
  – Definitions you will need to know
  – What organizations are covered entities?
  – What is the Privacy Rule?
  – What is the Security Rule?
  – What is meaningful use?
  – Breach notification
  – Enforcement
■ What is HIPAA?
  – In 1996, the U.S. Congress enacted the Health Insurance Portability and Accountability Act (HIPAA) in response to the concern about fraud or compromise of sensitive information regarding the increased use of technology in the healthcare industry.

- As a result of the Administrative Simplification provisions of HIPAA, the following rules were developed:
  - The Privacy Rule
  - The Electronic Transactions and Code Sets Rule
  - The National Identifier Requirements, and
  - The Security Rule
- What is the HITECH Act?
  - As part of the American Recovery and Reinvestment Act (ARRA) of 1999, the Health Information Technology for Economic and Clinical Health (HITECH) Act revised HIPAA and amended enforcement regulations.
- Definitions
  - *Disclosure*—Release of information outside of the entity holding that information.
  - *Health information*—Any information, in any form or medium, that relates to the past, present, or future physical or mental health, condition, provision of healthcare, or future payment for the provision of healthcare of or to an individual.
  - *Individually identifiable health information*—Includes many common identifiers such as name, address, and Social Security number.
  - *Electronic protected health information (EPHI) or protected health information*—Individually identifiable health information transmitted by electronic media, maintained in electronic media, or transmitted or maintained in any other form or medium, whether electronic, paper, or oral.
  - *Direct identifiers*—Include the following 18 items:
    - Names
    - All geographic subdivisions smaller than a state, including street address, city, county, precinct, zip code, and their equivalent geocodes, except for the initial three digits of a zip code if, according to the current publicly available data from the Bureau of the Census:
    - The geographic unit formed by combining all zip codes with the same three initial digits contains more than 20,000 people
    - The initial three digits of a zip code for all such geographic units containing 20,000 or fewer people are changed to 000
    - All elements of dates (except year) for dates directly related to an individual, including birth date, admission date, discharge date, date of death; and all ages over 89 and all elements of dates (including year) indicative of such age, except that such ages and elements may be aggregated into a single category of age 90 or older
    - Telephone numbers
    - Fax numbers
    - Electronic mail addresses
    - Social Security numbers

- Medical record numbers
- Health plan beneficiary numbers
- Account numbers
- Certificate/license numbers
- Vehicle identifiers and serial numbers, including license plate numbers
- Device identifiers and serial numbers
- Web Universal Resource Locators (URLs)
- Internet Protocol (IP) address numbers
- Biometric identifiers, including finger and voice prints
- Full face photographic images and any comparable images
- Any other unique identifying number, characteristic, or code

■ *Healthcare*—"Care, services, or supplies related to the health of an individual. It includes, but is not limited to, the following:
  (1) Preventive, diagnostic, rehabilitative, maintenance, or palliative care, and counseling, service, assessment, or procedure with respect to the physical or mental condition, or functional status, of an individual or that affects the structure or function of the body; and
  (2) Sale or dispensing of a drug, device, equipment, or other item in accordance with a prescription."

■ *Individual*—"The person who is the subject of protected health information."

■ *Use*—"with respect to individually identifiable health information, the sharing, employment, application, utilization, examination, or analysis of such information within an entity that maintains such information."

■ *Required by law*—"a mandate contained in law that compels an entity to make a use or disclosure of protected health information and that is enforceable in a court of law."

■ Covered entities
  – *Health plan* (or a group health plan)
  – *Healthcare clearinghouse*—Processes or facilitates the processing of health information or receives a standard transaction and processes or facilitates the processing of health information.
  – *Covered healthcare provider*—A healthcare provider that conducts certain transactions.

■ Covered transactions
  – Healthcare claims or equivalent encounter information transactions
  – Eligibility for a health plan transaction
  – Referral certification and authorization transaction
  – Healthcare claim status transaction
  – Enrollment or disenrollment in a health plan transaction
  – Healthcare payment and remittance advice transaction
  – Health plan premium payment transaction
  – Coordination of benefits transaction

- Business associates
  - At times, covered entities require certain functions, activities, and services be performed by other companies that are not a member of a covered entity's workforce that may involve the use or disclosure of individually identifiable health information.
  - Companies that provide these types of functions, activities, and services to covered entities are known as "business associates."
  - If services of a company do not involve the use or disclosure of protected health information or if access to such information is incidental, then the organization or person providing these services is not considered a business associate.
- Business associate contracts
  - For a covered entity to utilize another company for business-associate-type services, the covered entity must have a contract or other agreement in place with the business associate to ensure the protection and safeguard of the covered entity's individually identifiable health information.
  - The covered entity must obtain satisfactory assurance that the business associates:
    - Will use the protected health information only for its intended use
    - Will safeguard the information from inappropriate use
    - Will assist the covered entity in complying with the Privacy Rule
- Privacy Rule: Permitted use and disclosure
  - Without specific authorization from an individual, a covered entity is permitted to use or disclose protected health information for the following situations:
    - To the individual
    - Treatment, payment, healthcare operations
    - Uses and disclosures with opportunity to agree or object
    - Incidental use and disclosure
    - Public Interest and Benefit Activities
    - Limited data set
  - A covered entity must obtain an individual's written authorization for any other purposes.
- Privacy Rule: Minimum Necessary
  - A covered entity must make a reasonable effort to allow only the minimum necessary use and disclosure of protected health information.
- Privacy Rule: Notice and Other Individual Rights
  - A covered entity must provide a notice of privacy practices to individuals.
  - This notice must contain certain elements related to the use and disclosure of protected health information and the rights the individual has on such information.

- The individual has the following rights:
  - To receive the notification at any time upon request and the covered entity should make every reasonable attempt to acknowledge such receipt of notification.
  - The rights to access, amend, and restrict the use or disclosure of their protected health information.
  - The right to receive an accounting of disclosure, with certain limitations, and request to receive confidential communications in an alternative method.
- Privacy Rule: Administrative Requirements
  - Privacy policies and procedures
  - Designation of a privacy official
  - Training of workforce and management in the policies and procedures
  - Implement data safeguards to secure protected health information
  - Develop mitigation strategies
  - Establish complaint or reporting procedures
  - Records retention
- Security Rule
  - The objectives of the stricter Security Rule were to promote the expanded use of electronic health information in the healthcare industry.
    - Security Rule intended to protect certain electronic healthcare information
    - Information is supposed to be protected while allowing the proper access and use of the information.
  - The covered entity's policies and procedures
- Security Rule vs. Privacy Rule
- Security Rule: Administrative Safeguards [provide details based on policies and procedures]
  - Security Management Processes
  - Assigned Security Responsibility
  - Workforce Security
  - Information Access Management
  - Security Awareness and Training
  - Security Incident Procedures
  - Contingency Plan
  - Evaluation
  - Business Associate Contracts and Other Arrangements
- Security Rule: Physical Safeguards [provide details based on policies and procedures]
  - Facility access controls
  - Workstation use
  - Workstation security
  - Device and media controls

- Security Rule: Technical Safeguards [provide details based on policies and procedures]
  - Access control
  - Audit controls
  - Integrity
  - Person or entity controls
  - Authentication
  - Transmission security
- Meaningful Use
  - To achieve health and efficiency goals, the Centers for Medicare & Medicaid Services (CMS) has implemented an Electronic Health Records (EHR) Incentive Program.
  - This program is designed to provide financial incentives for the meaningful use of certified EHR technology.
  - There are three main components of meaningful use. These are:
    - The use of certified EHR technology in a meaningful manner
    - For electronic health information exchanges
    - For clinical quality submissions
- Breach Notification
  - Increased breach notification requirements came about as part of the HITECH Act enacted under the American Recovery and Reinvestment Act of 1009 (ARRA) on February 17, 2009.
  - These breach notification provisions apply to HIPAA covered entities and business associates that access, maintain, retain, modify, record, store, destroy, or otherwise hold, use, or disclose unsecured protected health information.
  - In short, if a covered entity discovers a breach of unsecured protected health information, it is required to promptly notify the affected individuals and the Secretary of Health and Human Services.
  - If a business associate of a covered entity discovers that it had a breach, it must notify the covered entity of the breach.
  - In some cases, the media must also be notified of such a breach, and for any breach involving more than 500 individuals, the Secretary of Health and Human Services is required to post a list of covered entities on the Health and Human Services' Web site.
- Enforcement Rule
  - The Department of Health and Human Services (HHS) strengthened HIPAA enforcement as a response to the HITECH Act that was enacted as part of the American Recovery and Reinvestment Act of 2009.
  - New, stricter civil money penalties were enacted for violations of the HIPAA Act occurring after February 18, 2009.
  - The revisions included four categories of violations along with four different, incrementing tiers of monetary amounts.

- The modifications capped each violation at $50,000 per violation with an aggregate limit for identical violations set at $1.5 million per calendar year. The new requirements also provided an affirmative defense, waiver, and notice of proposed determination.

13.6 Summary

In this chapter, developing a security awareness training program was discussed in detail. Providing security awareness training to workforce members, executives, and individuals that may have access to protected health information is a requirement of the HIPAA Security Rule. It also can be one of the most important security controls that can be implemented at an organization. Since workforce members are the front line of any security program, providing the appropriate training to these members is essential.

A specific training strategy needs to be developed and an adequate training plan needs to be carried out that has upper management support. An individual or group of individuals should be directly responsible for providing a comprehensive security awareness training program that is ongoing. This training program should complement other training provided in the organization.

There are some very specific items that should be covered within the security awareness training material. An outline of these topics should be developed so as not to miss any essential components or address important items related to security. There are several methods by which training can be distributed to workforce members. It will be up to the individuals responsible for the security awareness training program to decide on the most appropriate method for the organization.

When the security awareness training is provided, documentation should be kept that will be utilized to track the progress of the program. To demonstrate compliance, a log should be maintained of all workforce members that attend the training. In addition, the specific content provided during this training should be documented. To improve the security awareness training program, the training should be evaluated and monitored. This review may provide insight into additional topic items that may need to be added to the training or questions that arise that may need to be addressed by policies or procedures.

Chapter 14

Security Rule: Incident Response

Objectives

The objectives of this chapter are as follows:

- Determine what standard format will be utilized to cover security incidences within the covered entity.
- Understand the steps involved in handling a security incident.
- Understand what type of notifications should be made during a security incident.
- Determine what details should be collected during the investigation of a security incident.
- Determine who will be responsible to handle a security incident.
- Understand the types of actions to take to resolve a security incident.
- Understand the types of recommendations that may be a result of a security incident taking place.

Background

In this chapter, the actual steps involved in handling a security incident will be discussed. Remember, a *security incident* is any inadvertent or intentional use or disclosure of protected health information. A *breach*, on the other hand, is defined as "the loss of control, compromise, unauthorized disclosure, unauthorized acquisition, unauthorized access, or any similar term referring to situations where persons other than authorized users and for an other than authorized purposes have access or potential access to personally identifiable information, whether physical or electronic" (OMB Memorandum M07-16). A covered entity is required to have policies and procedures implemented to properly handle any security incident that may occur covering a wide variety of situations. This chapter is dedicated to developing a standard format to handle these types of situations and refers to NIST SP 800-61, Computer Security Incident Handling Guide (January 2004) for further information.

14.1 Standard Format

When handling a security incident, it is important that a standard format is followed to include all necessary items. Setting up a standard framework for incident handling will allow the collection of all the information needed and to track the actions taken. It is important, for regulatory and possible law enforcement purposes, to document these actions. Since a lot of security incidents tend to be of a criminal nature, it is essential that accurate notes and proper documentation is kept.

A security incident normally involves a situation being discovered and being reported to the security official. A standard form should be developed for the initial report of the incident. This form should include, at a minimum, the following items:

- Name of the individual making the report
- Contact information for the reporting individual, to include phone, e-mail, and address
- Location where the incident took place
- Date and time that the incident occurred
- A brief synopsis of the incident including what happened, what systems were affected, what information may have been affected, and possible causes of such an incident occurring
- The rationale behind making the report

This should provide the security official enough information to begin an investigation into the security incident following the steps that will be discussed in the next section.

14.2 Steps

There are several steps that should be followed in the proper handling of a security incident that will be discussed, specifically:

- Confirmation
- Analysis

- Notification
- Containment
- Eradication
- Recovery
- Review

It is important that documentation of every action is taken during each of these steps. See Figure 14.1 for further information.

The first step of any incident is to confirm that an incident actually occurred. There are several factors that will be taken into consideration when confirming an incident. For instance, the covered entity needs to determine exactly what happened that caused a report to be generated. Some questions that need to be answered are the following:

- Was there an inadvertent disclosure of information?
- Was there an intentional exposure of this information?
- What type of information was exposed?
- How much of this information was exposed?
- Is this information considered protected health information?
- Would gaining access to this information allow an unauthorized individual to utilize the information for further harm?

Based on the answers to these questions, along with the other factors related to the incident, a decision will be required to be made on how the incident will be handled. Based on the impact with which the incident could cause harm to the covered entity in relation to financial, reputational, or regulatory risks, the handling of the incident should be prioritized. This will assist in the determination of the types of resources that will or may be required to mitigate further damage.

Once confirmation has been made that a security incident occurred, an analysis should be conducted. The analysis should take the current and potential technical impact of the incident and prioritize the resources affected accordingly.

Based upon the analysis conducted and depending on the thresholds set by the incident policy and procedures, notifications should be made. These notifications may include internal personnel or external groups. These individuals should have already been identified internally as part of the incident response team members. Notification procedures will be discussed further in the next section.

After notifications have been made, the incident needs to be contained. This containment may include procedures to acquire, preserve, secure, and document evidence of the security incident. One of the steps that could be taken in containment may be to take the affected system offline to prevent further damage. Depending on the situation, the incident response procedure should cover specific steps to take over a variety of situations. During the containment process, additional external resources may be required for this specific technical containment if

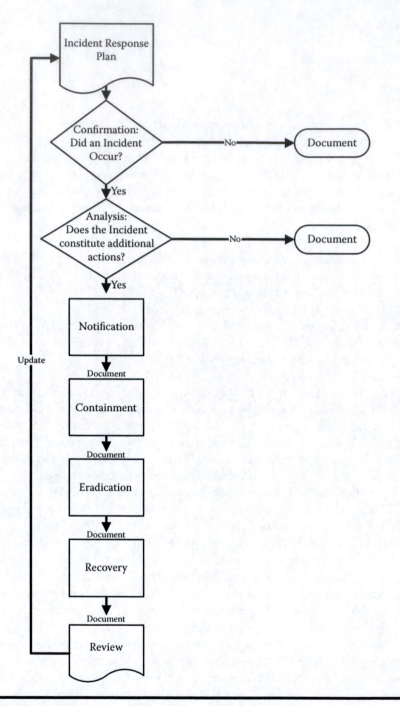

Figure 14.1   Incident response flowchart.

there is not an expert available internally. As previously recommended, the covered entity should have vetted a digital forensic partner beforehand that could assist in providing this expertise if necessary.

After the incident has been contained, the incident needs to be eradicated. The covered entity needs to identify and mitigate the vulnerabilities that were exploited that caused the incident in the first place. This could include removing any malicious software, disabling remote connections, or deleting inappropriate material.

Once the incident has been eradicated, the process moves into the recovery phase. The affected systems must be returned to their original operational state with any vulnerable issues identified in the previous step mitigated. This could be completed through restoring the system back from known good media and then reapplying any patches as mitigation, if applicable. Once the systems are operational, the covered entity needs to confirm that it is functioning normally. The covered entity may also want to consider implementing additional monitoring solutions to verify that there will be no unusual activity occurring in the future that may have been caused by the original security incident.

Finally, the covered entity will want to review the handling of the incident and make the appropriate changes to the incident response plan, if applicable. The follow-up report may be required to be distributed to the board of directors, executive management, or regulators depending on the severity of the incident.

14.3 Notification

There are six elements identified in OMB Memorandum M-07-16 regarding safeguarding against and responding to the breach of personally identifiable information that should be addressed in the procedures as the rationale in making external notifications:

- Breach notification required by law
- Timeliness in making notifications
- Source of the breach
- Content of the information used or disclosed
- Means to providing notification
- Recipients required to be notified

Chapter 8 should be reviewed to determine what types of external notifications are required based on the risk of harm caused by the breach and the level of risk sustained by the breach. The risk of harm takes into consideration five factors:

1. Nature of the data elements that were breached
2. The number of individuals that are or could have been affected by the breach
3. The ability for the information to be accessed and utilized

4. The possibility that additional harm could occur from the breach
5. Mitigation factors

In regard to timeliness of notification, a covered entity is required to notify an individual of a breach in a reasonable time and in no case later than 60 days after discovery of a breach. A breach is determined to be *discovered* by a covered entity as of the first day in which the breach was known or, by exercising reasonable diligence, should have been known by the covered entity.

Breach notifications should be made at the highest level within the organization. Per the policy or procedure, the breach notification may be made by the security official for internal notifications or the covered entity may have a specific public relations official that will make appropriate notifications to external entities.

Chapter 8 specifically identifies the content of the notifications, how notifications should take place, and who should be notified of any security breaches.

As mentioned earlier, full documentation should be kept on the individuals that were notified both internally and externally. This documentation should also include the following:

- Date of notifications
- Times of notifications
- Method of notifications (i.e., phone, fax, e-mail, letter, etc.)
- Titles or responsibilities of individuals notified
- Any other appropriate information related to notification of internal and external resources

14.4 Incident Details

Some additional information that the security official may want to document includes the following:

- Assign the incident a tracking number
- Assign a specific incident handler (Note: This could be the security official)
- Keep track of the status of the incident and the actions currently pending on the incident
- Document the type of information breached
- Document the sensitivity of this information
- Document the technical impact
- Identify the sources of the incident (including any hostnames or IP addresses of the possible source, if applicable)
- Detail the incident and how the incident was detected
- Describe the resources affected including hostnames or IP addresses, if applicable

- Determine the priority factor (functional impact, information impact, recoverability, etc.)
- Determine the mitigation factor (e.g., stolen laptop containing sensitive data using full disk encryption)
- Document response actions taken
- Document any other organizations that may have been contacted related to the incident such as software vendor or third-party service provider
- Provide any additional comments related to the incident that may be important

14.5 Incident Handler

For the individual assigned responsibility over the incident, the following additional information may be documented:

- The current status of the incident response
- Summary of the incident
- Action logs
- Contact information for all individuals involved in the incident
- List of inventory of all evidence gathered or collected
- Possible causes of the incident
- Incident cost
- The impact of the incident on the covered entity
- Any additional comments related to the incident

14.6 Actions Taken or Recommended Actions

Documentation is essential when dealing with security incidents as has been reiterated throughout this chapter. It is imperative that all actions that have been taken in the handling of the incident be tracked. This includes the date, time, and details of the actions taken and should be kept in sequential order. This will develop a timeline of the incident. Any recommended actions noted throughout the process, such as mitigation efforts or advice from external consultants that may have been contacted for assistance, should be documented. A disposition of these recommended actions should also be noted as necessary.

14.7 Other Recommendations

The following is a list of recommendations to assist in handling security incidents as paraphrased from the National Institute of Standards and Technology (NIST) Special Publication 800-61 Revision 2 (Draft) (January 2012):

- Determine and obtain the tools and resources that may be valuable during an incident.
- Attempt to prevent an incident from occurring in the first place by implementing adequate security controls.
- Implement several different types of monitoring systems that alert on suspicious activity. Review any alerts to identify precursors and indicators to an incident.
- Outside parties should be required to report incidents to the covered entity. Develop procedures for reporting of outside parties.
- Develop procedures for logging and auditing on all information systems. There should be a minimum standard of logging and auditing set with a stricter requirement for information systems handling electronic protected health information or other critical items.
- Determine the normal activities for the network, information systems, and applications.
- Develop a policy for log retentions.
- Correlate events.
- Keep information systems' internal clocks synchronized.
- Develop and maintain a knowledge base to assist incident handlers to reference information that may be available from previous incidents.
- Document the incident and all actions taken as soon as possible.
- Secure all data related to the incident.
- Based on relevant factors, prioritize handling activities.
- Ensure that the incident response policy contains provisions for incident reporting.
- Establish procedures for incident containment.
- Establish proper evidence collection procedures.
- Develop procedures for capturing volatile data.
- System snapshots should be taken through the use of a full forensic disk image and not through backups.
- After-action reviews should be performed after a major incident occurs.

14.8 Summary

A step-by-step process of handling a security incident was discussed throughout this chapter. This process is also summarized in Chapter 21, Section 21.3 and crisis handling steps are provided in Section 21.4. Determining a standard methodology for handling security incidents is the first step in handling a security incident. Having a plan of action prior to an incident occurring will prevent a lot of wasted resources and provide a little more control over an otherwise unpredictable situation.

Most, if not all, security incidents can be handled appropriately by following these steps:

- Confirming an incident
- Analyzing an incident
- Making proper notifications
- Containing an incident
- Eradicating an incident
- Recovering from an incident
- Conducting an after-action review of the incident to improve procedures for next time

There are special requirements and regulations regarding the appropriate notification process when dealing with breaches. It is important to document the details of an incident. It is also essential to track and monitor the incident appropriately. Upon the resolution of an incident, certain actions will be required and recommendations provided to prevent the incident from occurring in the future. An after-action review of the entire process should be conducted to improve the handling of security incidents.

Chapter 15

Security Rule: Business Continuity Planning and Disaster Recovery*

Objectives

The objectives of this chapter are as follows:

- Understand the requirements for a business continuity and disaster recovery plan under the HIPAA Security Rule.
- Understand requirements under the contingency plan.
- Determine requirements for the data backup plan.
- Determine requirements for the disaster recovery plan.
- Understand requirements under the emergency mode operation plan.
- Develop testing and revision procedures.
- Understand requirements to conduct analysis on applications and data criticality.
- Develop a plan to address both operational and regulatory requirements.

---

* The following chapter on business continuity and disaster recovery planning is provided with permission by Mike Stankiewicz, a subject matter expert on business continuity and disaster recovery planning.

Background

The areas of business continuity, business continuity planning, and disaster recovery are, and should be, considered as corporate or entity-level governance. Although many people may argue that business continuity and disaster recovery are specific to the information technology department, this line of thinking is outdated and ineffective for the recovery and restoration of businesses in the 21st century. For housekeeping purposes, the covered entity should understand that within this chapter, the terms *business continuity, business contingency, disaster recovery, disaster restoration,* and *business recovery planning* may be used interchangeably. Each of these is encompassed and should be considered as covered under the umbrella of what this book will term *business continuity.*

Business Continuity and Disaster Recovery pieces of the Health Insurance Portability and Accountability Act of 1996 (HIPAA) are included in the Administrative Safeguards section of this regulation. Many individual components of compliance within 45 CFR § 164.308(a)(7) fall under the realm of a business's technology professionals as a result of healthcare entities' increased dependence on technology for the management, processing, and storage of electronic protected health information (EPHI). Although many components will need to be restored by the restoration of computers and information systems, the criticality of both the data and timely restoration of operations for healthcare entities makes oversight a role for executive management. As such, the Administrative Safeguards section of the HIPAA framework is an appropriate location to address business continuity planning.

The Business Continuity and Disaster Recovery Planning requirement of the HIPAA regulation is split into a total of six subsections. Four of the six subsections are required, meaning that healthcare providers must comply with these four areas, while the other two subsections are addressable. It can be speculated that the two subsections that are currently labeled as "addressable" will become "required" at some point in the near future. Specifically, the HIPAA required subsections of BCP compliance are:

- Contingency Plan
- Data Backup Plan
- Disaster Recovery Plan
- Emergency Mode Operation Plan

Additionally, the two subsections that are not yet required are Testing and Revision Procedures, and Applications and Data Criticality Analysis. See Table 15.1.

The subsequent pages will provide details of the requirements on the subsections of 45 CFR § 164.308. The components or areas of required and addressable compliance will be detailed, followed by practical methodologies or ways to

Table 15.1 HIPAA Security Rule Standard Implementation Specification for Business Continuity/Disaster Recovery

Security Standards		
Administrative Safeguards		
164. 308(a)(7)		**Contingency Plan**
164. 308(a)(7)(ii)(A)	R	Data Backup Plan
164. 308(a)(7)(ii)(B)	R	Disaster Recovery Plan
164. 308(a)(7)(ii)C	R	Emergency Mode Operation Plan
164. 308(a)(7)(ii)(D)	A	Testing and Revision Procedures
164. 308(a)(7)(ii)(E)	A	Applications and Data Criticality Analysis
Physical Safeguards		
164. 310(a)(1)		**Facility Access Controls**
164. 310(a)(2)(i)	A	Contingency Operations
164. 310(d)(1)		**Device and Media Controls**
164. 310(d)(2)(iv)	A	Data Backup and Storage
Technical Safeguards		
164. 312(a)(1)		**Access Control**
164. 312(a)(2)(ii)	R	Emergency Access Procedure

Note: A = addressable, R = required.

evaluate the covered entity's healthcare information environment to ensure compliance with the HIPAA Security Rule.

15.1 Contingency Plan—45 CFR § 164.308(a)(7)(i)

The contingency plan is the master or summary-level of documentation required to be within compliance with the HIPAA Security Rule. Within the contingency plan are defined and succinct pieces that must be present to meet regulatory compliance. All staff involvement is usually required to adequately address each of the necessary components. The presence of an adequate contingency plan is the combination of all of the following components (please note that this is not an all-inclusive list):

■ A policy briefly stating that a business continuity plan (BCP; contingency plan) is in place, is supported and managed by executive management

- Creating and performing a business impact analysis (BIA) to identify:
  - Risks (man-made, technical, natural, etc.) to an entity (process, system)
  - Analysis of various data (EPH, EPHI, NPI, etc.) to an entity's operation
  - Analysis of facilities, paperwork, processes, or systems critical to an entity's operation
- Primary and backup plans to perform "critical tasks" vital to the entity's operation
- Evacuation and emergency procedures
- Employee communication
- Executive communication
- Partner/vendor communication
- A road map (the plan and support files) for any person in the business to perform the critical operational tasks and duties to ensure the solvency of the entity

15.2 Data Backup Plan—45 CFR § 164.308(a)(7)(ii)(A)

The contingency plan contains specific focus areas to ensure the restoration of the healthcare entity's business. The data backup plan is exactly how it sounds; it is the plan (and its details) for the backup, recovery, and restoration of data that resides on a computer or other information system. Additionally, the data backup plan must include provisions to ensure the confidentiality, integrity, and availability of an information system's data under normal conditions (rest, storage, transmission) as well as during and immediately after a disruptive event. In short, procedures should be established and maintained that detail the following:

- Critical information systems
- Critical data on information systems
- Backup, recovery, and restoration procedures for both data and information systems.

As such, the successful completion of this control set will require involvement from executives, technology persons, and staff from all operational business units. Table 15.2 details persons, roles, and responsibilities related to ensuring the organization's data backup plan is functional and that critical data to all business areas can be backed up, recovered, and restored in a time frame that is acceptable to the owner of the business file or document.

As previously mentioned, although the information technology (IT) department is the equivalent of a majority shareholder in the data backup plan and process, all business units' needs should be considered, and at day's end, it is executive management's role to ensure that both IT and other business units have the critical tools required to ensure business functionality after a disaster or other disruptive act.

Table 15.2 Roles and Responsibilities

Person(s)/Departments	Roles and Responsibilities
Executives	Provide support to business areas as needed; provide oversight to ensure functionality of overall plan; provide purpose, scope, and accountability and ensure enforcement
Information technology designees	Create formal data backup plan; ensure all critical data identified by business units is backed up; detail backup types, locations, frequencies, encryption/decryption, accessibility, data retention, data destruction, data security, and data recovery testing as applicable
Business unit representatives	Identify data needs/requirements for job duties; identify financial, operational, and regulatory requirements for processing of data previously identified, identify workarounds or backup procedures for processing of data previously identified; assist in testing/validation of data recovery testing

15.3 Disaster Recovery Plan—45 CFR § 164.308(a)(7)(ii)(B)

The disaster recovery plan requirement, as defined by the HIPAA Security Rule, is the culmination or completion of the entire business continuity management process. A comprehensive and completed business continuity plan both contains an outline of normal operations and is a game plan for the declaration, response, recovery, restoration, and return to normal operations for the entire entity. The plan will provide corporate-level governance, recovery and restoration (short- and long-term) for all critical applications, data, facilities, processes, tasks, and so on required to maintain the business.

Recovery plans for corporate and department-level reconstruction are traditionally written by either the critical "item" that requires recovery and restoration, or per business unit with all critical "items" required for the recovery and restoration of that business unit. In a perfect world, all critical items could be restored simultaneously with minimal downtime and impact on both entities and patients. Unfortunately, to be able to achieve this goal requires extensive resources (facilities, staff, and systems), which the vast majority of covered entities do not have at their disposal. Therefore, one of the most crucial attributes of the disaster recovery plan is to outline the "operational order of recovery and restoration" of critical items (data, facilities, information systems, processes, procedures, and other tasks). Since most covered entities have a finite amount of resources, the plan should define what steps are required to restore the business in the short- and long-term, and in what order items will be addressed. The idea is to address, plan, and make decisions for as many items or potential items that are "known to the business" as required for solvency prior to a disaster. This affords the business the opportunity to discuss and make decisions while under less stress (during normal conditions), instead of having to make decisions during or in the immediate aftermath of a chaotic and disruptive event.

Detractors or naysayers of the business continuity process may state that some things cannot be thought of or decided until the disruptive event occurs. That thinking is a fallacy, especially for those that study history. Hurricane Katrina was one of more recent and severe catastrophes in which the failure to perform some basic tasks rendered many businesses unable to fully recover from the event. Those businesses, as a result, likely went bankrupt or are insolvent. The Federal Financial Institutions Examination Council (FFIEC) published a whitepaper of lessons learned from Hurricane Katrina. To summarize, the major obstacles that affected financial institutions faced in recovery and restoration of businesses included "communication challenges in locating missing personnel, unplanned transportation interruptions, lack of redundant power or consideration to, physical facility destruction and lack of defined backup locations, and postal interruptions" (Federal Financial Institutions Examination Council 2006).

Hurricane Katrina provided some unique challenges to those affected. However, some pre-planning that could have been done in advance of this event may have led to a different result. Some things these financial institutions could have established ahead of time include:

- Creation, maintenance, and testing of employee contact trees (phone, e-mail, text)
- Consideration of a central telephone line for information and updates
- Generator purchase and deployment or procurement of generator (and fuel) in advance of the event since its onset was not sudden
- Creation, maintenance, and testing of business command centers, and alternate meeting and office locations
- Ensuring overstocks of supplies exist where applicable in case of transportation delays or interruptions

Though having or addressing all of these items in advance may not guarantee the successful restoration of the business, these preparations would have helped the business recovery cause by allowing executive management the ability to concentrate on the elements of this event that could not have been preplanned for (such as the ferocity of the storm and the duration of Katrina's effects on New Orleans). A good rule of thumb is, if something can be agreed upon and planned for (even in a limited scope or capacity) in advance of an event, the better chance the business has of an efficient and speedy restoration of services provided.

The disaster recovery plan, its content and criticality with respect to the public at large for healthcare entities, should be drafted, supervised by executive management, tested, analyzed, improved, redrafted, and retested. This will allow organizations both the ability to be in compliance with HIPAA guidance and also enable the business to better react to a disruptive incident when one really occurs.

15.4 Emergency Mode Operation Plan— 45 CFR § 164.308(a)(7)(ii)(C)

The emergency mode operation plan, as defined by the HIPAA Administrative Simplification Security Rule, is a subset of the disaster recovery plan for short-term processing and security of EPHI data. In essence, the emergency mode operation plan is the combination of the data processing central operations for the business as well as contingencies for every individual data processing task. The emergency mode operation plan is intended as a short-term checklist for the immediate or near-immediate recovery and restoration of business processes using backup and redundancies defined by each business unit. Based on the specificity that an emergency mode operation plan requires, input from representatives of all business areas is required if the end goal is a functional operation plan.

To build a functional emergency mode operation plan, there are specific areas at a minimum that should be considered. A covered entity's security official should implement, at a minimum, the following emergency mode operations plan procedures:

- Maintain alternate data processing sites
- Ensure that the primary and backup sites have compatible software and hardware requirements
- Provide alternative sources of power and communications
- Appoint emergency mode operation team members
- Ensure business associates are aware of the covered entity's emergency mode operation plan and the critical vendors that will be utilized when required
- Train workforce members in emergency mode operations. Training should include:
  - Plan initiation
  - Notifying patients
  - Notifying business associates
  - Restoring operations
- At least annually, test the emergency mode operations plan and modify accordingly
- Document actions taken during an emergency (Jones 2009)

In addition, creating and maintaining the following will greatly assist staff in recovery and restoration efforts:

- Critical vendor contact lists
- Vendor contingency plans
- Reciprocal business contracts
- Test plans and notes from operations at alternate command center location
- Providing staff with command center locations (as applicable)

Although the provided list will assist in the restoration of the business, the premise or assumption is that current workforce members are available to coordinate and perform the recovery and restoration duties needed by the covered entity to maintain stability.

Any executive worth her salt would be remiss if she did not ask herself, "what about a personnel recovery and restoration plan?" Unfortunately, this assumption may not always be correct based on the circumstances of the disruptive event. If the "disaster" is an epidemic, military-driven, pandemic, or other event that affects workforce members' (or their immediate family's) availability, health, and general well-being, this defines a disaster of another kind.

As with any other risk, steps can be taken to mitigate the exposure to covered entities with regard to "staffing emergencies." The first step is to have a plan in place that addresses unexpected absences from the covered entity. Thorough examination of the possibility of potential staffing issues uncovers a slippery slope of questions pertaining to compensation, short- and long-term replacement of staff (if needed), ensuring the lost skill sets unique to the healthcare entity are considered, and temporary versus permanent replacement of staff. The second step is to discuss and develop as much framework (such as policies) as possible to address these potential risks. Again, the rationale is to help the entity make better business decisions by making those choices during normal business meetings instead of on the fly immediately after a disastrous event. Items to consider including in the framework include:

- Paid time off and leave of absence provisions
- Position "holding"
- Staff quarantine protocols
- Maintenance of employee benefits during absences
- Staff scaling protocols
- Updated job descriptions including specialized skills
- Potentially an agreement or partnership with a regional or national staffing agency

Should a disaster occur that has an unusually great (and adverse) effect on staffing, plans should be implemented in advance to ensure that entities can provide both patient service, and security of EPHI and other sensitive data.

Advantages of contracting a staffing agency normally include individual background, financial, and professional records verification. Should a need arise to have to replace a great number of employees quickly, all of which have high levels of

EPHI access, a plan should be in place to allow for both rapid and secure hiring practices to ensure that patient care is uninterrupted or not compromised. The vetting that staffing agencies normally perform, prior to sending resumes to employers, saves the healthcare entity time and effort in locating potentially suitable replacement employees. It also ensures those employees will not abuse their access levels to EPHI and other confidential data. Working with agencies also affords the choice to management whether the requirement is a contractual hire or a full-time employee, since the agencies usually identify persons able or willing to accept a contract or contract-to-hire position. Whether the covered entity chooses to handle the applicant search portion of the human resources process or not, a comprehensive and succinct plan should be written and maintained to ensure that staffing needs can be adequately addressed for events that have both a slow and a fast onset.

The emergency mode operation plan is simply a short-term disaster recovery plan for processing and securing of EPHI data. The plan should address, in as much detail as possible, how to get critical operations restored as quickly and securely as possible. Its goal should be the short-term restoration of critical business functions that will eventually lead to the full recovery and solvency of the entity reviewed.

15.5 Testing and Revision Procedures— Addressable—45 CFR § 164.308(a)(7)(ii)(D)(b)

The Testing and Revision Procedures component of the Business Continuity Planning Process as defined by the HIPAA standards are currently listed as addressable versus required. Although testing and revision procedures are not yet required to ensure HIPAA compliance, a comprehensive BCP must include validation techniques. Testing the plan, validating specific procedures or statements within the plan, recording and addressing results from testing and validation steps, lessons learned, and plan redevelopment are necessities for a plan that management has confidence in using should the need arise.

In the business continuity world, testing of the plan is the final step in a comprehensive BCP management process or program. Simply stated, testing and validation of the details within the business continuity plan need to be done to ensure that the plan, as constructed, is:

1. Usable
2. Reasonable
3. Provides sufficient detail to replicate the performance of a task
4. Complete

Having a BCP document, policy, or other statement is a nicety, but will not help a business restore operations after it has been affected by the scope of a disruptive event.

Testing can take shape in many forms or manners, in both controlled and uncontrolled settings. Although a fully controlled testing environment is desired for BCP testing activities, unfortunately businesses do not always have that luxury. When unplanned issues do arise, a common mistake made by many organizations is the failure to fully document and learn lessons (where applicable) for unplanned events.

Types of testing (planned and unplanned) include but are not limited to:

- Performing emergency evacuation drills
- Testing staff call trees
- Tabletop testing (using a predetermined scenario)
- Component testing
- Procedural testing
- Data restoration and verification
- Full information systems and facilities cutover testing

While HIPAA requirements are specific to electronic data and the protection of EPHI, comprehensive testing will address both IT driven tasks as well as those to be performed by other business units. In summary, testing can take many forms and should be designed to test people, processes, and tasks to ensure proper functionality during an actual emergency.

Regardless of the test type, whether a test was planned or a real disaster occurs, fully documenting the actions taken once the BCP is enabled is a critical activity on many fronts. First, documentation during chaotic circumstances will allow for the most accurate summary or depiction of the events as they unfolded and the subsequent actions taken.

Second, in many instances, workforce members may be granted access rights outside of their normal scope. Although these access controls may need to be altered to continue or restore critical business components, failure to document access control changes will lead to what is known in the information security community as privilege creep. In short, *privilege creep* occurs when a workforce member with normal access rights is granted additional access rights; however, the additional (and in most cases temporary) extension of access rights is not subsequently revoked when no longer required. If documentation includes "special or additional access rights" provisioned for workforce members, a record should exist that can be later reviewed and acted upon; otherwise, the workforce member may attain additional access rights postdisaster in comparison to predisaster.

A third valid reason for complete documentation of the actions taken as the result of enacting the BCP is to later reflect upon, analyze, and learn from the test or real disruptive event that forced the enactment of the entity's BCP. Here is where the true value lies related to fully documenting the actions and decisions made during the course of a real disastrous event, or a planned or unplanned test of any part of the BCP. Analysis of testing or event results is useful for future improvement. Should an entity fail to log or document the actions and decisions made, analysis of the scenario and full recollection of the events as unfolded is not realistic. As time passes from the exact moment of the event or test, details become increasingly skewed, which can result in inaccurate analysis. In many cases, failure to document events as they unfold can lead business process owners to assume that procedures would be found, adhered to, and so on. This can lead business process owners and business owners to believe (erroneously) that the current BCP, as constructed, is functional.

Having accurate documentation of the entire disruptive test event also enables business entities to evaluate what pieces were performed well, what can be done better in the future, and what parts failed miserably. Although it is human nature to desire success, the creation and management of a successful business continuity management process must include reflective evaluation. It can be simple to recognize and amplify the successes while minimizing the shortcomings of a test or event, especially if results are solely evaluated and measured by workforce members within the entity. Therefore, independent valuation of all event or test documentation, logs, notes, and so on is the most objective way to obtain a reflection of what is great, what is average, what can be improved upon, and what is flat-out bad related to resulting actions and decisions performed once an event occurs or a test is declared.

As such, the most effective ways to ensure objective analysis of BCP event or testing documentation is to invoke separation of duties. In other words, the person(s) evaluating the event's actions and decisions, or the testing processes' resultant actions and decisions, should not be involved in the business restoration process. Businesses can choose to segregate this duty by either entering into an agreement or partnership with a service provider or by involving a noncustomer centric business division (examples include internal audit, project management offices, and quality assurance) to act as the independent test evaluator, also referred to as the *proctor*.

Although the analysis is a process that requires interaction from all areas of the business, persons without direct involvement should be accountable for the analysis and reporting of the plan test or the actual event's resultant actions to ensure objectivity. In addition, oversight of the BCP management process needs to be defined. To reiterate a previous point, the BCP management process is of corporate level. As such, the executive management team must ensure the BCP is and continues to remain on the radar of the individual business process owners (IT and otherwise). To recap, effective segregation of BCP oversight duties requires input from at least four entities:

1. Business process owners
2. IT in support of business process owners
3. Independent evaluation
4. Executive oversight

Assuming the previous steps have been followed, the next logical step or procedure is to redevelop or improve the existing documentation. The independent analysis detailed previously becomes crucial in ensuring that future BCP document

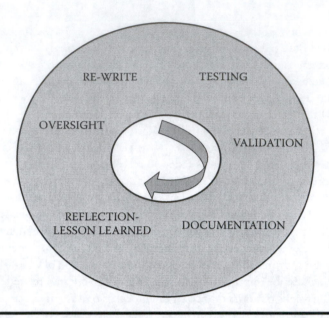

Figure 15.1 Testing and revision process.

versions are better, more complete, have increased accuracy, and contain all identified items. Once weaknesses in the existing plan or plan documentation are identified through testing and testing documentation, the entity has the opportunity to address the limitation(s) identified during the disruptive event or test event. Now that deficiencies have been identified, documented, validated, and remedied, it is time to repeat the process.

In summary, BCP testing and revision processes are circular in that the process never really has an end and once the "end" is reached, the process must be restarted. This circular process is visually explained in Figure 15.1.

This circular process should be comprehensive in its design to ensure that all critical needs are addressed and tested. In short, the BCP testing process should test modules of the overall BCP, the data backup plan, disaster recovery plan, and emergency mode operation plan. Subsequent tests should be designed to test or assess different components of the business continuity, data backup, disaster recovery, and emergency mode operation plans to ensure compliance with all facets of the HIPAA regulation as written.

15.6 Applications and Data Criticality Analysis— Addressable—45 CFR § 164.308(a)(7)(ii)(E)(b)

The Applications and Data Criticality Analysis portion of the Business Continuity Planning process as defined by the HIPAA standards is currently listed as addressable versus required at the date of publishing. Although an applications and data criticality analysis is not yet required to ensure HIPAA compliance, a comprehensive BCP must be comprised and constructed from the applications and data criticality analysis process. Without performing a criticality assessment of all data and applications residing on entity information systems, decisions on the recovery order of information systems and applications will be left solely to the discretion of the IT department.

Although 99% of IT departments are versed in performing their own job duties, it is not their function or responsibility to instruct or direct the operations of other departments. Therefore, the completion and subsequent creation of a game plan resulting from the applications and data criticality analysis should allow for:

- Business process owners to explain needs, requirements and timelines
- Discuss available process workarounds (if applicable)
- Create a net criticality rating
- Identification of net criticality ratings for all data and all business areas
- Analyze data, determine financial and operational impact, and rank or rate data based on net criticality
- Identify critical applications and information systems that data is dependent upon for business process owners to perform job duties
- Determining prerequisites and interdependencies for all previously identified and ranked critical data, applications, information systems, networks, and interconnectivity to other networks (Cloud, Internet, and VPN)
- Create a chronological order to recover information systems, applications. and data as the end result of the analysis
- Test, evaluate, edit and re-start the processes (just like the figure of the wheel depicted for BCP testing)

According to HIPAA Training and Supremus Group, LLC, required areas to be specifically addressed within an applications and data criticality analysis include "a completed and approved Business Impact Analysis prior to this analysis. In addition, the analysis will address information, specifications, users, vendors, vulnerabilities, recovery complexity, recovery plans, recovery history, standard operating procedures, source code and backup detail, dependencies and data reconstruction variables for all applications, databases, information systems and networks" that comprise the healthcare entity (Supremus Group 2012).

In understanding the business continuity planning and development processes, it would seem logical that the applications and data criticality analysis should be a precursor to the creation of the BCP document. With respect to HIPAA, however, this item is listed as addressable only at this time. During the next section of this chapter, a different approach will be shared with regard to when to perform the BIA, risk assessment, and applications and data criticality analysis within the BCP management process. Although HIPAA regulations touch upon all key areas, increased synergy in the creation and management of the plan, its documents, the performing of analyses, and compliance with regulations can be attained through a number of avenues. This volume will attempt to provide its readership with another perspective on how to achieve compliance with all six of the BCP-centric safeguards through a single and concentrated effort.

15.7 A Plan Addressing Both Operational and Regulatory Requirements

The purpose of this section is to concisely detail how to meet regulatory requirements while creating a functional and useful BCP. Using this author's experiences, common practices within the business continuity planning community, and successfully used framework as supporting references, a comprehensive oversight process will be outlined to assist readers with either creating a new HIPAA-compliant set of business recovery documents; or validating existing business resumption planning documents, plans, or binders. The following pages will provide one specific methodology for the oversight, development, and management of an entity's BCP. Although the provided approach is not "the only right way to develop a BCP program," it is a proven one that has resulted in organizations being able to successfully recover and restore critical operations and business as usual.

Based on initial articles, reports, and whitepapers surrounding HIPAA requirements, the first phase or iteration of evaluating an entity's BCP environment currently appears to be primarily concerned with the availability of data, postevent, with lesser focus on data's confidentiality and integrity. The purpose of this book is to guide entities through the full process and not just ensuring EPHI is made available, postincident. Therefore, from this point forward, we will discuss the how-to related to the successful completion of the BCP program as well as outline specific areas that are on HIPAA's radar currently. Finally, the remainder of this chapter will help guide those entities (both large and small) through a comprehensive process.

To have a workable or viable BCP, the previously identified method and framework is being provided for the reader's consideration. Based on this author's 10-plus years working in roles that include business continuity responsibilities, it is safe to state that a successful plan starts at the top of the organization. The first steps to a BCP's success or failure, simply stated, require executive buy-in authorizing those creating the plan and framework to cut across organizational silos that still exist in many organizations, and especially in larger institutions. This author, in the past, has experienced a direct correlation between the levels of real buy-in from executives, for example, in direct relation to the overall effectiveness of the program. In short, if the decision makers do not take business continuity seriously as both a business operations and business security issue, the resultant plan and framework will be more likely to fail and will be susceptible to more "break points" or more points of failure.

Having executive buy-in for the project has multiple positive ramifications including:

- Increased buy-in from subordinates
- Peer pressure of employees not wanting to be the one holding up the project
- Future planning includes the necessary BCP considerations (if any)
- If necessary, the use of the "executive's heavy hand" if the BCP project management team is not obtaining the resources it needs to advance the plan and project as previously scheduled and agreed upon

Usually, this is measured by the project manager (especially if that is an outside entity) to determine how the project may expect to proceed. Finally, executive management is usually those with fiscal responsibility over the organization and as such, is ultimately accountable for the creation, maintenance, testing, and updating of BCP and supporting documents.

Assuming the provider's executive team or person(s) are on board, the entity should specifically define a project manager or enlist the use of an outside consulting agency to manage the project. Since each type of organization is unique, there is not a right or wrong answer with respect to outsourcing or keeping BCP project management in-house. The critical success factors for the person, committee, or consultancy that is assigned accountability over the project include:

- A person with the ability to multitask and remain detail oriented
- Someone with the skills to understand the business as a whole as well as how work areas intricately affect the overall success of the entity
- Someone with both the knowledge and time that can be dedicated or devoted to managing the BCP project's progress
- The ability to remain objective to ensure that the "overall entity's" risks are addressed versus addressing a preferred subset of persons or departments;
- The ability to set deadlines that will be enforced and invoked by executives
- The ability to hold unsupervised interviews with various management and staff-level employees, from each business unit to discuss their business entity, their operations, and such

The first milestone step for the project manager (in-house or outsourced) is to create the project plan and timeline. Project management applications and other tools can sometimes be useful, especially when managing large or complex projects. The project plan should include the usual milestones and dependencies, provide areas for status updates, and projected completion dates, and assign accountability for the completion of the step.

In the most basic of BCP project development, the following steps can be used as high-level milestones:

■ Provide agenda for staff meetings
■ Schedule staff meetings with various business unit personnel
■ Provide/schedule dates to deliver the draft and final versions of the staff meeting summary with business units
■ Provide/schedule dates to deliver the draft and final versions of the assessment of risks and threats to the organization—risk assessment
■ Provide/schedule dates to deliver the draft and final versions of the business impact analysis to the covered entity—risk assessment detailed
■ Provide/schedule dates to deliver the draft and final versions of the report document and accompanying support documents (as needed)
■ Provide/schedule dates to attain approval of the plan (the BCP)
■ Provide/schedule dates to schedule a test of the BCP:
    – Test data recovery and resumption/use
    – Test critical documentation recovery and resumption/use
    – Test person recovery and resumption/use
    – Test facility/location recovery and resumption/use
    – Test telecom recovery and resumption/use
■ Provide annually recurring schedule of events centric to the maintenance, testing, and updating of the BCP and supporting documents

For smaller entities, this may seem to be overkill and the result may be a very simplistic risk assessment and business impact analysis. For larger healthcare entities, however, in addition to the listed high-level dates, it is also recommended to create more detail-oriented milestones upon the completion of a significant task or part of the plan.

One of the other expectations of the BCP is a direct correlation between a covered entity's size and complexity of operations and the size and complexity of its BCP. Usually there is far less confusion if a project schedule is mutually agreed upon prior to engaging in the project. Having this in place also assists in setting clear expectations for both the project manager and business owners.

The first actionable step in the process between the business process owners and the BCP project manager is to verbally cut across the organizational silo by organizing and executing meetings with people representing all areas of the business. If the entity is a one-doctor practice, interviews may be limited to the doctor, nurse, executive assistants, and vendors (IT support and otherwise). In larger entities, it is most beneficial to meet with all business areas, regardless of the department's "perceived value." The defined prerequisites not only open the proverbial lines of communication, but in many cases, have reaped tidbits of gold regarding a need for a critical operation or task.

One simple example regarding tidbits of gold and with the prevalence of the Internet is the backup and recovery of "bookmarks" or "favorites" from within a Web browser. For example, it is wonderful that Mary knows to click onto her favorites and enter her credentials to access a Web site for payment processing, billing, or some other critical revenue-producing function of the healthcare provider. If the computer is not there, such as would be the case if the computer dies, is temporarily being upgraded, or Mary is forced to work from another computer, she is more than likely to know her username and passphrase, but how about the URL/Web site address?

One of the many benefits of performing unsupervised interviews is that workforce members feel less inhibited to just say what is on their minds. It is also beneficial to get workforce members chatting about their jobs as they become more likely to mentally retrace their steps, especially if rapport is built between the project manager and the interviewees. As part of retracing the steps, the workforce member, in many cases, thinks of something not previously mentioned and later it is determined to be quite important. Case in point, there is one commercial Web site that requires all of the following to authenticate to their Web site to begin "their work":

- A valid username
- A valid password
- A software certificate preinstalled on the PC being used to connect
- An RSA SecurID token with passphrases changing every 60 seconds
- The correct routable (public) IP address

As such, without a workaround, all of these factors are critical for immediate recovery and restoration if the underlying process or task is critical to the covered entity's success.

As the project manager for the BCP works through departments or business units, commonalities will quickly be identified and can then be easily noted as priority items (function, process, task, etc.) for restoration. Services such as access to files on internal networks, Intranets, or secured Internet-based portals will more than likely be identified as a recurring need. Recurring needs are granted a higher level of priority for securing, recovering, and restoring over those that may be helpful but not as important. If the choice is to care for an injured or sick patient and ensuring the insurance billing processes are followed, patient care will come first. Therefore, part of this process includes feedback on "what is important, what is core business to the entity and what does the entity always need to provide." If the response is to service the clients (i.e., patients), which results in revenue and profits, then the covered entity needs patients, invoicing systems, and interconnectivity to the covered entity's banking accounts. Although performing a Risk assessment or business impact analysis is not this easy, it outlines the essential end goals that are to identify risks and threats to the organization as a whole.

From there, risks and threats are identified. Risks can be found within the covered entity's ability to provide services; maintain the confidentiality, integrity, and availability of EPHI; and each person's ability to perform normal job functions. Threats can be identified that would cause a disruption of normal operations. Upon completing the interviews with various business units, it is this author's preference to interview the facilities and IT teams last. In short, the facilities and IT teams are those that most all other business areas are dependent upon. The rationale is to exercise certain scenarios with these teams to determine their levels of tolerance for business interruptions or outright disasters.

As majority stakeholders over BCP, facilities' and IT's ability to recover directly and indirectly affects how effectively a business will recover from an outage. For example, if a workforce member works from an office and there is no office to get to tomorrow or the workforce member arrives to find the building uninhabitable, where does the workforce member go? Does the workforce member know whom to call? Does the workforce member have their cell or home phone numbers handy? Are the workforce members being paid? Can the workforce member be asked or forced to report to work at an alternate location? Does staff unionization (where applicable) become a factor in resuming business operations? Therefore, facilities or operational staff that manage offices or facilities are nearly as important in the short-term recovery and restoration as other business functions.

The first step is to correlate all of the data obtained during on-site interviews. The results, as previously mentioned, will include common responses from a variety of business areas that need to be accounted for and later ranked. Depending on the size and complexity of the covered entity, a chart, spreadsheet, or database could be used to account for each of these items. It is within this step of the overall process that the identification of critical applications, data, and information systems is attained.

The next step is to perform analyses of the risks and threats the covered entity is subject to. Risks and threats come in many varieties and can include:

■ Man-made or created events (strikes, wars, or human corruption)
■ Naturally occurring events (weather, travel prohibitions, etc.)
■ Pandemic events (mass sickness, epidemics, etc.)
■ Regulatory events (inability to comply with regulations, etc.)

Thereafter, the project manager should take into account which types of risks and threats may pose challenges and stress to the organization. For example, an electrical power outage may have a significant impact on a one-location office; however, if a generator is in place at the location and it allows for restoration of electricity to the organization, that risk is mitigated (addressed).

Each risk and threat as well as threat mitigation factors already in place need to be considered in the process of the risk assessment. Later these risks will be tallied to include risk mitigation measures in place (if any) to help determine the importance or criticality of the application, data, facility, or system in place. The combination of risks and threats coupled with the most critical applications, data, facilities, information systems and staff with a ranking is the essential crux of what is called a business impact analysis .

The BIA is really the framework, outline, or guideline that should be used to create the BCP. So far, the data gathering, correlation, and placement of said data into the BIA has been covered. At this point, the BIA and its requirements should help provide a guide to the project manager with regard to recovery and restoration of critically identified items. How will the BIA guide the ranking and subsequent recovery and restoration of critical business items, one may ask? Simply stated, the use of common sense, practicality, and input from various persons in IT will provide the much-needed responses to craft a viable BIA.

The common sense and practicality factors are both simpler to explain and to demonstrate; therefore those will be discussed first. The example to be considered moving forward would be:

> A healthcare provider sustains water damage from a disruptive event that makes all information systems and data residing in the server room (or data center) inaccessible. The facility is accessible (offices, desks); however, anything related to electronic data and the primary location where that data resided is no longer accessible. The event occurred 4 hours ago and there are no time estimates for even gaining access to the server room, and all electricity and communication is turned off.

Some of the common sense prerequisites in such a scenario would include:

1. Does this scenario force the organization to enable or enact the BCP?
    a. If not, the exercise or scenario needs to be adjusted to force the enactment of the BCP.
2. Assuming this scenario would indeed enact the BCP, some prerequisites that must be put into motion would include:
    a. Securing the affected location(s)
    b. Human safety and tending to injured or ill persons
    c. Notify emergency services as needed
    d. Perform a damage assessment—preliminary
    e. Declare alternate command centers:
        i. Where are applications, data, and systems recovered?
        ii. Where do non-IT workforce members report to or do they remain in the office without communications or electricity?
        iii. How are applications, data, people, and systems "reconnected" to begin initial steps of restoring the business?
        iv. Etc.
3. Notify patients or partners directly affected by this event.

Prior to even considering whom, when, where, and how information systems, applications, and data residing on those systems (computers) will again be accessible and ready for use, the organization must render choices to all of the aforementioned items and in many cases, additional tasks based on the complexity of the organization and the specific event at hand. Once these decisions are made and executive team members are armed with the information available for future decision making, the restoration of information systems, applications, and EPHI data can then be considered.

Before proceeding with the more technical aspects of the BIA, please reflect back to the on-site data gathering process. During the on-site data gathering process, let's suppose that data set "Q" was deemed absolutely essential to business operations. Data set Q is considered critical to over three-quarters of the business units of the organization and of those, 100% are forward facing (impacts patients or patient care). During the interview process, business units might state that they could get away with not having data set Q for 1 day maximum. Data set Q is part of the data, applications, and information systems affected in the aforementioned example and now the organization essentially has between 16 and 20 hours to restore data set Q, the information system it lives upon, the application used to reach the data, and the communications to allow a PC to connect and work with data set Q. Now that the example groundwork has been provided, the more technical aspects of the BIA will be covered.

The components of the BIA that are considered to be most difficult to attain, calculate, and measure the impact of are recovery point objectives (RPOs), recovery time objectives (RTOs), and maximum acceptable losses (MALs). To most easily detail these terms, how they are affected, how they are calculated, and how loss is estimated, see Table 15.3.

Some additional rules of thumb related to RPO, RTO, and MAL calculations are:

■ RPO, where applicable, cannot be less than RTO.
■ RPO is only required where data is electronically backed up and has a backup "point in time."
■ All applications, data, information systems, and critical business activities must have an RTO value assigned to it, as a core component of the BIA.
■ The RPO and RTO values should, if possible, be aligned with business goals.
■ The RPO and RTO values should, if possible, be acceptable to all departments.
■ MALs must be acceptable to the business owners or stakeholders, and in some cases, are thought of as an insurance deductible (i.e., if an accident occurs, the covered entity is going to be out of pocket X dollars before insurance activates).

The RPO data is going to be obtained from IT stakeholders for the organization. Since IT has constructed and manages the networks, systems, data, and applications,

Table 15.3   RPO/RTO/MAL

Acronym	Applicability	Definition	Impact
RPO	EPH/ EPHI— IT centric	RPO is the last time or date a backup was performed and is available for use.	More frequent backups are more expensive but make recovery easy as fewer records must be manually reentered.
RTO	Global	RTO is the time in which the application, data, event, or task must be finished within.	Failure to meet RTOs can lead to lost revenue, market share, regulatory punishments, and increased financial loss.
MAL	Global	MAL is the maximum acceptable loss the business stakeholders are willing to incur as the result of data set Q, based on data set Q's RPO and RTO	Traditionally lower RPO and RTO lead to lesser financial losses. The impact is that keeping losses low will cost the business more up front to ensure data Q is recovered rapidly.

these folks should have a firm grasp of realistic RTOs, provide RPO details (how often data sets are backed up), and estimate the impact of being without.

The RTO data should be a collaborative effort from all areas of the organization. Although the ultimate accountability falls within the laps of executive stakeholders, staff that are in the trenches can in many cases provide valued insight that may be otherwise missed.

MAL values will normally be calculated by an accounting or finance department. Although input will be required from all business areas to assist accounting in understanding the impact, the financial calculations/estimations should originate from those within the organization that best understand finance.

Referencing the previous scenario, to restore data set Q and have it usable by staff within 24 hours, Table 15.4 is a basic concept of the BIA for purposes of this example. In this example, the RPO for all data is 1 hour, which means that IT is performing off-site backups for data set Q hourly and could access them during the immediate aftermath of a disaster. The RPO of 12 of PC restoration is based on a backup of network PCs and their configurations every 12 hours. If this does not occur as frequently in the environment under review, it may be unreasonable to expect a RTO value of 24. So in essence, all of these items need to be in place within the RTO defined for the recovery of the organization and the data set Q to be considered a success.

Table 15.4   Business Impact Analysis

Critical Item	Who Uses	Who Recovers	RPO	RTO (hours)
Physical security	All	Facilities	N/A	1
Physical office	All	Facilities	N/A	1
Data security	All	All areas with EPH access	N/A	1
Staff accountability and roll call	All management	All areas	N/A	2
Command center establishment	All	Facilities, affected area(s)	N/A	4
IT command center	IT	IT, executives	N/A	4
Critical vendor contact	All, as applicable	All areas	N/A	6
Network reconstruction	All	IT	1	8
Information server Q restoration	Most departments	IT	1	12
Application Q restoration	Most departments	IT	N/A	12
Data Q restoration	Most departments	IT	1	16
Application, data, server Q testing	Most departments	IT	N/A	20
PC restoration	All	IT	12	24
Q data integrity testing	Most departments	IT	N/A	24
Q restoration	Most departments	IT	N/A	24

The essence of what to consider is that based on the scenario of being without data set Q for 24 hours, what will it cost the organization to be without? Include real costs and attempt to estimate as closely as possible the impact of not having data set Q for one full day. In many cases, these figures will tend to drive one another. For example, if Q being down for one day is too costly (too high an MAL), then more frequent backups of data, PCs., and servers may be evaluated to determine if that can cut downtime. The organization may also have a backup "hot site" or a disaster recovery backup location equipped with computers, networks, and a good percentage of the primary server room's capacity for more rapid recovery. Although the costs of configuring, maintaining, and securing the hot site may be considerable, MAL calculations may determine that it is far less costly to maintain a hot site versus running the risk of not having data set Q for any sustained period of time.

At this juncture, the covered entity would prioritize its BIA taking all previously discussed items into consideration. The BIA would then essentially be the outline for each business area's business continuity plan or business recovery plan. The BIA and BCP should be, and in many industries, must be reviewed, updated, and reaffirmed at least annually. This author concurs with the necessity of revisiting the BIA and BCP annually or more frequently. First, this ensures that executive stakeholders are aware, reminded, and can take future growth into consideration as it relates to business needs (and BCP needs) to ensure their business can restore operations for its customers and remain solvent. Second, this allows management-level staff from each area to have their executive marching orders. Since executives have already reviewed, adjusted, and approved the BIA and BCP, these are predetermined decisions made by the business pre-event to help ensure a smoother and better thought-out restoration.

Making as many decisions as possible ahead of time is an advantage to those organizations. This allows executive team members to deal with the crises at hand and allows operational business areas to do what needs to be accomplished to get the business back on its proverbial feet.

It is the experience of this author that many organizations pine over having their first BCP 100% comprehensive, exact, and accurate. In some cases, this causes undue delays in the initial creation of the BCP and can lead to wanting to ensure the document contains everything. It is prudent to ensure that although business process owners and stakeholders want a functional BCP document, it is a living, breathing document that will need to evolve and change in harmony with the business and how customers are served. As such, it would be this author's recommendation to complete the document, get to a fixed point in time, and call the document final (for now).

With approved BIA and BCP in hand, it is time for testing and recovery of the BCP and critically identified components to ensure that plans are realistic and can be performed when required to recover the business. The HIPAA/Health Information Technology for Economic and Clinical Health (HITECH) Act guidance at this time denotes testing and recovery as addressable. However, a robust test will address required components including: data backup plans, disaster recovery plans, emergency mode operating plans, and emergency access procedures. Each of these should be tested at least annually to ensure the recovery and emergency plan can be successfully completed. If exposure exists in any piece or an entire area of a safeguard, the covered entity is much better served to learn this through testing and recovery exercises versus a catastrophic failure subsequent to a real act or event that has affected the covered entity.

Testing can be performed in a myriad of ways and can be of the following types: planned or unplanned tests. Unfortunately, many covered entities fail to take advantage of the silver lining of what could be termed as unscheduled tests of the data backup plan, disaster recovery plan, emergency mode operation plan, or emergency access procedure. For example, a smoke detector malfunctions and forces an evacuation of the main facility and data center. Smart business stakeholders will document and detail the malfunction, pursuant events, evacuation, head counts, staff communication, and correspondence with emergency services personnel. Although the smoke detector's malfunction was unplanned, the result was a valid, albeit unscheduled, test of the facility and datacenter's evacuation plan.

Even though the provided example is quite simplistic, it is proven that in the majority of cases where a BCP is enacted, it is the result of a failure of "a subset of critical faculties" versus a complete and cataclysmic event. Therefore, the information nugget to take away from this example is to ensure that all unplanned outages are documented and inclusive in annual BCP or disaster recovery testing. Business events including data and file restoration to information systems, network connection issues, Internet and VPN connection issues, use of backup procedures due to information system outages, and any other event that occurs that forces the business to use its data backup, disaster recovery, emergency mode operation plans, or its emergency access procedure should be documented for both business and contingency purposes.

Planned testing, on the other hand, can take a variety of forms. Tests of the BCP documents include:

- Tabletop testing
- Process testing
- Data restoration tests
- Hot site or alternate recovery location tests
- Full spectrum tests

Although HIPAA/HITECH security standards are most concerned with data backup and recovery, emergency operations, and restoration components, it is always good practice to ensure that backup or workaround procedures, data restoration, offsite work, and so forth will function as expected during a controlled exercise instead of during the aftermath of a disastrous event that adversely affects the covered entity.

Any testing performed should then be analyzed and evaluated for effectiveness. Simply stated, how does any covered entity understand the effectiveness of its plans? Through results analysis, of course!

The famous philosopher and poet George Santayana once stated that "those who cannot remember the past are condemned to repeat it," and with regard to testing and analysis of a BCP, the quote fits perfectly into the analysis and lessons learned from the execution of BCP testing.

The idea that the BCP and supporting data within constitutes a living, breathing document takes shape at this point, during the analysis process. A thorough test (planned or unplanned) should reveal weaknesses or shortcomings, as previously stated. This author's preference is to perform a *SWOT analysis* (SWOT: strengths, weaknesses, opportunities, and threats) of all tests. The SWOT analysis will not only provide direction to improve later revisions of the BCP document, it will also provide a more objective view for stakeholders to read and better understand. Finally, it is recommended that the SWOT analysis be performed (or at least validated) by an independent party. The independent party can consist of a vendor, oversight committee, or business area that is not considered as operationally significant. For example, if the IT department executes its data backup plan, someone outside of the IT department should validate or verify what occurred, what went well, what tasks were not performed smoothly, and to help identify opportunities to better or improve the plan or any supporting document the plan relies upon.

Referring back to Figure 15.1, five of the six steps identified as required for BCP oversight have been completed. The final task is to begin the improvement process of the contingency plan.

The last step identified to close the loop of the BCP management process is to take everything compiled and begin the rewrite or revision process of the:

- Data backup plan
- Disaster recovery plan
- Emergency mode operation plan
- Emergency access procedures
- Business impact analysis (BIA), and applications and data criticality analysis
- Contingency plan/business continuity plan

Since the first revision of the BCP was built from the outline that was the first revision of the BIA, usually the first step in the revision process is to revisit the BIA. The BIA (and applications and data criticality analysis) should be reviewed to ensure that all of the following items are considered: changes in business, patient billing, patient care, and processes or systems used to run the business. In addition, any testing performed over the past year should be reviewed to ensure threats or weaknesses identified from testing activity are adequately addressed (if applicable) within the new BIA revision.

To continue to improve the business and to help ensure its solvency postdisaster, business process owners and stakeholders need to ensure the covered entity's contingency plan is well aligned with its actual operational plans. The best manner to accomplish proper maintenance and updating of the plan is to ensure changes to normal operations are reflected within the BCP and that the covered entity learns from past mistakes as the result and analysis of BCP testing.

15.8 Summary

This chapter should assist its readers in meeting HIPAA/HITECH Security Rules and Safeguards that are required, as well as those areas currently considered addressable. More important, this chapter should provide a high-level overview of how to create, manage, and improve a functional contingency plan for a covered entity. Regulatory risk from noncompliance with HIPAA/HITECH Security Rules is just one risk to address. Therefore, merely writing a contingency plan to meet HIPAA/HITECH regulatory guidance is shortsighted since threats such as financial, operational and reputational risks are not considered. On the other hand, following this chapter to create, maintain, test, and revise contingency plan items will lead to both addressing the regulatory risk, as well as financial, operational and reputational risks of the covered entity.

Chapter 16

Security Rule: Compliance Assessment

Objectives

The objectives of this chapter are as follows:

- Understand how to conduct a policy and procedure gap analysis.
- Understand the process to developing or modifying policies and procedures.
- Determine what is required to approve policies and procedures.
- Understand how to effectively implement policies and procedures.
- Determine what planning is required to test the adequacy of policies and procedures.
- Understand what is required to conduct an assessment.
- Determine the differences between a nontechnical and a technical evaluation.
- Understand the requirements for conducting a periodic technical and nontechnical evaluation contained in the HIPAA Security Rule.
- Determine what is required to conduct a reassessment of policies and procedures.

Background

As claimed earlier, one of the most important requirements of the Health Insurance Portability and Accountability Act (HIPAA) Security Rule states that a covered entity is required to "perform a periodic technical and nontechnical evaluation, based initially upon the standards implemented under this rule [the Security Rule] and subsequently, in response to environmental or operational changes affecting the security of electronic protected health information, that establishes the extent to which an entity's security policies and procedures meet the requirements [of the Security Rule]" as specified in 45 CFR § 164.308(a)(8). This requirement, in its simplest form, states that a covered entity needs to be in compliance with the HIPAA Security Rule. The question that many may be asking is how does a covered entity become compliant?

In this chapter, some steps that a covered entity can take to validate compliance will be discussed. As the covered entity may, or may not know, the Department of Health and Human Services (HHS) does not recognize any certification program for compliance with the HIPAA Privacy or Security Rules. It is left up to the covered entity to assure compliance and when the Office for Civil Rights (OCR), the enforcement arm of the HHS, comes knocking on the door the covered entity will have to defend its position of being compliant. Or when a complaint is filed for a violation of these rules, the OCR will begin its investigation into the alleged complaint. It is believed to be too late for a covered entity if it comes to these points, unless the covered entity takes a proactive approach to its compliance efforts.

The steps to compliance are as follows:

1. Define the requirements based on regulations (federal, state, and local), the covered entity's needs, and the resources available.
2. Identify all policies and procedures that are currently in place to meet requirements.
3. Conduct a gap analysis to determine if policies and procedures adequately meet the requirements or need improvements.
4. Develop or modify policies and procedures to meet the requirements.
5. Approve policies and procedures.
6. Implement policies and procedures or solutions that satisfy the policies and procedures.
7. Develop test plans that will prove solutions implemented to satisfy policies and procedures are working as expected. Develop test plans that validate policies and procedures are being followed.
8. Conduct assessment utilizing test plans to validate compliance. Note: Testing procedures can be done through interview, observation, or sampling to validate compliance.
9. Correct any findings that the assessment identifies.
10. Reassess.

See Figure 16.1.

The material in this book covers, in detail, the requirements of the HIPAA Privacy and Security Rules. Since it is pretty self-explanatory to identify the covered entity's existing policies and procedures, this chapter will start with step 3, conducting a gap analysis, discussed in the next section.

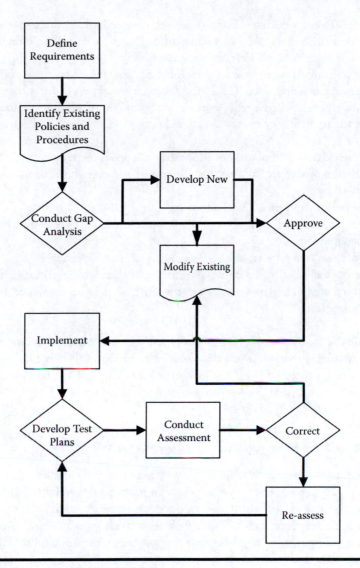

Figure 16.1 Compliance assessment steps.

16.1 Gap Analysis

A *gap analysis* is a methodical review of requirements compared to existing policies and procedures. As a reminder, requirements or regulations provide the basis for most of the policies and procedures developed. Throughout this book the author has made it a point to reference a standard framework along with the regulations to assist in the development of the policies and procedures. The author utilized the National Institute of Standards and Technology (NIST) framework or guidelines that are believed to be one of the easier set of standards to follow. The NIST framework is also referenced many times throughout the guidance offered by the Department of Health and Human Services (HHS).

Once a list of all requirements is established, a review of existing policies and procedures can be conducted. Codifying the policies and procedures may assist in the mapping of them to the requirements or regulations. Questions that should be asked throughout this review are the following:

1. Is there a policy in place that adequately addresses the requirement?
2. Is there a procedure in place that adequately addresses how the policy is to be carried out?
3. Are policies and procedures approved?
4. Are policies and procedures fully implemented or are they still under development?
5. What requirements are not covered by a policy or procedure?
6. How can an existing policy or procedure be modified to meet the requirements?
7. Does a completely new policy or procedure need to be developed to meet a requirement?

This is the basic concept of a gap analysis. When completed, a documented list of items will be identified. There may be a lot of items on the list that need to be developed or modified. It is suggested to prioritize these items or break these items into smaller parts so that the work is not so overwhelming.

16.2 Develop or Modify Policies and Procedures

Through the gap analysis, the covered entity may realize that a lot of procedures may already be in place but may not have been formally documented. The covered entity may be able to utilize different workforce members to assist in writing a formal procedure for these activities that are already taking place within the covered entity. It is recommended to modify existing procedures as opposed to developing them from scratch. Unless these procedures do not satisfy the requirements and modifying them will not help, it is easier to modify than redevelop.

16.3 Approve Policies and Procedures

Once policies and procedures have either been modified or developed based on the gap analysis, they need to be approved. Normally, policies are approved at the board level or executive level while procedures that implement the policies are approved at management level. Policies are usually more general and broad while procedures are usually more specific and narrowly defined to implement the policy.

Policies and procedures need to be reviewed and an approval process needs to be developed to track these policies and procedures. Policies and procedures need to be disseminated and followed accordingly by all workforce members. As mentioned, a top-down management approach is the best and validates the commitment by management to the governance process.

16.4 Policy and Procedure Implementation

Having formally documented policies and procedures is just the first phase of compliance. The true testament to the adequacy of these policies and procedures are highlighted in the second phase, which is the implementation of these policies and procedures. To implement certain policies and procedures, certain solutions may be developed. Especially in cases where technology applies, these technical solutions need to be configured properly to carry out their specified functions. For example, if the policy says that complex passwords are supposed to be utilized on information systems or applications, a procedure should be in place to specify that at least eight-character passwords with complexity options be enabled. The technical solution should be configured to enforce eight-character complex passwords on the information system or application.

16.5 Test Plans

Testing of policies and procedures can be done in basically three ways: interview, observation, or sample testing. *Interviewing* is asking questions or surveying how policies and procedures are carried out. *Observation* is the direct review of policies and procedures taking place. *Sampling* is taking a small portion of items and reviewing these items to make sure that they meet policies or procedures identified.

Test plans, or procedures, should be developed that establish the validity of policies and procedures that are being followed. In keeping with the example regarding password complexity, one of the testing procedures is to verify that all passwords are at least eight characters. A sampling approach could be used to test the passwords of a small portion of accounts established for a particular application or on a particular information system. There are testing applications that can assist in verifying the complexity of account passwords. The covered entity could also validate the configuration of a system by attempting to establish an account with a password less than eight characters. If the account is established in this way and is functional, then the configuration of the technical control to enforce such password complexity could be proven to be ineffective in carrying out the procedure as intended. The control in this case may need correcting or the procedure may need to be modified if there is no control to enforce the actions.

Test plans could be a little tricky in developing cases where it may be hard to validate that certain activities are taking place. In some situations, interviewing workforce members as to their activities or how they handle certain situations may be the only way to ensure policies and procedures are being followed. A little slogan that can be used when conducting an assessment is "trust, but verify." Although the author might *trust* what an individual is telling him, the author wants to *verify* that it is actually true. This testing takes all human senses into consideration: what is *heard*, what is *smelled*, what it is *tasted*, what can be *touched*, and what can be *seen* (or observed). This is how testing procedures should be developed. This is the essence of compliance.

16.6 Assessment

Now that testing procedures are in place, the covered entity is ready to perform these procedures to validate compliance. In the assessment step, it is imperative that the covered entity understands the concept of *independence*. Assessments should be performed by competent, knowledgeable, and independent parties. These parties could be internal or external to the covered entity. If the assessor works internally, the question arises whether the assessor has the ability to make an objective opinion as to the state of compliance. For instance, if the assessor works for the information manager that is responsible for writing policies and procedures and implementing solutions to carry out these policies and procedures, how well does the covered entity think the assessor can do his or her job when it comes to critiquing the effectiveness of the solution? Does the assessor have enough authority within the organization to independently request certain documentation or interview work-force members to obtain the information necessary to derive at a conclusion? Does the assessor have the qualifications or experience to conduct a thorough assessment as required?

For these reasons, it is recommended to consider using a third-party assessor for this type of evaluation. As a word of caution, this assessor should be highly qualified and understand the environment under review. The assessor should provide a scope of work and describe a methodology that they follow to conduct the assessment. This methodology should have some cohesiveness with the covered entity's compliance framework or else the work performed may not be meaningful or provide value to the covered entity.

As required by the HIPAA Security Standard, technical and nontechnical evaluations should be performed on the covered entity. It is recommended that this evaluation be conducted on an annual basis and that the assessment be conducted on-site to include both the technical and nontechnical portions. If the covered entity has any external or publicly facing devices, a technical evaluation should be performed on these devices at least once every 6 months. The primary focus of the compliance assessment should be the HIPAA Security Standards that were developed to implement appropriate security safeguards for the protection of electronic protected health information that may be at risk while permitting authorized workforce members to access and use this information as necessary. The assessment should consider the three fundamental security parameters: confidentiality, integrity, and availability of electronic protected health information. The covered entity should go through what the assessment overview should cover, at a minimum, in the next sections.

16.6.1 *Nontechnical Evaluation*

The assessment should review the accessibility of electronic protected health information to verify that it is not altered or destroyed in an unauthorized manner and that it is available, as needed, to authorized individuals. As it relates to the nontechnical portion of the evaluation, the assessment should review the following implementation standards:

- Administrative Safeguards
- Physical Safeguards
- Organizational Requirements (if applicable)
- Policies, procedures, and documentation requirements

Under the Administrative Safeguards, the following areas, at a minimum, should be reviewed:

- Security management process
- Assigned security responsibility
- Workforce security
- Information access management
- Security awareness training
- Security incident procedures
- Contingency planning
- Evaluation

Under Physical Safeguards, the following areas, at a minimum, should be reviewed:

- Facility access controls
- Workstation use
- Workstation security
- Device and media controls

Under Organizational Requirements, where applicable, the following areas, at a minimum, should be reviewed:

- Business associate contracts or other arrangements
- Requirements for group health plans

Of course, policies, procedures, and documentation of these policies and procedures should be reviewed as required by the HIPAA Security Standards.

16.6.2 Technical Evaluation

As it relates to the technical portion of the evaluation, the assessment should review the following technical safeguards:

- Access control
- Audit controls
- Integrity
- Person or entity authentication
- Transmission security

As a word of caution, technical evaluations may involve the use of testing or auditing software that could cause disruptions to network systems. These types of evaluations, which may include vulnerability and penetration tests, should be conducted by highly skilled, qualified, and knowledgeable assessors. It can take a number of years along with a lot of experience to obtain the necessary skill set to conduct a thorough technical evaluation of this type. That is why in some situations, when conducting a compliance assessment, a team of individuals may be required. Some individuals may have the prerequisite qualifications to conduct the technical aspects, whereas others may have the nontechnical background necessary to conduct these assessments.

When conducting technical evaluations, concerns or constraints of such testing should be identified prior to testing. The scope of the engagement should define what is acceptable and what is not acceptable when conducting this type of testing. As a point of reference, when discussing technical evaluations, there are usually two types:

- Vulnerability assessment
- Penetration test

To explain the difference between them, the author likes to use an analogy. If a burglar targeted a house to break into, he or she may canvas a neighborhood to pick an unsuspecting victim. The burglar may try to open doors by rattling their handles or shaking window frames to see which ones may open. This is synonymous with a vulnerability assessment. This type of assessment is basically knocking on doors and windows to see if there is a house that is potentially interesting for the burglar to target. Vulnerability assessments may provide a lot of potential false positives and due to certain configurations may not provide accurate information. Although vulnerability software tools are getting better, they still have some drawbacks.

To continue with the analogy, once the burglar discovers a door will open on a certain house by jiggling the handle, the burglar can enter the house. This is where the penetration test takes the technical evaluation to the next level. Once a vulnerability has been discovered, in this case the door not being locked, the burglar (or penetration tester) could exploit this vulnerability and see what is in the house (or system). The burglar may not find any valuables in the house; however, he or she may find a key to the next-door neighbor's house. From there, the burglar could gain access to the neighbor's house. In penetration testing, the initial vulnerability may not be all that crucial; however, leveraging this access could disclose other additional critical vulnerabilities. These vulnerabilities would not be discovered unless someone actually figures out what extent or access they can leverage.

The author will not go through the complete details of technical testing since this is outside of the scope of this book. Suffice it to say, there is a minimum standard of technical testing that should be conducted in the assessment. In regard to specific technical testing, the following should be performed and at least two methods (i.e., testing or auditing software applications) should be performed for each. Note: One of these methods could also involve manual processes and some tools can perform multiple types of tests.

- *Port scanner*—This type of testing determines what ports are open on each device tested.
- *Simple Network Management Protocol (SNMP) scanner*—This protocol is utilized in the management of network devices. There are several known vulnerabilities or wrong configurations that could lead to severe issues with devices utilizing this protocol on the network. This type of testing evaluates the proper configuration of this protocol.
- *Enumeration*—This type of testing is utilized to determine what types of services are running on identified open ports and what type of operating systems along with version information are running on devices. Depending on the information, targeted exploits could be developed for known vulnerabilities of the systems identified.
- *Wireless enumeration*—Wireless access has become prevalent in networks and this type of testing determines the level of security implemented on these wireless solutions.
- *Vulnerability scanning*—This type of testing determines the presence of known vulnerabilities.
- *Host evaluation*—This type of testing is performed on servers and workstations to confirm that security configurations are implemented to meet the covered entity's policies and procedures.
- *Network device*—This type of testing determines the adequacy of controls around the gatekeepers of the networks (i.e., routers, switches, hubs, etc.).

■ *Password compliance*—Since passwords are the norm for authentication, the verification of compliance should be required as part of the technical testing process.
■ *Application-specific scanning*—This type of testing takes into consideration specific applications utilized by the covered entity. This testing could also include the specific database applications that house electronic protected health information and the technical safeguards securing this information.
■ *Network sniffing*—This type of testing is considered passive testing insofar as a network connection is established and all traffic going across the wireless is being captured. This type of testing is synonymous with telephone wiretapping but conducted on a network. If data is not encrypted in transit, it could be viewed through this type of sniffing activity.

16.7 Reassess

The assessment should provide a covered entity with the assurance that it is complying with the implementation standards of the HIPAA Security Rule along with providing recommendations based on other relevant guidance. If deficiencies are noted, the covered entity should attempt to correct or mitigate these findings to an acceptable level. Since the compliance program is an ongoing process, once corrective action is taken, additional reassessments should be performed to ensure that compliance is being met and no changes took place that caused additional issues in compliance.

16.8 Summary

Compliance assessment, as required by the HIPAA Security Rule standards, was discussed in detail throughout this chapter. A gap analysis is an essential first step in performing compliance activities. Through a methodical approach, a determination of specific requirements can be made in implementing policies and procedures. Through the gap analysis, a determination can appropriately be made in regard to what policies and procedures need to be developed or modified to meet the requirements of the organization. Once policies and procedures have been developed, management needs to review and approve them. Again, the security culture of an organization is determined by the approach of management and the seriousness that it takes in protecting the organization's assets.

After policies and procedures have been accepted and approved, they must be implemented. This implementation usually comes in the form of training workforce members in the expected actions that they should be making in regard to the approved policies and procedures. Most organizations have to deal with fluid environments, and for this reason, processes need to be developed so that policies and procedures can be formally changed to the current state of the organization. To ensure the effectiveness of policies and procedures, test plans should be developed. These test plans should be integrated into the assessment process.

To reiterate, one of the most important standards required by the HIPAA Security Rule is the requirement to conduct periodic technical and nontechnical evaluations. Without these types of reviews, the organization cannot determine how well their policies, procedures, and other compliance efforts are working. These evaluations, especially the technical portions, should be performed by qualified independent assessors. These assessors could be internal to the organization, but it may be best to consider external sources to complete these types of assessments. Compliance is an ongoing effort, and even though an evaluation has been performed, it needs to be done periodically to ensure that risks are mitigated and the security posture of the organization is maintained at a consistently strong level. It is recommended that at least an annual evaluation is performed on the internal systems or the evaluation is performed whenever there is an instrumental change in the organization's environment. For external systems or public-facing devices, a technical evaluation should be performed at least semiannually or whenever changes may mandate a review of the configurations.

Chapter 17

Security Rule: Physical Safeguards

Objectives

The objectives of this chapter are as follows:

- Understand what is required to physically secure a facility.
- Determine what needs to be addressed under contingency operations.
- Determine what needs to be addressed in a facility security plan.
- Understand what types of procedures need to be implemented for access control and validation.
- Determine what needs to be addressed in maintaining records.
- Understand the requirements for controlling the use of workstations.
- Determine what security measures are required for workstations.
- Understand the controls in place for devices and media containing electronic protected health information.
- Determine what type of requirements there are for disposing of devices or media containing electronic protected health information.
- Determine what is required to reuse media with electronic protected health information on it.
- Understand how to address and account for devices or media containing electronic protected health information.
- Determine what requirements need to be addressed to conduct data backups and storage.

■ Determine how electronic protected health information will be protected while being accessed, stored, or transmitted on mobile devices.
■ Determine what types of controls are necessary when implementing a wireless local area network.

Background

One of the first layers of defense for any organization is the physical layer. This primarily includes the controls around the physical access to the facility or structures that may store protected health information. These safeguards also involve the controls surrounding procedures and maintenance of documents or hardware that contain protected health information. The Health Insurance Portability and Accountability Act (HIPAA) Security Rule separates physical safeguards into two primary areas: facility access controls and device/media controls. Both of these areas have several subsections of controls that are either required or addressable under the HIPAA Security Rule standards. See Table 17.1 for further information on addressable and required areas of the Physical Safeguards standards.

Table 17.1 Security Standards: Physical Safeguards

Security Standards		
Physical Safeguards		
164.310(a)(1)		**Facility Access Controls**
164.310(a)(2)(i)	A	Contingency Operations
164.310(a)(2)(ii)	A	Facility Security Plan
164.310(a)(2)(iii)	A	Access Control and Validation Procedures
164.310(a)(2)(iv)	A	Maintenance Records
164.310(b)	R	Workstation Use
164.310c	R	Workstation Security
164.310(d)(1)		**Device and Media Controls**
164.310(d)(2)(i)	R	Disposal
164.310(d)(2)(ii)	R	Media Re-use
164.310(d)(2)(iii)	A	Accountability
164.310(d)(2)(iv)	A	Data Backup and Storage

Note: A = addressable, R = required.

17.1 Facility Access Controls

A covered entity should have policies and procedures in place that adequately limit the physical access to electronic information systems and protected health information. This includes the facilities that these systems are located in such as data centers, workstation locations, information technology (IT) workforce member areas, medical records areas, and other areas. There, of course, is a fine balance between limiting unauthorized access and access that must be allowed to conduct business. Policies and procedures should reflect this balance keeping in mind the minimum necessary rule. These policies and procedures should identify workforce members, by title or job function, that are authorized to have physical access to the facilities that house the electronic information systems. In addition, business associates, contractors, subcontractors, or any other individuals that may require access to the covered entity's facilities should be addressed in the policies and procedures. Policies and procedures should also address maintaining proper access levels in the event of repairs, upgrades, or modifications made to the facility or controls in place to secure the facility. A current list of workforce members having authorized access to the facility and specific access to certain areas containing protected health information needs to be developed and maintained. This list should be reviewed to ensure the appropriate access levels to the facility are being kept.

The physical and environmental protection policy should cover at least the following components: the purpose, scope, responsibilities, management commitment, coordination among different departments, and compliance. These policies should be formally documented, disseminated, and reviewed and updated on a periodic basis (i.e., annually or upon any major changes that affect physical or environmental security). These policies should define the covered entity's overall objectives and include all areas where protected health information is utilized. Remember, the goal of physical and environmental protection is to secure protected health information along with the security of the facility and workforce members working within the facility.

Policies and procedures should also address the methods or types of physical controls that are implemented to secure protected health information. Some of these items that may be addressed include door locks, cipher locks, biometrics, access control systems to include badge or fob access, security guards, surveillance equipment, and burglar alarms. Locks on doors or combinations should be periodically changed or changed whenever keys are lost, codes are compromised, or workforce members having access leave or no longer require the access to these areas.

There should be a specific workforce member assigned the responsibility for correcting any physical deficiencies, monitoring physical access, and ensuring that authorized access is permitted. This responsibility normally falls under the security official. As a special note, in this author's experience, he has seen this type of physical security responsibility fall under the facilities manager. Although this would seem reasonable since these workforce members are responsible for correcting most of the physical deficiencies of the facility, it is strongly recommend that physical security responsibilities be brought under a more senior-level workforce member. Remember, physical security is the first line of defense in the overall security and needs to have some of the highest priority and considerations. Physical security needs to be recognized as important and the individual responsible needs to be highly qualified and knowledgeable in this area.

A covered entity should establish a room where records are kept. This room should be utilized for secure record-keeping only. The walls surrounding this room should extend all the way to the ceiling so that someone is not able to crawl through the spacing of a drop-down ceiling to circumvent any other controls that may be in place. The records room should be locked at all times utilizing metal keys, badges, cipher locks, or some other method to authenticate authorized entry. Any other paper records that are not stored in this designated area should be stored in locked filing cabinets or by some other secured method. Surveillance cameras should be installed to capture any activity that may occur in this room to include the monitoring of individuals entering the room and covering the records residing in the room. The records room should also be alarmed after hours to alert for any unauthorized access. In addition to making sure the records are not being accessed by unauthorized individuals, the records should be protected from damage. Consideration should be made for the installation of fire detection and suppression solution in the records room.

Physical locations of workstations need to be considered. Monitors should be facing away from external windows to mitigate the risk of viewing these screens from the outside. If locations of monitors cannot be adjusted, the covered entity should consider utilizing privacy filters on the monitors, tinting on the windows, or blinds on the windows to protect from unauthorized viewing. Printers or other devices such as faxes, audio devices, or other output devices also need to be secured from unauthorized access. In addition, the physical locations of information system distribution points or transmission lines such as wiring closets need to be secured. Cabling or spare communication jacks need to be secured from tampering or unauthorized access.

All areas that contain electronic protected health information or other protected health information that should not be available to the public need to be restricted. These entrances and exits should be controlled by badge access, locked doors, or some other means that require authentication to enter. On external entrance and exit doors, alarms should be installed along with surveillance to capture the faces of individuals entering these areas. Any operable windows should be locked when necessary (i.e., after hours) and consideration of glass break sensors or appropriate motion detector sensors should be installed throughout the main hallways. In addition, motion detection should be considered in highly sensitive areas such as the records room discussed earlier and the data center that houses critical information systems.

As part of the annual testing, physical access testing should also be conducted. This access testing can take the form of social engineering-type testing. What is being talked about is the ability for an unauthorized person to trick or convince a workforce member into allowing them access to areas of the facility that they would normally not have access to. An example of this would be to allow an individual to utilize the restroom in the back area, but then allowing this individual to wander around the halls alone. Another example would be to utilize a fake badge or authorization letter that would convince a workforce member to allow an individual access to restricted areas without making sure the individual is authorized to access these areas. There are several ways in which social engineering can be utilized and entire books have been written on this topic. One of the best books that this author has read on this topic is *Social Engineering: The Art of Human Hacking* by Chris Hadnagy. This book goes into detail about social engineering and how effective these types of methods can be in gaining unauthorized access to information. A rule of thumb to follow is that no matter how many technical controls are in place, the human factor is still one of the weakest areas and can be easily exploited if the proper training or awareness is not provided to workforce members. This is why it is very important that workforce members are trained in facility access procedures as part of their security awareness training along with refresher training conducted periodically.

Along the same lines as physical testing, a complete inventory of all assets should be conducted periodically (i.e., annually). Utilizing this inventory, an analysis should be performed to determine if there are any threats to these assets through the current physical security controls implemented. Vulnerabilities discovered should be rated based upon their degree of impact if exploited and mitigated to an acceptable level. Any decisions on mitigating or actions taken to correct deficiencies should be formally documented.

The covered entity should refer to the following references for further details related to facility access controls:

- NIST SP 800-53 PE-1 Physical and Environmental Protection Policy and Procedures
- NIST SP 800-53 PE-2 Physical Access Authorizations
- NIST SP 800-53 PE-3 Physical Access Control
- NIST SP 800-53 PE-4 Access Control for Transmission Medium
- NIST SP 800-53 PE-5 Access Control for Output Devices
- NIST SP 800-66 4.10 Facility Access Controls
- NIST SP 800-66 4.10.1 Conduct an Analysis of Existing Physical Security Vulnerabilities
- NIST SP 800-66 4.10.2 Identify Corrective Measures

17.1.1 Contingency Operations—Addressable—45 CFR § 164.310(a)(2)(i)

Although this should be addressed under the business continuity and disaster recovery plan, it is also being addressed under facility access since a covered entity should establish procedures that will allow authorized access to facilities to restore data in the event of an emergency. The plan should cover all appropriate potential disasters such as a flood, fire, or earthquake. The plan should also cover all of the covered entity's facilities, not just the main office.

Since it is recommended that backups are kept off-site at a secure location, there have to be procedures in place to retrieve this data under the disaster recovery plan and emergency mode operations plan. At the off-site facility, a list of authorized individuals that can retrieve data backups should be kept current. Once the backup media is obtained, procedures should be implemented that will allow access to backup facilities to restore the data. These procedures should be tested to affirm that those workforce members responsible for data restoration are able to follow them without any issues. Of course, security considerations should be made so that unauthorized individuals will not have access to the facilities or the backup media.

The procedures should address any individual that has authorization to reenter facilities that may have been evacuated under an emergency situation to restore the systems back to normal operations. These procedures should be included or combined with the contingency plans very consistently.

Another consideration should be made for these backup facilities to have emergency power supplies in case of power loss. These emergency power supplies could come in the form of temporary generators or permanent generators attached to the facilities' power systems. This emergency source of power should be supplied, at a minimum, to the server room or critical systems, alarm systems, and surveillance systems. This redundant power source should be able to run for at least 72 hours without refueling or have refueling supply contracts from two different sources that can provide fuel in emergency situations. These generators can be very expensive so the covered entity will have to address this standard based on the risks specific to the covered entity. At the end of the day, the covered entity will have to determine how much downtime it can afford before its business and clients will suffer. There have been companies in the past that have not prepared for such emergency situations and are no longer in existence. A company that prepares for the worst and properly plans for contingencies will be able to survive most any type of emergency situation.

The covered entity should refer to the following references for further details related to contingency operations:

- NIST SP 800-53 PE-17 Alternate Work Site
- NIST SP 800-66 4.10.5 Establish Contingency Operations Procedures

17.1.2 Facility Security Plan—Addressable—45 CFR § 164.310(a)(2)(ii)

A covered entity should address and implement adequate policies and procedures to safeguard the facility and the equipment within from unauthorized access, tampering, or theft. There should be controls in place such as locking doors, surveillance cameras, alarms, and other controls to protect property and personnel as previously recommended. The covered entity should have an inventory of all of these physical access control assets along with current maintenance records and history of any changes, upgrades, or modifications to these controls. Let's take a minute to further discuss these controls.

A covered entity should know how many entrances and exits are available to the facility. All doors and locking mechanisms should be free of defects. One of the first things this author looks for is a gap between the door and the door frame. This is a good indication that a door was not installed properly. This author has seen many external doors installed in this way throughout his assessments. When traveling, the author usually asks for two card keys at the hotel. The question is asked, why? And no, it is not because the author is a forgetful person and loses them. On the contrary, the author utilizes one of the cards to attempt to bypass the lock at the client's building. By wedging a credit card (or hotel key card in my case) between an improperly installed lock and doorjamb, a door may sometimes slip open allowing unauthorized access to the facility. It has been the experience of the author that once an individual has gained access to the facility, they are assumed to be authorized and are very rarely questioned by workforce members.

Does the covered entity put up signs warning that a certain area is restricted? What are the procedures in place if someone is caught in an area that is designated as restricted? Are workforce members trained to question these individuals, confront these individuals, call a supervisor, call the police, and so forth? Are visitors given a physical token like a visitor badge to identify them as nonemployees? Does the covered entity have proper lighting around the facility to illuminate the dark areas at entry points or where workforce members tend to travel? These are just some of the questions that should be answered when addressing physical security concerns.

In today's society, there is a surveillance camera on just about every street corner. People go throughout their day not even realizing that they have probably been captured on many different cameras multiple times. Every time an individual gets cash out of an ATM, buy groceries, put gas in the car, or even drives down the highway, the individual's picture has been captured. It should go without saying that it is important to document who is doing what in the covered entity's facility and when. A covered entity should consider installing cameras to cover all entrances and exits to the facility. These cameras should be of good quality to capture the faces and be able to identify the individuals entering and leaving the facility. In addition, cameras should be installed to capture the activity that occurs in critical areas such as the server room and record rooms. These cameras should be able to identify who is entering these rooms and what type of activity is occurring in these areas.

Surveillance technologies have advanced over the years, and the standard is now recording video on digital media. This usually takes the form of a digital video recorder (or DVR). New technology has allowed for the recording of several hours of real-time footage to be compressed into a small amount of memory space. Although camera equipment is better, cameras and recordings still need to be checked on a daily basis to make sure that the system is working properly, date and time stamps are accurate, and to follow up on any events that may have occurred throughout the previous day. The video solution should be able to store at least three months worth of video before it is overwritten or should be able to be archived on removable storage devices and kept for at least this period of time. The equipment should also be protected, stored in a secure location with proper ventilation, and treated as one of the critical systems.

Besides entering and exiting through the doors, a covered entity should look at other ways someone may enter the facility such as through windows or roof access. Facilities with windows that open should place alarm contacts on them. If possible, windows should be equipped with glass break sensors, or motion detection should be installed appropriately in all critical areas and common passageways. If there is a roof access from inside the facility, this access should also be secured with alarm contacts and locks to prevent entry from the outside.

An alarm system should be installed in the facility. As already addressed, alarm contacts should be installed on all entry and exit doors, on doors protecting critical areas such as server rooms and record rooms, and should include adequate motion detection to cover other areas that may be susceptible to unauthorized intrusions. Specific individuals should be responsible for disarming the alarm when opening and arming the alarm at night. If a cleaning crew works after hours, the alarm should automatically be set at a certain time in case one of these crew members forgets to set it. The alarm system should be under a maintenance contract and tested periodically (at least monthly) for proper operations. In addition, the control panel for the alarm system should be out of the view of the public either in a secure back area or by an entry door that is only used by workforce members.

All equipment should be properly inventoried and tagged with an asset control number or engraving. Inventory should be conducted on a regular basis to make sure that no equipment has been lost or stolen. If janitorial services are provided by a cleaning company, this company should be bonded and insured. Since these individuals may have access after-hours to areas that may be restricted, the companies and the individuals being employed by this company should be trusted. A covered entity could require that employees of the cleaning company go through the same background checks as other workforce members as part of the contractual relationship between the covered entity and the janitorial service. The covered entity could also restrict janitorial services to certain times when workforce members are present to monitor their activities.

Not only is a covered entity responsible for protecting its equipment, it must also provide a safe working environment for its workforce members. Personnel could be considered a company's greatest asset and should be treated as such. It is recommended that workforce members be given photo identification badges that are required to be worn. There should be procedures in place that anyone not wearing their identification badge will be detained and questioned. There may also be sanctions against those workforce members that do not comply with these procedures.

Visitors should be given physical tokens or badges to identify them as nonworkforce members. This badge should be turned in at the end of each day and should expire when authorization is no longer required. All visitors should be escorted by a workforce member in any nonpublic areas of the facility. A visitor log should be maintained for at least 3 months and detail the following:

- Visitor's name
- The company the visitor represents
- Time and date of the visit
- The purpose for the visit
- The workforce member authorizing the visit

If the covered entity has the resources available, a private security service company may be hired to provide patrols of the facility. It should be noted that even though a security company is hired to protect the facility, this does not necessarily mean that the facility will not be compromised. The hiring of a security company may provide a false sense of security for the covered entity. Do not forget that it is every workforce member's responsibility to protect the covered entity's assets and to follow policies and procedures regarding physical security.

It cannot be stressed enough how important it is to assign a workforce member, such as the security official, responsibility over the facility security plan. This facility security plan needs to be consistent with the covered entity's overall facility architecture. It needs to define the system's authorization boundaries or systems that directly fall under the control and responsibility of the covered entity. The security plan needs to describe the interconnectivity or relationship between information systems. Information systems need to be categorized on the basis of their operations or business processes, and the appropriate physical security controls should be implemented to secure any electronic protected health information stored on these systems. Along with the security category of the systems, the facility plan should document the rationale for the type of security controls implemented on the systems and security requirements of the systems along with the environment that the information system operates under. Furthermore, the plan should address the coordination of security activities such as assessments, maintenance on hardware and software, and contingency plan testing to minimize the operational impact on the information systems and workforce members. The plan needs to be reviewed and approved by the appropriate official prior to implementation. The plan also needs to be reviewed on a periodic basis to keep it updated when changes are made or if deficiencies are discovered through the security controls assessment.

The covered entity should refer to the following references for further details related to the facility security plan:

- NIST SP 800-53 PE-9 Power Equipment and Cabling
- NIST SP 800-53 PE-10 Emergency Shutoff

- NIST SP 800-53 PE-11 Emergency Power
- NIST SP 800-53 PE-12 Emergency Lighting
- NIST SP 800-53 PE-13 Fire Protection
- NIST SP 800-53 PE-14 Temperature and Humidity Controls
- NIST SP 800-53 PE-15 Water Damage Protection
- NIST SP 800-53 PE-16 Delivery and Removal
- NIST SP 800-53 PE-18 Location of Information System Components
- NIST SP 800-53 PE-19 Information Leakage
- NIST SP 800-53 PE-20 Port and I/O Device Access
- NIST SP 800-53 PL-2 System Security Plan
- NIST SP 800-53 PL-4 Rules of Behavior
- NIST SP 800-53 PL-7 Security Concept of Operations
- NIST SP 800-53 PL-8 Security Architecture
- NIST SP 800-66 4.10.3 Develop a Facility Security Plan

17.1.3 Access Control and Validation Procedures— Addressable—45 CFR § 164.310(a)(2)(iii)

Some controls have already been discussed that can be used to provide physical protection to the facility. Now these controls must be addressed in the standard operating procedures that all workforce members should abide by. The covered entity also needs to have monitoring solutions implemented to track appropriate access. A workforce member's access to the facility is based on his or her job role and function. Using an ID badge validates the workforce member as being authorized to access the facility or certain restricted areas within the facility. Visitors should sign a log and be escorted throughout the facility. Procedures should be defined to describe the methods by which access and validation controls are implemented.

In addition, there should be procedures developed to define the controls in place for accessing software programs to test and modify these programs. Controlling such access to these software programs will assist in reducing errors and limiting the possibility of introducing bad coding instructions to the software.

To demonstrate compliance and verify that procedures are being followed, management should regularly review the list of individuals with physical access to restricted areas along with monitoring the actual access of these individuals. Unusual or suspicious times should be noted of workforce members entering restricted areas above and beyond their normal job functions. These incidents should be investigated to determine if there is a reasonable explanation for the discrepancy or if there are other issues to address. The results of this review or investigation should coincide with the covered entity's incident response procedures for suspicious activities.

Management should pay special attention to workforce members that hold the door open in restricted areas to other members when these areas utilize measures that are supposed to log entry and exit activities. An unauthorized workforce member could gain access to these restricted areas by piggybacking authorized personnel. This could lead to circumventing the controls that have been implemented to restrict access.

As mentioned earlier, a covered entity should consider changing locks on doors or combinations whenever a workforce member is terminated, transferred to another area that no longer needs the initial access level, or whenever it is believed that a key or code has been compromised. If punched cipher locks are used to control access to certain areas, can someone view these codes "over the shoulder" or do workforce members utilize their bodies to protect someone from viewing code entry? A covered entity should require all workforce members to sign for the possession of badges, metal keys, or codes. Workforce members should understand their responsibilities in protecting these items and the procedure to follow in case these items were lost or stolen. Most covered entities will have spare or master keys to the facility. All keys or badges should be accounted for using a key inventory sheet. Extra keys should be kept secure and may be under dual control whereby two different individuals may be required to retrieve these extra master keys.

The covered entity should refer to the following references for further details related to access control and validation procedures:

- NIST SP 800-53 PE-6 Monitoring Physical Access
- NIST SP 800-53 PE-8 Visitor Access Records
- NIST SP 800-66 4.10.4 Develop Access Control and Validation Procedures

17.1.3.1 Sample of Access Controls Policy

PURPOSE OF POLICY

To ensure that individual's protected health information is used or disclosed in an appropriate manner and protected from unauthorized use or disclosure as set forth in the Privacy and Security Rules.

POLICY DETAIL

[The covered entity] must implement facility and device access controls to protect electronic assets that store electronic protected health information. These access controls include but are not limited to: key locks, alarm systems, intrusion detection solutions, visitor escorts, name tags, fire detection and suppression, access profiles, and other construction materials.

17.1.3.2 Sample of Facsimile Machine Policy and Confidentiality Statement

PURPOSE OF POLICY

To ensure that the individual's protected health information is used or disclosed in an appropriate manner and protected from unauthorized use or disclosure as set forth in the Privacy and Security Rules.

POLICY DETAIL

Facsimile machines may be used to transmit protected health information provided HIPAA policies and procedures are observed. Frequently used numbers may be preprogrammed on these devices as long as they have been verified prior to transmitting any protected health information. Faxes must include a cover sheet with the following confidentiality statement:

> Confidentiality Statement: The documents accompanying this transmission contain protected health information that is privileged and confidential. This information is intended only for the use of the individuals or entities listed above. If you are not the intended recipient, you are hereby notified that any disclosure, copying, distribution, or action taken in reliance on the contents of these documents is strictly prohibited. If you have received this information in error, please notify the sender immediately to arrange for the return or destruction of these documents.

17.1.3.3 Sample of E-Mail Policy and Confidentiality Notice

PURPOSE OF POLICY

To ensure that the individual's protected health information is used or disclosed in an appropriate manner and protected from unauthorized use or disclosure as set forth in the Privacy and Security Rules.

POLICY DETAIL

Only under limited situations should protected health information be sent utilizing e-mail transmission solutions. In these cases, all protected health information is required to be encrypted prior to transmitting via e-mail. [The covered entity] will provide the workforce member with the specific encryption solution and training on how to properly encrypt e-mail. Workforce members should verify the address of a sender prior to e-mailing any messages or attachments. For all e-mail correspondence, the following confidentiality notice will automatically be attached:

> Confidentiality Notice: The information contained in this electronic communication, including any attachments, is confidential and intended only for use by the recipients named above. If the reader of this message is not the intended recipient, you are hereby notified that any review, use, dissemination, distribution, or copying of this communication (or any of its contents) is strictly prohibited. If you have received this communication in error, please notify the sender immediately and permanently remove the original message (or any copies) from your system immediately.

17.1.4 Maintenance Records—Addressable—45 CFR § 164.310(a)(2)(iv)

It is important to address the maintenance of the physical components that are used to secure the facility. Only certain workforce members should be authorized to make changes or conduct repairs on the physical security systems. Policies and procedures should be implemented to specify how repairs or modifications are made to these components. These policies and procedures need to indicate what components are required to have documentation maintained on them and those individuals responsible for maintaining this documentation. Policies and procedures should also detail the special circumstances when repairs or modifications to the physical security components are required.

The information system maintenance policy should cover at least the following components: purpose, scope, responsibilities, management commitment, coordination among different departments, and compliance. These policies should be formally documented, disseminated, and reviewed and updated on a periodic basis (i.e., annually or upon any major changes that affect information system maintenance and associated system maintenance controls). These policies should define the covered entity's overall objectives and include all areas where maintenance is required. Remember, the goal of maintenance on information systems is to maintain the security environment and controls that are utilized to secure protected health information.

The information system maintenance procedure should include scheduling, performing, documenting, and reviewing the maintenance records and any repairs on information systems or their components. These schedules should be in accordance with manufacturers' specifications. The procedures should also include control over all maintenance activities whether performed on- or off -site. If systems need to be removed off-site for repairs, the procedure should require approval from a designated official. Any equipment that may store electronic protected health information needs to be sanitized prior to the removal from the facility. Once a system is returned from repair, it needs to be fully checked for any potential security modifications and verified that it meets the security standards set for the equipment prior to placing it back into production. Some critical systems may have service level maintenance agreements for parts or components from the vendor. If this is the case, these designated time frames to obtain replacement parts need to be specified in the procedures or within the business continuity and disaster recovery plan.

The covered entity should refer to the following references for further details related to maintenance records:

- NIST SP 800-53 MA-1 Maintenance
- NIST SP 800-53 MA-2 Controlled Maintenance
- NIST SP 800-53 MA-3 Maintenance Tools

- NIST SP 800-53 MA-4 Non-Local Maintenance
- NIST SP 800-53 MA-5 Maintenance Personnel
- NIST SP 800-53 MA-6 Timely Maintenance
- NIST SP 800-66 4.10.6 Maintain Maintenance Records

17.2 Workstations Use—Required—45 CFR § 164.310(b)

A covered entity is required to have policies and procedures regarding the proper functions that are to be performed on a workstation. These policies and procedures need to be developed and implemented to identify the manner in which these functions are to be performed on a workstation. In addition, the policies and procedures need to identify the physical attributes of specific workstations or class of workstation that is authorized to access electronic protected health information. This means that the policies and procedures should describe which workstations have access to electronic protected health information and which ones are restricted from this access.

An asset inventory list should be maintained specifying the types of electronic devices and locations of these devices throughout the covered entity to include, but not limited to, workstations, laptops, PDAs, tablets, smart phones, and printers. The inventory should contain the classification of these devices, their capabilities, and the common functions utilized by these devices. A workforce member, or a group of workforce members, should be assigned responsibility to conduct this inventory and keep it current. Since each device has its own unique security concerns, the covered entity should ensure that its policies and procedures address these issues. For example, mobile devices like tablets have a lot of storage and computing power. Since they are smaller and more portable than a workstation, they could have a tendency of getting lost or stolen if they are taken out of the facility. There should be some procedures in place to ensure that these devices will not contain electronic protected health information or if they do, they are fully encrypted with password protection. Just as this example demonstrates, the covered entity needs to identify certain risks that each of these devices may have and train its workforce members on possible breaches of these devices.

Policies and procedures should cover the placing and positioning of workstations so as to only allow authorized individuals to view the information on the monitors. Policies and procedures should also describe any additional security measures that may be utilized to secure electronic protected health information such as the use of privacy screens on monitors, forcing the use of a password-protected screensaver after a certain period of user inactivity, or shutting down workstations when they are not in use. Not only should policies and procedures cover controls around workstations at a certain location, but also workstations that may be used by workforce members to access electronic protected health information from remote sites such as from the workforce member's home in cases of telecommuting work.

A covered entity should consider providing users with the minimum necessary privileges on their workstations needed to perform their job functions. This means that users should not be administrator level or power users on their local workstations. Users should be restricted from installing any programs on their systems that are not approved by IT management. In addition, IT staff members should have technical controls in place to monitor for any software or programs that are legitimately or illegitimately installed on the workstations.

Since the Internet can be a dangerous place to traverse and many people have become victims of hacking or other malicious attacks from Internet activity, a covered entity should consider restricting or filtering Internet access. A Web filtering solution should be considered to protect the covered entity from workforce members going to liable Web sites such as the following categories of sites:

- Pornography
- Anonymizer or proxy avoidance
- Hacking
- Online chat
- Web mail
- Social media
- Remote or online storage

This Web filtering solution should be able to log users by a unique identifier so that workforce members will be accountable for their actions.

All workstations owned by the covered entity or that may have access to electronic protected health information should contain a log-on warning banner. This banner should contain the following elements:

- The system is owned by the covered entity.
- It is for business purposes only.
- Workforce members do not have any expectation of privacy.
- The systems are monitored.
- Information about the use of the system can be turned over to law enforcement.
- By using the system, it is implied the workforce member agrees to the terms of use.
- Any improper use of the system can be subject to sanctions.

See a sample of a log-on warning banner in Section 17.2.1 for additional information.

The covered entity should have security controls in place to secure electronic protected health information that is being stored, being processed, or being transmitted. Policies and procedures should be able to correlate these attributes with the information systems controls. When dealing with remote access capabilities, for instance, policies and procedures should document the authorized access to these information systems. For each method of remote access, procedures should be established to restrict usage of these methods. There should also be monitoring in place for unauthorized remote access and prior authorization should be met before the connection is made. Finally, remote connections should have these and other security requirements enforced prior to gaining access to the information systems.

Examples of controls have already been provided surrounding mobile devices, but just as with remote access capabilities, the covered entity needs to document the authorized access to these mobile devices. Monitoring needs to be implemented so that unauthorized connections of mobile devices that may be made to other information systems are detected and notification is made to the appropriate workforce member. Security requirements need to be enforced on mobile devices such as encryption and password protection as necessary. Furthermore, automatic execution of code without user direction should be disabled on these mobile devices. In cases where workforce members travel to areas where the covered entity may be of significant risk, these mobile devices should be specifically configured to address these concerns and should be reviewed upon return. This review process and preventative measures may include wiping the mobile device and restoring it back to known good condition prior to allowing additional access to information systems.

The covered entity should refer to the following references for further details related to workstation use:

- NIST SP 800-53 AC-8 System Use Notification
- NIST SP 800-53 AC-9 Previous Logon (Access) Notification
- NIST SP 800-53 AC-16 Security Attributes
- NIST SP 800-53 AC-17 Remote Access
- NIST SP 800-53 AC-19 Access Controls for Mobile Devices
- NIST SP 800-66 4.11 Workstation Use
- NIST SP 800-66 4.11.1 Identify Workstation Types and Functions for Use
- NIST SP 800-66 4.11.2 Identify Expected Performance of Each Type of Workstation
- NIST SP 800-66 4.11.3 Analyze Physical Surroundings for Physical Attributes

17.2.1 Sample of Log-On Warning Banner

BANNER HEADER
WARNING, PLEASE READ CAREFULLY

BANNER BODY
This computer system is the property of [the covered entity]. It is for authorized business purposes only. Authorized or unauthorized workforce members have no explicit or implicit expectation of privacy. Any and all uses of this

system may be monitored, intercepted, recorded, copied, audited, inspected, and disclosed to [the covered entity's] management, law enforcement personnel, as well as any other authorized officials of other authorized agencies. By using this system, the workforce member consents to such monitoring, interception, recording, copying, auditing, inspection, and disclosure at the direction of [the covered entity's] management.

Unauthorized or improper use of this system may result in sanction actions, civil, and/or criminal penalties. By continuing to use this system, you indicate your awareness of and consent to these terms and conditions of use. DO NOT LOG ON if you do not agree to the conditions stated in this warning.

17.2.2 Sample of Workstation Use and Location Policy

PURPOSE OF POLICY

To ensure that the individual's protected health information is used or disclosed in an appropriate manner and protected from unauthorized use or disclosure as set forth in the Privacy and Security Rules.

POLICY DETAIL

[The covered entity] will provide secure workstations and other electronic devices with physical and technical safeguards to minimize the use or disclosure of electronic protected health information to unauthorized individuals. Asset inventory tracking solutions will be utilized to account for all electronic devices accessing or storing electronic protected health information. All electronic devices will have an asset tracking number permanently attached. Workstations at [the covered entity's] facility will be secured to desks by physical locking solutions and access to these workstations will be permitted by authorized personnel only utilizing unique usernames/password authentication. Laptops assigned to remote workforce members will have their entire hard drives encrypted.

Computer monitors will be positioned or located where only authorized workforce members can view them. If monitor screens are visible by unauthorized individuals, privacy screen filters will be installed on these monitors. Systems will be configured with a password protected screen saver after 10 minutes of user inactivity. Workforce members are required to lock their workstations when leaving their work areas.

Any documents containing protected health information will be secured in locked desk drawers or locked filing cabinets when not being used. All temporary shred boxes need to be emptied into the secure shred bins located throughout the facility prior to the end of the workforce member's shift.

17.3 Workstation Security—Required—45 CFR § 164.310(c)

A covered entity is required to implement physical safeguards to protect workstations that may access electronic protected health information and to restrict access to these workstations to authorized workforce members only. The policies and procedures should identify all types of electronic devices that may access electronic protected health information such as laptops, desktops, personal digital assistants (PDAs), mobile phones, tablets, etc. The controls in place on all these devices need to be adequate to protect from unauthorized use or disclosure of electronic protected health information.

The covered entity should document the different ways in which electronic devices can be accessed by workforce members or others. If workstations are located in public areas of the facility, the covered entity should document the rationale behind this access and determine if there are other controls in place to limit the access to electronic protected health information such as logical controls, segmentation of networks, password protection, etc. As mentioned earlier, laptops or tables may have the same capabilities as workstations in accessing information. There should be specific policies and procedures documented for this type of access. With this type of access comes greater risk or exposures, and the covered entity should identify this enhanced risk and other access that may have greater threats to the security of electronic protected health information.

A review of the areas that secure your electronic devices should be assessed to determine which areas are more vulnerable to theft, viewing, or the use of these devices. This review should be conducted on a periodic basis and could be incorporated into the security assessment. The covered entity should determine if current access configurations can be modified if deficiencies are discovered during the review.

A covered entity should consider establishing a secure room for critical servers or workstations. This server room should only be used to house these critical systems. The walls to this room should extend all the way to the ceiling to prevent anyone from crawling through drop down ceiling space. This server room should be locked at all times and only accessible by authorized personnel. The server room should utilize an access control system such as keys assigned to specific workforce members, badge access, or cipher code locks to allow only authorized personnel access. For any additional visitors, a log sheet should be present upon entry to sign and visitors should be escorted at all times in this area by an authorized workforce member.

To protect this server room from damage caused by fire, an acceptable fire detection and suppression solution should be installed. This is recommended to be an inert gas system (like FM-200) as opposed to a Halon gas suppression system that could be hazardous to personnel. The author has seen several server rooms contain sprinkler systems like other areas. It is strongly recommended not to utilize these types of fire suppression systems. Although it will mitigate fire damage, electrical devices and water do not necessarily agree with each other. The damage caused by water may be greater to the equipment than the damage caused by the fire that it was supposed to protect against.

The server room should be in an area that is not susceptible to flooding and all electronic devices should be at least 3 inches off the floor. Equipment in the server room should be protected by universal power supplies (UPS) to prevent against damage from electrical spikes and to maintain continuity, albeit for a short time, in cases of power loss. These UPS systems should be connected to an emergency power shutoff switch or have the ability to be disconnected from a power source breaks in cases of emergency. The fire department does not want to enter a room containing charged power supplies if a fire broke out without the ability to turn them off from a central location. This will mitigate possible electrical hazards that the UPS systems may pose. Just as a vehicle's oil is changed every 3,000 miles, the equipment in this server room should be routinely inspected and maintained in proper working condition.

Not only should the electronic devices be secure, but security needs to be implemented on electronic media that may store electronic protected health information. The covered entity should have policies and procedures in place for removable information system media such as tapes, hard drives, USB thumb drives, CDs, DVDs, and other such media. These media items should be accordingly marked to designate their limitations of distribution or classification along with handling procedures applicable to the type of data the media may store. Some of this media may be exempt from security marking if it remains in defined controlled areas as long as the covered entity has specifically defined this exemption. These defined controlled areas should have sufficient physical controls and other measures implemented to securely store this media. Media containing electronic protected health information needs to be secured until it is destroyed by an approved sanitation method such as wiping or physical destruction of the media is performed.

The covered entity should refer to the following references for further details related to workstation security:

- NIST SP 800-53 AC-7 Unsuccessful Login Attempts
- NIST SP 800-53 CM-1 Configuration Management Policy and Procedures
- NIST SP 800-53 CM-2 Baseline Configuration
- NIST SP 800-53 CM-3 Configuration Change Control
- NIST SP 800-53 CM-4 Security Impact Analysis
- NIST SP 800-53 CM-5 Access Restrictions for Change
- NIST SP 800-53 CM-6 Configuration Settings
- NIST SP 800-53 CM-7 Least Functionality
- NIST SP 800-53 CM-8 Information System Component Inventory
- NIST SP 800-53 CM-9 Configuration Management Plan
- NIST SP 800-53 CM-10 Software Usage Restrictions
- NIST SP 800-53 CM-11 User-Installed Software
- NIST SP 800-53 PE-18 Location of Information System Components
- NIST SP 800-53 SA-18 Tamper Resistance and Detection
- NIST SP 800-53 SA-19 Anti-Counterfeit
- NIST SP 800-66 4.1.2 Workstation Security
- NIST SP 800-66 4.12.1 Identify all Methods of Physical Access to Workstations

- NIST SP 800-66 4.12.2 Analyze the Risk Associated with Each Type of Access
- NIST SP 800-66 4.12.3 Identify and Implement Physical Safeguards for Workstations

17.4 Device and Media Controls

A covered entity needs to have policies and procedures to identify the types of hardware and other electronic media that must be tracked. The receipt and removal of hardware and electronic media in and out of a facility along with the movements of these items within a facility should be addressed in these policies and procedures. Hardware and electronic media include:

- Hard drives
- Magnetic tapes or disks
- Optical disks
- Digital memory cards
- Removable thumb drives
- Any other items that may contain electronic protected health information

The media protection policy should cover at least the following components: purpose, scope, responsibilities, management commitment, coordination among different departments, and compliance. These policies should be formally documented, disseminated, and reviewed and updated on a periodic basis (i.e., annually or upon any major changes that affect media protection). These policies should define the covered entity's overall objectives and include all areas where media protection is required. Remember, the goal of media protection is to maintain the security over electronic protected health information that removable media stores.

A covered entity should have a current inventory of system components that identifies the information system boundaries and contains the necessary information to keep proper accountability of the systems. The inventory list needs to have enough details to efficiently, and accurately, track and report on system components. The inventory list should also be available for review and audited by a designated workforce member that is responsible for attesting to its accuracy.

The covered entity should have security measures in place to protect and control digital and nondigital media transported outside of secure areas. This transportation should be accounted for and tracked. Responsibility for transporting such media should be restricted to authorized workforce members or designated individuals such as a trusted third-party courier service. Remember that media containing electronic protected health information needs to be secured until it is destroyed by an approved sanitation method such as wiping or physical destruction. If a wiping solution is implemented, this solution should be Department of Defense-grade sanitation. As a note, this sanitation process may take some time depending on the size of the media being wiped. There is other degaussing equipment that may be considered to wipe media, but in certain cases this may be cost prohibitive. A determination of how or what solution is implemented in handling the disposal of media should be conducted based on the resources the covered entity has available. This will be discussed further in the next section.

The covered entity should refer to the following references for further details related to device and media controls:

- NIST SP 800-53 CM-8 Information System Component Inventory
- NIST SP 800-53 MP-1 Media Protection Policy and Procedures
- NIST SP 800-53 MP-2 Media Access
- NIST SP 800-53 MP-3 Media Marking
- NIST SP 800-53 MP-4 Media Storage
- NIST SP 800-53 MP-5 Media Transport
- NIST SP 800-53 MP-6 Media Sanitization
- NIST SP 800-53 MP-7 Media Use
- NIST SP 800-53 MP-8 Media Downgrading
- NIST SP 800-66 4.1.3 Device and Media Controls

17.4.1 Disposal—Required—45 CFR § 164.310(d)(2)(i)

A covered entity is required to develop and implement policies and procedures that address the disposal of hardware or electronic media that stores electronic protected health information. The disposal process must make the electronic protected health information stored on hardware or electronic media unusable or inaccessible. The technology, such as software or specialized hardware, used in the disposal process should be identified in the policies and procedures. It is recommended that a wiping software approved by the Department of Defense, specialized degaussing equipment, or the physical destruction of hardware or electronic media be utilized in the disposal process. These procedures should be used by all workforce members authorized to dispose of electronic protected health information.

Although these standards specify hardware or electronic media, policies and procedures should also identify how the covered entity is disposing of documents containing protected health information. It is recommended that cross-cut shredders be used to dispose of these documents or a covered entity may decide to contract with a third party service provider that will provide shredding services. These types of service contractors usually provide secure shred bins that should be placed in convenient areas for the use of workforce members. If these shred bins are not convenient and workforce members utilize shred boxes under their desks, they should be required to empty these boxes into the secure shred bins at the end of each work day. Service contractors should be bonded and consideration should be made for them to shred documents on-site in the presence of authorized workforce members. If these services are providing disposal services for hardware or electronic media, a covered entity should receive a document of destruction that certifies the items were disposed of properly and in accordance with the covered entity's procedures.

Some covered entities may still utilize typewriters to fill out certain paper forms. If this is the case, special consideration should be made for the type of ribbon that is used on the typewriter. Some ribbons may store typed information and if an individual reverses the ribbon, the information could be recreated. A covered entity should consider what type of information this typewriter may be used to transmit and what happens once these ribbons need to be replaced. Does this ribbon store protected health information? Does the ribbon go into the trash? Does it get destroyed under the same types of procedures as other electronic media containing protected health information? These questions should be answered and addressed within the covered entity's policies and procedures.

The covered entity should refer to the following reference for further details related to disposal:

■ NIST SP 800-66 4.13.1 Implement Methods for Final Disposal of ePHI

17.4.2 Media Reuse—Required—45 CFR § 164.310(d)(2)(ii)

If the electronic media is going to be reused, a covered entity is required to have procedures implemented to remove electronic protected health information before reusing it. These procedures should address specific situations when electronic protected health information should be permanently deleted or only reformatted so that the files are not accessible by unauthorized workforce members. An individual workforce member or department should be responsible for coordinating the disposal or reuse of any hardware, media, or software across the organization. As part of the security awareness program, workforce members should be trained in the proper destruction procedures and risks involved with the reuse of hardware, media, or software.

The covered entity should refer to the following reference for further details related to the reuse of media:

■ NIST SP 800-66 4.13.2 Develop and Implement Procedures for Reuse of Electronic Media

17.4.3 Accountability—Addressable—45 CFR § 164.310(d)(2)(iii)

A covered entity needs to address a process to maintain a record of the movements of hardware and electronic media containing electronic protected health information. These processes should address the workforce member responsible for maintaining these records. In addition, if the covered entity allows workforce members or other authorized individuals to remove media that contains electronic protected health information, the covered entity should have a way in which to track this media. The records should identify all devices or media that need to be tracked under the policies and procedures. If the multiple devices are of the same type, the logs need to reflect these devices separately such as through the serial number, asset number, or some other tracking mechanism. Radio frequency ID (RFID) is newer technology that may be utilized to track movements and log devices and media that store electronic protected health information.

As previously described, a covered entity should have a current inventory of system components that identifies the information system boundaries and contains the necessary information to keep proper accountability of the systems. The inventory list needs to have enough details to efficiently and accurately track and report on system components. The inventory list should also be available for review and audited by a designated workforce member that is responsible for attesting to its accuracy.

The covered entity should refer to the following references for further details related to accountability of hardware and electronic media:

■ NIST SP 800-53 CM-8 Information System Component Inventory
■ NIST SP 800-66 4.13.3 Maintain Accountability of Hardware and Electronic Media

17.4.4 Data Backup and Storage—Addressable—45 CFR § 164.310(d)(2)(iv)

A covered entity should address processes that specify authorized movement of equipment. If equipment is moved, consideration should be made, when needed, that an exact copy of any electronic protected health information stored on this equipment is created and retrievable. The process should identify situations where this data backup is required. In addition, the process should identify the workforce member responsible for creating this retrievable, exact copy and by what specific method this copy will be obtained. A common solution for making an exact copy is by ghosting or imaging the data. These processes create a bit-by-bit exact replica of the electronic protected health information and can satisfy this standard. Backup files should be kept off-site in a case where data in transit may be lost. This information could be recreated from the backups. A review of the covered entity's business continuity and disaster recovery plan should be conducted to determine if there is any impact to business functions in cases where data may be unavailable while media is being relocated.

The covered entity should refer to the following reference for further details related to the backup and storage of data:

■ NIST SP 800-66 4.13.4 Develop Data Backup and Storage Procedures

17.5 Remote Use and Mobile Device Controls

Recently, the Office of the National Coordinator for Health Information Technology's (ONC's) Office of the Chief Privacy Officer (OCPO) launched a Privacy and Security Mobile Device Project in collaboration with the Office for Civil Rights (OCR). The goal of this project is to provide better security for mobile devices that contain protected health information. Some examples of these mobile devices are tablets and smart phones. Although the Department of Health and Human Services published security guidance related to remote use (December 28, 2006), it appears that covered entities have not taken this area of security seriously.

> There have been a number of security incidents related to the use of laptops, other portable and/or mobile devices and external hardware that store, contain or are used to access Electronic Protected Health Information (EPHI) under the responsibility of a HIPAA covered entity. All covered entities are required to be in compliance with the HIPAA Security Rule, which includes, among its requirements, reviewing and modifying, where necessary, security policies and procedures on a regular basis. This is particularly relevant for organizations that allow remote access to EPHI through portable devices or on external systems or hardware not owned or managed by the covered entity. (Department of Health and Human Services 2006)

The guidance separates risks and possible mitigating strategies into three areas of concern over electronic protected health information: accessing, storing, and transmitting.

The covered entity should refer to the following references for further details related to remote use:

- NIST SP 800-53 AC-20 Use of External Information Systems
- NIST SP 800-53 SC-18 Mobile Code

17.5.1 Accessing Electronic Protected Health Information on Mobile Devices

When accessing mobile devices containing electronic protected health information, one of the major concerns is the potential unauthorized access, viewing, or modification of electronic protected health information on these mobile devices. This could occur through the loss of log-on credentials or as a result of a stolen mobile device.

Some possible mitigating strategies that could be implemented to protect against this unauthorized access are the implementation of two-factor authentication that is required to access the mobile devices. This authentication process goes beyond just usernames and passwords, and requires an additional authentication process such as answering an additional security question. Unique usernames should also be used on mobile devices and authentication of workforce members that use mobile devices should be conducted prior to allowing them access to any internal network resources.

Another concern in using mobile devices is that workforce members may access electronic protected health information while working off-site. To mitigate this risk, covered entities should have proper clearance procedures in place to specify where and how access to electronic protected health information is permitted. All workforce members should be trained and acknowledge these policies and procedures. As discussed, workforce members' roles and responsibilities will dictate the access levels granted to electronic protected health information, and mobile devices along with their applications should follow these specific business requirements. Sanction policies should appropriately address the issue of accessing electronic protected health information remotely if this is considered prohibited activity.

Mobile devices could enable workforce members the ability to work from home or other remote off-site locations. One of the concerns is the potential risk of leaving these mobile devices unattended. To mitigate this risk, procedures should be implemented to establish inactivity time-out session terminations for mobile devices. Most current applications come with this type of configuration option.

One of the final concerns related to accessing electronic protected health information on mobile devices is the risk of virus infections. Personal firewalls and updated virus-protection software should be configured and implemented on all mobile devices that connect to the network. These applications should not be able to be turned off or modified in any way by the workforce member using the mobile device.

The covered entity should refer to the following reference for further details related to the access controls for mobile devices:

■ NIST SP 800-53 AC-19 Access Control for Mobile Devices

17.5.2 Storing Electronic Protected Health Information on Mobile Devices

Mobile devices can store large amounts of electronic protected health information. If one of these devices were to be lost or stolen, this information could potentially be improperly accessed. The following are some mitigating strategies to prevent this unauthorized access of stored electronic protected health information:

■ Develop an inventory control system to identify and track all mobile devices, both hardware and electronic media such as hard drives, magnetic tapes/disks, optical disks (CD/DVD), digital memory devices (USB/SD cards), and other security equipment.
■ Use locking mechanisms to secure unattended mobile devices such as laptops.

- Protect files with passwords that contain electronic protected health information.
- Protect all mobile devices with passwords that store electronic protected health information.
- Employ strong encryption solutions on all mobile devices that store electronic protected health information.
- Ensure mobile devices are kept updated with the appropriate security updates.
- Consider using a biometric solution (i.e., fingerprint reader) to authenticate access to mobile devices.

Some mobile devices will synchronize information with the main database. When this occurs, there may be a possibility that information on the remote mobile device is lost or corrupted. If this occurs, it is important that mobile devices have appropriate backups to maintain the operationally critical electronic protected health information required to be stored on the device. Of course, these backups should also be encrypted to ensure the security of electronic protected health information that may be stored on mobile devices.

Mobile devices have a short life expectancy. Smart phones are usually updated every 2 years and other mobile devices may be damaged over time. It is important that proper disposal procedures are implemented for the wiping or destruction of electronic protected health information stored on these devices.

Mobile devices have a tendency to be accidentally left at remote locations such as libraries or hotel business centers. For this reason, it is important that electronic protected health information is not downloaded or left on these devices if there is no business justification for this information to be stored on these devices. Workforce members should be trained on deleting files from the mobile devices that should not be stored on these devices. For applications that use browser-cached data, this type of caching should be minimized and these temporary files should be automatically deleted from mobile devices.

17.5.3 Transmitting Electronic Protected Health Information on Mobile Devices

There are multiple ways that mobile devices can connect to internal networks. Mobile devices are generally designed to be able to connect to the Internet through several different channels such as through services offered through communication carriers or through Wi-Fi connections. Since data may be transmitted through unsecured channels, it is essential that the following mitigation strategies are implemented:

- Prohibit electronic protected health information to be transmitted through open networks like the Internet except when encrypted

- Prohibit the use of unsecured access points to be utilized for e-mail or other secure tasks
- Enforce the use of more secure connections such as receiving e-mail through Secure Socket Layer (SSL)-type connections or securing this communication through encryption
- Set standards to use when transmitting electronic protected health information across public network connections such as enforcing SSL as a minimum requirement for all Internet-facing systems that manage electronic protected health information

The covered entity should refer to the following references for further details related to the transmission of electronic protected health information on mobile devices:

- NIST SP 800-53 AC-18 Wireless Access
- NIST SP 800-53 SC-19 Voice Over Internet Protocol
- NIST SP 800-53 SC-42 Wireless Link Protection

17.5.4 Securing Wireless Networks

Users no longer have to be plugged into the network to work. Through the use of wireless network devices throughout an office building utilizing radio frequencies, workforce members can work on this wireless local area network (WLAN) to perform the same types of electronic transactions anywhere in the facility as if they were sitting stationary at their desks. A lot of individuals have some concerns surrounding security related to this type of technology; however, if proper steps and considerations are made prior to deploying this solution, wireless network connectivity can be as secure as plugging the device into the local area network.

NIST has recently released Special Publication 800-153, Guidelines for Securing Wireless Local Area Networks (WLANs) that provides a detailed step-by-step process of implementing a wireless solution in an organization. The following are summarized recommendations to consider when implementing WLAN solutions:

1. Standardized security configurations—Common WLAN components such as client devices and access points should have strong security configurations.
2. Consider security throughout—Implement security controls not only in the WLAN solution but also consider how this solution may affect the security of other networks.
3. Have WLAN policies—Develop policies that clearly state how the WLAN will be utilized. For instance, the policy may state that if a workforce member is plugged into the network, then the wireless connection should be disabled. It may also state that if the wireless network is being utilized, a physical con-

nection should not be made. There should be appropriate security controls implemented to enforce these policies.

4. Enforce configurations—Controls should be implemented to enforce compliance of policies on mobile devices and access points. Configurations that are compliant with the policy should be enforced on these devices at all times.
5. Monitor—Security of the WLAN should be monitored both for attacks and vulnerabilities.
6. Assess—Conduct regular periodic technical security assessments on the WLAN.

The covered entity should refer to the following references for further details related to wireless security:

- NIST SP 800-53 AC-3 Access Enforcement
- NIST SP 800-53 AC-4 Information Flow Enforcement
- NIST SP 800-53 AC-18 Wireless Access
- NIST SP 800-53 AC-19 Access Control for Mobile Devices
- NIST SP 800-53 AC-20 Use of External Information Systems
- NIST SP 800-53 AU-2 Auditable Events
- NIST SP 800-53 CA-2 Security Assessments
- NIST SP 800-53 CA-7 Continuous Monitoring
- NIST SP 800-53 CM-6 Configuration Settings
- NIST SP 800-53 IA-2 Identification and Authentication (Organizational Users)
- NIST SP 800-53 IA-3 Device Identification and Authentication
- NIST SP 800-53 IA-5 Authenticator Management
- NIST SP 800-53 IA-8 Identification and Authentication (Non-Organizational Users)
- NIST SP 800-53 PE-18 Location of Information System Components
- NIST SP 800-53 RA-3 Risk Assessment
- NIST SP 800-53 RA-5 Vulnerability Scanning
- NIST SP 800-53 SC-7 Boundary Protection
- NIST SP 800-53 SC-8 Transmission Integrity
- NIST SP 800-53 SC-9 Transmission Confidentiality
- NIST SP 800-53 SI-2 Flaw Remediation
- NIST SP 800-53 SI4 Information System Monitoring

17.6 Summary

As discussed throughout this chapter, one of the first layers of defense to form a strong security posture is the physical layer. In most cases, if unauthorized physical access to a piece of equipment is obtained, it can be considered compromised.

Through the use of facility access controls, risk to unauthorized physical access can be limited. It is important that a facility security plan is developed and procedures to control access to the facility are enforced. It is also important that the plan considers contingency operations so when emergencies occur, security is still maintained.

A covered entity should have procedures over access control and validation. Only authorized individuals that have been vetted should have access to the information that they will need to perform their assigned jobs. Being able to validate the identity of an individual and ensuring that the individual is who they say they are is essential in maintaining proper control over protected health information. In most cases, this is done by assigning a unique user identifier along with a secured password that the individual can utilize to validate his or her authenticity. As companies grow their business, so does the volume of information they obtain grow. There needs to be procedures in place that can address the maintenance of a company's records in a secure fashion.

A covered entity should have policies related to the acceptable and permitted use of workstations assigned. These workstations should only be utilized for business purposes and have the least amount of privileges necessary for workforce members to perform their assigned tasks. Along with documented policies and procedures, technical controls should be implemented to enforce security on workstations such as session timeouts with protected screensavers, logon banners, enforcement of strong passwords, and encryption.

Not only do the workstations require security controls, but other media or portable devices containing electronic protected health information require the same levels of protection. There should be policies and procedures in place that address the appropriate disposal process of media, when or how media can be reused, an inventory of all media or other devices containing electronic protected health information, and backup or storage of these sensitive devices.

The chapter ends with recommendations that a covered entity should take if consideration is being made to use wireless technology. Although there may be some concerns surrounding wireless technology, if the proper steps are taken, configurations made, and security controls implemented, a wireless solution could be as safe as physically plugging a device into the local area network.

Chapter 18

Security Rule: Technical Safeguards

Objectives

The objectives of this chapter are as follows:

- Understand the technical safeguards that are required to be implemented by the Security Rule.
- Understand access control requirements.
- Determine what type of unique user identifier is appropriate for the covered entity.
- Understand what type of procedure is required for emergency access capabilities.
- Determine how the information system addresses automatic log-off functions.
- Determine what type of encryption should be utilized on information systems, devices, media, and so on, and what capabilities are available for these items.
- Understand the types of audit controls an information system has in place.
- Understand what is meant by integrity.
- Determine what mechanisms are required to authenticate access to electronic protected health information.
- Understand what is required to authenticate individual or entity access levels.
- Understand what is meant by transmission security.
- Determine what type of integrity controls can be implemented to address the security of electronic protected health information in transit.
- Determine what types of encryption are available to secure electronic protected health information.

Table 18.1   Technical Safeguards

Security Standards		
Technical Safeguards		
164.312(a)(1)		**Access Control**
164.312(a)(2)(i)	R	Unique User Identification
164.312(a)(2)(ii)	R	Emergency Access Procedure
164.312(a)(2)(iii)	A	Automatic Logoff
164.312(a)(2)(iv)	A	Encryption and Decryption
164.312(b)	R	Audit Controls
164.312c(1)		**Integrity**
164.312c(2)	A	Mechanism to Authenticate Electronic Protected Health Information
164.312(d)	R	Person or Entity Authentication
164. 312(e)(1)		**Transmission Security**
164.312(e)(2)(i)	A	Integrity Controls
164.312(e)(2)(ii)	A	Encryption

Note: A = addressable, R = required.

Background

As technology advances in the healthcare industry, it is becoming imperative to increase the level of security in this technology. Covered entities are expected and required to implement an adequate level of security for safeguarding their electronic protected health information. As part of the requirements under the Health Insurance Portability and Accountability Act (HIPAA) Security Rule, covered entities must implement security measures to comply with these standards. The objective of these safeguards is to mitigate the risk of electronic protected health information being used or disclosed in an unauthorized manner. These technical safeguards include the following measures: access control, audit controls, integrity, person or entity authentication, and transmission security. See Table 18.1 for a list of required and addressable controls.

18.1 Access Control

The access control standard requires a covered entity to implement adequate technical policies and procedures for electronic information systems that maintain electronic protected health information in such a way as to allow access only to those workforce members that have been granted access rights under the information access management policies and procedures. This includes restricting certain software programs and allowing only authorized workforce members to utilize these programs that have access to electronic protected health information.

The access control policy should cover at least the following components: purpose, scope, responsibilities, management commitment, coordination among different departments, and compliance. These policies should be formally documented, disseminated, and reviewed and updated on a periodic basis (i.e., annually or upon any major changes that affect access control). These policies should define the covered entity's overall objectives and include all areas where access control is required. Remember, the goal of access control is to allow only authorized workforce members (or other individuals) access and restrict those workforce members (or other individuals) that should not have access to use or disclose electronic protected health information and the devices that store and process this information.

To maintain an acceptable level of access control the covered entity should implement safeguards, not only for the information systems such as workstations and laptops, but also for the network as a whole. This would include placing firewalls between internal networks and external networks, the use of port security or network access control to limit unauthorized devices from connecting to the network, and deploying encryption capabilities.

The covered entity should determine what type of access control would work best in its environment. For instance, would identity-based, role-based, or attribute-based policies work best in the covered entity's environment? Identity-based access control (IBAC) utilizes the user's identity to grant access to specific objects or data. For example, each workforce member may have access to their own private working directory but not have access to each other's directory based upon their own unique log-in credentials. In role-based access control (RBAC), the access is determined by the information system rather than the individual owner. For example, a workforce member is assigned a "nurses" role. This means that this workforce member would have access to any information that the system recognizes as being authorized for that role. Based on the role and the role authorization, transactions can be performed such as editing a patient's electronic medical record based upon the transactions that are allowed under the workforce member's role. In attribute-based access control (ABAC), access is granted to workforce members based on their attributes rather than their rights. For example, let's say that information about a patient may only be seen by workforce members that are over 18 years of age. In this case, any workforce member that can prove the claim of being over 18 will be granted access to this specific information.

The covered entity should be able to document the roles of each user for each application, information system, server, or other device that may hold electronic protected health information. In addition, the covered entity should determine the access capabilities of their systems such as creating, viewing, modifying, or deleting the information. Access enforcement mechanisms should be used such as access control lists, matrices, encryption, and other controls that will be discussed later. Not only does the covered entity want to control access at the physical level, but also it needs to control access at the network and application levels. In case of emergency situations, these automatic controls should have an override that can be issued and audited in accordance with the covered entity's business continuity and disaster recovery policies and procedures.

The documentation of roles is important to determine if there are separations of duties to prevent against fraud or collusive acts. For example, a workforce member conducting a transaction should not be the same individual that reviews or audits the report of those transactions. Some other duties that should be considered to be separated between different workforce members are operational functions and informational support functions. Related to information support functions, duties should be separated for system administrative functions and security testing functions. The individual writing software code should not be the same individual testing the code. In addition, workforce members that administer access control functions should not be the same workforce members that audit or review these functions. Finally, it is recommended that system administrator accounts are set up for different roles and accounts should be assigned at the least privilege with only the amount of privileges necessary to perform the assigned function.

Wireless networks have become mainstream and are now being widely deployed throughout healthcare providers' networks. There are, however, some special considerations and configurations that should be implemented when utilizing this technology. For instance, wireless network devices deployed on a network should have all of their default configurations modified. This includes not broadcasting the Server Set Identifier (SSID), changing the SSID to a unique identifier, not utilizing Wired Equivalent Privacy (WEP), placing a firewall between a wireless access point and the local area network, utilizing strong Virtual Privet Network (VPN) encryption technology, copying wireless audit logs to a secure log server, and routinely searching for rogue wireless access points that may not belong to the covered entity. A workforce member, or other individual, that may be authorized to use the wireless technology should accept a liability disclaimer that releases the covered entity from any damage and identifies the appropriate use of this technology.

All devices connected to the network should require authentication prior to gaining any access to the resources on these devices. For example, there should not be any directories that are accessible or shared with everyone on the network. In addition, File Transfer Protocol (FTP) that is generally used to transfer files from one system to another should be limited. Due to the insecure nature of FTP, it is recommended not to be used; instead, SSH File Transfer Protocol (SFTP) or FTP over Secure Socket Layer (SSL)/Transport Layer Security (TLS) (or FTPS) should be considered. If FTP is being utilized on the local area network (LAN), then it needs to require authentication. Anonymous FTP servers are strongly discouraged.

All network devices or services should be kept up to date to mitigate known vulnerabilities. These devices should not be deployed in production environments with any default configurations still set. For instance, network devices such as routers or switches need to have their account usernames and passwords changed for their administrative consoles or configuration sessions. In cases of software packages or Web server interfaces, the administrative accesses should not be left as default. It has been my experience that vendors, even those in the security arena, may install their information systems on the network without changing their settings. I have, on several occasions, compromised the entire network by targeting these vendor systems and leveraging their access levels on the network to gain total control of the network. Any devices connecting to the network become the covered entity's responsibility and should be tested to verify that the proper security controls are implemented on these systems.

Firewalls are an essential piece of network equipment that can be utilized to comply with the access standards. Firewalls should provide "stateful inspection," or dynamic packet filtering, that only allows established connects to enter the network. Firewalls can be a bit difficult to configure and it is recommended to employ the resources of an outside expert if these resources are not available in house. Firewalls normally work from a standpoint of access control lists (or ACLs). ACLs only allow those networks or devices that are implicitly identified in their rules access to other resources or devices on the network. All other networks or devices have an explicit "deny all." Firewall rules should be designed to allow access specifically from one source to one destination over specific protocols or ports. These firewall rules should be reviewed on a regular basis and any entries into the ACL should be justified and documented.

The covered entity should refer to the following references for further details related to access control:

- NIST SP 800-53 AC-1 Access Control Policy and Procedures
- NIST SP 800-53 AC-3 Access Enforcement
- NIST SP 800-53 AC-4 Information Flow Enforcement
- NIST SP 800-53 AC-5 Separation of Duties
- NIST SP 800-53 AC-6 Least Privilege
- NIST SP 800-53 AC-24 Access Control Decisions
- NIST SP 800-53 SC-1 System and Communications Protection Policy and Procedures
- NIST SP 800-66 4.14 Access Control
- NIST SP 800-66 4.14.1 Analyze Workloads and Operations to Identify the Access Needed by Users
- NIST SP 800-66 4.14.2 Identify Technical Access Control Capabilities

18.1.1 Unique User Identification—Required—45 CFR § 164.312(a)(2)(i)

Each and every workforce member should have a unique user identifier when logging onto the workstation, network, or software program that has access to electronic protected health information. In many cases, this unique user identifier is known as the *username* or the *user ID*. This unique identifier should be utilized to track the user's activity within the information system and users should be restricted from sharing this information with anyone else. To authenticate the user, a password is generally used with the unique user identifier.

The covered entity should have a formal access control policy in place that should help guide the development of procedures related to the implementation of access control authorization and restrictions. Access control procedures should include the management of information system accounts. Management of accounts includes:

- Account establishment
- Account activation
- Account modification
- Account termination
- Eventual account removal

In addition, the access control procedures should include the process for initial access, process for increasing or restricting access, and a process for providing access to different applications or other systems that the user may need. Once the access control procedures have been developed, they will need to be effectively implemented, communicated to all workforce members, and compliance with these policies and procedures need to be enforced. A designated workforce member, such as the security official, should be responsible for managing the procedures for access control.

One of the ways that access control policies and procedures can be communicated to the workforce members is through training specific to access control and management of access control. All new workforce members should be instructed on these policies and procedures and others related to securing electronic protected health information. All workforce members should have refresher training and be advised of any updates to the access control policies and procedures.

Information system accounts, as per policy and procedures, should be managed in a certain way. System accounts should be identified by account type. For example, there may be individual accounts or group accounts set up for an information system. There may also be system or application level accounts for a particular information system or application. Finally, there may be guest, anonymous, or temporary accounts that may need to be treated with special care, such as additional monitoring for these accounts, or disabled entirely from the information system.

One of the easiest ways to manage system accounts is by setting up group memberships. These groups may correspond to the roles of the individual workforce

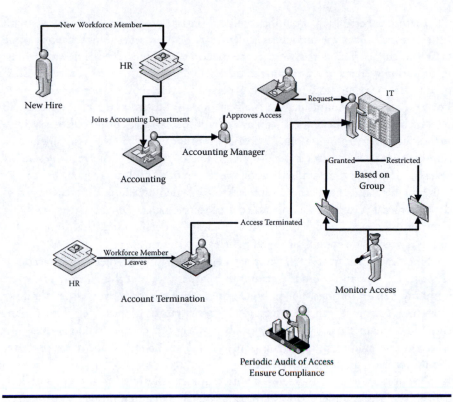

Figure 18.1   Workflow of account establishment and termination.

members within the covered entity. Conditions will need to be established on group memberships for the appropriate access levels required on the information system and appropriate requests for approval to these groups need to be established. For instance, the covered entity may have an accounting group established in a specific information system or application. One of the conditions placed on this group is that only workforce members working in the accounting department will be authorized to be a member of this group. The manager of the accounting department should send a request to the IT department to establish an account in this group for one of their workforce members. Once the account is set up within the group, the individual will inherit all of the rights or restrictions placed on this group. Depending on the information system and its function, the accounting group, for example, may or may not have privileges to access this information system or other information systems that do not run accounting functions. If the workforce member leaves or transfers positions, procedures should be implemented to modify or terminate the workforce member's access. A review or audit of system accounts needs to be conducted on a periodic basis to ensure compliance with access control policies and procedures. See Figure 18.1 for additional details on this process.

There has been a lot of emphasis placed on the protection of passwords with little thought about the unique user identifiers or usernames. Since the username is half of the username–password authentication scheme widely deployed in most information systems, the username should be protected just as the password. Most organizations set up accounts using a person's name or a portion of the name. For example, an account may be the first initial and last name of the person to which that account belongs. This may be easy to manage, but it is also easy for a malicious person to figure out. A possible solution could be the assignment of a number that may be a little more difficult to identify as part of this security schema for username–password authentication. Furthermore, this unique identifier can be different for different types of applications or when accessing different types of data. Remember, unique identifiers are used to track all system activities involving electronic protected health information back to a specific user. This audit trail is necessary to ensure compliance with policies and procedures.

Since most information systems are deployed with a privileged user account, "super user" account, or "root" account, it is imperative that this account is not left with any default settings. For instance, the administrator account in a Windows operating system is generally named "administrator." If possible, this account should be renamed or disabled after another account is created to take its place. In addition, for auditing purposes, accounts should not be reused and every new user should receive a unique user account.

Passwords are normally required with a unique user identification to authenticate a user. There are several ways that passwords are compromised. Most of these have to deal with the lack of control that a user places over the security of their passwords. One example of this is by using simple passwords. A password like "123456" or "11111111" is not appropriate and provides just a little more protection than if the password was just blank in the first place. Common passwords such as "Password1" and "qwerty" should also not be used. Most password hacking programs utilize a dictionary list that can automatically insert passwords into the password field. It is recommended that passwords do not contain any type of words that may be found in a dictionary, common misspellings of these words, these words spelled backwards, or slang terms. Passwords should also not be the same as the unique user identifier or a hybrid combination of the name of the covered entity such as "[covered entity name]1234."

Since passwords are used for all types of resources on the Internet and other applications, it is recommended not to use the same password across different sites. For instance, e-mail passwords should be different than banking passwords that are different than passwords for social media sites. If the passwords were all the same for these accounts than if one of these resources were compromised, all the applications could be compromised as well.

The following are some recommendations that could be followed to keep passwords secure (Siciliano 2011):

1. Do not tell anyone your password.
2. If passwords need to be written down to remember them, make sure they are secured. Replace a password list with a "tip list" to assist in remembering passwords.
3. Change passwords on a routine or periodic basis.
4. When entering passwords, cover the keyboard and make sure no one is around that is watching.
5. Make passwords at least eight characters long with a mix of uppercase, lowercase, numbers, and symbols.
6. Use strong passwords that can be remembered but cannot be guessed. For instance, use a phrase from a song and replace symbols with similar characters or words like "to" with a number "2".
7. Use the keyboard as a palette to make shapes. For instance, to make a V shape, use "$rfvGY7." Slide your fingers up or down the keyboard to create different combinations.
8. Avoid entering passwords into unknown systems or public-use systems like Internet cafes. These systems could have software installed that could be used to capture the credentials entered.
9. Avoid entering passwords over unsecured Wi-Fi connections. Make sure that any site requiring passwords has a secure connection (i.e., through HTTPS).
10. If a site provides a password strength analyzer to determine how strong a password is, make sure to follow its advice and make the password as strong as possible.

The covered entity should refer to the following references for further details related to using unique user identifiers:

- NIST SP 800-53 AC-2 Account Management
- NIST SP 800-53 AC-14 Permitted Actions Without Identification or Authentication
- NIST SP 800-53 IA-1 Identification and Authentication Policy and Procedures
- NIST SP 800-66 4.14.3 Ensure That all System Users Have Been Assigned a Unique Identifier
- NIST SP 800-66 4.14.4 Develop Access Control Policy
- NIST SP 800-66 4.14.5 Implement Access Control Procedures using Selected Hardware and Software
- NIST SP 800-66 4.14.6 Review and Update User Access

18.1.2 Emergency Access Procedure— Required—45 CFR § 164.312(a)(2)(ii)

A covered entity should identify all workforce members that may need access to electronic protected health information in the event of an emergency. A covered entity is required to have policies and procedures in place to provide appropriate access to these workforce members in emergency situations. In addition, a covered entity should have a policy in place that designates a responsible workforce member to make a decision about activating emergency procedures and the appropriate time these should be activated. These emergency procedures should contain methods of supporting continued operations in situations that affect normal operations. It should be determined whether the information systems can allow for the automatic failover to emergency configurations or will a workforce member have to manually configure these failover procedures.

The covered entity should refer to the following reference for further details related to emergency access procedures:

■ NIST SP 800-66 4.14.7 Establish an Emergency Access Procedure

18.1.3 Automatic Logoff—Addressable—45 CFR § 164.312(a)(2)(iii)

Covered entities should implement an automatic log-off of information systems after a period of workforce member inactivity. This automatic log-off capability is generally seen within a Windows network through a group policy that can enforce a password protected screensaver after a certain period of inactivity. This inactivity period is generally recommended to be 10 minutes but could be adjusted for a group of workforce members that may require a little more time. This could also be adjusted in cases where certain processes are running on information systems but may not be picked up as activity, and if the session was terminated, the process may not complete as desired. The automatic log-off feature should be activated on all workstations with access to electronic protected health information.

The covered entity should refer to the following references for further details related to automatic log-off:

■ NIST SP 800-53 AC-11 Session Lock
■ NIST SP 800-10 SC-10 Network Disconnect
■ NIST SP 800-66 4.14.8 Automatic Logoff and Encryption and Decryption

18.1.4 Encryption and Decryption—Addressable—45 CFR § 164.312(a)(2)(iv)

A covered entity needs to identify or address all electronic protected health information that requires encryption so that it is restricted from access by individuals or other software programs that may not be granted access rights to this information. The encryption should be reasonable and appropriately implemented to prevent unauthorized access to electronic protected health information. The covered entity may decide to encrypt electronic protected health information in transit and while being stored depending on the risk of exposure of the information in these two states.

The covered entity should refer to the following references for further details related to encryption and decryption of data:

- NIST SP 800-53 AC-11 Session Lock
- NIST SP 800-66 4.14.9 Terminate Access If It Is No Longer Required

18.2 Audit Controls—Required—45 CFR § 164.312(b)

A covered entity is required to implement audit control mechanisms to record and examine activity in information systems that contain or use electronic protected health information. Most current information systems have built-in audit control capabilities and the covered entity should identify what type of logging is currently in place. Audit controls need to be adequately implemented to allow the covered entity to adhere to its policies and procedures regarding compliance with the implementation specifications for information system activity review.

The audit and accountability policy should cover at least the following components: purpose, scope, responsibilities, management commitment, coordination among different departments, and compliance. These policies should be formally documented, disseminated, and reviewed and updated on a periodic basis (i.e., annually or upon any major changes that affect auditing). These policies should define the covered entity's overall objectives and include all areas where access control is required. Remember, the goal of auditing is to record and examine activity in information systems that affect electronic protected health information. This includes any hardware, software, or procedural controls in place to track such activity as modifying electronic protected health information within information systems.

Based on the covered entity's risk assessment and other business needs, it should be able to define a list of events that need to be audited. These events should cover a cross-section of audit-related information supported by input from departments across the entire covered entity. There should be a documented rationale behind the list of events chosen to adequately support an investigation after a breach or incident occurs. The audit records generated from logging should, at a minimum, detail the type of event, the date and time of an event, the possible identity of the subject of the event, and the information that may have been affected by the event. There also needs to be a workforce member or designated group that is responsible for the overall audit process and reporting. Time frames for audits should be defined within the audit policies and procedures.

Auditing or logging could take up a lot of hard drive space on an information system. Depending on the types of events that are recorded, storing this information could become exceedingly difficult or expensive. It may not be feasible or necessary to record every possible event, so it is important to decide what reporting is essential to the covered entity's needs. Storage of audit logs should be carefully monitored so that important reporting information is not overwritten in the event that capacity is exceeded. Since these logs could be extremely large, it is important that a solution is implemented to filter or aggregate the data into an easily readable format so that unusual activity can be identified and findings reported to the designated workforce member such as the security official. These thresholds also need to be analyzed so that false positives are kept to a minimum and resources are not wasted in tracking down nonevents. Consideration may be made to store audit logs on a completely separate server with all the necessary controls implemented to ensure the integrity of the logs stored within.

The auditing or logging process should be flexible. It should monitor for the creation, review, modification, or deletion of electronic protected health information. Based on analysis, reporting, or other audit reviews, auditing should adjust for changes in risk levels of the covered entity obtained by credible sources such as law enforcement or other intelligence agencies. The auditing process should also include reporting that approaches almost near real-time review or notification capabilities to allow for the immediate reaction to any suspicious activities identified. This suspicious activity, for example, could include any unauthorized or inappropriate access to electronic protected health information.

The auditing process should be reviewed on a continuous basis and at least annually along with updating the system capabilities as necessary. This audit process should have metrics designed to assess the effectiveness of the process and to assist in the determination of improvements. One of the methods that I have seen performed to ensure the effectiveness of the audit process is by testing. When security testing is performed, such as a penetration test, an evaluation on the auditing process can be conducted. Does the monitoring or logging implemented pick up the scanning activity? If access is gained on the system through an exploitable vulnerability, did the audit events log such activity? Did the appropriate workforce members receive notification that any suspicious activity was occurring during the security testing? These are some of the questions that should be answered and items reviewed during these types of exercises. If the auditing process does not provide the expected results, it should be updated appropriately.

Some recommendations regarding the configurations of firewalls have already been touched upon, but along with the access controls that these firewalls provide, they should also provide logging capabilities. Firewalls should be audited for failed and successful connections. Each time a device connects or attempts to connect to another device through the rules provided for in the ACL, the firewall should be logging this activity. These firewall logs should be reviewed on a daily basis by someone with the experience to identify suspicious activity. In addition, these firewall logs should be stored, for a duration of 6 years, in accordance with the policies and procedures as previously addressed in Chapter 11, Section 11.4.4.

The covered entity should refer to the following references for further details related to audit controls:

- NIST SP 800-53 AC-9 Concurrent Session Control
- NIST SP 800-53 AU-1 Audit and Accountability Policies and Procedures
- NIST SP 800-53 AU-2 Auditable Events
- NIST SP 800-53 AU-3 Content of Audit Records
- NIST SP 800-53 AU-4 Audit Storage Capacity
- NIST SP 800-53 AU-5 Response to Audit Processing Failures
- NIST SP 800-53 AU-6 Audit Review, Analysis, and Reporting
- NIST SP 800-53 AU-7 Audit Reduction and Report Generation
- NIST SP 800-53 AU-9 Protection of Audit Information
- NIST SP 800-53 AU-11 Audit Record Retention
- NIST SP 800-53 AU-12 Audit Generation
- NIST SP 800-53 AU-14 Session Audit
- NIST SP 800-53 AU-15 Alternate Audit Capability
- NIST SP 800-53 AU-16 Cross-Organizational Auditing
- NIST SP 800-53 CA-5 Plan of Action and Milestones
- NIST SP 800-66 4.15 Audit Control
- NIST SP 800-66 4.15.1 Determine the Activities That Will Be Tracked or Audited
- NIST SP 800-66 4.15.2 Select the Tool That Will Be Deployed for Auditing and System Activity Reviews
- NIST SP 800-66 4.15.3 Develop and Deploy the Information System Activity Review/Audit Policy
- NIST SP 800-66 4.15.4 Develop Appropriate Standard Operating Procedures
- NIST SP 800-66 4.15.5 Implement that Audit/System Activity Review Process

18.3 Integrity

Integrity deals with the alteration or modification of data. A covered entity must implement policies and procedures to secure electronic protected health information from unauthorized alteration, modification, or destruction. Information systems and software programs should have the capabilities of maintaining the integrity of electronic protected health information through the use of integrity verification solutions that can identify information that has been modified through human error, omission, or malicious tampering.

The system and security information integrity policy should cover at least the following components: purpose, scope, responsibilities, management commitment, coordination among different departments, and compliance. These policies should be formally documented, disseminated, and reviewed and updated on a periodic basis (i.e., annually or upon any major changes that affect integrity). These policies should define the covered entity's overall objectives and include all areas where access control is required. Remember, the goal of integrity is to restrict any unauthorized modification to electronic protected health information.

A covered entity should have policies and procedures in place that detail how workforce members (and other users) are authorized to access electronic protected health information. These procedures should include a list of all users that have access to electronic protected health information and detail the rationale behind the access granted such as the roles or responsibilities that require certain workforce members authority to access the information based on their job requirements. Their job roles or requirements should detail the ability to alter or destroy certain electronic protected health information.

A covered entity needs to train its workforce members on how to use electronic protected health information. Workforce members need to be aware that there are audit trails available that establish monitoring of access to electronic protected health information. Workforce members also need to be aware that sanctions can and will be disseminated based on violation of the covered entity's access policies and procedures. Any additional training should be considered to mitigate human errors when dealing with the integrity of the data.

Through a risk assessment or analysis, the covered entity should have identified situations where unauthorized modifications could be made to electronic protected health information such as from disgruntled workforce members, hackers, third-party providers, or possibly business competitors. The covered entity should determine what it can do to secure electronic protected health information in these systems and mitigate the risk of unauthorized access to an acceptable level. Examples of some mitigation controls could be access controls to information systems that store electronic protected health information and encryption while this electronic protected health information is in transit.

The risk assessment should also document the integrity requirements for the electronic protected health information. These requirements should be supported by management or any other designated workforce member responsible for security-related functions. These integrity requirements should also be disseminated to the workforce members utilizing the information systems through written policies or procedures. It is important that audit controls take into account methods to adequately address the integrity of electronic protected health information. There may be a situation where current integrity controls are not enough and additional solutions such as a quality control process may need to be implemented to ensure the data is accurate.

As it relates to integrity, the covered entity should determine what types of periodic backups will be conducted. These backups could be conducted on user-level information, system-level information, or both. System and security documentation should also be considered as critical data that require periodic backups. Backups should be treated as confidential, and integrity controls need to be implemented to secure this information especially at off-site storage locations and during transit outside of controlled areas. Backups should be restricted and only authorized workforce members or designated individuals should be allowed access to them. If backups are done through digital methods, the information should be protected across both the internal and external network connections.

The covered entity should refer to the following references for further details related to integrity:

- NIST SP 800-53 AU-8 Time Stamps
- NIST SP 800-53 AU-10 Non-Repudiation
- NIST SP 800-53 CP-9 Information System Backup
- NIST SP 800-53 SC-2 Application Partitioning
- NIST SP 800-53 SC-3 Security Function Isolation
- NIST SP 800-53 SC-4 Information in Shared Resources
- NIST SP 800-53 SC-8 Transmission Integrity
- NIST SP 800-53 SC-11 Trusted Path
- NIST SP 800-53 SC-20 Secure Name/Address Resolution Service (Authoritative Source)
- NIST SP 800-53 SC-21 Secure Name/Address Resolution Service (Recursive or Caching Resolver)
- NIST SP 800-53 SC-22 Architecture and Provisioning for Name/Address Resolution Service
- NIST SP 800-53 SC-28 Protection of Information at Rest
- NIST SP 800-53 SC-29 Heterogeneity
- NIST SP 800-53 SI-1 System and Information Integrity Policy and Procedures
- NIST SP 800-53 SI-7 Software and Information Integrity
- NIST SP 800-53 SI-9 Information Input Restrictions
- NIST SP 800-53 SI-10 Information Input Validation
- NIST SP 800-53 SI-11 Error Handling
- NIST SP 800-53 SI-12 Information Output Handling and Retention
- NIST SP 800-53 SI-14 Non-Persistence
- NIST SP 800-66 4.16 Integrity
- NIST SP 800-66 4.16.1 Identify All Users Who Have Been Authorized to Access ePHI
- NIST SP 800-66 4.16.2 Identify any Possible Unauthorized Sources That May Be Able to Intercept the Information and Modify It
- NIST SP 800-66 4.16.3 Develop the Integrity Policy and Requirements
- NIST SP 800-66 4.16.4 Implement Procedures to Address these Requirements

18.3.1 Mechanism to Authenticate Electronic Protected Health Information— Addressable—45 CFR § 164.312(c)(2)

A covered entity needs to determine if existing information systems have functions or processes available that will automatically check the integrity of the data stored on these systems. This integrity checking can be done in the form of checksum verification or digital signatures. In checksum verification, a block of data is processed through a checksum function (or checksum algorithm) to calculate a fixed number. It is assumed that if the block of data was changed from its original version, the ending checksum value would change. Thus, if two blocks of data were processed with the same checksum value, it proves that the data was not corrupted and the integrity of this block of data is intact.

A digital signature is primarily used to verify authenticity of a message but can also be used to check for integrity of a block of data. A digital signature scheme normally consists of three parts. The first is a key generation algorithm that generates a private and public key combination. The second is a signing algorithm that uses the private key to produce a signature for a block of data. The final part is a signature-verifying algorithm that uses the public key along with a signature to determine the authenticity of the block of data. In the signing process, data is calculated into a hash value. This hash value is then encrypted using the signer's private key to create a signature. This signature is sent along with the original data and the data is said to be digitally signed. In the verification process, the digitally signed data is broken into two parts: the data part and the signature part. The data part is recalculated using the same hashing algorithm that was originally used by the signing process to obtain a hash value. The signature part is decrypted using the signer's public key that the verifier of the message received prior. This decrypted hash value is compared to the data part hash value. If these values are equal, the signature is valid and the message is authenticated. This means that the message came from the sender and the data was not manipulated during the period of time when it was signed to the time it was verified. See Figure 18.2 for further information.

The covered entity should routinely review existing processes to ensure that objectives are being addressed when it comes to authentication and integrity controls around electronic protected health information. These processes need to be reassessed as technology and operational environments change within the covered

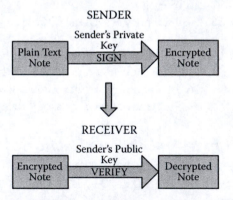

Figure 18.2   Public/private keys.

entity. There should be some established metrics that can validate any integrity issues are being corrected as the related procedures are implemented. These metrics should establish assurance that integrity of the electronic protected health information is being maintained.

The covered entity should refer to the following references for further details related to authentication mechanisms:

- NIST SP 800-53 IA-5 Authenticator Management
- NIST SP 800-53 IA-6 Authenticator Feedback
- NIST SP 800-53 IA-7 Cryptographic Module Authentication
- NIST SP 800-53 SC-14 Public Access Protections
- NIST SP 800-53 SC-15 Collaborative Computing Devices
- NIST SP 800-53 SC-17 Public Key Infrastructure Certificates
- NIST SP 800-53 SC-23 Session Authenticity
- NIST SP 800-66 4.16.5 Implement a Mechanism to Authenticate ePHI

18.4 Person or Entity Authentication— Required—45 CFR § 164.312(d)

A covered entity must implement an authentication mechanism to electronic protected health information that will validate the person or entity accessing this information is the authorized person or entity verified to have access to this information. The risk assessment will assist in determining the proper authentication method implemented within the covered entity. Authentication can be conducted by utilizing one or more of the following three factors:

1. An authorized individual is required to present something that only they would know prior to gaining access.
2. An authorized individual is required to present something that they would only have prior to gaining access.
3. The authorized individual is presenting something unique to only that individual prior to gaining accesses.

A covered entity may consider using a multifactor authentication process that involves utilizing two of the three factors. Some examples of these authentication factors are passwords or personal identification numbers (PINs). These are something that only an authorized individual should know and no one else could obtain or guess. Smart cards, tokens, or even a key are other examples of something that an authorized individual may possess. Unique items that authorized individuals may use for authentication could be biometrics (i.e., fingerprints), voice recognition, facial patterns, or iris patterns. These are items that, in theory, no other individual would possess or could not be duplicated.

A covered entity needs to have documented authentication policies and procedures that are clearly communicated throughout the organization and to all workforce members. These authentication procedures need to be maintained and updated for all information systems, software applications, network devices, and auditing or monitoring tools utilized within the covered entity. Workforce members need to be trained in the proper authentication methods and there should be trained staff maintaining these systems. Remember that the goal of authentication is to verify and validate that the workforce member is who he or she claims to be. As part of the security testing, the authentication method utilized by the covered entity needs to be tested to validate that the solution is working as expected.

A covered entity should determine the reasonable and appropriate level (or type) of authentication that should be utilized to grant access to information systems containing electronic protected health information. As discussed, there are several different types of authentication methods that a covered entity could consider using. The main factor in deciding which is best is ultimately determined by the culture of the covered entity. If security is considered a high priority, then the most stringent authentication methods will probably be deployed such as multifactor authentication using tokens or biometrics along with username–password combinations. On the other hand, if security is lax, the culture of the covered entity may dictate only username–password combinations to authenticate to the information system rather than the added second layer of authentication. There will always be a battle between functionality and security, but in the end, work still has to get done and reasonable security controls still need to be implemented.

In addition to authenticating individuals or users of the information systems, the information systems themselves need to be hardened. All information systems or devices on a network should require some form of authentication. Networking devices such as routers, switches, firewalls, intrusion detection systems, and intrusion prevention systems need to have unique passwords set and be configured in such a manner that only authorized individuals can access them.

Maintenance accounts, such as the "SA" account on SQL databases, need to be secured so that only authorized administrators can access these databases. As a note of reference, the authentication process implemented should not compromise the authentication information itself. For instance, if passwords are utilized for authentication, the password file that stores this information should be encrypted.

The covered entity should refer to the following references for further details related to person or entity authentication:

- NIST SP 800-53 IA-2 Identification and Authentication (Organizational Users)
- NIST SP 800-53 IA-3 Device-to-Device Identification and Authentication
- NIST SP 800-53 IA-4 Identifier Management
- NIST SP 800-53 IA-8 Identification and Authentication (Non-Organizational Users)
- NIST SP 800-53 IA-9 Service Identification and Authentication

- NIST SP 800-53 IA-10 Alternative Authentication
- NIST SP 800-53 IA-11 Adaptive Identification and Authentication
- NIST SP 800-53 IA-12 Re-authentication
- NIST SP 800-66 4.17 Person or Entity Authentication
- NIST SP 800-66 4.17.1 Determine Authentication Applicability to Current Systems/Applications
- NIST SP 800-66 4.17.2 Evaluate Authentication Options Available
- NIST SP 800-66 4.17.3 Select and Implement Authentication Option

18.5 Transmission Security

A covered entity needs to implement adequate technical security measures to guard against unauthorized access to electronic protected health information being transmitted over an electronic communications network. This is especially important if electronic protected health information is being transmitted across a public accessible network like the Internet. This data needs to be encrypted. In an internal network, controls implemented in the network devices such as switches, routers, and firewalls may provide the necessary levels of security to guard against unauthorized access to electronic protected health information being transmitted on the LAN.

A covered entity should have formal policies and procedures in place to detail the methods that will be used to secure electronic protected health information while in transit. Procedures should identify any methods that will be used to implement the transmission security policy. These methods may include hardware or software to secure the transmission of electronic protected health information. Trained workforce members should be monitoring this transmission to ensure that the information is secure. The procedures should also formally document the requirements for transmitting this type of information that is approved by management or a designated official. Through the covered entity's risk assessment, scenarios that put this information at risk should be identified. Through security testing, electronic protected health information in transit should be verified and secured from unauthorized access. Any deficiencies discovered through this review should be corrected accordingly.

To further limit unauthorized access, it is recommended that all ports or protocols not being utilized for business purposes should be disabled on the information systems. Protocols such as the Simple Network Management Protocol (SNMP), Finger, Trivial File Transfer Protocol (TFTP), or other unnecessary protocols should be restricted on the network.

The covered entity should refer to the following references for further details related to transmission security:

- NIST SP 800-53 SC-9 Transmission Confidentiality

- NIST SP 800-53 SC-16 Transmission of Security Attributes
- NIST SP 800-66 4.18 Transmission Security
- NIST SP 800-66 4.18.1 Identify Any Possible Unauthorized Sources That May Be Able to Intercept and/or Modify the Information
- NIST SP 800-66 4.18.2 Develop and Implement Transmission Security Policy and Procedures

18.5.1 Integrity Controls—Addressable—45 CFR § 164.312(e)(2)(i)

A covered entity needs to address controls to maintain the integrity of data traversing the network. During the risk analysis, scenarios should be identified that may result in the modification of electronic protected health information by unauthorized sources during transmission of this information. Solutions or mitigating controls should be implemented to secure electronic protected health information during transit. Assurances that this information is not altered during transmission needs to be implemented.

An intrusion detection system (IDS) or intrusion prevention system (IPS) could be installed on the network. These devices should be located outside and inside of the external firewalls or on network segments that may transmit electronic protected health information. IDS/IPS solutions are different than firewalls. Although some newer firewall models may have built-in IDS/IPS solutions, there are some differences between the functions. A firewall, through the use of its configured access control lists, determines whether traffic is allowed to pass through it. If the conditions allow for specific traffic to pass, then the firewall allows it; otherwise, the packets are denied and dropped. An IDS solution, on the other hand, reviews and analyzes the packets transmitted across the network. It can detect anomalies between normal traffic behaviors and suspicious traffic that may indicate possible unauthorized access. If unusual traffic is discovered, an IPS could be utilized to determine the origination of this traffic and shut it down. These types of devices can provide a lot of security but could also create issues on a network if they are not configured properly or monitored on a continuous basis. For this reason, it is recommended that if the covered entity does not have dedicated IT resources, an IDS/IPS solution should be monitored and controlled by a third-party expert provider. This service provider should be able to provide continuous, real-time response to any potentially dangerous activities discovered.

The covered entity should refer to the following references for further details related to integrity controls:

- NIST SP 800-53 SC-8 Transmission Integrity
- NIST SP 800-66 4.18.3 Implement Integrity Controls

18.5.2 Encryption—Addressable—45 CFR § 164.312(e)(2)(ii)

A covered entity needs to identify how it transmits electronic protected health information. The risk analysis conducted should determine the amount and frequency of electronic protected health information transmitted throughout the entire network. The risk analysis conducted should also determine whether encryption is needed to secure the electronic protected information transmitted.

There are many different types of encryption methods and algorithms. Each has its own pros and cons along with its own feasibility and costs associated with its implementations. A determination should be made as to what encryption method would be best for the covered entity's specific application and environment. Depending on the encryption method chosen, the covered entity may require additional skilled staff to configure and maintain the encryption solution. Furthermore, some encryption technology requires the use of cryptographic keys that come with their own security requirements that need to be managed.

The covered entity should refer to the following references for further details related to encryption:

- NIST SP 800-53 SC-9 Transmission Confidentiality
- NIST SP 800-53 SC-12 Cryptographic Key Establishment and Management
- NIST SP 800-53 SC-13 Cryptographic Protection
- NIST SP 800-66 4.18.4 Implement Encryption

18.6 Summary

A covered entity is required to have certain technical safeguards in place to secure electronic protected health information from unauthorized use or disclosure. One of the first technical safeguards to implement is controlling access to the electronic protected health information. Normally, this is done by assigning unique user identifiers to individual workforce members and providing certain privileges to these users based on their job roles or functions. Procedures also need to be developed to maintain security at all times even in emergency situations. Some of the other items included under technical access controls are logging off sessions automatically after a certain amount of inactivity time and encrypting electronic protected health information while it is being stored or transmitted.

To determine the effectiveness of technical controls, certain audits should be conducted. Most modern information systems have built-in capabilities for maintaining audit functions. These audit controls should assist in determining suspicious activities and track all access to electronic protected health information. Special care should be made to monitor the activities of privileged users since these users have the greatest rights on the systems.

Integrity deals with the alteration or modification of data. This is one of the three components of the security triad (i.e., confidentiality, integrity, and availability). There should be appropriate mechanisms in place to authenticate all users prior to allowing access to any electronic protected health information on an information system. The mechanisms by which this is accomplished will be determined by the information systems in place. They should all follow the same basic principle of allowing only access to the minimum amount of information necessary to individuals based upon their roles. There should also be other controls to verify that information is not being changed or modified in an unauthorized manner either accidentally, intentionally, or through any type of corruption that may be caused by errors in the information system itself.

Although data may be very secure within an information system, as soon as this information leaves the system, the security of this information may be an issue. Since most systems are not parts of networks and networks are part of each other, it is essential that controls are in place to secure electronic protected health information while in transit. This is usually done by encrypting the data. There are several different types of encryption solutions, each with their own pros and cons. Based upon the capabilities, functions, and resources available to the covered entity, a decision will need to be made as to what encryption solution will work the best. This may be a time that an expert would be called on to assist in evaluating the chosen solution to make sure it is the best option for the covered entity.

Chapter 19

Security Rule: Organizational Requirements

Objectives

The objectives of this chapter are as follows:

- Understand what elements or components are required in a business associate contract.
- Determine some of the new regulations with the Omnibus Rules.
- Understand what type of liability a covered entity has under a business associate agreement or contract.
- Understand what rights or requirements a business associate has under an agreement with a covered entity.
- Understand some of the other arrangements that could be developed between another organization and a covered entity.
- Determine what specific requirements there are for group health plans regarding the security of electronic protected health information.

Background

As discussed in Chapter 1, Section 1.6, covered entities sometimes require certain services from third-party providers. These services could include:

- Claim processing
- Data analysis
- Utilization reviews
- Billing
- Legal services
- Accounting/financial services
- Consulting services
- Administrative services
- Accreditation
- Other health-related types of services

In the process of providing these services to the covered entity, the third-party service provider may be required to use or disclose protected health information. If this occurs, the company that provides the service is considered to be a *business associate* to the covered entity as defined in 45 CFR § 160.103. A business associate is required to have a contract with the covered entity to safeguard electronic protected health information. See Table 19.1 for additional requirements of the business associate.

45 CFR § 160.103 provides some examples of business associates that "include third party administrators or pharmacy benefit managers for health plans, claims, processing or billing companies, transcription companies, and persons who perform legal, actuarial, accounting, management, or administrative services for covered entities and who require access to protected health information." It is important to note that a notice of proposed rule making (NPRM) was proposed as of July 14, 2010 (also known as the Omnibus Rule [OR]) that would include the following in the definitions of a business associate: patient safety organizations (PSOS), health information organizations (HIO), e-prescribing gateways, other persons that facilitate data transmission, vendors of personal health records, and subcontractors that

Table 19.1 Organizational Security Standards

Security Standards		
Organizational Requirements		
164.314(a)(1)		**Business associate contracts or other arrangements**
164.314(a)(2)(i)	R	Business Associate Contracts
164.314(a)(2)(ii)	R	Other Arrangements
164. 314(b)(1)		**Requirements for Group Health Plans**
164.314(b)(2)	R	Implementation Specifications

Note: R = required.

will now be defined as "a person who acts on behalf of a business associate, other than in the capacity of a member of the workforce of such business associate."

Another major change in this NPRM involves the liability of the covered entity over its business associates. In the existing regulation 45 CFR § 160.402(c), an exception has been included for the liability held by the covered entity for the acts of its agents in cases where the agent was a business associate and where a business associate contract requirement was met. If a violation occurred and the covered entity did not know of the practices with the covered entity that caused the violation, the covered entity had an affirmative defense to the liability. In addition, if the covered entity acted in response to the requirements of the Health Insurance Portability and Accountability Act (HIPAA) Privacy or Security Rules with respect to such violation, it may have been exempted from any liability of the business associate. Fortunately, the proposal will remove this exception and hold the covered entity responsible for the failure of its business associate to perform the obligations required on the covered entity's behalf.

According to the recent annual Ponemon Institute study, 46% of the total number of breaches occur with third-party providers. The new requirements will no longer make it acceptable just to accept a SSAE16 (recently replacing the SAS70) audit to supply proof that a provider is protecting sensitive data, but rather it will become the personal responsibility of covered entities to review security procedures themselves (Voelker 2012).

19.1 Business Associate Contracts— Required—45 CFR § 164.314(a)(2)(i)

A covered entity is required to have a contract with business associates. This contract must contain certain elements required to be followed by the business associate. The first required element of the business associate contract is that the business associate must "implement administrative, physical, and technical safeguards that reasonably and appropriately protect the confidentiality, integrity, and availability of the electronic protected health information that [the business associate] creates, receives, maintains, or transmits on behalf of the covered entity." This means that all of the security standards followed by the covered entity must also be followed by the business associate in securing electronic protected health information. For this reason, the NPRM dated July 14, 2010, will simplify this element by indicating a business associate's obligation to comply with the HIPAA Security Rule. Don't forget that one of the important elements of the HIPAA Security Rule is the performance of a risk assessment. The business associate contract should specify that the business associate will conduct a risk assessment that addresses its risk (i.e., administrative, physical, and technical) to provide for the protection of electronic protected health information.

The second element of the business associate contract is that the business associate is required to "ensure that any agent, including a subcontractor, to whom [the business associate] provides such [electronic protected health information] agrees to implement reasonable and appropriate safeguards to protect [the electronic protected health information]." So not only does the business associate need to comply with the security standards, this also means that any '"business associate" of the business associate must comply with the security standards. The NPRM dated July 14, 2010, modifies this element as follows: "ensure that any subcontractors that create, receive, maintain, or transmit electronic protected health information on behalf of the business associate agree to comply with the applicable requirements of [the Security Rule] by entering into a contract or other arrangement that complies with this section."

The third element of the business associate contract is that the business associate must "report to the covered entity any security incident of which [the business associate] becomes aware." This goes along with the covered entity's security incident response policy requiring third-party providers or other contractors (i.e., business associates) to report a security incident detailing the process by which the incident should be reported. The NPRM dated July 14, 2010, includes the reporting of "breaches of unsecured protected health information as required by [45 CFR] § 164.410 [Notification by a business associate]." Details of this notification requirement are discussed further in Chapter 8.

The final element of the business associate contract is that the covered entity may terminate the contract with the business associate "if the covered entity determines that the business associate has violated a material term of the contract." The covered entity should probably define what violates a "material term of the contract." However, suffice it to say that if the business associate is not taking reasonable and appropriate measures to secure electronic protected health information as part of the business associate contract, the covered entity would be within its rights to terminate this contract with the business associate. In the NPRM dated July 14, 2010, this element was removed since there is a parallel provision that existed in the HIPAA Privacy Rule 45 CFR § 164.504(e)(2)(iii). Since a business associate is obligated to follow the standards under the HIPAA Security Rule, it is also considered a business associate under the HIPAA Privacy Rule and therefore required to meet these standards as well. If termination of a business associate contract is not feasible and a breach occurs, the issue must be reported to the Office for Civil Rights of the Department of Health and Human Services.

An assessment of risk should be performed on business associates as part of the information acquisition contracting process. Based on this risk assessment, the covered entity should include functional security requirements or specify what steps the business associate should take to secure electronic protected health information. The covered entity should be requesting security-related documentation requirements from its business associate based on any applicable regulations or guidance. In addition, the covered entity should receive development and evaluation-related assurances that all security requirements are met to safeguard electronic protected health information. In addition, it is imperative that a procedure is implemented by the covered entity for the reporting of any security incident that the business associate is obligated to report. For example, the security official could be the point of contact for such notification and this individual has in place a reporting process described in Chapter 14.

The covered entity should refer to the following references for further details related to business associate contracts:

- NIST SP 800-53 SA-4 Acquisitions
- NIST SP 800-66 4.19 Business Associate Contracts or Other Agreements
- NIST SP 800-66 4.19.1 Contract Must Provide That Business Associates Adequately Protect ePHI
- NIST SP 800-66 4.19.2 Contract Must Provide That Business Associate's Agents Adequately Protect ePHI
- NIST SP 800-66 4.19.3 Contract Must Provide That Business Associate Will Report Security Incidents
- NIST SP 800-66 4.19.4 Contract Must Provide That Business Associate Will Authorize Termination of the Contract if it Has Been Materially Breached

19.1.1 Sample Business Associate Contract

The following is the paraphrased and summarized components of the business associate contract sample provided by the Department of Health and Human Services at http://www.hhs.gov/ocr/privacy/hipaa/understanding/coveredentities/contract-prov.html:

DEFINITIONS

This section should include meanings of the following terms defined in the HIPAA Privacy Rule under sections 45 CFR § 160.103, 45 CFR Part 160, 45 CFR Part 164, and Subparts A and E: Business Associate, Covered Entity, Individual, Privacy Rule, Protected Health Information, Required By Law, and Secretary. (Note: The covered entity could utilize the definitions for these terms already previously discussed.)

OBLIGATIONS AND ACTIVITIES OF BUSINESS ASSOCIATE

Business associate agrees to the following:

- Not to disclose or use protected health information in an unauthorized manner, against the agreement, or as required by law.
- Use appropriate safeguards to prevent unauthorized disclosure of protected health information to include administrative, technical, and physical safeguards as required by the HIPAA Security Rule and will perform a risk assessment to address these administrative, technical, and physical risks.

- If a violation of the agreement requirements occurred, the business associate needs to mitigate any harmful effect.
- Report any disclosure or use of protected health information against the agreement or unsecured protected health information to the covered entity and to document such disclosure or any other relevant information related to such disclosure. [Enter the point of contact for the covered entity that should be notified in cases of security incidents.]
- Ensure any subcontractor that may be working with the business associate or receives protected health information from the business associate will also be obligated to the same restrictions and conditions of the agreement by entering into an agreement or other arrangement with the subcontractor.
- Terms that allow the Covered entity to access and verify that the business associate is complying with the agreement including the disclosure of risk assessments, security testing documentation, internal practices, books, records, and policies/procedures related to the use and disclosure of protected health information.

PERMITTED USES AND DISCLOSURES BY BUSINESS ASSOCIATE

- Specify purposes that the business associate may use or disclose of the covered entity's protected health information.
- Provide the minimum necessary policies and procedures of the covered entity that relate to the underlying services provided by the business associate.
- The business associate may provide data aggregation services relating to the healthcare operations of the covered entity.

OBLIGATIONS OF COVERED ENTITY

Covered entity shall notify business associate of the following to the extent that such restrictions may affect business associate's use or disclosure of protected health information:

- Limitation(s) in its notice of privacy practices of the covered entity in accordance with 45 CFR § 164.520.
- Any changes in, or revocation of, permission by individual to use or disclose protected health information.
- Any restrictions to the use or disclosure of protected health information that covered entity has agreed to in accordance with 45 CFR § 164.522.

PERMISSIBLE REQUESTS BY COVERED ENTITY

Covered entity shall not request business associate to use or disclose protected health information in any manner that would not be permissible under the Privacy Rule, if done by the covered entity.

TERMS AND TERMINATION

Term: The term of agreement shall be effective as of the date of the contract and terminated when all of the protected health information provided to the business associate has been destroyed or returned to the covered entity.

Termination for cause: Upon knowledge of a material breach, the covered entity shall either:

- Provide an opportunity for business associate to cure the breach or end the violation.
- Immediately terminate the agreement.
- If neither termination nor cure is viable, report the violation to the Secretary of the Department of Health and Human Services.

Effect of termination: Business associate shall return or destroy all protected health information to the covered entity or provide the conditions that make the return or destruction of the information infeasible.

MISCELLANEOUS

This section should contain any regulatory references, amendments, survivability, interpretations, and so on.

19.2 Other Arrangements—Required—45 CFR § 164.314(a)(2)(ii)

If a covered entity and its business associate are government entities, then the covered entity should be entering into a memorandum of understanding (MOU) with the business associate. The MOU should contain all of the elements of the business associate contract discussed earlier. There could be other laws or regulations adopted by the covered entity and its business associate that may accomplish the objectives of the business associate contract that are applicable to the business associate.

A covered entity should make every effort to ensure that the HIPAA Security Standards are met by the organizations involved in an MOU. If for any reason this assurance cannot be met, the covered entity should document the reasons for not being able to obtain applicable documentation. There may be some situations where the termination requirement is removed from the MOU under statutory obligations. If a covered entity's MOU cannot be terminated, there should be other reasonable and appropriate enforcement procedures in place to ensure compliance with HIPAA Security Standards.

The NPRM dated July 14, 2010, will apply the requirements of the business associate contract to arrangements between a business associate and another subcontractor of that business associate. These requirements are the same as those that apply to the arrangements or contracts between a covered entity and the business associate. Furthermore, any agent provided electronic protected health information should agree to "implement reasonable and appropriate security measures to protect the information." A covered entity or business associate, from time to time, may change its policies and procedures to come into compliance with the Security Rule. These changes should be documented and implemented accordingly.

The covered entity should refer to the following references for further details related to other arrangements:

- NIST SP 800-66 4.19.5 Government Entities May Satisfy Business Associate Contract Requirements through Other Arrangements
- NIST SP 800-66 4.19.6 Other Arrangements for Covered Entities and Business Associates

19.3 Requirements for Group Health Plans—Implementation Specifications—Required—45 CFR § 164.314(b)(2)

Just like the business associate contract discussed earlier, group health plans must incorporate certain provisions in their plan documentation related to the security of electronic protected health information. More specifically, the health plan documentation should reference the implementation of administrative, physical, and technical safeguards. These safeguards must reasonably and appropriately protect the confidentiality, integrity, and availability of electronic protected health information. This protection should cover the information that the group health plan creates, receives, maintains, or transmits. The security measures must ensure the reasonable and adequate separation between the group health plan and the plan sponsor as required in the HIPAA Privacy Rule [45 CFR § 164.504(f)(2)(iii)]. The plan documentation must address assurance that any subcontractor of the group health plan must also implement reasonable and appropriate security measures to protect the electronic protected health information. Finally, the group health plan documents should contain a provision that any security incident of which it becomes aware should be reported to the group health plan.

The group health plan documents should adequately separate the group health plan from the plan sponsor or other individuals that may be given access to electronic protected health information, such as the sponsor's employees. In addition, the group health plan documents should specify requirements that the health plan sponsor implements administrative, physical, and technical safeguards for the security of electronic protected health information. This caveat could be very important especially if the plan sponsor creates, receives, maintains, or transmits electronic protected health information on the group health plan's behalf.

Provisions in the group health plan documents should address the requirements for implementing appropriately reasonable safeguards for the health plan sponsor's agents or subcontractors that may have access to electronic protected health information. As with the business associate contract, plan sponsors should be required to report any security incident to the group health plan following the procedures that the health plan has implemented. These procedures should also include a response plan to handle any security incident reported by the plan sponsor.

The covered entity should refer to the following references for further details related to group health plan requirements:

- NIST SP 800-66 4.20 Requirements for Group Health Plans
- NIST SP 800-66 4.20.1 Amend Plan Documents to Address Plan Sponsor's Security of ePHI
- NIST SP 800-66 4.20.2 Amend Plan Documents to Address Adequate Separation
- NIST SP 800-66 4.20.3 Amend Plan Documents to Address Security of ePHI Supplies to Plans Sponsor's Agents and Subcontractors
- NIST SP 800-66 4.20.4 Amend Plan Documents to Address Reporting of Security Incidents

19.4 Summary

From time to time, covered entities will require the resources of third-party providers to assist them in their business operations. When certain arrangements are made between a covered entity and a third-party provider that may have access to or be disclosed electronic protected health information maintained by the covered entity, a business association has been formed. The covered entity is required to have specific agreements or contracts in place with these business associates as to the obligations, rights, and responsibilities these associates have toward the security of electronic protected health information. There are several specific elements that any business associate agreement or contract must cover. Under new rulings, a covered entity must ensure that business associates are maintaining control and security over all electronic protected health information that may be passed on to them through the services that a business associate provides to a covered entity. In addition, any business associate that does business with other third-party contractors must also obtain agreements similar to the existing business associate contract it has in place with the covered entity.

Due to recent issues arising from breaches occurring with business associates, it is imperative for covered entities to affirm and validate that proper controls over their electronic protected health information is taking place. Although it is not very clear how this validation should be performed, covered entities should develop reasonable procedures in conducting their due diligence on their vendors.

There are specific arrangements that may be made between healthcare providers and government entities such as memorandums of understanding. In addition, there are specific requirements related to group health plans and their plan sponsors related to securing electronic protected health information.

Chapter 20

Frequently Asked Questions

1. What is the appropriate HIPAA relationship between a business associate (company A) and another vendor (company B) that is providing services to a covered entity related to hosting the covered entity's data in the cloud?

Company A is providing services to a covered entity that requires it to be a business associate of the covered entity along with requiring it to sign a business associate contract (BAC) with the covered entity. The BAC should have a stipulation that any subcontractor (in this case, Company B) of Company A be required to secure electronic protected health information (EPHI) just as Company A is required by the BAC to secure EPHI. You could think of it as an "inherent requirement" that will require Company A to ensure that Company B is meeting the Health Insurance Portability and Accountability Act (HIPAA) security requirements that Company A has agreed to with the covered entity.

On July 14, 2010, a notice of proposed rule making (NPRM), the Omnibus Rule (OR), was published that would include other persons that facilitate data transmission and subcontractors that will now be defined as "a person who acts on behalf of a business associate, other than in the capacity of a member of the workforce of such business associate." Company B, by this definition, would also be considered a business associate and may be required sign a BAC with the covered entity. (This ruling, as I am aware, has not been finalized yet but may be in the near future.) If a BAC is not completed between Company B and the covered entity, there should be at least a service level agreement (SLA) between Company A and Company B that specifies the responsibilities related to securing EPHI as per the HIPAA Security Requirements.

If a breach occurs at Company B, it would be required to notify Company A and mitigate any damage of the breach. Likewise, Company A would have to notify the covered entity and also mitigate the damage. If it was discovered that Company B, as a subcontractor for Company A, was not complying with the BAC, the covered entity could terminate its contract with Company A under the terms of the BAC.

2. Should a Scenario Where Paper Medical Records Cannot Be Located Be Considered A Breach?

Note: There is no indication that the records were used or disclosed in an unauthorized manner; the records simply cannot be located.

This simple question is actually more complex than you may think. It involves many different components of the current regulations to consider. I will attempt to provide an answer to this question as it relates to the specific federal breach notification requirements along with providing my own personal opinion as to how this scenario should be handled. State laws may be more specific and supersede federal breach notification regulations in this scenario.

As a general rule, a covered entity is required to notify any individual whose unsecured protected health information has been breached. There are basically two elements to this general rule. First, is the information considered unsecured protected health information, and second, is there a breach, by definition, that has occurred?

Let's recall that unsecured protected health information is defined as "protected health information that is not rendered unusable, unreadable, or indecipherable to unauthorized individuals through the use of a technology or methodology specified by the Secretary of Health and Human Services."

For the sake of argument, an assumption is going to be made that the paper medical records contain 1 or more of the following 16 direct identifiers: names; postal address information (other than town or city, state, and zip code); telephone numbers; fax numbers; electronic mail addresses; Social Security numbers; medical record numbers; health plan beneficiary numbers; account numbers; certificate/license numbers; vehicle identifiers and serial numbers (including license plate numbers); device identifiers and serial numbers; Web Universal Resource Locators (URLs); Internet Protocol address numbers; biometric identifiers (including finger and voice prints); or full-face photographic images and any comparable images. Based on our assumption, this would imply that protected health information was involved. For this scenario and based on our previous definitions, we are going to consider the information contained in the lost paper medical records as unsecured protected health information. So we have one of the elements of our rule.

Under 45 CFR § 164.402, a *breach* is considered to be the acquisition, access, use, or disclosure of protected health information in a manner not permitted under the Privacy of Individually Identifiable Health Information that poses a significant risk of financial, reputational, or other harm to the individual. Again, this breach definition has two parts: (1) the unauthorized acquisition, access, use, or disclosure of protected health information; and (2) a significant risk of financial, reputational, or other harm to the individual. Here is where it gets a little trickier to figure out and there are also three examples of *specific breach exclusions* that we should consider since this scenario may fall under one of these exceptions that would automatically identify this scenario as a breach or not.

First, does this scenario involve a workforce member, person acting under the authority of a covered entity, or a business associate unintentionally acquiring, accessing, or using protected health information as long as it was done in good faith and within the scope of its authority, and, in addition, was the further use or disclosure of this protected health information in a manner permitted under the Privacy of Individually Identifiable Health Information? We really cannot say with 100% certainty that this exception would apply to our scenario since we do not know if there was any unintentional acquiring, accessing, or using of protected health information as it relates to good faith or within the scope of authority. There still may be a breach situation occurring. Let's look at the next exception.

Second, does this scenario involve any inadvertent disclosure by a person who is authorized to access the protected health information at a covered entity or business associate to another person authorized to access protected health information at the same covered entity or business associate, or organized healthcare arrangement in which the covered entity participates, and is the information received as a result of such disclosure not further used or disclosed in a manner not permitted under the Privacy of Individually Identifiable Health Information? Again, we cannot positively say that there was not any inadvertent disclosure of this information; we just cannot locate the record.

Finally, does this scenario involve a disclosure of protected health information where a covered entity or business associate has a good faith belief that an unauthorized person to whom the disclosure was made would not reasonably have been able to retain such information? Since this information is considered unsecured protected health information and is provided in paper form, it could be easily retained by an unauthorized person, if it were found. Since the breach exclusions do not specifically apply to this scenario, let's go back to the definition of a breach and see if the scenario qualifies.

Thus far, we determined that the report was lost and it contained unsecured protected health information. The next question we need to ask is did this protected health information get acquired, accessed, used, or disclosed in an unpermitted manner? Unfortunately, we cannot say that it did or did not with affirmation since we really do not know what happened to the medical record. This being the case, I would recommend erring on the side of caution and assume that it could have been acquired, accessed, or used, or the information disclosed in an unauthorized fashion.

374 ■ *Complying with the HIPAA/HITECH Privacy and Security Rules*

This brings us to the final and maybe one of the hardest questions to answer: Does this scenario "pose a significant risk of financial, reputational, or other harm to the individual"? This is where a risk analysis of the specific type of incident is involved. We already answered, or assumed a few items as part of our decision making process, but we would also like to know the likelihood of this information being utilized. For this specific scenario, I would recommend developing a risk matrix utilizing a scoring as follows: 1 is considered low risk, 2 is considered a medium risk, and 3 is considered a high risk.

As I mentioned earlier, I would provide my recommendations based on this scenario utilizing the following risk analysis:

a. We already determined that the information is considered unsecured protected health information. What information, specifically, was available? For instance, could the information allow someone to conduct medical identity theft or other financial crimes? If so, the risk may be considerably higher. In my opinion, we will assume, for the sake of argument, that there was no specific information that could lead to financial risk. I would rank this as low risk, assigning 1 point.

b. We could not determine if there was any unauthorized acquisitions, access, use, or disclosure of this information. For this reason, I would rank this as a medium risk, assigning 2 points to this area of concern due to the possibility of access or disclosure.

c. We could not determine if there was any access to this information by workforce members, or any other individual, conducted in 'good faith' or otherwise. For this reason, I would rank this as a medium risk, assigning 2 points to this area of concern due to inadvertent or intentional possibilities of access or disclosure.

d. Taking into consideration the types of services that the covered entity provides would definitely be a factor in the risk of the potential use of the information. For instance, if the covered entity provides sensitive treatment, such as HIV, cancer, substance abuse, or genetic disorder, this information may create some reputational risk for the individual. For our scenario, I am going to assume that the covered entity does not provide any sensitive treatment and rank this as a low risk, assigning 1 point to this area of concern.

e. Are there any other areas of harm that we may not have considered? Based upon other possible harm scenarios regarding specifics of the situation, a risk assignment should be made. Do not forget to include any specific state or local requirements within the basis of the evaluation. Each state may have different requirements regarding notification that may be more specific than the federal regulations. In this case, however, we are just looking at the federal HIPAA regulations related to breach notification. In our scenario, I would rank this as a low risk, assigning 1 point to this area of concern.

In total, I have assigned 7 risk level points out of a possible 15 points in my analysis. This comes to just over 46% on our risk-level scale. If we define our scale as anything over 80% as being a significant risk, 50% to 79% as being a medium risk, and anything less than 50% as a low risk, we can make the argument that this scenario would not pose a significant risk of financial, reputational, or other harm to the individual and therefore would not be considered a breach under the HIPAA Breach Notification Requirements.

In an Office of Management and Budget (OMB) Memorandum M-07-16, *Safeguarding Against and Responding to the Breach of Personally Identifiable Information*, dated May 22, 2007, the department noted concerns raised by experts for unnecessary notification and the effect it may have on the public. The memorandum suggests that "agencies should consider the costs to individuals and businesses of responding to notices where the risk of harm may be low. Agencies should exercise care to evaluate the benefit of notifying the public of low impact incidents."

Although this may not meet the federal statutory requirements of a breach, I would caution the covered entity in the proper course of action. It could be in the best interests of a covered entity to at least informally notify the individual that is affected by the lost records, letting him or her know of the event and the actions that the covered entity is taking to find the records. The covered entity could explain the rationale behind any concerns that the information may have been used or disclosed in an unauthorized manner and the likelihood that this could have occurred. Furthermore, the covered entity could keep the individual updated with any information regarding the status of this lost record and possible tips to ensure that the individual will not be harmed due to this situation. If nothing else, this shows a true commitment that the covered entity cares about the individual's information and demonstrates good ethical business practices.

Make sure you document the situation as part of your incident response and tracking procedures, and document the rationale that the covered entity utilized in the decision of whether to make a breach notification. If this scenario would have constituted a breach, refer to Chapter 8 for further requirements on breach notifications. See Figure 20.1 for further information.

3. What Is the Difference between IT Security and Information Security?

A lot of people may think that these terms are synonymous, but they are very different. Information technology (IT) security deals primarily with the configuration and hands-on work of information systems or other network devices. IT security narrowly concentrates on electronic data, and individuals working in this role generally work under the direction of IT management. IT security is normally managed at the chief information officer (CIO) or chief technology officer (CTO) level.

Information security, on the other hand, is broadly based. It looks as information in all of its forms, including digital and paper records. It encompasses several different areas of concern, including physical security, business continuity,

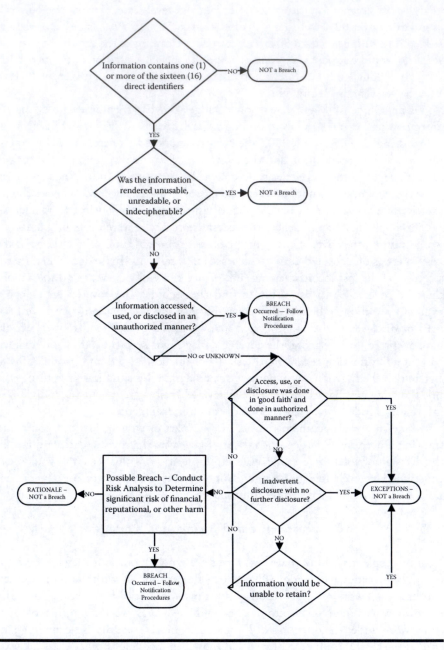

Figure 20.1 Flowchart of a data breach.

awareness, disaster recovery, technology, and administration. Individuals in this position should be reporting to upper-level or executive-level management and have the broad-based authority to efficiently conduct their roles as it applies across the entire organization. Information security should be handled by the chief information security officer (CISO).

As I have argued in my book *The Executive MBA in Information Security* (CRC Press), the CISO should not be reporting to the CIO or CTO. The CISO should be reporting to a supervisory or security board (or committee) made up of key executives, but is outside of the realm of any one particular area of responsibility. Since security traverses the entire enterprise, the CISO responsibilities and roles will extend any single department (including legal or audit). Since every key stakeholder has some responsibility over information security, there needs to be an executive level (or board level) committee developed to oversee information security led by the CISO.

4. What Should Covered Entities Be Concerned with in the Upcoming Years Related to HIPAA/HITECH Requirements?

It looks like Health Information Technology for Economic and Clinical Health (HITECH) Act enforcement will be on the rise. Since this act allows attorney generals of the states to enforce noncompliance issues and since most states are having issues with their budgets, lawsuits against large covered entities or business associates may subsidize these shortcomings. Since most of these cases will be settled, it may not require attorney general's offices to devote a lot of time or resources to this enforcement endeavor. In addition, the audit firm of KPMG, LLP, will be conducting its "mandatory audits." Although the goal of these audits is to assist in compliance, findings may constitute fines that will go right back into the Department of Health and Human Services (HHS). Security breaches are not going away anytime soon and from all research conducted, breaches of privacy are increasing. As more and more consumers become victims, pressure will be put on Congress to tighten or enforce stricter regulations. This will, in turn, force HHS to take a more heavy-handed approach to compliance. With the likely passing of the Omnibus Rule, additional enforcement activities will occur against business associates. Prior to the HITECH rule, HIPAA regulations were not enforced. However, covered entities and business associates are going to find that noncompliance will no longer be accepted.

5. What Is One Thing That a Small Medical Practice Can Do to Better Its Security?

Although there are several things that a small medical practice can do to better its security, if the practice does not have internal resources to devote to technology, then it should look for outside expertise to help. Obtaining external support through a managed service provider can significantly increase the security posture of the provider.

6. How Do You Know If a Business Associate Is HIPAA/HITECH Compliant?

Although a covered entity may have a business associate agreement in place with a business associate, this does not mean that the business associate is compliant with the HIPAA/HITECH requirements. The business associate agreement, of course, has multiple elements that need to be met. One of the most important is for the business associate to use appropriate safeguards to prevent unauthorized disclosure of protected health information to include administrative, technical, and physical safeguards as required by the HIPAA Security Rule and will perform a risk assessment to address these administrative, technical, and physical risks. For a covered entity to know with certainty that safeguards are in place, the contract should also allow the covered entity to access and verify that the business associate is complying with the agreement including the disclosure of risk assessments, security testing documentation, internal practices, books, records, and policies and procedures related to the use and disclosure of Protected Health Information. Through a review of an independent HIPAA audit conducted on the business associate and other due diligence activities performed on the business associate by the covered entity, the covered entity should be able to make an accurate determination as to the state of the business associate's overall compliance efforts.

7. When Does the Time Frame for Breach Notification Begin?

Per the interim final breach notification rule, notification is required as soon as possible, but no later than 60 days from the date the breach is discovered or should have been discovered. Although a risk assessment may be performed to determine if notification is required in the first place due to the harm that a breach may have on an individual, once a decision is made to notify, the time started when the breach was discovered or should have been discovered. In some states, this notification timeline is shorter than the 60 days provided for in the federal regulations. A covered entity should know the specific notification requirements of its individual state.

8. How Does My Healthcare Provider Avoid Unintended Consequences of Electronic Health Records ?

The Agency for Healthcare Research and Quality (AHRQ) made a free online guide under contract by RAND, a nonprofit research organization, to assist in reducing any unintended consequences of electronic health records. This guide can be viewed at http://www.ucguide.org/index.html.

9. Is Cloud Computing the Right Option for Our Healthcare Organization?

There are many advantages and some disadvantages to using cloud services for healthcare. One of the clear advantages is the ability to access services from basically anywhere whenever you need to. In cases where technical staff is limited within the organization, cloud computing can provide incredible opportunities to improve services that would not otherwise be available. One of the biggest concerns is privacy and security. Although the vendor may say the information is kept "private," this does not necessarily mean that it is "secure." The risks that are usually seen within an internal network are basically the same seen with cloud services. Although a cloud service provider may have security experts on staff with highly skilled and qualified individuals working for it in-house, there are still some risks and uncertainty with a vendor having control over the covered entity's information. Does the covered entity really know who has access to this information or who has control over this information? Cloud computing services do come at a cost and with the rise of its popularity in the industry, the government is keeping an eye on what regulations or standards may be necessary for these service providers. The best recommendation is to conduct a thorough risk analysis taking into account all factors that could contribute in making a decision to move to cloud computing services within the organization.

10. How Can We Get Our Cloud-Based Healthcare Service or Product HIPAA Certified or Compliant?

If you are a cloud-based service provider that performs certain business functions on behalf of a covered entity and that covered entity provides you protected health information as part of the contracted services, the cloud-based service provider will be considered a business associate of the covered entity and should have a business associate agreement in place with the covered entity. To this end, the cloud-based service provider will be required to comply with the HIPAA Security Rule and other components of the business associate agreement. Currently, services or products cannot advertise as being HIPAA compliant since there is no official recognition of such a claim. Products and services can assist covered entities or other business associates in becoming compliant with the HIPAA/HITECH Privacy and Security regulations, but they are not necessarily HIPAA certified.

11. Is It a Violation of the HIPAA Privacy Rule If a Supervisor Shares Information That an Employee, Who Works for a Covered Entity, Is Out of Work on Family Medical Leave (i.e., Related to the Family Medical Leave Act)?

This question raises the issue of when HIPAA Privacy Rules apply and when they do not. It is important to determine the differentiating factors that require the application of the HIPAA Privacy Rules. Improperly applying these rules can lead to the requirement of notifications and other actions that may not be necessary and could lead to other significant exposures or damages. In this situation, information about the employee is related to the covered entity's status as an employer, not as a covered entity itself. It would not be a violation of the HIPAA Privacy Rule to share this information. However, sharing certain information about the situation may violate the Family Medical Leave Act laws pertaining to the privacy of an employee–employer relationship.

12. Is It a Violation of the HIPAA Privacy Rule If a Healthcare Provider Gives Gift Cards to Patients That Have Referred Other Individuals and Has Listed the Name of the Patient That Referred Them to the Healthcare Provider?

On the surface, this looks like a simple question to answer, however, it may be more complex than you think. First, we know that a name is a direct identifier under protected health information. Second, we may be able to assume certain healthcare services being provided based on the type of healthcare provider named on the gift card. For instance, if the card is being provided from a dental office that provides cosmetic dental surgery, then we can assume that the healthcare services provided are related to such dental work. The question here relates to the healthcare provider disclosing the name of one patient to another patient.

Let's determine if this disclosure is permitted. Does it fall within one of these permitted categories: to the individual; treatment, payment, healthcare operations; uses and disclosures with opportunity to agree or object; incidental use and disclosure; public interest and benefit activities; and limited data set. After reviewing each permitted use under Chapter 4, the closest related use may be incidental use, but if the healthcare provider is purposely releasing names, then this would not apply.

This situation may be considered a marketing exception. Any face-to-face communication made by the covered entity to an individual or a promotional gift of nominal value provided to the individual by the covered entity does not require an individual's authorization. Unfortunately, the healthcare provider in this situation is providing the name of the patient to another individual so it does not meet the marketing exception of disclosure.

If protected health information is not being used or disclosed for treatment, payment, healthcare operations, or otherwise permitted or required by the Privacy Rule, then the covered entity must obtain the individual's written authorization. Let's assume that the healthcare provider did not receive an individual's written authorization; then it would be the case that the practice of providing the name of a referral patient on the gift card is in violation of HIPAA Privacy Rules. The healthcare provider may still provide the gift card; however, the name of the referring patient should not be added.

13. What Does Compliance Mean to You? How Do You Know If You Are in Compliance?

First, to me compliance means that an organization has an overall effective information security program in place. Compliance is an ongoing process that involves all staff members at all levels within the organization. Through formal policies that lead to processes, tracking mechanisms must be implemented along with documentation that certain processes are taking place. Finalize it with testing or auditing and you have built a compliance culture within your organization along with determining the state of your compliance program. A little formula that you could utilize to determine the state of your compliance program is: Policies + Processes + Tracking Mechanisms = Documentation of Compliance + Testing (or Auditing) = The State of Your Compliance Initiative. I believe one of the only true ways to determine if you are in compliance is to have an independent assessment conducted on your organization. This assessment should be performed by experienced professionals and include both technical and nontechnical reviews of your HIPAA/HITECH policies, procedures, and processes and related required initiatives. Ultimately, the Department of Health and Human Services (HHS) has the final say as to its belief in your compliance state. However, with an independent qualified group of experts assisting in your compliance efforts, HHS may have a harder time justifying any negative actions taken against your organization.

14. What Are the Recommended Reviews and the Frequencies of Reviews That Should Be Conducted to Demonstrate HIPAA/HITECH Compliance on a Covered Entity or Business Associate?

It is recommended that a thorough technical and nontechnical evaluation be conducted on a covered entity or business associate related to HIPAA/HITECH compliance at least annually or when significant changes occur within a critical system that could affect the security of electronic protected health information. On-site assessments should be conducted annually that should include a review of policies and procedures, internal vulnerability and penetration testing, physical assessment, social engineering, and business associate and vendor due diligence reviews. At least semiannually, a vulnerability and penetration test should be conducted on all external systems or devices owned or operated by the covered entity or business associate. Documented mitigation lists should be tracked and assessments should tell whether the covered entity or business associate is improving (or declining) from year to year. The review should take into account new attack vectors and additional risks associated with the handling, managing, storing, transmitting, or other aspects of protected health information.

15. Are the U.S. Postal Service, United Parcel Service, and Delivery Truck Line Employees and Their Management Considered to Be Business Associates under the HIPAA Privacy Rules?

Per the Department of Health and Human Services, the answer is no. Since these organizations provide only conduits for protected health information, covered entities are not required to enter into a business associate contract with these organizations. As a conduit of transport, they do not necessarily access protected health information and there is no expectation of disclosure that is intended by the covered entity. The probability of disclosure is deemed to be very small; therefore, a conduit is not considered a business associate of a covered entity (Department of Health and Human Services 2006).

16. On the Same Premise As Question 20.15, Are Video-Conferencing Services, Such as Skype, Considered HIPAA Compliant?

If you consider Skype a "conduit" by which healthcare information is transported, then the answer is no. Based on the guidance provided to the Department of Health and Human Services, Skype is not required to be HIPAA/HITECH compliant. Since Skype, itself, would not be considered a covered entity by definition, it would also not be required to be HIPAA/HITECH compliant. Now, I am not saying that Skype should or should not be used, but rather a covered entity should conduct a risk assessment as to the security and protection of communication through this conduit or any other service provider providing similar services. The liability will ultimately rest on the covered entity in regard to protecting and safeguarding protected health information.

17. How Do I Learn to Respond to or Detect Intrusions (or Hacker Attempts)?

There are several ways to learn how to respond to or detect intrusion or hacker attacks. One of the first ways is to take a theoretical approach by imagining yourself creating some possible attacks on your network infrastructure. Ask yourself what you would do if you were going to try and hack into your systems. For example, if you were going to attack a Web server on your network, what type of tools would you use, what type of traffic would these tools create, and what type of logging is in place to pick up this traffic? After conducting this type of exercise, you may discover that you have some gaps within your ability to detect such activity.

You may need to implement certain solutions to mitigate the risk of intrusions going undetected. It is recommended that you thoroughly learn the solution implemented. This could be completed through training, reading manuals, or working with the solution in a test environment. Most vendors of intrusion detection solutions provide this type of training as part of their product or service offering.

From there, you may want to hire a third-party "red team." This team of experts can provide simulated attacks based on the scenarios and guidelines you set forth. As the exercises are occurring, you can determine how well certain solutions are working to track and monitor this activity.

After completing this testing, you should have a pretty good understanding as to your detection and response capabilities. You may want to rehire this red team to conduct another test. This time, the team will not have to follow the scenarios and can think out of the box to gain access to the systems under review.

Although some of this testing and the solutions implemented to assist in the detection and response of intrusions may have some associated costs, the results should provide the capabilities to sustain most types of real-world attacks (Bejtlich 2012).

18. Is Posting Pictures of Patients (or Discussing Patient Matters) on Social Media Outlets Like Facebook a HIPAA Violation?

Yes. It is a violation of HIPAA Privacy Rules to post a picture of a patient (or discuss patient matters) on Facebook. The patient may not have consented to taking a picture (or discussing the matter) in the first place, and even if he or she did, they would not have consented to having their picture (or problem) posted on the Internet. Although a past rule of thumb is that if you wouldn't discuss the matter in an elevator, you shouldn't discuss it on social media sites; this may not necessarily be taken to heart by many workforce members today. It may appear as a natural thing for anyone with a cell phone to take pictures of others, but there have been many workforce members fired for these types of actions. (See "When Facebook goes to the hospital, patients may suffer" at http://articles.latimes.com/2010/aug/08/local/la-me-facebook-20100809 (Hennessy-Fiske 2010) and "Five nurses fired for Facebook postings" at http://scrubsmag.com/five-nurses-fired-for-facebook-postings/ (Fink 2010).)

Covered entities and business associates should have policies and procedures in place to handle the use of mobile devices in restricted areas. They should also have restrictions from discussing or posting any pictures of patients on social media sites. Sanctions policies should address these situations, and penalties, as have been seen, are severe for these types of violations.

19. What Is the Difference between the HIPAA Security Rule and the HIPAA Privacy Rule?

The Security Rule is different from the Privacy Rule in that the Security Rule sets the requirements for only allowing those who should have access to electronic protected health information (EPHI) to actually have access to this information. The Security Rule only applies to EPHI, whereas the Privacy Rule applies to protected health information (PHI) that could be found in many different forms such as electronic, oral, or paper. The Security Rule defines administrative, physical, and technical controls to be implemented to protect the confidentiality, integrity, and availability of the EPHI. The Security Rule is a more detailed, comprehensive requirement than is found in the Privacy Rule.

20. If a Microsoft Exchange™ Server, behind the Organization's Firewall, Is Being Utilized, Would E-Mail Containing Protected Health Information Need to be Encrypted If Sent to or from E-Mails within the Same Domain?

The answer to this question is that it depends. Although this configuration would be considered a closed network, a closed network does not necessarily mean a secure network. There are a few things that need to be considered. Under 45 CFR § 164.312(a)(2)(iv), encryption and decryption need to be addressed under the HIPAA Security Rule. A determination must be made whether to encrypt data in transit or while being stored based on the risk of exposure of this information in these two states. The purpose for this determination is to validate that individuals (or other software programs) are restricted from accessing this information while in transit or being stored utilizing the "minimum necessary" requirements. The guidance provided by the Department of Health and Human Services is to encrypt or destroy (in paper or electronic form) protected health information so that it is unusable, unreadable, or indecipherable by unauthorized individuals. It is a fallacy to believe that this information is secured when it is within this closed network.

First, the protected health information in the e-mail could be "sniffed" (or viewed) while in transit if a device was planted or another system was compromised within the closed network if it is not encrypted in transit. Are there other mitigating controls implemented to prevent a compromise of systems or planting an unauthorized device on the closed network?

Second, a determination needs to be made on how this information is being stored in the Microsoft Exchange server and who has the ability to access this information. Is this information being stored in an unencrypted fashion on the server? Are remnants of these e-mails being stored on local devices? Would the individuals that have access to these e-mails normally be authorized to access protected health information?

Third, do all workforce members utilize separate e-mail accounts with unique user identifiers and have controls been implemented to restrict the viewing of other workforce members' e-mails? Are workstations locked when workforce members leave their areas? Are there password-protected screensavers implemented after a certain period of inactivity?

Finally, how are e-mails backed up or retained for purposes of satisfying e-mail retention requirements? Are they backed up on tape and are these tapes encrypted themselves?

As demonstrated, based on a thorough risk assessment conducted, it may be determined that e-mail may need to be encrypted (even in a closed network) if other mitigating controls are not present to secure this protected health information.

21. Top 10 Myths of HIPAA/HITECH Compliance

The following are the top 10 reasons (or myths) regarding HIPAA/HITECH compliance that I have heard in the healthcare industry over the past couple of years. There is no specific order in which these appear. However, I do attempt to explain the fallacy of these thought processes.

a. My Electronic Medical Record/Electronic Health Record Software Is HIPAA Compliant So That Makes Me HIPAA Compliant

Although the software you utilize to process, store, or transmit your patient information and other electronically protected health information is certified HIPAA compliant, this does not necessarily mean that the covered entity (as a whole) is compliant. The HIPAA Privacy and Security Rules cover the entire entity and software is just a minor subset of the standards. These rules cover administrative, physical, and technical safeguards that need to be implemented to satisfy the regulations and to put the covered entity into compliance.

b. My Business Associate Handles My Security and Makes Me HIPAA Compliant

A business associate, such as a managed IT service provider or other contractor, may be hired to assist the covered entity in managing its network and other IT-related services. This, however, does not by itself qualify a covered entity to claim that it is compliant with HIPAA regulations. The responsibility (and liability) still falls on the covered entity to validate and ensure compliance with the HIPAA Privacy and Security Rules. A covered entity must perform its own due diligence in an effort to validate compliance, and the business associate itself also needs to ensure its own compliance under the business associate agreement in regard to complying with the regulations. It should also be noted that there is a conflict of interest to have an IT service test or validate its configurations and security level. Assessors should be completely independent to allow for a more objective review of compliance. It has been my experience that sometimes vendors are not completing work or providing the best possible services as initially thought. Although you need to trust your vendors, you also need to verify what they are saying and doing. Ultimately, you, as the covered entity, are responsible for their actions (or lack of action).

c. I Have Policies and Procedures in Place, Now I Am HIPAA Compliant

Having policies and procedures in place is just the first step on the path to compliance. These policies and procedures need to be fully approved, implemented, and validated. Approval of these policies and procedures needs to come from the top executives and be disseminated to all workforce members. All workforce members need to fully adhere to these policies and procedures at all times or be subject to sanctions that are enforced. Assessments need to be performed to validate that all workforce members are following the policies/procedures as approved and adjustments need to take place to correct any deficiencies accordingly. Only after demonstrated proof that these steps are occurring within the covered entity on an ongoing basis can compliance be achieved.

d. I Conducted a Review of Compliance a Couple of Years Ago, Nothing Has Changed, I Should Still Be in Compliance

A compliance review being conducted in the first place is a huge start to an effective information security management program. However, compliance is an ongoing effort. Just because you were in compliance a couple of years ago does not mean that you are still in compliance. Regulations and standards are being updated and technology is ever changing. Since new vulnerabilities and threats change the risk environment, it is recommended that a compliance review be conducted on an annual basis. Deficiencies or mitigation efforts should be tracked and documented to validate improvements to the covered entity's security posture. These actions demonstrate a high level of commitment that is placed on securing protected health information.

e. I Won't Be Audited

Although the chances of being audited are very small (in the area of .02%), the financial risks associated with such audits are very high. Civil penalties can range in the area of several thousand dollars up to multimillion dollars depending on the violations uncovered. These penalties can come from both the state and federal levels, and being in noncompliance can raise the risk of actually having a breach. If a breach occurs, other costs are sure to follow such as those associated with making notifications, civil lawsuits, resource allocations, reputational, and other financial losses. It is recommended to be proactive in compliance efforts as opposed to rolling the dice and hoping that the Office for Civil Rights (or the attorney general) won't come knocking on your door.

f. I Am Not Subject to HIPAA/HITECH Regulations

It is recommended that you go through the process detailed in Chapter 1, Section 1.5 to confirm that your organization does not meet any of these guidelines to be classified as a covered entity. Although you may not meet these definitions, you still may be subject to HIPAA/HITECH Privacy and Security Rules if you are among one of the 1.5 million business associates that work with (or for) a covered entity. In addition, you may be a subcontractor for a business associate that has a business associate agreement with a covered entity. In this case, you may also be subject to meeting the HIPAA/HITECH Privacy and Security Rule based on your relationship with these business associates. The new Omnibus Rule will significantly change the responsibilities associated with agreements between business associates and covered entities.

g. I Won't Have a Breach

The probability of a breach is shown to be very high. Most security experts will say it is not a matter of if a breach will occur, but rather when a breach will occur. Unfortunately, it is usually the case that a breach will go unnoticed for a while since most covered entities do not take proactive steps to prevent or detect such a breach from occurring.

As indicated during a recent survey conducted in February 2012 by the Ponemon Institute of 700 healthcare practitioners, 91% of participants with 250 workforce members or less indicated that they suffered from at least one data breach over the past year. In addition, 23% of these respondents experienced at least one patient medical identity theft within their organization during the same time period (Bowman 2012).

h. I Do Not Need a Privacy Official or Security Official

Per 45 CFR § 164.530 (i), "A covered entity must designate a privacy official who is responsible for the development and implementation of the policies and procedures of the entity." Per 45 CFR § 164.308 (a)(2), "Standard: Assigned security responsibility. Identify the security official who is responsible for the development and implementation of the policies and procedures required by this subpart [Administrative safeguards] for the entity." There are no restrictions as to whether the same workforce member can handle these two roles.

i. I Do Not Need a Technical Review of My Systems

One of the most important requirements of the HIPAA Security Regulations involves the performance of a "periodic technical and nontechnical evaluation … that establishes the extent to which an entity's security policies and procedures meet the [Security Rule requirements]" (45 CFR § 164.308(a)(8)). In addition, under the core measures for meaningful use for eligible professionals, eligible hospitals, and critical access hospitals, electronic health information created or maintained by the certified electronic health record technology is protected through the appropriate technical capabilities that are implemented. This measure determines if a security risk analysis was conducted or reviewed as required under 45 CFR § 164.308(a)(1). In addition, this measure determines, as part of the eligible professional's risk management process, that security updates are implemented as necessary and security deficiencies identified are corrected. The full requirements of a risk analysis are discussed in Chapter 12.

j. It Is Cheaper to Pay a Fine Than It Is to Become Compliant

Although there have only been a couple of fines levied against covered entities such as the $4.3 million fine against Cigna Health, most covered entities settle on slightly lesser amounts. For instance, Mass General settled for $1 million for violations of the HIPAA Privacy regulations. With the recent authority by state attorney generals under the HITECH Act to bring actions against covered entities (and business associates), a couple of examples have been noted such as Health Net settling a complaint of $250,000 along with other conditions and a recent lawsuit being brought against Accretive Health, Inc., for an undisclosed amount.

If the covered entity can handle these possible financial penalties, then it may make more sense to settle. However, I would strongly caution against this rationale. There may be other costs above and beyond fines related to securing protected health information. Recent class-action lawsuits have been filed by individual patients regarding the privacy of their protected health information. In one case involving TRICARE, a $4.9 billion class-action lawsuit is being decided. We have not even touched on the cost of an actual breach due to safeguards not being implemented. If all of this is taken into consideration, it would be hard to rationalize how information security is not a priority in the organization or how a covered entity does not budget for compliance efforts.

Chapter 21

Checklists

In this chapter, a list of policies and procedures is provided that a covered entity and a business associate should have implemented within their organizations. Along with the policies and procedures, most assessors or auditors will want to take a look at the documents included in the document request list provided.

21.1 Policies and Procedures

Covered entities and business associates should have policies and procedures that address the following:

1. Establishing and terminating users' access to systems housing electronic protected health information (EPHI).
2. Emergency access to electronic information systems.
3. Inactive computer sessions (periods of inactivity).
4. Recording and examining activity in information systems that contain or use EPHI.
5. Risk assessments and analyses of relevant information systems that house or process EPHI data.
6. Employee violations (sanctions).
7. Electronically transmitting EPHI.
8. Preventing, detecting, containing, and correcting security violations (incident reports).
9. Regularly reviewing records of information system activity, such as audit logs, access reports, and security incident tracking reports.

10. Creating, documenting, and reviewing exception reports or logs. Please provide a list of examples of security violation logging and monitoring.
11. Monitoring systems and the network, including a listing of all network perimeter devices (i.e., firewalls and routers).
12. Physical access to electronic information systems and the facility in which they are housed.
13. Establishing security access controls (what types of security access controls are currently implemented or installed in hospital's databases that house EPHI data?).
14. Remote access activity, that is, network infrastructure, platform, access servers, authentication, and encryption software.
15. Internet usage.
16. Wireless security (transmission and usage).
17. Firewalls, routers, and switches.
18. Maintenance and repairs of hardware, walls, doors, and locks in sensitive areas.
19. Terminating an electronic session and encrypting and decrypting EPHI.
20. Transmitting EPHI.
21. Password and server configurations.
22. Antivirus software.
23. Network remote access.
24. Computer patch management.

21.2 Document Request List

Covered entities and business associates should have documentation that addresses the following:

1. A list of all information systems that are used to collect, store, process, or transmit electronic protected health information, as well as network diagrams, including all hardware and software that are used to collect, store, process, or transmit electronic protected health information.
2. A list of terminated workforce members within the last 6 months.
3. A list of all new workforce members within the last 3 months.
4. A list of encryption mechanisms utilized to secure electronic protected health information.
5. A list of authentication methods used to identify users authorized to access electronic protected health information.
6. A list of outsourced individuals and contractors (i.e., business associates) with access to electronic protected health information, if applicable. Include a copy of the contract (i.e., business associate agreement) for each of these entities.
7. A list of transmission methods used to transmit electronic protected health information over an electronic communications network.

8. Organizational charts that include names and titles for the management of information systems and information system security departments.
9. Enterprise-wide security program plans (i.e., system security plan).
10. A list of all users with access to electronic protected health information. Identify each user's access rights and privileges.
11. A list of systems administrators, backup operators, and users.
12. A list of installed antivirus servers including their software versions.
13. A list of software used to manage and control access to the Internet.
14. Identify the antivirus software used for desktop and other devices, including their software versions.
15. A list of users with remote access capabilities.
16. A list of database security requirements and settings.
17. A list of all primary domain controllers (PDCs) and servers (including Unix, Apple, Linux, and Windows). Identify whether these servers are used to collect, store, process, or transmit electronic protected health information.
18. A list of authentication approaches used to verify that a person has been authorized for specific access privileges to information and information systems.

21.3 Incident Handling Checklist

The following is a checklist to follow when handling a security incident as provided for in the National Institute of Standards and Technology (NIST) Special Publication 800-61, Computer Security Incident Handling Guide—Revision 2 (Draft) January 2012 (National Institute of Standards and Technology 2012):

Detection and analysis
1. Determine whether an incident has occurred
    a. Analyze the precursors and indicators
    b. Look for correlating information
    c. Perform research (e.g., search engines, knowledge base)
    d. As soon as the handler believes an incident has occurred, begin documenting the investigation and gathering evidence
2. Prioritize handling the incident based on the relevant factors (functional impact, information impact, recoverability effort, etc.)
3. Report the incident to the appropriate internal personnel and external organizations (notify United States Computer Emergency Readiness Team [US-CERT]).

Containment, eradication, and recovery
4. Acquire, preserve, secure, and document evidence
5. Contain the incident
6. Eradicate the incident
    a. Identify and mitigate all vulnerabilities that were exploited

       b. Remove malware, inappropriate materials, and other components
       c. If more affected hosts are discovered (e.g., new malware infections), repeat the detection and analysis steps (1a and 1b) to identify all other affected hosts, then contain (step 5) and eradicate (step 6) the incident for them
  7. Recover from the incident
       a. Return affected systems to an operationally ready state
       b. Confirm that the affected systems are functioning normally
       c. If necessary, implement additional monitoring to look for future related activity

Postincident activity

  8. Create a follow-up report
  9. Hold a lessons-learned meeting (mandatory for major incidents, optional otherwise)

21.4 Crisis Handling Steps

The following are the steps to follow when handling a serious incident as provided for in the National Institute of Standards and Technology (NIST) Special Publication 800-61 Revision 2 (Draft), January 2012:

1. Document everything
2. Find a coworker who can provide assistance
3. Analyze the evidence to confirm that an incident has occurred
4. Notify the appropriate people within the organization
5. Notify United States Computer Emergency Readiness Team (US-CERT) and/or other external organizations as appropriate for help
6. Stop the incident if it is still in progress
7. Preserve evidence from the incident
8. Wipe out all effects of the incident
9. Identify and mitigate all vulnerabilities that were exploited
10. Confirm that operations have been restored to normal
11. Create a final report

Acronyms

ABAC—Attribute-Based Access Control
ACL—Access Control List
AHRQ—Agency for Healthcare Research and Quality
AICPA—American Institute of Certified Public Accountants
AMAPCPI—American Medical Association Physician Consortium for Performance Improvement
ANSI—American National Standards Institute
ARRA—American Recovery and Reinvestment Act
ASC—Accredited Standards Committee
ASCA—Administrative Simplification Compliance Act
BAA—Business Associate Agreement
BAC—Business Associate Contract
BCP—Business Continuity Plan
BIA—Business Impact Analysis
CAH—Critical Access Hospital
CDC—Centers for Disease Control and Prevention
CDT—Current Dental Terminology
CEHRT—Certified EHR Technology
CERT®/CC—CERT® Coordination Center
CFR—Code of Federal Regulations
CHAMPUS— Civilian Health and Medical Program of the Uniformed Services
CLIA—Clinical Laboratory Improvement Act
CMS—Centers for Medicare & Medicaid Services
COLO—Colocation Data Center
CPOE—Computerized Physician Order Entry
CPT—Current Procedural Terminology
CQM—Clinical Quality Measure
CSMO—Code Set Maintaining Organization
DHHS—Department of Health and Human Services
DRP—Disaster Recovery Plan

DSMO—Designated Standard Maintenance Organization
EFI—Electronic File Interchange
EFIO—Electronic File Interchange Organization
EFT—Electronic Fund Transfer
EHR—Electronic Health Record
EIN—Employer Identification Number
EOB—Explanation of Benefits
EP—Eligible Professional
EPHI—Electronic Protected Health Information
ERISA—Employee Retirement Income and Security Act of 1974
ESI—Electronically Stored Information
FAEs—Filed Against Entities (i.e., complaints regarding a violation of the Privacy or Security Rule)
FBI—Federal Bureau of Investigation
FDA—Food and Drug Administration
FIPPS—Fair Information Practice Principles
FIPS—Federal Information Processing Standards
FRCP—Federal Rules of Civil Procedures
FTC—Federal Trade Commission
FTP—File Transfer Protocol
FTPS—SSL/TLS Protocol under FTP
HCPCS—Health [Care Financing Administration] Common Procedure Coding System
HHS—Department of Health and Human Services
HIO—Health Information Organizations
HIPAA—Health Insurance Portability and Accountability Act of 1996
HITECH—Health Information Technology for Economic and Clinical Health Act of 2009
HMO—Health Maintenance Organization
HMS—Hospital Management Systems
IBAC—Identity-Based Access Control
ICD-9CM—The International Classification of Diseases, 9th edition, Clinical Modification
IRB—Institutional Review Board
IRS—Internal Revenue Service
IT—Information Technology
LAN—Local Area Network
MAC—Media Access Control
MMS—Measures Management System
MOU—Memorandum of Understanding
MSHA—Mine Safety and Health Administration
MTD—Maximum Tolerable Downtime
NAICS—The North American Industry Classification System

NCPDP—National Council for Prescription Drug Programs
NCQA— National Committee for Quality Assurance
NDC—National Drug Code
NIST—National Institute of Standards and Technology
NIST SP—National Institute of Standards and Technology Special Publication
NPI—National Provider Identifier
NPPES—National Plan & Provider Enumeration System
NPRM—Notice of Proposed Rule Making
NPS—National Provider System
NQR—National Quality Forum
OCPO—ONC's Office of the Chief Privacy Officer
OCR—Office for Civil Rights, Department of Health and Human Services
OESS—Office of E-Health Standards and Services
OHCA—Organized Healthcare Arrangement
OIG—Office of the Inspector General
ONC—Office of the National Coordinator for Health Information Technology
OR—Omnibus Rule, or the Notice of Proposed Rule Making regarding sections of the HITECH Act dated July 14, 2010
OSHA—Occupational Safety and Health Administration
PHI—Protected Health Information
PSQIA—Patient Safety and Quality Improvement Act of 2005
PSO—Patient Safety Organizations
QDS—Quality Data Set
RBAC—Role-Based Access Control
RPO—Recovery Point Objectives
SAS—Statement on Auditing Standards (SAS 70)
SFTP—Secure File Transfer Protocol
SLA—Service Level Agreement
SMB—Small and Medium Business
SNMP—Simple Network Management Protocol
SSAE—Standards for Attestation Engagements (SSAE 16)
SSID—Server Set Identifier
SSL—Secure Socket Layer
SSO—Standard Setting Organization
SOC—Service Organization Controls (Type 1, Type 2, and Type 3); SOC1, SOC2, and SOC3
SOX—Sarbanes–Oxley Act
TLS—Transport Layer Security
WEP—Wired Equivalent Privacy
WLAN—Wireless Local Area Network

Glossary

Note: The quoted definitions that are not specifically identified come from the definitions of the HIPAA/HITECH Privacy Rule and Security Rule Regulations.

Access: "The ability or the means necessary to read, write, modify, or communicate data/information or otherwise use any system resource."

Addressable: Under the implementation specification, addressable means that the entity must determine if a safeguard is reasonable and appropriate for the covered entity. It is very important to note that addressable does not mean optional. A covered entity must analyze the specification as it relates to the likelihood of protecting the covered entity's electronic protected health information from reasonable threats. If a covered entity thinks the specification is reasonable to apply, then the covered entity should implement the specification. If the covered entity believes the addressable specification is not reasonable and appropriate for its environment, then the covered entity must document the rationale supporting the decision and either implement an equivalent measure that would accomplish the same purpose or not implement the specification as long as the standard for which the specification applies can still be met.

Administrative Safeguards: Defined under 45 CFR § 164.304 as "administrative actions, and policies and procedures, to manage the selection, development, implementation, and maintenance of security measures to protect electronic protected health information and to manage the conduct of the covered entity's workforce in relation to the protection of that information."

American National Standards Institute (ANSI): "An organization that accredits various standards-setting committees, and monitors their compliance with the open rule-making process that they must follow to qualify for ANSI accreditation. HIPAA prescribes that the standards mandated under it be developed by ANSI-accredited bodies whenever practical" (HIPAA Pedia 2009).

Authentication: "The corroboration that a person is the one claimed."

Availability: "The property that data or information is accessible and usable upon demand by an authorized person."

Breach: "The acquisition, access, use, or disclosure of protected health information in a manner not permitted under subpart E [45 CFR Subpart E—Privacy of Individually Identifiable Health Information] of this part which compromises the security or privacy of the protected health information [or poses a significant risk of financial, reputational, or other harm to the individual]."

Breach Discovery: A breach is determined to be discovered by a covered entity as of the first day in which the breach was known or, by exercising reasonable diligence, should have known by the covered entity.

Business Associate (BA): At times, covered entities require certain functions, activities, and services be performed from other companies that are not a member of a covered entity's workforce that may involve the use or disclosure of individually identifiable health information. Some of these functions, activities, and services may include, but are not limited to, claims processing, data analysis, utilization review, billing legal services, accounting/financial services, consulting, administrative services, accreditation, or other types of services. Companies that provide these types of functions, activities, and services to covered entities are known as business associates as defined in 45 CFR § 160.103.

Certified Electronic Health Record (EHR) Technology: Qualified electronic health records such as inpatient hospital EHR for hospitals, that meet certain standards that are applicable to certain record types. Note: There is no certification for HIPAA-auditing-type services (or software); only EHR products can become certified.

Claims (or Encounters): A detailed, itemized record of healthcare services performed by a healthcare provider on an individual.

Claim Adjustment Reason Codes: "A national administrative code set that identifies the reasons for any differences, or adjustments, between the original provider charge for a claim or service and the payer's payment for it. This code set is used in the X12 835 Claim Payment & Remittance Advice and the X12 837 Claim transactions, and is maintained by the Health Care Code Maintenance Committee" (HIPAA Pedia 2009).

Clinical Quality Measure (CQM): Used to quantify healthcare processes in an effort to measure the quality of healthcare services.

Code Set: "Any set of codes used to encode data elements ["the smallest named unit of information in a transaction"], such as tables of terms, medical concepts, medical diagnostic codes, or medical procedure codes." "A code set includes the codes and the descriptors of the codes [or "text defining a code"]". There are six code sets or clinical codes used in transactions to identify the type of procedures, services, and diagnoses pertaining to patient encounters.

Code Set Maintaining Organization (CSMO): The organizations that maintain or create the code sets. "Maintain or maintenance refers to activities necessary to support the use of a standard adopted by the Secretary [of Health and Human Services], including technical corrections to an implementation specification, and enhancements or expansion of a code set. This excludes the activities related to the adoption of a new standard or implementation specification, or modification to an adopted standard or implementation specification."

Confidential (or Proprietary) Information: Includes information that is owned, licensed, or possessed by the covered entity that must be protected. This information could be trade secrets or other information regarding the covered entities' business relationships.

Confidentiality: "The property that data or information is not made available or disclosed to unauthorized persons or processes."

Contingency Plan: The master or summary-level of documentation required to be in compliance with the HIPAA Security Rule. The contingency plan contains specific focus areas to ensure the restoration of the healthcare entity's business.

Coordination of Benefits (COB) Transaction: As defined in 45 CFR § 162.1801, "the transmission from any entity to a health plan for the purpose of determining the relative payment responsibilities of the health plan of claims or payment information for healthcare."

Covered Entity (CE) or Covered Healthcare Provider: A healthcare provider that transmits any information in an electronic form in connection with a covered transaction. Some examples of a covered healthcare provider are doctors, clinics, psychologists, dentists, chiropractors, nursing homes, and pharmacies. There are three elements that need to be fulfilled to be defined as a covered healthcare provider and required to comply with HIPAA/HITECH regulations. First, to be a covered healthcare provider, the organization or individual has to provide healthcare defined as "care, services, or supplies related to the health of an individual." Second, information must be transmitted in an electronic form or using electronic media, electronic storage media including memory devices in computers (hard drives) and any removable/transportable digital memory medium, such as magnetic tape or disk, optical disk, or digital memory card; or transmission media used to exchange information already in electronic storage media. Finally, the electronic exchange of information has to be related to a covered transaction.

Data at Rest: Data being stored on a hard drive, tape, or other media storage device along with being saved in a database or file system.

Data Backup Plan: The plan (and its details) for the backup, recovery, and restoration of data that resides on a computer or other information system.

Data Condition: "The rule that describes the circumstances under which a covered entity must use a particular data element or segment" (or "a group of related data elements in a transaction").

Data Content: "All the data elements and code sets inherent to a transaction, and not related to the format of the transaction. Data elements that are related to the format are not data content."

Data Disposed: Data that is being discarded on paper or electronic media.

Data in Motion: Data traversing a network through a wired or wireless connection.

Data in Use: Data that is being created, viewed, updated, deleted, or in general use. Note: Data in this state may not be encrypted due to the assumption that it is being used or disclosed in an authorized manner.

Data Set: "A semantically meaningful unit of information exchanged between two parties to a transaction."

Designated Record Set: "A group of records maintained by or for a covered entity that is: the medical records and billing records about individuals maintained by or for a covered healthcare provider; the enrollment, payment, claims adjudication, and case or medical management record systems maintained by or for a health plan; or used, in whole or in part by or for the covered entity to make decisions about individuals." In general, the designated record set "means any item, collection, or grouping of information that includes protected health information and is maintained, collected, used, or disseminated by or for a covered entity."

Designated Standard Maintenance Organization (DSMO): "An organization designed by the Secretary [of Health and Human Services] under [42 CFR] § 162.910(a)."

Direct Data Entry: "The direct entry of data that is immediately transmitted into a health plan's computer."

Direct Identifiers: Is information about an individual, relatives, employers, or household members of the individual as defined under 45 CFR § 164.514(e)(2) and include the following:

1. Names
2. All geographic subdivisions smaller than a state, including street address, city, county, precinct, zip code, and their equivalent geocodes, except for the initial three digits of a zip code if, according to the current publicly available data from the Bureau of the Census:
   a. The geographic unit formed by combining all zip codes with the same three initial digits contains more than 20,000 people
   b. The initial three digits of a zip code for all such geographic units containing 20,000 or fewer people are changed to "000"
3. All elements of dates (except year) for dates directly related to an individual, including birth date, admission date, discharge date, date of death; and all ages over 89 and all elements of dates (including

year) indicative of such age, except that such ages and elements may
be aggregated into a single category of age 90 or older

4. Telephone numbers
5. Fax numbers
6. Electronic mail addresses
7. Social Security numbers
8. Medical record numbers
9. Health plan beneficiary numbers
10. Account numbers
11. Certificate/license numbers
12. Vehicle identifiers and serial numbers, including license plate numbers
13. Device identifiers and serial numbers
14. Web Universal Resource Locators (URLs)
15. Internet Protocol (IP) address numbers
16. Biometric identifiers, including finger and voice prints
17. Full-face photographic images and any comparable images
18. Any other unique identifying number, characteristic, or code

Disclosure: The release of information outside of the entity holding that information. It also covers the transfer of, provision of, access to, and divulging in any other manner of that information. For example, a disclosure of information would be demonstrated by a healthcare provider providing information on a patient to the patient's health plan that would be responsible for paying for the services provided to the patient by the healthcare provider.

Electronic Form: Using electronic media, electronic storage media including memory devices in computers (hard drives) and any removable/transportable digital memory medium, such as magnetic tape or disk, optical disk, or digital memory card; or transmission media used to exchange information already in electronic storage media. Transmission media includes, for example, the Internet (wide open), extranet (using Internet technology to link a business with information accessible only to collaborating parties), leased lines, dial-up lines, private networks, and the physical movement of removable/transportable electronic storage media. Certain transmissions, including paper (via facsimile) and voice (via telephone) are not considered to be transmissions via electronic media, because the information being exchanged did not originally exist in electronic form before the transmission.

Electronic Media: "The mode of electronic transmission. It includes the Internet (wide open), extranet (using Internet technology to link a business with information only accessible to collaborating parties), leased lines, dial-up lines, private networks, and those transmissions that are physically moved from one location to another using magnetic tape, disk, or compact disk media."

Electronic Protected Health Information (EPHI) or Protected Health Information (PHI): Individually identifiable health information transmitted by electronic media, maintained in electronic media, or transmitted or maintained in any other form or medium, whether electronic, paper, or oral.

Eligible Professionals: Physicians that may be eligible to receive incentive payments for the adoption of meaningful use certified electronic health record (HER) technology.

Eligibility for a Health Plan Transaction (or Eligibility Inquiry/Response): As defined in 45 CFR § 162.1201, either "an inquiry from a healthcare provider to a health plan or from one health plan to another health plan, to obtain any of the following information about a benefit plan for an enrollee: eligibility to receive healthcare under the health plan; coverage of healthcare under the health plan; or benefits associated with the benefit plan," or "a response from a health plan to a healthcare provider's (or another health plan's) inquiry" for the information already described.

Emergency Mode Operation Plan: As defined by the HIPAA Administrative Simplification Security Rule, is a subset of the disaster recovery plan for short-term processing and security of electronic protected health information (EPHI) data. In essence, the emergency mode operation plan is the combination of the data processing centric operations for the business as well as contingencies for every individual data processing task.

Encryption: "The use of an algorithmic process to transform data into a form in which there is a low probability of assigning meaning without use of a confidential process or key."

Enrollment or Disenrollment in a Health Plan Transaction: As defined in 45 CFR §162.1501, "the transmission of subscriber enrollment information to a health plan to establish or terminate insurance coverage."

Essential Government Functions: Certain essential government functions do not require authorization to use or disclose protected health information. Such functions include: "assuring proper execution of a military mission, conducting intelligence and national security activities that are authorized by law, providing protective services to the President, making medical suitability determinations for U.S. State Department employees, protecting the health and safety of inmates or employees in a correctional institution, and determining eligibility for or conducting enrollment in certain government benefit programs."

Expected Benefits: As defined under 42 U.S.C. 300gg-91(c)(1), excepted benefits are "coverage for accident, or disability income insurance, or any combination thereof; coverage issued as a supplement to liability insurance; liability insurance, including general liability insurance and automotive liability insurance; workers' compensation or similar insurance; automobile medical payment insurance; credit only insurance; coverage for on-site medical clinics; other similar insurance coverage, specified in regulations, under which benefits for medical care are secondary or incidental to other insurance benefits."

Facility: "The physical premises and the interior and exterior of a building(s)."

Format: "Refers to those data elements that provide or control the enveloping or hierarchical structure, or assist in identifying data content of, a transaction."

Gap Analysis: A methodical review of requirements compared to existing policies and procedures.

Group Health Plan: An employee welfare benefit plan that includes insured and self-insured plans with 50 or more participants that is not administered by the employer for the purpose of providing medical care to include items and services paid for as medical care. An employee welfare plan, as defined in section 3(1) of the Employee Retirement Income and Security Act of 1974 (ERISA), 29 U.S.C. 1002(1)), "is any plan fund or program established by an employer, union, or both that provides a wide variety of benefits including medical, sickness, accident, unemployment, vacation, disability, day care, scholarships, training programs and prepaid legal services." Medical care as defined under 42 U.S.C. 3000gg-91(a)(2) as the "amounts paid for the diagnosis, cure, mitigation, treatment or prevention of disease, or amounts paid for the purpose of affecting any structure or function of the body" includes transportation primarily for and essential to this medical care and for insurance covering this medical care. A participant is defined as any employee (or former employee) of an employer or a member (or former member of an employee organization) that is eligible to receive benefits under an employer benefit plan. It also covers someone who may become eligible or whose beneficiaries may be eligible to receive benefits.

Guidelines: Common practices that are followed by employees of a covered entity and are normally the 'real-life' practices that are in place established by a given procedure.

Health and Human Services (HHS): Assigned the responsibility and oversight for the implementation and enforcement of the HIPAA/HITECH Privacy and Security Rule Regulations.

Health Information: Broadly defined as any information, in any form or medium, that relates to the past, present, or future physical or mental health, condition, provision of healthcare, or future payment for the provision of healthcare of or to an individual.

Health Information Technology for Economic and Clinical Health Act of 1999 (HITECH Act): As part of the American Recovery and Reinvestment Act (ARRA), revised HIPAA and amended the enforcement regulations as related to civil monetary penalties. This new rule-making gave the Department of Health and Human Services more control over enforcement and compliance of the HIPAA regulations with stiffer penalties. It also paved the way for the attorney generals of each state to take enforcement actions for violations of these regulations.

Health Insurance Portability and Accountability Act of 1996 (HIPAA): With the increased use of technology, it became apparent to the United States Congress that there could be potential fraud or compromise of sensitive information, leading the way to the establishment of security and privacy standards. In 1996, Congress enacted the Health Insurance Portability and Accountability Act (HIPAA) in response to these concerns.

Health Plan Premium Payment Transaction: As defined in 45 CFR § 162.1701, "the transmission of payment, information about the transfer of funds, detailed remittance information about individuals for whom premiums are being paid, or payment processing information to transmit healthcare premium payments (to include, payroll deductions, other group premium payments, or associated group premium payment information) from the entity that is arranging for the provision of healthcare or is providing healthcare covered payments for an individual to a health plan."

Healthcare: "Care, services, or supplies related to the health of an individual. It includes, but is not limited to, the following: (1) Preventive, diagnostic, rehabilitative, maintenance, or palliative care, and counseling, service, assessment, or procedure with respect to the physical or mental condition, or functional status, of an individual or that affects the structure or function of the body; and (2) Sale or dispensing of a drug, device, equipment, or other item in accordance with a prescription."

Healthcare Claim Status Transaction: As defined in 45 CFR § 162.1401, "an inquiry to determine the status of a healthcare claim or a response about the status of a healthcare claim."

Healthcare Claims or Equivalent Encounter Information Transactions: As defined in 45 CFR § 162.1101, either "a request to obtain payment, and necessary accompanying information, from a healthcare provider to a health plan, for healthcare," or "if there is no direct claim, because the reimbursement contract is based on a mechanism other than charges or reimbursement rates for specific services, the transaction is the transmission of encounter information for the purpose of reporting healthcare."

Healthcare Clearinghouse: Defined in 45 CFR § 160.103, as a "public or private entity ... that performs either of the following functions: (1) Processes or facilitates the processing of health information ... in a nonstandard format or containing nonstandard data content into standard data elements or a standard transaction. (2) Receives a standard transaction ... and processes or facilitates the processing of health information [in the standard transaction] into nonstandard format or nonstandard data content for the receiving entity."

Healthcare Operations: These are the core business and support functions for the treatment and payment of health services such as administrative, financial, legal, and quality improvement activities of a covered entity. As defined in 45 CFR § 164.501, healthcare operations are limited to the following activities: "Conducting quality assessment and improvement activities, population-based activities relating to improving health or reducing health-care costs, and case management and care coordination; Reviewing the competence or qualifications of healthcare professionals, evaluating provider and health plan performance, training healthcare and non-healthcare professionals, accreditation, certification, licensing, or credentialing activities; Underwriting and other activities relating to the creation, renewal, or replacement of a contract of health insurance or health benefits, and ceding, securing, or placing a contract for reinsurance of risk relating to healthcare claims; Conducting or arranging for medical review, legal, and auditing services, including fraud and abuse detection and compliance programs; Business planning and development, such as conducting cost-management and planning analyses related to managing and operating the entity; and Business management and general administrative activities, including those related to implementing and complying with the Privacy Rule and other Administrative Simplification Rules, customer service, resolution of internal grievances, sale or transfer of assets, creating de-identified health information or a limited data set, and fundraising for the benefit of the covered entity. General Provisions at 45 CFR § 164.506."

Healthcare Payment and Remittance Advice Transaction: As paraphrased from 45 CFR § 162.1601, the transmission of payment, information about the transfer of funds, or payment processing information from a health plan to a healthcare provider's financial institution, or the transmission of the explanation of benefits or remittance of advice from a health plan to a healthcare provider.

High Risk Pool: A mechanism established under state law to provide health insurance coverage or comparable coverage to eligible individuals.

Hybrid Entity: A single legal entity that conducts both covered and noncovered functions as it pertains to the HIPAA Privacy Rule.

Implementation Specification: Detailed instructions to implement a specific standard.

Individual: "The person who is the subject of protected health information."

Individually Identifiable Health Information: This is information that can identify or reasonably be used to identify an individual and is created or received by a healthcare provider, health plan, employer, or healthcare clearinghouse. This information can relate to past, present, or future physical or mental, condition, or payment for healthcare to an individual.

Information system: "An interconnected set of information resources under the same direct management control that shares common functionality."

Interviewing: Asking questions or surveying how policies and procedures are carried out.

Issuer of a Medicare Supplemental Policy: A private entity that offers a health insurance policy or other health benefit plan, to individuals who are entitled to have payments made under Medicare, which provides reimbursement for expenses incurred for services and items for which payment may be made under Medicare, but which are not reimbursable by reason of the applicability of deductibles, coinsurance amounts, or other limitations imposed pursuant to or other limitations imposed by Medicare. A Medicare supplemental policy does not include policies or plans excluded under section 1882(g)(1) of the Social Security Act. See 42 U.S.C. 1395ss (g)(1).

Limited Data Set: Protected health information where specified direct identifiers of individuals, their relatives, household members, and employers have been removed.

Local Code(s): Codes that different payer organizations, such as health plans including state Medicaid programs, devised to handle their own special circumstances. Unfortunately, under HIPAA, these local codes are not allowed to be used; thus, providers must replace these codes with the appropriate Healthcare Common Procedure Coding System (HCPCS) and Current Procedural Terminology (CPT-4) codes. Health plans are supposed to notify their providers with information to specify how the standard code sets will replace their local codes.

Malicious Software: A virus designed to damage or disrupt a system or that may target the availability of the information system causing the system to crash or to be unavailable for the users.

Marketing: Defined by the HIPAA Privacy Rule as making "a communication about a product or service that encourages recipients of the communication to purchase or use the product or service." Marketing is also defined as "an arrangement between a covered entity and any other entity whereby the covered entity discloses protected health information to the other entity, in exchange for direct or indirect remuneration, for the other entity or its affiliate to make a communication about its own product or service that encourages recipients of the communication to purchase or use that product or service."

Meaningful Use: Using certified electronic health record (EHR) technology in a meaningful manner, for electronic health information exchanges, and for clinical quality submissions.

Minimum Necessary: Means that the covered entity's workforce members will only be provided the least amount of an individual's information that is necessary for them to perform their jobs.

Multiemployer Welfare Benefit Plan: Defined under 45 CFR § 160.03 as "an employee welfare benefit plan or any other arrangement that is established or maintained for the purpose of offering and providing health benefits to the employees of two or more employers."

National Provider Identifier (NPI): A unique 10-digit identifier that is ambiguous of any identifiable information assigned to a healthcare provider. As part of the HIPAA Administrative Simplification Standard, all covered healthcare providers, health plans, and healthcare clearinghouses must use their NPIs in any administrative or financial transactions.

National Provider System (NPS): The National Provider System is assigned responsibility for the management of healthcare providers' unique health identifiers.

Nonmedical or Nonclinical Code Sets: Code sets that characterize a general administrative situation as opposed to a medical condition or service.

Observation: The direct review of policies and procedures taking place.

Office for Civil Rights (OCR): One of the offices within the Department of Health and Human Services (HHS) responsible for investigating violations of the HIPAA/HITECH Privacy and Security Rule along with conducting enforcement actions.

Organized Healthcare Arrangement: "(1) A clinically integrated care setting in which individuals typically receive healthcare from more than one healthcare provider; (2) An organized system of healthcare in which more than one covered entity participates and in which the participating covered entities: (i) Hold themselves out to the public as participating in a joint arrangement; and (ii) Participate in joint activities that include at least one of the following: (A) Utilization review, in which healthcare decisions by participating covered entities are reviewed by other participating covered entities or by a third party on their behalf; (B) Quality assessment and improvement activities, in which treatment provided by participating covered entities is assessed by other participating covered entities or by a third party on their behalf; or (C) Payment activities, if the financial risk for delivering healthcare is shared, in part or in whole, by participating covered entities through the joint arrangement and if protected health information created or received by a covered entity is reviewed by other participating covered entities or by a third party on their behalf for the purpose of administering the sharing of financial risk. (3) A group health plan and a health insurance issuer or HMO with respect to such group health plan, but only with respect to protected health information created or received by such health insurance issuer or HMO that relates to individuals who are or who have been participants or beneficiaries in such group health plan; (4) A group health plan and one or more other group health plans each of which are maintained by the same plan sponsor; or (5) The group health plans described in paragraph (4) of this definition and health insurance issuers or HMOs with respect to such group health plans, but only with respect to protected health information created or received by such health insurance issuers or HMOs that relates to individuals who are or have been participants or beneficiaries in any of such group health plans."

Passwords: "Confidential authentication information composed of a string of characters."

Patient Safety Work Product: Patient safety information that is provided Federal privilege and confidentiality protections under the Patient Safety and Quality Improvement Act of 2005 (PSQIA).

Payer: An individual or health plan that reimburses a healthcare provider for healthcare services.

Payment: Encompasses the various activities of healthcare providers to obtain payment or reimbursement for services rendered. In the case of a health plan, it is the ability to obtain premiums and to fulfill their obligations under the plan.

Personal Representative: A person legally authorized to make healthcare decisions on an individual's behalf or to act for a deceased individual or the estate. Parents are considered the personal representatives of their minor children.

Physical Safeguards: Defined under 45 CFR § 164.304 as "physical measures, policies, and procedures to protect a covered entity's electronic information systems and related buildings and equipment, from natural and environmental hazards, and unauthorized intrusion."

Policies: Intentions of management to come into compliance with regulations. Policies are high-level requirements that are documented and approved by management to direct employees in the process of complying with the stated objectives.

Privilege Creep: Occurs when a workforce member with normal access rights is granted additional access rights; however, the additional (and in most cases temporary) extension of access rights is not subsequently revoked when no longer required.

Procedures: More detailed than policies and normally provide step-by-step instructions to follow in complying with the policy. Normally, there is one policy statement and several procedures on what the covered entity should do to carry out the policy.

Psychotherapy Notes: Special protected health information that requires an individual's authorization to disclose under any circumstance.

Public Health Authority: As defined in 45 CFR § 164.501, "an agency or authority of the United States government, a State, a territory, a political subdivision of a State or territory, or Indian tribe that is responsible for public health matters as part of its official mandate, as well as a person or entity acting under a grant of authority from, or under a contract with, a public health agency."

Public Information: Information that is available to the public. Examples of public information include marketing and advertising information that may be available on the covered entity's Web site.

Quality Data Set (QDS) Elements: Model of information that contains the standard element, the quality data element, and the data flow attributes. QDS is used to describe clinical concepts in a standardized fashion so that there is no unambiguous interpretation of the data. The data can then be clearly located and clinical performance can be monitored.

Reasonable Cause: "Circumstances that would make it unreasonable for the covered entity, despite the exercise of ordinary business care and prudence, to comply with the administrative simplification provision violated."

Reasonable Diligence: "The business care and prudence expected from a person seeking to satisfy a legal requirement under similar circumstances."

Referral Certification and Authorization Transaction: As defined in 45 CFR § 162.1301, "a request for the review of healthcare to obtain an authorization for the healthcare, a request to obtain authorization for referring an individual to another healthcare provider, or a response to a request" for such information.

Remittance Advice: An explanation of claim or encounter processing and/or payment sent by a health plan to a provider.

Required by Law: In 45 CFR § 164.103, defined as "a mandate contained in law that compels an entity to make a use or disclosure of protected health information and that is enforceable in a court of law."

Residual Risk Factor: The percentage of risk left over that needs to be mitigated.

Risk Analysis: "An accurate and thorough assessment of the potential risks and vulnerabilities to the confidentiality, integrity, and availability of electronic protected health information held by the covered entity."

Risk Mitigated Factor: The percentage of risk perceived to be mitigated by controls that are currently implemented to protect against certain vulnerabilities.

Risk Mitigation: The process of implementing solutions or performing actions to ultimately reach the goal of decreasing the risk level or the impact of the event to an acceptable level.

Sampling: Taking a small portion of items and reviewing these items to make sure that they meet policies or procedures identified.

Security or Security Measures: "Encompass all of the administrative, physical, and technical safeguards in an information system."

Security Incident: "The attempted or successful unauthorized access, use, disclosure, modification, or destruction of information or interference with system operations in an information system."

Standard Transaction: "A transaction that complies with the applicable standard adopted under this part [45 CFR § 162]." It can include the following types of information transmissions:
1. Healthcare claims or equivalent encounter information
2. Healthcare payment and remittance advice
3. Coordination of benefits
4. Healthcare claim status
5. Enrollment and disenrollment in a health plan
6. Eligibility for a health plan
7. Health plan premium payments
8. Referral certification and authorization
9. First report of injury
10. Health claims attachments
11. Other transactions that the Secretary of Health and Human Services may prescribe by regulation.

Standards: Set by policies that help produce the procedures that will be followed to carry out the objectives of the policies. Standards attempt to tie the procedures with their policies.

Summary Health Information: Information that summarizes claims history, claims expenses, or types of claims experience of the individuals of the plan that is stripped of all individual identifiers.

Systems: "Normally include hardware, software, information, data, applications, communications, and people."

Technical Safeguards: Defined under 45 CFR § 164.304 as "the technology and the policy and procedures for its use that protect electronic protected health information and control access to it."

Threat: From NIST SP 800-30, is "the potential for a person or thing to exercise (accidentally trigger or intentionally exploit) a specific vulnerability."

Threat Source: The intent or method by which an exploitation of vulnerability occurs. A threat source could also be a situation or method by which vulnerabilities are triggered by accident.

Treatment: "The provision, coordination, or management of healthcare and related services among healthcare providers or by a healthcare provider with a third party, consultation between healthcare providers regarding a patient, or the referral of a patient from one healthcare provider to another."

Unsecured Protected Health Information: "Protected health information that is not rendered unusable, unreadable, or indecipherable to unauthorized individuals through the use of a technology or methodology specified by the Secretary of Health and Human Services." The guidance provided by the Department of Health and Human Services is to encrypt or destroy (in paper or electronic form) protected health information so that it is unusable, unreadable, or indecipherable by unauthorized individuals.

Use: "With respect to individually identifiable health information, the sharing, employment, application, utilization, examination, or analysis of such information within an entity that maintains such information."

Users: "Persons or entities with authorized access."

Virtual Private Network (VPN): "A technical strategy for creating secure connections, or tunnels, over the internet" (HIPAA Pedia 2009).

Vulnerability: Defined in NIST SP 800-30 as "a flaw or weakness in system security procedures, design, implementation, or internal controls that could be exercised (accidentally triggered or intentionally exploited) and result in a security breach or a violation of the system's security policy."

Willful Neglect: "Conscious, intentional failure or reckless indifference to the obligations to comply with the administrative simplification provision violated."

Workforce Member: Any employee, volunteer, trainee, or individual under direct control of the covered entity whether paid or not.

Workstation: "An electronic computing device, for example, a laptop or desktop computer, or any other device that performs similar functions, and electronic media stored in its immediate environment."

References

Akwaja, Chima. "Cyberspace War: Is Your Business Protected?" *Leadership*. January 24, 2012. http://leadership.ng/nga/articles/14234/2012/01/24/cyberspace_war_your_business_protected.html (accessed January 24, 2012).

American National Standards Institute (ANSI). "PHI." *The Financial Impact of Breached Protected Health Information*. February 14, 2012. http://webstore.ansi.org/phi (accessed March 8, 2012).

Anderson, Howard. "Breach Tally Surpasses 19 Million." *Healthcare Info Security*. January 23, 2012. http://www.healthcareinfosecurity.com/articles.php?art_id = 4426&opg = 1 (accessed January 24, 2012).

———. "Computer Theft Affects 4.2 Million." *Healthcare Info Security*. November 16, 2011. http://www.healthcareinfosecurity.com/articles.php?art_id = 4250 (accessed January 24, 2012).

———. "Interview: The New HIPAA Enforcer." *Healthcare Info Security*. October 3, 2011. http://www.healthcareinfosecurity.com/podcasts.php?podcastID = 1258 (accessed October 10, 2011).

———. "McAndrew Explains HIPAA Audits." *Healthcare Info Security*. July 15, 2011. http://www.healthcareinfosecurity.com/podcasts.php?podcastID = 1190 (accessed October 10, 2011).

———. "More Breach Class Action Lawsuits Filed." *Healthcare Info Security*. November 23, 2011. http://www.healthcareinfosecurity.com/articles.php?art_id = 4275 (accessed January 24, 2012).

b, P. "Biggest Security Threats in 2012 Are Cyber Espionage, Privacy Violations." *CXOtoday*. January 2, 2012. http://www.cxotoday.com/story/biggest-security-threats-in-2012-are-cyber-espionage-privacy-violations/ (accessed January 12, 2012).

Bejtlich, Richard. "I Want to Detect and Respond to Intruders But I Don't Know Where to Start!" *TaoSecurity*. February 13, 2012. http://taosecurity.blogspot.com/2012/02/i-want-to-detect-and-respond-to.html (accessed February 14, 2012).

Bowman, Dan. "91% of Small Healthcare Organizations Suffered a Data Breach in the Last Year." *FierceHealthIT*. February 17, 2012. http://www.fiercehealthit.com/story/91-small-healthcare-organizations-suffered-data-breach-last-year/2012-02-17 (accessed February 19, 2012).

Centers for Medicare & Medicaid Services (CMS) Office of E-Health Standards and Services (OESS). "2009 HIPAA Compliance Review Analysis and Summary of Results." *Health and Human Services*. September 22, 2009. http://www.hhs.gov/ocr/privacy/hipaa/enforcement/cmscompliancerev09.pdf (accessed November 21, 2011).

Clark, Cheryl. "Meaningful Use Incentive Payouts Top $3B." *HealthLeadersMedia*. February 17, 2012. http://www.healthleadersmedia.com/content/TEC-276732/Meaningful-Use-Incentive-Payouts-Top-3B (accessed February 21, 2012).

Department of Health and Human Services (HHS). "III. Section-By-Section Discussion of Comments." n.d. http://aspe.hhs.gov/admnsimp/final/PvcPre03.htm (accessed March 10, 2012).

——. "Business Associates." March 14, 2006. http://www.hhs.gov/hipaafaq/providers/business/245.html (accessed February 11, 2012).

——. "Remote Use." HIPAA Security Guidance. December 28, 2006. http://www.hhs.gov/ocr/privacy/hipaa/administrative/securityrule/remoteuse.pdf (accessed February 16, 2012).

——. Office for Civil Rights. "Are We Required to 'Certify' Our Organization's Compliance with the Standards of the Security Rule?" n.d. http://www.hhs.gov/ocr/privacy/hipaa/faq/securityrule/2003.html (accessed March 4, 2012).

——. Office for Civil Rights. "Mass General Hospital Settles Potential HIPAA Violations." February 14, 2011. http://www.hhs.gov/ocr/privacy/hipaa/news/mghnews.html (accessed January 20, 2012).

——. Press Office. "HHS Imposes a $4.3 Million Civil Money Penalty for Violations of the HIPAA Privacy Rule." February 22, 2011. http://www.hhs.gov/news/press/2011pres/02/20110222a.html (accessed February 20, 2012).

Dunn, John E. "US hospital hit by data-stealing malware." *ITWorld*. February 7, 2012. http://www.itworld.com/security/247824/us-hospital-hit-data-stealing-malware (accessed February 7, 2012).

Eisenberg, Carol. "Theft of Digital Health Data More Often Inside Job, Report Finds." *BusinessWeek.com*. September 22, 2011. http://www.businessweek.com/news/2011-09-22/theft-of-digital-health-data-more-often-inside-job-report-finds.html (accessed October 10, 2011).

Federal Financial Institutions Examination Council. "Lessons Learned from Hurricane Katrina: Preparing Your Institution for a Catastrophic Event." June 13, 2006. http://www.ffiec.gov/katrina_lessons.htm (accessed February 9, 2012).

Fox News. "Cyber-Threats Will Become Top Worry, FBI Director Says." *Fox News*. March 2, 2012. http://www.foxnews.com/scitech/2012/03/02/cyber-threats-will-become-top-worry-fbi-director-says/ (accessed March 3, 2012).

Gartner. "Gartner Says SAS 70 Is Not Proof of Security, Continuity or Privacy Compliance." *Gartner Newsroom*. July 14, 2010. http://www.gartner.com/it/page.jsp?id = 1400813 (accessed March 4, 2012).

Goedert, Joseph. "Huge Breach at TRICARE." *HealthData Management*. September 29, 2011. http://www.healthdatamanagement.com/news/breach-tricare-notification-hipaa-privacy-43288-1.html?ET = healthdatamanagement:e2013:144085a:&st = email&utm_source = editorial&utm_medium = email&utm_campaign = HDM_Daily_092911 (accessed October 11, 2011).

Grimes, Roger A. "Why Internet Crime Goes Unpunished." *Infoworld*. January 10, 2012. http://www.infoworld.com/d/security/why-internet-crime-goes-unpunished-183605?page = 0,0 (accessed January 12, 2012).

Help Net Security. "48% of Enterprises Targeted by Social Engineering Attacks." *Help Net Security*. September 21, 2011. https://www.net-security.org/secworld.php?id = 11665 (accessed October 10, 2011).

Hennessy-Fiske, Molly. *Los Angeles Times*. August 8, 2010. http://articles.latimes.com/2010/aug/08/local/la-me-facebook-20100809 (accessed August 15, 2012).

HIPAA Pedia. "Glossary of HIPAA Terms." October 27, 2009. https://www.hipaapedia.com/twiki/bin/view/Main/DefinitionsGlossary (accessed February 18, 2012).

Homeland Security. "Healthcare and Public Health Sector: Critical Infrastructure and Key Resources." Sector Overview. June 25, 2008. http://www.dhs.gov/files/programs/gc_1188490299862.shtm (accessed February 20, 2012).

———. "Sector-Specific Plans." December 17, 2003. http://www.dhs.gov/files/programs/gc_1179866197607.shtm#content (accessed February 20, 2012).

Jones, Ed. "Contingency Plan: Emergency Mode Operation Plan—What to Do and How to Do It." 2009. http://www.hipaa.com/2009/04/contingency-plan-emergency-mode-operation-plan-what-to-do-and-how-to-do-it/ (accessed February 9, 2012).

Kennedy, Tony. "Minnesota Sues Consulting Firm over Lost Health Data." *Star Tribune*. January 19, 2012. http://www.startribune.com/local/137678533.html?source = error# (accessed January 21, 2012).

Kingsley-Hughes, Adrian. "DigiNotar Files for Bankruptcy Following Hack Attack." *Hardware 2.0 Blog*. September 20, 2011. http://www.zdnet.com/blog/hardware/diginotar-files-for-bankruptcy-following-hack-attack/14878 (accessed October 10, 2011).

Klein, Mike. "AICPA Fumbles Audit Standards at the 5-Yard Line." *Data Center Knowledge*. January 19, 2012. http://www.datacenterknowledge.com/archives/2012/01/19/aicpa-fumbles-audit-standards-at-the-5-yard-line/ (accessed March 4, 2012).

Lamkin, Elizabeth. "HIPAA Compliance Audits: The Newest Risk for Providers?" *RAC Monitor*. February 2, 2012. http://www.racmonitor.com/news/27-rac-enews/749-hipaa-compliance-audits-the-newest-risk-for-providers.html (accessed February 11, 2012).

Los, Rafal. "Psychology of Information Security—The God Complex." *InfoSec Island*. January 27, 2012. http://www.infosecisland.com/blogview/19374-Psychology-of-Information-Security-The-God-Complex.html (accessed January 28, 2012).

Manning, William L. "Summary of The Medicare and Medicaid Patient Protection Act of 1987 (42 U.S.C. 1320a-7b)." *NetReach.net*. 1996. http://www.netreach.net/~wmanning/fasumm.htm (accessed January 12, 2012).

Maynard, Shereese. "2012 Predictions: What Providers Should be Preparing For." *Maynard Health Blog*. December 30, 2011. http://maynardhealth.blogspot.com/2011/12/2012-predictions-what-providers-should.html (accessed January 27, 2012).

Mediati, Nick. "6 Security Trends to Watch For." *PCWorld*. March 2, 2012. http://www.pcworld.com/businesscenter/article/251211/6_security_trends_to_watch_for.html (accessed March 3, 2012).

Menn, Joseph. "They're Watching. And They Can Bring You Down." *FT Magazine*. September 23, 2011. http://www.ft.com/cms/s/2/3645ac3c-e32b-11e0-bb55-00144feabdc0.html#axzz1YxxLFtOB (accessed October 10, 2011).

Millard, Mike. "Medical Identity Theft on the Rise." *HealthcareIT News*. March 15, 2011. http://www.healthcareitnews.com/news/medical-identity-theft-rise (accessed January 11, 2012).

"'Monetary Enforcement' Is the New Aim of OCR, Following $1.5M BCBST Settlement." *AISHEALTH*. April 2012. http://aishealth.com/archive/hipaa0412-03#.t4ofusdqi0k. mailto (accessed April 15, 2012).

Morrissey, John. "iGovernance." *Hospitals & Health Networks.* February 2012. http://www.hhnmag.com/hhnmag_app/jsp/articledisplay.jsp?dcrpath = HHNMAG/Article/data/02FEB2012/0212HHN_Coverstory&domain = HHNMAG#rlz = 1C1LENP_enUS460US460&sourceid=chrome&ie=UTF-8&q=Kaloramahttp%3A%2F%2Fwww.hhnmag.com%2Fhhnmag_app%2Fjsp%2Farticledisplay.jsp% (accessed March 7, 2012).

Nicastro, Dom. "HIPAA Auditor Involved in Own Data Breach." *Health Leaders Media.* August 8, 2011. http://www.healthleadersmedia.com/page-1/PHY-269480/HIPAA-Auditor-Involved-in-Own-Data-Breach (accessed November 21, 2011).

Painter, Mark. "Healthcare Organizations Not Ready for New Security Standards." *The HP Security Laboratory Blog.* September 2011. http://h30499.www3.hp.com/t5/The-HP-Security-Laboratory-Blog/Healthcare-organizations-not-ready-for-new-security-standards/ba-p/5339745 (accessed October 10, 2011).

Ponemon Institute. "Ponemon Study Shows the Cost of a Data Breach Continues to Increase." *Ponemon Institute.* January 25, 2011. http://www.ponemon.org/news-2/23 (accessed October 10, 2011).

Ponemon Institute, LLC. "Second Annual Survey on Medical Identity Theft." *ProtectMyID.* March 2011. http://www.protectmyid.com/images/education_center/pdf/050TypesofFraud/1_types%20of%20fraud_medical%20study.PDF (accessed January 11, 2012).

Proskauer Rose, LLP. "New HIPAA Cop: First AG Settlement for HIPAA Violations." *Proskauer.* July 14, 2010. http://privacylaw.proskauer.com/2010/07/articles/medical-privacy/new-hipaa-cop-first-ag-settlement-for-hipaa-violations/ (accessed January 3, 2012).

PRWEB. "NetClarity Announces Top Ten Cybercrime and Cyberwar Predictions for 2012." February 14, 2012. http://www.prweb.com/releases/prweb2012/2/prweb9194477.htm (accessed February 18, 2012).

Roberta. "The New Certified EHR Technology." *HITECHAnswers.* February 28, 2012. http://www.hitechanswers.net/the-new-certified-ehr-technology/ (accessed March 2, 2012).

Sells, Toby. "BlueCross BlueShield of Tennessee to pay $1.5M penalty for data loss." *The Commercial Appeal.* March 14, 2012. http://www.commercialappeal.com/news/2012/mar/14/bluecross-blue-shield-pay-15m-penalty-data-loss/?CID=happeningnow (accessed March 18, 2012).

Siciliano, Robert. "15 Tips To Better Password Security." *McAfee.* June 29, 2011. http://blogs.mcafee.com/consumer/15-tips-to-better-password-security (accessed March 7, 2012).

Stech, Katy. "Burglary Triggers Medical Records Firm's Collapse." *Bankruptcy Beat.* March 12, 2012. http://blogs.wsj.com/bankruptcy/2012/03/12/burglary-triggers-medical-records-firm%E2%80%99s-collapse/?blog_id=108&post_id=17940 (accessed March 19, 2012).

Supremus Group. "Applications and Data Criticality Analysis Template." *Supremus Group.* 2012. http://www.supremusgroup.com/compliance_template/Applications_Data_Criticality_Analysis.htm (accessed April 8, 2012).

Tripathi, Micky. "First-Hand Experience with a Patient Data Security Breach 12/3/11." *HISTalk Practice.* December 3, 2011. http://www.histalkpractice.com/2011/12/03/first-hand-experience-with-a-patient-data-security-breach-12311/ (accessed January 20, 2012).

Voelker, Michael P. "After 'Year of the Data Breach,' Carriers Increase Capacity, Competition for Cyber Risks." *Property Casualty 360.* February 6, 2012. http://www.propertycasualty360.com/2012/02/02/after-year-of-the-data-breach-carriers-increase-ca?t = commercial&page = 2 (accessed February 10, 2012).

Washington Post editorial. "Cybersecurity Boost Can Wait No Longer." *The Journal Gazette.* February 16, 2012. http://www.journalgazette.net/article/20120216/EDIT05/302169947/1147/EDIT07 (accessed February 20, 2012).

Weigel, Jen. "Cybercrime: A Billion-Dollar Industry." *Chicago Tribune.* September 20, 2011. http://www.chicagotribune.com/features/tribu/ct-tribu-weigel-cyber-crime-20110920,0,3910462.column (accessed October 10, 2011).

Whitehouse. "Consumer Data Privacy in a Network World: A Framework for Protecting Privacy and Promoting Innovation in the Global Digital Economy." *WhiteHouse.Gov.* February 23, 2012. http://www.whitehouse.gov/sites/default/files/privacy-final.pdf (accessed February 26, 2012).

Wikipedia. "Hippocratic Oath." January 2010. http://en.wikipedia.org/wiki/Hippocratic_Oath (accessed January 12, 2012).

Wilson, Tim. "IT Security Employment Rising Rapidly, Study Says." *Dark Reading.* January 10, 2012. http://www.darkreading.com/security/news/232400019/it-security-employment-rising-rapidly-study-says.html (accessed January 13, 2012).

Additional Resources

Books and Articles

Fair, Lesley. "Taking the Lead to Prevent Identity Theft." Bureau of Consumer Protection, http://business.ftc.gov/documents/taking-lead-prevent-identity-theft.

Hadnagy, Chris. *Social Engineering: The Art of Human Hacking.*, Wiley, 2011.

Trinckes, John J. Jr. *The Executive MBA in Information Security*. CRC Press, 2010.

Organizations and Businesses

Centers for Medicare & Medicaid Services, www.CMS.HHS.gov

Healthcare Info Security, www.HealthcareInfoSecurity.com

National Institute of Science and Technology (NIST), Special Publications

800-12, An Introduction to Computer Security: The NIST Handbook, October 1995

800-14, Generally Accepted Principles and Practices for Security Information Technology Systems, September 1996

800-18, Guide for Developing Security Plans For Information Technology Systems, December 1998

800-26, Security Self-Assessment Guide for Information Technology Systems, November 2001

800-27, Engineering Principles for Information Technology Security (A Baseline for Achieving Security), January 2004

800-30, Risk Management Guide to Information Technology Systems, January 2004

800-34, Contingency Planning Guide for Information Technology Systems, June 2002

800-35, Guide to Information Technology Security Services, October 2003

800-36, Guide to Selecting Information Security Products, October 2003

800-37, Guide for the Security Certification and Accreditation of Federal Information Systems, May 2004

800-42, Guideline on Network Security Testing, October 2003

800-44, Guidelines on Security Public Web Servers, September 2002

800-47, Security Guide for Interconnecting Information Technology Systems, September 2002

800-50, Building an Information Technology Security Awareness and Training Program, October 2003

800-53, Recommended Security Controls for Federal Information Systems, Revision 4, February 2012

800-55, Security Metrics Guide for Information Technology Systems, July 2003

800-60, Guide for Mapping Types of Information and Information Systems to Security Categories, March 2005

800-61, Computer Security Incident Handling Guide, January 2004

800-61, Computer Security Incident Handling Guide (Draft), January 2012

800-63, Electronic Authentication Guide: Recommendations of the National Institute of Standards and Technology, June 2004

800-64, Security Considerations in the Information System Development Life Cycle, October 2003

800-65, Integrating Security into the Capital Planning and Investment Control Process, January 2005

800-66, An Introductory Resource Guide for Implementing the Health Insurance Portability and Accountability Act (HIPAA) Security Rule, March 2005

800-153, Guidelines for Security Wireless Local Area Networks (WLANs), February 2012

Guidelines and Toolkits

Agency for Healthcare Research and Quality, "Guide to Reducing Unintended Consequences of Electronic Health Records," http://www.ucguide. org/index.html

Centers for Medicare & Medicaid Services, Education Materials, www.cms.hhs.gov/EducationMaterials/

Data Backup Plan Template, http://www.training-hipa a.net/template_suite/Dat a_backup_plan.htm

Department of Health and Human Services, Office for Civil Rights, "Health Information Privacy", www.HHS.gov/ocr/hipaa

Disaster Recovery Plan (DRP) Template to Achieve HIPAA Security Compliance, http://www.training-hipaa.net/templ ate_suite/Disast er_recovery_plan.htm

Federal Information Processing Standard (FIPS) 140-2, Security Requirements for Cryptographic Modules, June 2001

Federal Information Processing Standard (FIPS) 199, Standards for Security Categorization of Federal Information and Information Systems, February 2004

Harmonic Data Associates, "HIPPA Security Rules Guidelines," http://www.harmonic-da ta.com/hipaamatrix.pdf

HIPAA Security Rule Toolkit, http://scap.nist.gov/hipaa/

HIPAA Survival Guide, http://www.HIP AASurvivalGuide.com/

Office of Management and Budget (OMB) Memorandum M-03-19, Reporting Instructions for the Federal Information Security Management Act and Updated Guidance on Quarterly IT Security Reporting, August 6, 2003

Patient Safety Rule, http://www.gpo.gov/fdsys/pkg/FR-2008-11-21/pdf/E8-27475.pdf

Symantec/Ponemon's Institute, Data Breach Calculator, http://databreachcal culator.com. sapin.arvixe.com/ Default.aspx

Index